HOW TO EUROPE

HOW TO EUROPE

EUROPE

The Complete Travelers Handbook

by John Bermont

Murphy & Broad
Midland, Michigan

HOW TO EUROPE
Edition 4
Revised 2ⁿᵈ Printing, September 2003

© 1981, 1982, 1984, 1986, 1987 Murphy & Broad Publishing Co.
© 2001, 2002, 2003 James J. Broad

James Broad
Murphy & Broad Publishing Co.
212 West Pine Street
Midland, Michigan 48640-4970

989-633-8395

http://www.enjoy-europe.com/

bermont@enjoy-europe.com

ISBN 0-940792-69-9

Printed in the United States of America

This publication is offered on a best efforts basis, produced with my limited budget and schedule and is as up to date as possible under these constraints. I was not paid to write this nor have I accepted gratuities from any business in the travel industry. No liability whatever is assumed for real or imagined damages caused in any way by your reliance on what you read here. It is incumbent on you to verify all terms, conditions, and specifications with the original sources before buying, acting, or committing yourself to anything. Do not assume. Do not extrapolate. It is your time, money, and comfort at stake. Have fun and bon voyage.

Dedication

In memory of Annette Kampinga of Haarlem, The Netherlands. Annette was my secretary and companion, and became a stewardess to roam the world. It was her invitation that led me to return to Europe, and her encouragement that got me to write this book. Annette, 25, was murdered in a terrorist bomb blast at the Norfolk Hotel in Nairobi, Kenya on New Years Eve of 1981.

Note: This is the same dedication I made in my first edition in 1982. The terror of the first few years of the 21st century is not anything new. It's been around and it will stay around. See more on this in chapters 1 and 20.

Thanks

MENTORS, PATRONS, AND CREW

A lot of people have helped to rake the weeds and water the plants in this garden, from the first edition 21 years ago to the present. They have given me everything from encouragement and information to editorial advice and graphical assistance to financial help and a free place to sleep while I struggled to finish. Some of you didn't know you were helping, but I give you credit anyway.

I thank all who contributed. This list is in no particular order and I hope that I remember everybody. Paula Warmerdam, the Böhmer family (Connie, Uwe, Rita, and Tina), Orest Kromenko, Boris Rekhles, Elizabeth Varga, Stephanie Broad, the Novarro family (Giampietro, Anita, Annaperina, and all the rest in Italy), Aafje Rietveld, Ida Richle, Geoffrey L. Guenther, Valerie Beardwood, Bill Hunter, Phil Lisle, Chi Chi Juaneza, Cheryl Rianda, Meri Gephart, Jeff Ruiz, Paul Millner, Karen Linden, Nancy Simpson, Thom West, Cal's Camera's, the Papadakis Taverna, Ken Jesperson, Jannie de Groot, John Koster, Cathy Billington, Brigitte Kohlenberg, my parents Walter and Mary Broad, Gregory, Michael, and Anthony Broad, Jackline Knable, Corrie Dil, Kieth Morey, Cameron James Quinn, Fokker Hoffman, Dianne Gill, Guiseppe de Grisantis, Peggy Glen, Heidi Tritten, Cindy Cooper, Dan Poynter, Doris Cartin, Jairo Buitrago Pim, Christina Vazquez, Cheryl Russell, and Jeanne Guenther and her niece "Fred."

I remain grateful to Gerhard F. Markus of the Austrian National Tourist Office and Y. Pekka Kurki of the Finland National Tourist Office for their detailed critiques of the first edition. And I am thankful to the reviewers for their many kind comments on my earlier editions, snippets of which are on the back cover.

It's not easy being in the travel book authoring business and every bit from everyone above is sincerely appreciated. If you have a comment, criticism, or contribution please send it over for the benefit of future editions.

Have a good trip in life.

John Bermont

Table of Contents

Foreword

How To Europe is a phoenix. This 21st anniversary edition, its first publication since 1987, has ingredients and a flavor you won't find anywhere else.

John Bermont started his European life in 1975 when the company he worked for gave him a two year transfer to Haarlem, a beautiful city just west of Amsterdam in The Netherlands. He traveled throughout western Europe in the car he shipped over, and always had a camera and notebook at his side. The result of these travels and others was the first edition of *How To Europe* in 1982. The second edition was published from 1985 through 1987. Since that second edition he has also lived in Germany, France, and Switzerland. These experiences have given birth to new chapters on living in Europe and working in Europe.

Whole new fields for independent travel opened up in the 1990s when the communist domination over eastern Europe suddenly imploded with a whimper. Bermont took advantage of these new travel opportunities. *How To Europe* now has extensive coverage of eastern Europe — from Berlin overland to Istanbul and to the eastern end of The Ukraine — all based on Bermont's adventures on the rails and roads. On one trip he drove right into the former "Evil Empire" after buying a visa at the Polish-Ukrainian frontier, and frontier it is.

Many of the original 140+ photographs are still here in the 4th edition. These illustrations of everyday artifacts and infrastructure are part of the uniqueness of this book. About 200 new photographs along the same lines — telephones, train facilities, street signs, electrical connections, gas stations, people having fun, etc., etc., — continue to show the way things are, and are done, in Europe. No book or video available anywhere approaches the scope and detail of *How To Europe* in describing and illustrating the *mode de la vie* of Europe. Bermont took all of these photographs, except the few where you see his own face and/or those credited to his ex-wife Elizabeth and daughter Stephanie.

How To Europe is not a travel guidebook, as you'll see, and it is not meant to be carried along in your travels. It is too heavy, for one thing. But more importantly it is meant to be read before you go, long before you go. As several reviewers have commented, this book is the one to read before you buy a guidebook or a suitcase.

Code	Country	EU	EZ	SZ
AL	Albania			
AND	Andorra			
A	Austria	Yes	Yes	Yes
BY	Belarus			
B	Belgium	Yes	Yes	Yes
BiH	Bosnia & Herzegovina			
BG	Bulgaria	A		
HR	Croatia			
CY	Cyprus	AA		
CZ	Czech Republic	AA		
DK	Denmark	Yes		Yes
EW	Estonia	AA		
FIN	Finland	Yes	Yes	Yes
F	France	Yes	Yes	Yes
D	Germany	Yes	Yes	Yes
GR	Greece	Yes	Yes	Yes
H	Hungary	AA		
IS	Iceland			Yes
IRL	Ireland	Yes	Yes	
I	Italy	Yes	Yes	Yes
LV	Latvia	AA		
LT	Lithuania	AA		
FL	Liechtenstein			

Code	Country	EU	EZ	SZ
L	Luxembourg	Yes	Yes	Yes
MK	Macedonia			
M	Malta	AA		
MD	Moldova			
MC	Monaco			
NL	Netherlands	Yes	Yes	Yes
N	Norway			Yes
PL	Poland	AA		
P	Portugal	Yes	Yes	Yes
RO	Romania	A		
RUS	Russia			
RSM	San Marino			
SCG	Serbia and Montenegro			
SK	Slovakia	AA		
SLO	Slovenia	AA		
E	Spain	Yes	Yes	Yes
S	Sweden	Yes		Yes
CH	Switzerland			
TR	Turkey	A		
UA	Ukraine			
GB	United Kingdom	Yes		
V	Vatican City			

EU = European Union (15)   EZ = Euro Zone (12)   SZ= Schengen Zone (15)
AA= Application approved (10)   A = Applying (3)   See the index for EU, EZ, and SZ.

Chapter 1
What's It All About?
In Europe Travel Like a Native

You can't swim in a car pool.

AN ALMOST FATAL MISTAKE

Transfer To The Netherlands
My boss walked in one morning and asked how I would like a two year transfer to the company's office in The Netherlands. After a couple of days thinking it over I decided what the heck and accepted. A few weeks later I landed on a drizzly October morning at Amsterdam's *Schiphol* airport to begin an adventure in Europe, though I was lucky to live through the first month.

Just a Leaf
Shortly after arriving, I borrowed a friend's car to run some errands. While driving on a narrow street, another car suddenly came speeding from the opposite direction. The Dutch driver flashed his lights and honked his horn but continued to race ahead as if I was just a leaf on the pavement. He seemed eager for the inevitable head-on collision.

My only escape was to jump the curb and drive across someone's front lawn. Then I circled the block to see what, if anything, I had done wrong. The only visible sign at the street where I turned in was a round red board with a white band across it. That was something I had never seen before. Later, a Dutch neighbor explained that this road sign means "Do Not Enter — Wrong Way." It's always posted at the exit end of one-way streets.

GENESIS OF A BOOK

Living and Working in Holland
Within a few weeks I had found an apartment and started to settle in. I made the short drive to the office every day, by car or bike. Though it was the same work I had done in California, the environment and worker attitude were totally different.

After work was much different also. Being single, I didn't have much in common with most of the Americans in Holland. Most of them had families and socialized through the American Women's Club. My life was almost entirely among the Dutch and I got to know them quite well.

Shipping my car over turned out to be an excellent move. I put it to good use on the roads all over northern Europe. Drives up to Stockholm, over to the former East German border, down to the Italian Riviera, and many areas in between were covered on weekend and one-week trips. I learned how to drive in Paris like a local, drive 120 mph on the German *Autobahnen* (expressways), and maneuver around Sunday strollers on rural roads

No, this is not Venice. My first home in Europe in 1975 was in Haarlem, The Netherlands, about 17 minutes from the heart of Amsterdam. For two years I lived in the ground floor apartment of the house on the right. The Teylers Museum is six doors to the left, the building with the wings on top. The Sint Bavo Kerk towers above the city and is visible for miles. Most of the houses in this neighborhood are about 300 years old. The counter-weighted lift bridge is attended full time during working hours, and is raised dozens of times a day to let boats pass up and down the Spaarne River. [0117]

Returning for Adventure

After two years in Holland I went back to California but it wasn't long before I started to regret leaving Europe. I decided to return, but this time strictly as a traveler. I was still single and had saved enough money to take some time off..

To get ready for the return trip, I quit my job and spent two months in full-time preparation. While sorting through most of the popular guidebooks, plus a library of books, pamphlets, and maps accumulated while living in Holland, it appeared that a new book would be helpful. For example, you will not to this day find a description, much less a reasonable illustration, of the "Do Not Enter" sign in any European guidebook. Maybe the guidebook authors do not drive in Europe?

The bottom round one with the white belt is "Do Not Enter." Learn more about the rest of those important round signs in chapter 18, "On the Roads of Europe; Travel by Car, Van, or Motorcycle." Seeing as how this is Amsterdam, a city with one of the finest public transportation systems and most confusing driving conditions on the whole planet earth, just don't drive here, unless you can read those little white boards with other qualifiers written in good crisp Dutch while a taxi snooks up your tailpipe and two bicycles brush you on the right as a pedestrian and dog step out in front of you on the left. If you feel lucky enough to drive in A'dam you should take a taxi to the casino where all you can lose is your cash and not your life. [0115]

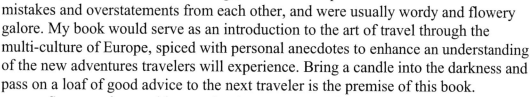

    My nearly fatal mistake on the one-way street was only one of many "dumb foreigner" blunders in Europe. Each cost me time, cash, or grief, or all of the above. Sometimes the local citizens were not very amused. Many things are different over there and I had to learn it all the hard way. As I learned the ropes, it became apparent that other Americans on their first trip were just as confounded by the mores of Europe as I was initially.

    At the time many of the available books presented little more than superficial facts, presumed a reader's familiarity with the new surroundings, sometimes copied mistakes and overstatements from each other, and were usually wordy and flowery galore. My book would serve as an introduction to the art of travel through the multi-culture of Europe, spiced with personal anecdotes to enhance an understanding of the new adventures travelers will experience. Bring a candle into the darkness and pass on a loaf of good advice to the next traveler is the premise of this book.

    So a year later, with a notebook, a camera, and a three-month EurailPass, I covered most of Europe in almost constant travel, from Bordeaux to Vienna to Narvik in the north of Norway. Then I spent an additional three months visiting and studying in Amsterdam, Paris, and London. After another three-week refresher trip through nine countries in 1981, I published the first edition of *How To Europe* the following spring.

    The book reviews were very nice. The American Library Association's *Booklist* said ". . . outstandingly practical . . ." *The Los Angeles Times* said ". . . exceedingly complete . . ."*The International Travel News*, the best travel journal there is, said "Bermont has a knack for picking out and clarifying the things that usually baffle American visitors." Many others echoed the same sentiments.

    The following year I was back again hitting the four corners of then Western Europe — Helsinki, Dublin, Lisbon, Athens — crisscrossing by train and boat for ten weeks ending in early 1984. The second edition went to press later that year and sold out three printings in three years.

Uh oh, they saw my camera. This couple with their pet grizzly came quickly to get a donation. We were stuck in traffic in Constanta, Romania but got moving before they reached us. [0104]

The Changing Times

Welcome to the fourth edition. Since the last printing of *How To Europe* in 1987 Europe has undergone incredible changes in some aspects, but most things are still the same.

Eastern Europe: The most significant change is that the Berlin Wall is down and the communist dictatorships are gone. We are now free to travel in most of what was once a huge prison, the so-called Peoples Democratic Republics. There are still a few of these bastardizations left in other parts of the world but Europe is rid of them.

New Technology: Also, the technological revolution of the 1990s has helped Europe immensely. It has brought the archaic telecommunications systems up to and above the quality we enjoy in the USA. The caliber of transportation — plane, train, and auto — has improved dramatically. Unfortunately so has the frequency of traffic jams and overcrowded trains.

Living in France and Germany: I've also changed. I moved to Paris in the summer of 1986 to study French and to work on the next edition. There I met Elizabeth and *amour*, which lasted about 10 years. We were transferred to Germany in 1991 for a two year period. Taking advantage of the new freedoms in the east I drove throughout eastern Europe, going into the Ukraine twice. We finished up the German experience with a one month drive as far as Istanbul, returning back to Germany via Bulgaria, Romania, Poland, and several other countries. This edition will get you up to speed on travel in the former "Evil Empire."

Unmovable Artifacts: But for the most part the character and charm of old Europe remains — the monuments are still where they have been for hundreds of years. Notre Dame Cathedral plus a thousand monuments and museums have not moved a millimeter in a millennium, and won't.

WHAT IS THIS BOOK?

Most people think of travel books as guidebooks. *Au contraire, mon ami*, for *How To Europe* is not really a travel guidebook. This means that it is not a catalog of hotels, restaurants, and sights, telling you what is "comfortable" or "cheap" or "charming" or whatever. There are many good and not so good guidebooks. You'll find recommendations in chapter 10, "Guidebooks, Maps, Dictionaries; You Too Can Be Your Own Tour Guide."

A Travelers Handbook

Rather than a specific guidebook, *How To Europe* is a general and practical handbook for Americans planning a trip to Europe. It is essential reading for first-time travelers and will probably enlighten and amuse even experienced Europhiles. I've received letters from native Europeans telling me how much they learned from this book.

How To Europe is zero-base. This means it does not presume that you know how to drive on a German expressway, use a French telephone, get service in a Dutch restaurant, find a hotel in the Ukraine, or board an Italian train. Amongst many other things, what it does do is show you how to find the best values in any city in Europe without guiding you and a thousand other Americans to the same cheap hotels and restaurants. You'll learn how to travel like a European, thus getting the most from your time and money while dodging the travel gremlins.

At least as important as anything, *How To Europe* teaches you how to avoid becoming another victim of the ever-present pickpockets and baggage thieves operating throughout Europe. Thieves are concentrated in the major cities and resort areas, but can strike anywhere and anytime. This ubiquitous army of villains, usually not native to the locale, can mess up your trip — very seriously. Security should always be on your mind. See the first section of chapter 8, "Cash, Check, and Credit Card; Travel with Some of Each in Europe."

Photos To Learn By

Together with the captions, the photographs explain many of the mundane but essential points of life in Europe, those things that differ from our upbringing in America. Reviewers of the first two editions have especially noted the uniqueness and value of these photos. I took all of the pictures except for a few as noted or as obvious.

Really Straight Talk

Here and there in this book I have recommended some products, publications, and services, and have found a few words of caution to offer about other things which did not measure up. I paid retail for everything and received no payment or other consideration for any comment in this book. I mention this because virtually all travel writers accept free air travel, ground transportation, hotels, and/or meals from companies in the travel business. That is why you rarely, if ever, read a travel article with the least bit of criticism of anything. Those who bite the golden hand are not invited to eat again. I didn't take any freebees so I can tell it like it is.

The Fifth Arrondissement (ward) of Paris welcomes visitors with this street side map locating hotels and sights. The bulls eye is accompanied by the words vous etes ici (you are here). My Paris apartment was just a tad southeast of the bull's eye on rue des Trois Portes, 200 yards from the back door of Notre Dame Cathedral. Check the inset "Paris V" to see where you are in the city — I should say THE City. [0108]

I have been to every place I've discussed in this book. I did not hire others to "research" or write this book or take the photos. If you see a book with a famous author's name on the cover — it is marketing bull. Most of the popular guide books these days are written by hired writers for politically imperfect corporations.

From the Algarve to the eastern Ukraine, Iceland to Istanbul, Narvik to Naples, I've traveled the rails and roads throughout Europe. I've slept in hotels deluxe and on deck chairs, dined in gourmet restaurants and picnicked on park benches, and walked the boulevards and back alleys of cities big to small. I was lost and found, rained on, frozen, sun burnt, insulted, complimented, ripped off, embraced, and scorned. *How To Europe* gives it to you straight, no matter what your schedule, budget, or attitude.

EUROPE, WHY NOT?

Why go to Europe? Curiosity, culture, entertainment, sports, adventure, relatives, roots, education, business, a job, diet, or just plain fun may entice you. If you haven't made the decision yet, the holdup is probably due to one of three things: money, time, or timidity.

Can't Afford It?

A major problem is cost. Travel is expensive. But some things are cheaper in Europe, most are negotiable, and airline and hotel bargains can be found with diligent searching. Despite the high cost of travel, you can budget accurately with the information presented in the next chapter. The key to low cost travel is up-front smarts and cautious shopping. Do a little home budget swapping to tide you over. You might want to postpone buying a new car to put some European flavor in your life.

A couple of celebrants brandish their beers at the annual Queen's Day festival in Amsterdam, The Netherlands. I kept pace. What a beautiful day. If you suffer from ochlophobia stay out of Amsterdam on April 30. [0109]

Don't Have Time?

Another problem for most of us is lack of time. A standard corporate vacation of two or three weeks is hardly enough to see one country, much less the 45 or so in Europe. Request an extra four or five weeks of unpaid leave from your job and go on your own. A longer tour will enable you to get your feet on the ground and wander off the trampled tourist trail.

By the way, Europeans are horrified when you tell them that you are allowed a two week vacation. In most of Europe the standard vacation is four to six weeks. Some companies pay their employees for a "13th month" so they have enough money to enjoy themselves on vacation.

Afraid of All Those Foreigners?

Aside from the limitations of time and money, many Americans are afraid to go. The adventure of travel is not always fun. On the road, aggravations often outnumber the laughs. Travel is not always relaxing. It can be tiresome visiting strange places with different languages, money, customs, food, and poor service. Why leave the security and comfort of home to find yourself lost in France in the rain? Look at this from another perspective: your nest is just another place on our earth and those strangers are just as human as you and your home town neighbors.

If you really do find yourself in trouble over there, help is readily available and it usually comes with a bigger heart because you are a foreigner. Just ask. Women, of course, must be a little more careful than men. For encouragement and advice, ladies should consult the books of Mesdames Kaye, Hesse, Zobel, Bereny, and Baxel.

After reading *How To Europe* you should have as much confidence in visiting Europe as you have in going to your corner grocery store.

The Terror

The unspeakable monstrosity which struck America and civilization on 9/11 cannot be ignored by those planning a trip, or even by those going to work every day. A new and brutal war without limits or front lines is all around us. It is just beginning. The enemy is well organized, financed, and concealed. The head of the evil is at large. When that head is cut off another will take its place.

I personally experienced the effects of terror years ago. My first edition published in 1982 and subsequent editions are dedicated to a victim of a terrorist bombing, Annette Kampinga. She was murdered on December 31, 1980 in Nairobi, Kenya. The coward who killed her and 15 other people placed a bomb in his closet at the Norfolk Hotel and then flew off to Malta and then on to Saudi Arabia without checking out of his room. The time bomb exploded just above the ballroom as the New Year's Eve party was getting underway.

Closer to my own body, I was evacuated from Los Angeles International Airport along with hundreds of others when someone phoned in a bomb threat. I flew to Amsterdam and traveled on to Paris just a few days after President Reagan bombed Libya in April 1987, amidst talk of war. I flew into Frankfurt in January 1991, a few days before the Gulf War started and flew out a week later on PanAm while the other five in our group jumped ship and thought they would be safer on Lufthansa. I was in Al Khobar, Saudi Arabia in July 1996 on the night that a terrorist gang blew up the Khobar Towers and murdered 19 American servicemen. That bomb went off a couple of miles from my apartment with effects remarkably like the Oklahoma City bombing. The truth on the Khobar Towers attack is still concealed, though Osama bin Laden was the mastermind whispered about at the American Consulate at the time, 5 years before 9/11.

On the other hand, one of my brothers was murdered in Chicago. He stopped his taxi for the wrong "customer" who immediately shot him. The Chicago cops supposedly know who did it but never arrested anybody.

The point is that you never know when or where or how your Maker is going to call you back. Look at the situation in our schools. Teachers and students are killed in their classrooms every year. This is murder and mayhem and a violation of citizens rights, but typically the only rights being respected are those of the mad dogs who do the crime, even when they are filmed in the act and caught with blood on their hands.

Have no fear, but be alert and ready for action. Those people on the "shoe bomber" flight from Paris to Miami saved themselves. Perhaps, some day, so must you.

Security is tight and causes delays in airports. You are advised to get to the airport early. I arrived at Los Angeles airport in January 2002 before the Northwest Airlines people opened check-in. After checking in I went to security and they hadn't opened yet. I had to wait a half hour till 5:00 am to get clearance to enter the boarding area. I found a place to plug in my laptop and work on this book for a few hours. If you're not writing a book, bring one and relax.

The bottom line on mass murder by terror is that it can and probably will happen again. But the odds are that it won't happen to you if you fly every day for the next 50 years. Let your Maker select your inevitable last day. You enjoy your life while you have it. Don't let the bastards get you down.

You Are Already Too Thin?

My last reason for not going to Europe is not especially profound. (A double negative can be used in this sentence because the negatories apply to different subjects.) If you've watched the evening news at all for the past few years you certainly have heard about the French paradoxes. One has to do with their extraordinary consumption of wine and their less than (American) average incidence of heart disease. The other has to do with their dietary intake of beautiful rich foods — lamb, duck, paté, cheeses — with their inverse correlation to the American waistline. You rarely see fat French people. So, if you don't want to lose weight, don't go on a one-month French restaurant crawl. Especially, I encourage everyone to stay out of *Bourgogne* (Burgundy), one of the least touristed regions of France and my favorite for food and wine.

WHEN AND WHERE

In Season

Americans traditionally travel in the summer. That's equally true in Europe. Northern Europeans head for the sand and sun around the Mediterranean in July and August. Many also take winter holidays, skiing in the Alps and other cold climes.

Out of Season

Those who have the opportunity to travel off-season are lucky. You can travel more economically and in far less crowded circumstances with a spring trip. Air fares are drastically lower off-season, and the roads and trains are noticeably less crowded. Off-season is anytime other than July and August and the holiday period around Christmas and Easter. April through June is the best off-season travel period.

The obvious feature of off-season travel is that it is cooler in the south and colder in the north. The opposite is true of in-season travel, since it can get uncomfortably hot and humid in southern Europe during the summer. Spring is the driest time of year in northern Europe. You are less likely to get rained on in April and May, and the length of daylight is about the same as in July and August.

A significant problem when traveling in the fall is that hotel space may be scarce or impossible to find. This is caused by the plethora of annual trade shows and business conventions in major cities. These are known as *fairs* and *congresses* to most Europeans. If you have a chance, go to one. These exhibitions feature everything from French cuisine to hazardous waste, and many are open to the public, not just to those in the trade.

Municipally operated tourist offices in most cities of Europe give you maps, hotel lists, and current information on sights and events. This is the entrance to the Informazioni Turistiche Alberghiere *in Firenze (Florence), Italy. Photo by Elizabeth. [0106]*

All the Seasons

Those with a transportable profession can enjoy Europe throughout the year, and have someone else pay the bill. Just get a job in Europe. That's easier said than done. I've lived and worked in The Netherlands and in Germany. Not only do you get a salary boost but there can be other financial rewards as well, depending on your employer. Most companies have an overseas transfer policy and some are decidedly more civil than others. See more about this in chapter 21, "Working in Europe" and chapter 22, "Living in Europe."

Special Events

Your interest in special events may dictate your timing. Oktoberfest, for instance, is held in late September in Munich. The tulips bloom at Keukenhof, Holland, in early spring, weather permitting. These and other events can live with you for life.

Pick Your Own Pleasure

Friends and students are always asking me which place in Europe I like the most. My preferences would be of little value to anyone else. These places are mostly associated with memories of the people I met there, whether locals or other travelers.

Pick your own pleasure. Prepare thoroughly for your travels using the general and specific information in this book, as well as other books discussed in chapter 10, "Guidebooks, Maps, Dictionaries." Make your own itinerary based on your lifestyle and preferences. Chapter 30, "Melding with Europe" offers an overview of the kinds of activities that are possible, although I don't pretend to list everything. Nobody can prescribe a universal list of the "good stuff." This is just a peek at the menu. You must make your own selections.

Enjoy Tivoli Garden from May to mid September. Tivoli is an amusement park in Copenhagen, Denmark. It is great for all ages and not as stodgy or as expensive as another famous place which seems to have copied some of its designs, and added a talking mouse. [0113]

HOW TO GO

Should you travel alone, with a friend, or with a group? Each way has its advantages.

Solo

When single I usually traveled alone. This offers the best opportunities for meeting local citizens and other travelers. Getting in a train compartment or sitting at a table on a ship, I would tell the others "Sorry, I only speak English." At least half the time, this would result in a non-stop conversation with a local citizen that lasted until one of us got off the train or the boat docked. Sometimes I would practice my French or German or Dutch, depending on the situation. If I happened to meet another vagabond we would sometimes team up for a couple of days. You're never alone unless you want to be.

When traveling with a EurailPass in first class, you are likely to meet educated Europeans and other travelers from the United States, Canada, Australia, South America, Japan, and China. It is even easier to meet others on the overnight ferries between Ireland and France and between Greece and Italy. Seating in the bars and cafeterias is crowded, and you'll have a lot of spare time. Only a hermit could avoid meeting someone on board. Travelers have a great deal in common, develop camaraderie, and help each other with tips on hotels, cafes, sights, and rip-offs.

You don't have to be a man to travel alone. I've met American and Australian college girls, and even a few ladies in their sixties, on their own, all over Europe. At the Romanian border leaving Bulgaria we met a young French woman, traveling in a Citroën 2CV with her dog. That's adventure in a tin can, the auto known as the "duck" or "doe-che-voh."

Use a coin or a card. The German phone on the left accepts coins. The one on the right accepts telephone cards. This picture reminds me of a study done by a sociology professor at the University of Aachen, Germany. On side by side phones he put a "Nur Herren" (men only) sign on one and a "Nur Frauen" (women only) sign on the other. He and his class observed at a distance. All the men used the men's phone and all the women used the women's phone, with one exceptional exception. They rushed over to interview the woman to discover why she had shown contempt for the German obsession with obedience. She was French! [0105]

With Friends

Traveling with a friend, or friends, requires compromises from each. Preferred itineraries must be agreed on, and it sure helps if everybody is on the same general budget. Being with a small group puts you in a better bargaining position when negotiating the room price with a hotel keeper, and gives each a bit more courage walking the streets at night. Another advantage of traveling in company is that the hotel rooms are better. You get a lot more comfort at a lower per person cost in a double room.

Family With or Without Child

When I was married, most of my traveling was with Elizabeth, and often with our daughter Stephanie in the car or on the train. Family people will recognize the pilot/navigator scenario with nearly constant back-seat commentary "Are we there yet?" until the little one falls asleep. The extra hotel cost is usually none or negligible, though the cost of a soft drink for the kid is usually more than a glass of beer or wine.

Excess baggage in the extreme was a problem when traveling on the trains and negotiating the train stations with two-year old Stephanie. A kid of that age has more luggage than two adults. Families have the option of parking the kid(s) with a relative so mom and dad can have a vacation on their own.

Package Group Tours

It can be a lot of work traveling on your own. Do-it-yourselfers make many decisions every day. If you choose to travel with a group on an organized tour, you'll find that tour directors do most of the work and make most of the decisions for you.

Group tours usually include hotels, air and ground transportation, guided sightseeing excursions, many meals, and time off for independent side trips.

Advertised prices are always per person, double occupancy. Solo travelers pay a "single supplement." Tours are ideal for the timid, for those who do not have time or inclination for detailed travel planning, and for those who would rather sit back, enjoy the sights, and leave all the routine details in the hands of experienced tour managers.

I scoff at package group tours for anyone except the physically handicapped. Tours are overpriced, rigid in schedule, and full of Americans looking out the bus window. Anybody who has graduated from high school can travel independently in Europe, especially after reading *How To Europe*

THE COST OF TRAVEL

Prices of products and services are mentioned on a very limited basis in this book. *How To Europe* is designed to be valid for several years into the future so specific prices are not included. Most books which include prices are in error before they are printed, which is about six months before you get your hands on them. The "2003" editions of some travel books were available in October, 2002 with information from the previous spring or summer. The next chapter describes in detail how to make a budget. First, here are some general notes to keep in mind.

Prices

In virtually any city you can find meals for $5 or $200. The same goes for sleeps. Be a frugal traveler, but don't pick the cheapest places to bunk in. Select what appears to be clean and amenable. Pass it up if the price is not right. For hotels, negotiate — <u>always</u>. See the detailed discussion on negotiating in chapter 14, "Hotel, Hostel, B&B, Private Home." You can save 20% to 50% at almost any hotel with any number of stars almost every night almost anywhere no matter what your budget and no matter how expensive the hotel.

Inflation

Another reason prices are not given in *How To Europe* is that dirty "I" word — inflation. As we all know, prices are always changing, usually up. In some European countries inflation is much higher than in America. In others it is less.

However, the inflation rate for the overall economy does not translate equally to the inflation rate for the discretionary economy. Travel services are cyclic in demand, but fixed in supply. They don't truck extra hotel rooms into Paris when tourist season starts. Small changes in demand can move the price dramatically. Big changes in demand, for instance between off season and in season, can change prices by an order of magnitude. Nothing demonstrates this better than the price of flying to Europe. Compare a ticket in May to one in July.

In those chapters dealing with air travel, hotels, and dining, I present tried and true strategies for reducing your outlay regardless of your budget. You might think it cheesy to negotiate and/or shop around over these things, but just call it a game for profit because you can save beaucoup bucks. Depending on your situation you can save enough for a tea kettle or a new Porsche.

Traveling off-season in May I was probably the only guest in this Biarritz, France hotel. This economical, clean, and comfortable little hotel is way up the hill from the city, and there is a great Spanish restaurant a few blocks away. [0110]

Dollar Exchange Rate

Another cost factor in the travel equation is the value of the dollar. Currency exchange rates change continuously. The dollar may be worth more or less in European currency at the time of your travels. The dollar dipped to record lows in 1978. For a number of years it was on a strong upward trend. It set record highs against many European currencies in 1985. Then by the mid-1990's the dollar fell well below its levels of ten years prior.

As of 2003, the dollar had ended its upward trend and has gone below par with the *euro*, the new currency of the European Union, most of the members that is. More about the *euro* in later chapters. By late summer the dollar had moved up a bit, but where the dollar goes from here can only be determined with tomorrow's newspaper — something like the weather.

GET READY

"If it wasn't for the last minute, a lot of things wouldn't get done." But a successful and favorably memorable trip requires careful preparation. You are better off planning far ahead and using that last minute to eat the last good hamburger you will have until you get home.

Your Schedule

There are many things to do before you go. The first is to make a planning schedule, notwithstanding the old adage about the plans of mice and men. This assures that you will get everything done without a last-minute panic. The earlier you begin, the easier it will be. Two months of preparation is appropriate, but six months would not be out of order for a long journey. If you wait until the last minute you will have to hurry and be faced with the old Dutch adage: "The hurrier you go the behinder you get."

For a planning schedule, a large wall calendar, self-made on drafting paper, the back of shelf liner, or any large sheet of plain paper will do. A square of about 2" by 2" for each day, plus a six-inch wide margin for each week for additional notes will suffice. Or use a calendar desk pad, available at stationery stores. Keep it in a conspicuous place as a daily reminder.

This beautiful walk street in Salzburg, Austria, can turn your clock back a few decades. Parking within reach of the No Parking sign (blue and round with a red slash) is a common European pastime. The other sign prohibits entry to bicycles and mopeds. [0102]

Lists

Next, begin your check lists. A long piece of adding machine paper is ideal. Have at least three lists: "Things to do before leaving," "Things to buy before leaving," and "Packing list." Carry these lists in your pocket, reviewing them daily, scratching off items as they are done, and adding new items which come to mind. Review chapter 5 "What to Wear in Europe" and chapter 6 "A Packing List for Europe" to get you started. A summary packing list is presented in the appendix, "Last Call."

Additional lists such as "Things to buy in Europe" and "Things to do" can be made as you study guidebooks and tourist brochures and talk to other travelers.

GENERAL NOTES

Redundancies

Because of the relationship between several topics in the book and my objective of making every chapter as complete as possible on the subject at hand, there are some redundancies in the book. These second looks are not long and usually concern items like the Michelin, Berlitz, and Thomas Cook publications, and *The International Travel News*. These should be emphasized anyway.

Terminology

For brevity, throughout the book, certain areas of Europe are referred to without listing each of the countries to which a comment is applicable. The conventional and created terms used throughout the book are:

The Continent: all of Western Europe excluding Ireland and Great Britain.
The Islands: Ireland and Great Britain.
Scandinavia: Denmark, Norway, Sweden, Iceland, and Finland.

Iberia: Portugal and Spain.
The Mediterranean countries: Portugal, Spain, Italy, Greece, Cyprus, and Malta.

The dining car crew consented to pose with a smile during my 21 hour voyage across the Ukraine, from Kiev to nearly the eastern border. [0116]

The Eastern countries: All of those formerly under communist domination. The names have changed and some have broken up into pieces. As of this writing, the names are Russia, Ukraine, Belarus, Moldavia, Romania, Bulgaria, Albania, Macedonia, Yugoslavia (which prefers to call itself Serbia and Montenegro), Bosnia and Herzegovina, Croatia, Slovenia, Hungary, Czech Republic, Slovakia, Poland, Lithuania, Latvia, and Estonia. Former East Germany is not necessarily in this group. It received special privileges from former West Germany which is bringing it into the modern world much faster than the others from the former Soviet Bloc. Some people in these countries prefer to say they are in "central" Europe. Technically they are correct. The center of my National Geographic map of Europe is in southeastern Poland. But, for the time being, Eastern Europe is still that part of Europe formerly known as "peoples democratic republics" — the countries from which citizens would flee at the risk of their lives. I know one man who made it out alive. Many were shot in the back.

Of course, Portugal does not front the Mediterranean, but France does, and some people do not consider Finland to be part of Scandinavia. But these six groupings indicate convenient demarcations in customs, food, weather, and the general character of the peoples. Examples will be seen throughout the book.

A small piece of Turkey lies in Europe. This is a good enough reason to go to Istanbul, a fascinating city.

Spellings

There is no consistency in this book on spellings of cities and places. I did that on purpose. There is no consistency anywhere on this point. You have to stay loose and get a smell for things — like Corinth and Kórinthos, Munich and München, Göteborg and Gothenburg, Basel and Bâle, and scores of other places with two or more names.

Generally, foreign words are *italicized* in this book with the American translation in (parentheses) right next to it. I say American translation, not English, because there are some dialectical differences between American and British "English." See more on this subject in chapter 26, "Languages, Numbers, Alphabets; Encounter the Tower of Babel in Europe."

While having paella at the La Barraca restaurant in Madrid, Spain these university students came in and serenaded every table. [0112]

Chapter 2
On Budget in Europe
Travel Expenses

Everybody's life is on a budget.

STAYING ON A BUDGET

Making a travel budget is relatively easy. Staying on one is the real challenge. It's like being on a diet.

Budget vs. Expense

A budget is the amount you plan to spend. An expense is the amount you actually spent.

The purpose of this chapter is to provide information on getting the cost data together so that you can make your budget. In other words, make an estimate of your expenses for the trip. Later in the book you will learn many ways to save money compared to the first-cut estimates you will make now. Since it is a natural human tendency to spend more than is planned, make sure that you have the finances to cover your budget. If you have a surplus in the last week of your trip you will certainly find a way to take care of that "problem."

Even if you feel that you don't need to budget, the exercise will be enlightening. When you're traveling, money is always flowing and it helps to know just how much. Keep an eye on your funds to prevent rip-offs. Declare a victory when you score good bargains which you can brag about at home, whether it's a humble tea pot or a new Porsche.

Cash Draw System

There are a number of ways to put your budget into practice. One method I have found very effective is to go on a weekly cash draw system. Every Wednesday morning, say, get the cash that will carry you through the following week. If you're running out on the following Tuesday morning, just starve or stop shopping until Wednesday morning. That may be unpleasant but it will save you from the jam I saw others fall into. They failed to monitor cash flow and found themselves with the inevitable unpleasant surprise — an empty wallet. Waiting for money from home is certainly the worst way to spend time in Europe.

MAKING YOUR BUDGET

How much does it really cost to travel in Europe? Are you put off by travel agents quoting you hotel rates of $200 per night, or are you enraptured by reports of $5 dollars a day, room, meals, *and* transport included? Both are true. In fact the extremes are further apart than this. Those who have it can spend any amount. Those who don't have the financial means can try to beg or pick grapes to earn traveling money, though you will have a hard time at it. With luck and beyond, you can theoretically live off the land and keep going forever, or until you must have a real hamburger again. If you are the super adventuring sort and have no wallet, read Ed Buryn's book "Vagabonding in Europe and North Africa." He did it by thumb and by sleeping in barns, in addition to more conventional travel by VW bus in the early 1970s. Ed Buryn's book is a classic for adventure travel.

Most of us have limited funds and limited time, though, and do not want to just survive just to be in Europe. The following sections will enable you to make a budget to suit your own personal travel plans and standard of living. Your lifestyle, rather than where you are, is the major determinant of your expenses.

There are a few dozen categories of expenses you will encounter on a trip to Europe. A general list is presented below.

The first three items are the essentials and the things you think about first. But the sum of the thirty or so miscellaneous items can easily exceed any one of the big three, or even the sum of the three if you insist on spending and spending.

Hotels in France usually display a board showing room prices. Here at the Hotel Paul in Aix-en-Provence the first column gives the room numbers, the second the number of beds, the third whether it has a douche *(shower) or W.C. (toilet) or just a* lavabo *(wash basin), and then the price according to the number of guests. Since January 1, 2002 France and most of central Europe uses the euro, €. The euro is one of the greatest blessings that has ever fallen on travelers,*

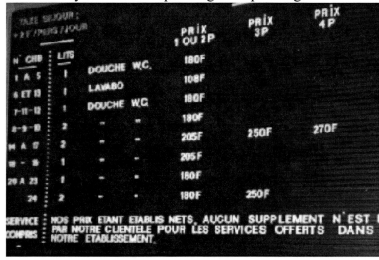

making it so much easier to cross borders without needing to change money immediately on arrival. [0211]

Now let's look at the nitty gritty of putting your budget together. Remember, this does not need to be extremely accurate, and in fact you should budget a little high just to be safe.

The Big Three
- Lodging
- Food
- Transportation

Thirty (or so) Miscellaneous Items

- Guidebooks
- Maps
- Souvenirs
- Medicine
- Gifts
- Toilet tips
- Guitar case donations
- Fees
- Cleaning
- Money changing
- Film
- Guided tours
- Museums, theaters, shows
- Bus, tram, and metro tickets
- Taxis
- Bike rental
- Film processing

- Telephone calls
- Internet café time
- Smokes
- Entertainment
- Drinks
- Postage
- Toothpaste
- Postcards
- Soap
- Haircuts
- Taxes
- New shoes
- New clothes
- Casino losses
- Pickpocket losses
- Whatever else

Here are the sources of information to help you set up your own budget. This covers the big three — lodging, food, and transportation.

LODGING

There are many sources of prices for hotel rooms and other accommodations. The sources readily available to you are:
- Individual hotels
- City tourist offices
- Michelin Red Guides
- Official national tourist offices
- Travel agents
- Budget travel guides

These sources are arranged in order of decreasing reliability. There are exceptions, as there must be in any such generalization.

Individual Hotels

The best source is the hotel itself. You can write and request prices for the type of room you want for the date you want it. Enclose a self-addressed envelope with an International Reply Coupon (available at your post office) to insure a reply. Most hotels have published rate cards so you should get an early response.

It is better to phone if you want an immediate response. Most hotels have someone on duty who speaks English. You can use a fax to confirm a reservation, but most hotels will not respond to fax inquiries because of the expense. Many hotels have a web site with descriptions of their facilities and prices.

Determine whether a bath/shower, toilet, taxes, "service charges," and breakfast is included in the price or is extra. If you are planning to drive ask if they have on-site parking and if it is included in the price of the room. Parking is usually an extra cost option at hotels in major cities. Street parking is usually free but can be difficult to find. In some cities street parking is restricted to residents and special permit holders. Road side motels usually have plenty of free parking. If you use a "discount" hotel internet booking service to find a hotel it would be a good idea to call the hotel before making your reservation. You are paying for the service, and the hotel often has a better rate, and you can negotiate a better deal.

City Tourist Office

The next best source of room price information is the tourist office in the city you are planning to visit. You may obtain detailed hotel lists describing services, facilities, and prices by writing directly to the local city tourist office. Allow yourself weeks for a reply. If you receive last year's listed prices, adjust them for inflation and exchange rate changes to come up with a budget figure. Do not expect a firm price until your cash is in the hands of the hotel operator. Also ask the tourist office for information about the city and its surroundings. You will probably receive a 2 pound package of information, and they pay the postage. An alternate to writing is to seek out the web site of the city or region you plan to visit. Use a search engine and just enter the city name. You will have more hits than you would expect. To save time use the "city tourist office" category of the *TRAVELERS YELLOW PAGES* on my web site *www.enjoy-europe.com* to be connected to official tourist offices in many cities of Europe.

Michelin

The Michelin Red Guides published by the Michelin Tire Company in France are an outstanding source of hotel price information. Red Guides are available for most of the countries of Europe and regions of France. There is a small guide to the major cities of Europe, ideal for business travelers. Major virtues of Michelin Red Guides are that the directories are comprehensive and they are readily available from American book retailers, either regular bookstores or on the internet. These books do not list all hotels, but they do list hotels in all price ranges and in virtually every city and village. AAA Guides, published by the American Automobile Association, list only the most expensive establishments, approved for "American comfort." For hostel price information, obtain the official guidebook from the American Youth Hostels. This is available from the AYH in Washington, DC and in bookstores at hostels in the USA. Note that a hostel is not a hotel — it is more like a bunkhouse.

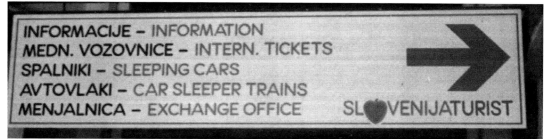

INFORMACIJE – INFORMATION
MEDN. VOZOVNICE – INTERN. TICKETS
SPALNIKI – SLEEPING CARS
AVTOVLAKI – CAR SLEEPER TRAINS
MENJALNICA – EXCHANGE OFFICE   SL♥VENIJATURIST

The Slovenijaturist *office welcomes you in English. Otherwise most of us would not know what is happening in Ljubljana. Slovenia was part of Yugoslavia until 1990 but got away with a 10 day war for independence. Go to Slovenia for a pleasant time without spending a lot of money. [0202]*

National Tourist Offices, NTOs

Another good source of hotel price information is the official national tourist office for the country you are planning to visit. Each European country maintains a tourist office in New York City or a consulate in Washington, and some have offices in other major American cities. Write and allow several weeks for a reply. Request a list of hotels for the cities on your itinerary. Again, most of these countries maintain a web site, and again, the TRAVELERS YELLOW PAGES on *www.enjoy-europe.com* has a directory of these offices with direct links.

Travel Agents

You can get confirmed prices (and reservations) at your travel agent. You must be well-heeled or on an expense account to find this practical since a travel agent will provide this service only if you are going to stay in the world class hotels. They pay a commission to the travel agent for the booking service. Generally this means a minimum of $200 per nose per sundown.

Budget Guidebooks

Lastly, use one of the budget guidebooks. All too often the cheap hotel prices are either completely bogus, out of date, or for only a few rooms which are perpetually booked. Additionally, if you do get a room in a hotel mentioned in one of these books, you will find the place full of Californians, Texans, and New Yorkers. You went to Europe for that?

Prices in many publications are out of date before they are printed because of the long lead time between field research, if any, and publication date. Some of the travel books with a big date on the cover are published in the previous fall to take advantage of the Christmas buying season. Well known books dated 2003 were in the bookstores in October 2002. If you are using these in the following summer you have stale information.

There are very few guidebooks which I have found reliable and relatively free of errors. Chapter 10 has a review of most of the current crop.

Looking out from the inside of a café in Toul, France while I take the two sips of my wake up espresso. It is often less expensive and more interesting to have breakfast in a café like this rather than in your hotel. [0201]

FOOD

In Europe, you will find few American restaurant choices and many more that will be completely new to you. The feature common to almost all food in western Europe is that it will cost more than it does at home. You can budget for it. In eastern Europe, the prices are far more reasonable.

There are not as many sources of information on the cost of eating as there are on the cost of sleeping. But again, here is a list, starting with the best source.
- Michelin Red Guides
- Official National Tourist Offices
- Budget guidebooks

When you are using these or other sources for food price information, always remember that the listed prices do not include the price of drinks, coffee, or desserts. In all of the Scandinavian countries, two beers with dinner can double the cost of a meal. Almost everywhere, one or two mixed drinks can do the same thing. In many countries, a soft drink will cost more than a glass of beer or wine. Spain, Portugal, Italy, and Greece all have good quality inexpensive table wine, a nice complement to the good and relatively low-cost meals, compared to northern Europe.

Coffee generally costs the equivalent of one or two dollars for the European half cup, with no free seconds, not to mention thirds or a pot on the table. In eastern Europe, local beers and spirits are inexpensive, with the quality varying from superb to unmentionable.

But the good news in Europe is that all posted menu prices include *value added tax* (sales tax) and virtually all include a *service charge* (tip). Sometimes the bill looks strange because they have broken out the tax and tip and show them as separate line items. Darn accountants are everywhere just to confuse us.

A major exception to the practice of including the tip is Italy where all restaurants have a "bread and cover" charge for each occupied chair. This is a buck or two plus about 5% and is added to your bill. And if you see *service 15% non-compris* on your French menu, it means that 15% will be added to your bill. That's the tip, though it will not insure promptness.

Michelin Red Guides

Very convenient sources of good dining cost information are the annual Michelin Red Guides. These books (discussed above and elsewhere herein) select some restaurants, give them ratings, and state minimum and maximum dinner prices. Restaurants in all price ranges and in virtually every city are covered. Again, the cost of beverages is not included in the price ranges.

Official National Tourist Offices

The NTOs do not generally publish information or advice on specific eateries. They do advise on approximate costs for meals in several categories, from luxury to budget.

Hotels and restaurants are not recommended in this book. On the other hand I can't remember how many times I've enjoyed the reasonable prices, good food, great service, friendly clientele, and beautiful interior of Le Bistro de la Gare in Paris. If you have to wait for a table, enjoy an aperitif and chat with other customers while you are standing in line. [0206]

Budget Guidebooks

Even though prices for meals as given by the popular guidebooks are more reliable than their data on hotel prices, take them lightly. Whatever research that is done for these annually "updated" books is 12 months old before you are likely to buy them. It is probable that a few restaurants will have closed, moved, changed owners, or simply changed menus by the time you get there. If prices are given in a publication, make adjustments for inflation and exchange rate fluctuations since the year before the copyright date of the book. The better books wisely do not state prices but simply indicate low, moderate, or high prices.

Economy Tip

Even if you don't have to do it to stay within your budget, picnic occasionally. Time savings can also be substantial. Simply visit any market or grocery store to buy bread, cold meats, fish, cheese, yogurt, fruit, and a bottle of wine. Hot roasted chicken is available in some super markets. On days when you picnic, your food bill can easily be kept under $10. Outdoor farmer's markets generally have the lowest priced groceries. Peel or wash the fruit and veggies to clean off the insecticides, herbicides, and fertilizer. You can eat in your room or on a park bench.

TRANSPORTATION

Getting there, getting around in Europe, and getting back will cost a lot. Transportation within cities is not included in this section. The cost of taxis, buses, and metros is very indeterminate and is grouped in bulk under the thirty miscellaneous items.

Flying to Europe

Getting there and getting back can be wrapped up quickly. Call a few airlines and get prices for flight plans that suit your schedule. Easier yet, walk into any travel agency. They should have the information at their fingertips. Or use one of the popular internet travel or airline sites. These can give you a vast amount of information. But don't use the lowest price from Travelocity.com or Excite.com for your budget unless you buy it immediately. These prices can vaporize in minutes. Before you actually buy a ticket, see chapter 4, "Flying to Europe," to learn how to save significantly on the cost of your flight.

Or, if you have enough frequent flyer miles with one of the international airlines you can budget close to zero for your airfare. Reserve early for summer travel and beware of blackout dates and premium flying dates. Many airlines raise the required FF miles from 40,000 to 50,000 for flights to Europe between mid June and mid September. You will be asked to pay the September 11 security fee for all flights.

Travel Within Europe

Getting around once you're there is a more difficult budgeting problem. The two best means of travel are car and train. Air travel within Europe is wrong unless you are in a hurry. It is expensive and all you see are the interiors of the same planes and the tops of the same clouds that we have at home.

Trains

The cost of train travel is relatively easy to determine, so that comes first. For any decent amount of scooting around, the EurailPass or one of it's siblings is the way to go.

Here's one that flies low, the French TGV, Train a Grande Vitesse (high speed train). Even when parked in a station c'est formidable. *You must pay for a seat reservation, but the supplement fee is waived for Eurailpass holders.* [0208]

The principle of Eurailpass is to allow the holder unlimited travel on virtually all the trains and on some ferries. These passes allow you to ride the rails anywhere in 15 countries of continental Europe plus Ireland. Great Britain is not included in Eurailpass, but it issues similar passes for England, Scotland, and Wales at comparable prices. Also, French, German, Dutch, and many other national railroads issue passes for unlimited travel within their country for slightly less than the cost of Eurailpass.

Passes are available for periods of 15 days, 21 days, one month, two months, and three months. Children under 12 pay half price, and those under four travel free. The Eurailpass Youth is available to those who are 25 and younger. Other options include Eurail Selectpass and Eurailpass Flexi, both with restrictive features but at a lower cost than regular Eurailpass. For example, Flexi can give you 10 or 15 days of travel in a two month period.

Go to any travel agency and ask for the free Eurail or Britrail brochure with current prices, conditions, and maps. You will need to bring your passport when you buy it. For detailed information on riding the rails in Europe see chapter 17, "Riding the Rails and Waves."

Rental Car

The cost of auto travel is variable galore. You can rent one, buy one, or bring your own. In any case, you are in one way or another paying for gas, oil, maintenance, depreciation, insurance, and taxes. Ouch.

For the purposes of budgeting, auto rental prices will be discussed in this section. Information on shipping yours over is given in chapter 22, "Living in Europe."

Rental car prices are available from Hertz, Avis, National, Budget, and specialized agencies with offices in the United States, e.g. Foremost Euro Car. Call the toll free 800 number of one of these companies and request a worldwide directory. This free directory lists car types, locations, prices, and rental terms. Many car rental companies also have web sites allowing you to view the goods and make a reservation. See my site *www.enjoy-europe.com* , the TRAVELERS YELLOW PAGES category "Auto Rental," for URL addresses of many companies renting cars in Europe.

Many companies do not rent to young people. The lower age limit may be 21, 25, or 30, depending on their policies. Some also have an upper age limit.

Daily rates for just basic transportation for two people are high, and rates for a luxury Mercedes or BMW will be astronomical. Savings can be had by shopping around so don't sign up for the first offer you see. Rates vary from country to country for each rental company, and different equivalent models are available in each price category. Take note in the brochures of the rather outrageous drop charges. It pays to travel in a circle and return the car to the office where you picked it up.

Weekly unlimited mileage (kilometers over there) rates can save you bundles if you are scooting around a lot. VW camper vans are available in a few places.

Determine if insurance and taxes are included in the quoted rates. These can possibly exceed the rental rate of small cars. You will also have some tolls to pay on expressways in France and Italy. A fee for the privilege of driving on expressways is charged as you enter Switzerland, Austria, and some other countries. An annual sticker is placed on your windshield, but you must pay even if you are just driving through for the day, unless the car already has a valid sticker. Gasoline is not included in rental prices. *Benzin, petrol, essence,* or some other local name for gasoline costs around $4 per gallon.

There is no need to drive in the cities, big or small. Here is a well marked bus stop in Monza, just north of Milan. [0209]

To estimate the cost of driving, a fairly definite itinerary is needed. I've driven all over Europe, east and west. The only way that it can be recommended is if two or more share the expenses and the work. With three in the car you are approximately at the break even point with the cost of rail passes. You have more freedom of movement with an auto, but you give up much of the experience of Europe that train travelers enjoy.

You are better off paying with a credit card in order to avoid leaving a large cash deposit. And make sure you have a valid drivers license and an International Driving Permit, IDP. True, you are usually able to rent a car without the IDP but it would be better to have it considering its nominal cost. The police in some countries ask for it and in others they seem to not know what they are looking at when you hand it to them.

OTHER COSTS

Thirty (Or So) Miscellaneous Items

The cost of all the other items in the expense list depends on your personal habits. Budget as closely as you can for the Three Basic Biggies — lodging, food, and transportation — and then add 50% to cover everything else. If you don't allow for all those nickel and dime items, you will have an uncomfortable time and/or have to come home early.

Pre-Trip Expenses

There will probably be expenses in preparing for your journey. You may need a new suitcase, voltage transformers, a passport, etc. Costs of these items are not included here since only you know what you need to purchase, and you can readily get the prices of most items at your local department store. See chapter 6, "A Packing List for Europe; Travel Accessories" for a suggested list. Remember that you can buy toiletries in Europe so don't bother loading up for the duration of your trip.

Looking for a B&B in The Netherlands? Also keep your eye out for a zimmer mit frühstück *because most of the visitors are from* Germany and this is the way it's spelled in German. [0210]

EUROPE ON WHAT! PER DAY

I kept detailed records of my expenses during my early days traveling in Europe. Details of these expenses are in the appendix to this chapter.

Based on current prices of goods, services, and the exchange rate of the dollar, here is an approximate set of budgets for travelers in Europe. The costs are shown as low, moderate, and high. If I was writing the script for the face of a cereal box, these would be large, family size, and jumbo.

Cost data can be divided between variable costs, i.e. so much per day while you are traveling, and fixed costs, i.e. so much per trip to Europe. The fixed cost is your plane fare. Even this can be variable because the fares for most airlines increase dramatically when you stay for more than 30 days. Eurailpass costs increase for longer passes, but not proportionally. The longer your pass is valid, the lower the per diem cost. Also, there are family and group rail passes offering a savings.

Except for very short trips, the variable costs will be more than your fixed costs. You will need to feed and house yourself daily, and you will be subject to additional costs for ground transportation, entertainment, souvenirs, and other items.

2004 Budget

Table 2-1 is an estimate of the cost of traveling in Europe in 2004. It is based on staying in tourist hotels (not always in the major cities), eating in local establishments (not always on the major boulevards), using a Eurailpass, and buying a restricted airline ticket. This is per person for about one month. To refine the budget for your own circumstances go through the budget process above. These estimates are just "ballpark figures."

For 30 days your costs will run from around $5,000 to $15,000 per person in my estimation. If the minimum figure is beyond your interest, wait until next April or May to get an early start and save, especially on air fare.

The total costs should in truth be reduced by your cost of staying home. Variable costs you have at home will be eliminated and that money can be used to partially offset the cost of your European expedition.

Table 2-1
2004 Rough Cost Estimates

	Your Budget Level		
	Low 0 and 1 star	Medium 2 and 3 star	High 4 and 5 star
Room, daily average	$40	80	200
Food, daily average	$20	40	80
Transportation (daily pro rata)	$60	60	60
Sub Total	$120	180	340
Thirty Miscellaneous Items	$60	90	170
Daily TOTAL	$180	$270	$510

To stay comfortably on the "low" budget, spend most of your time in southern and eastern Europe. If you really want to save money and have an interesting time, go on over to Romania, Bulgaria, Turkey, and other countries in the east.

If you are a backpacker and camper you can travel for much less, though much of your time will be spent just managing your daily chores and getting back to town from the campground. Hostels are another low cost room option, though they are not often centrally located.

TIPPING

Some guidebooks have a special section telling you how much to tip the taxi driver, bell captain, porters, waiter, theater ushers, ad infinitum. These advisories are generally designed to waste your money. I've talked with some Dutch waiters who gleefully told me about the extra 20% that American tourists leave on the table.

Already Included

Most services for which you pay in Europe already include a 15% *service charge*. The service charge goes to the person who personally provides the service, or into a kitty to be shared by everyone on the staff. The service charge is the tip but it is obligatory. Listed prices on menus usually include this service charge, but when they don't, the house always adds it to your bill. You may leave a few coins of the change, round up by 1% to 3%, as a tip. In fact, often such amounts are not even returned when change is due.

*This menu posted at a Marseille café shows the cost of doing business. You can save a dime per drink if you stand at the bar (*comptoir*) rather than take a seat at a table in the room (*salle*). Prices include tax and tip. If you are a beer drinker learn how to say* pression *(draft) and/or* demi *(25 cl).*
[0204]

Before getting in a taxi, ask a local citizen about the custom for tipping or not tipping the driver. Do not ask after the ride. Tip is a word that is not in the vocabulary of most languages so ask if you should pay an additional service gratuity or not.

Regular Customer

One place where it is helpful to tip is in a café or bar if you are, or are planning to be, a regular customer. This will help to insure promptness on your subsequent visits, and they'll remember your name.

Toilets
In a few cases, most notably washrooms, tips are expected. There is invariably someone in there or at the door who is responsible for keeping it clean. Don't be surprised if you gentlemen notice a woman mopping the floor next to you as you use the urinal.

Toilets almost everywhere, except on the trains, require or request a donation. The usual approach is to have a saucer on a table outside the toilet. Sometimes the requested amount is stated on a hand written sign, and sometimes the toilet attendant is sitting there hovering over the saucer of coins. Donate whatever coin you see in the saucer, equivalent to maybe a dime.

To Tip or Not To Tip
In cases when a service is provided without charge, use your judgment and give what you think is appropriate.

Europeans are accustomed, for example, to tipping the hotel chamber maid, something not done in America. You should leave a few coins on the pillow. In ritzy hotels on the Riviera I have seen places where the hotel price does not include "service" charges so 15% will be added to your bill. If you can afford $500 for the room I guess you can afford another $75 for having your bed made.

Another appropriate tippee would be a table to table musician or group, playing and starving while they watch you eat. They also work on the streets and the Metros and appreciate all the coins you toss in their open guitar case.

When driving in some countries, kids run out to the cars at stop lights with a wash bottle and rag to do the windshield. Make sure they clean it, not just smear the dirt around.

Keep some small bills and change in your pocket. Do not reach for your wallet for these worthy of a gratuity. In all other cases, save your money.

APPENDIX — Historical Cost Data

Back in the days when the title of a famous travel book boasted that you could travel in Europe for about the price of a steak dinner at home I kept detailed records of my expenses. I only include this material now because of the notes which explain the costs. The costs are out of date, but the notations are still of value. You may want to compare your costs with mine 20 years ago, or with those of a British traveler 7 decades ago. In my library I have a book titled "Holland on £10." That was per week, back in 1936.

1980 at $115 per Day
For the three week trip I made in March 1980 through ten countries of northern Europe, I spent an average of $115 per day. The cost analysis is shown in Table 2-2

NOTES to Table 2-2:

1.) Room costs ranged from $10 to $40 per day for a single room equivalent to a two or three star hotel in France. This average figure of $23 included sleeping "free" one or two nights a week on an overnight train. The minimum figure applies to smaller cities, and got me a small single on the fourth floor, no elevator, narrow stairways, no toilet or shower in the room, and maybe a breakfast. But it was clean, warm, and comfortable nine times out of ten. The upper figure, $40, fetched a comfortable, well-plumbed double in a major city.

2.) Food costs ranged from $5 to $50 depending on appetite and location, service and tax included. My $18 average figure included some restaurants and some picnics. A rough estimate of prices in average restaurants can be used to make up your budget. In countries like Germany, with all-you-can-eat breakfasts, I could get by with a light lunch for about $3, and top off the day with dinner at $15 to $25. In countries like France, where breakfast will barely open your eyes, a hearty lunch cost about $7, and a good dinner $12 to $20. These costs included liberal quantities of house wine or beer, and coffee. Soft drinks and bottled water cost about the same as locally fermented products.

Table 2-2
1980 Travel Cost Analysis

Room, daily average		$23	Note 1
Food, daily average		$18	Note 2.
Transportation (daily pro rata)		$36	Note 3.
	Sub Total	$77	
Thirty Miscellaneous Items		$38	Note 4.
	Daily TOTAL	$115	Note 5

Table 2-3
1980 Transportation Costs

Air Fare (LA/Gatwick/LA on Laker Sky Train)	$438
Train/Boat (Gatwick/Oostende/Gatwick)	$80
Eurailpass (21 days in Western Europe)	$270
TOTAL transportation cost	$788
Averaged over 22 days, cost per day	$36

3.) The transportation figure is based on a three-week trip consisting of: Laker Airways round trip from Los Angeles to London; a train/boat round trip London to Oostende, Belgium; and a 21-day Eurailpass. Sadly, Laker Airlines Skytrain went out of business on the day that the first edition of *How To Europe* came off the press, February 5, 1982. Costs in March 1980 are shown in Table 2-3.

4.) Thirty miscellaneous items averaged out to $38 per day. You may wonder how in the world you can spend that much on miscellaneous items. Somehow, I managed to do it. Look at the list in this chapter again to get some idea of where all that money goes. One or two rolls of film a day can eat up pocket money like a paper shredder.

5.) After summing it up, my frugal trip cost me $115 per day way back in 1980. Multiplying this out, my 22 days cost $2,530. That includes *everything*, so don't compare that to the cost of a guided tour until you crunch the numbers. Tour costs never include *everything*. And the famous book from Frommer says, on page 2, that transportation is not included in his $5 a day, or the $70 in the year 2002. Let me get this straight. A guy writes a travel book and does not include the cost of transportation in the ridiculous $5. How does one actually do the traveling? Walk?

1984 at $98 per Day

From October 1983 through January 1984, I traveled for ten weeks through fourteen countries and spent slightly less per day than I did in 1980. This was due largely to a stronger dollar and partly to the fact that I spent half of the second trip in the Mediterranean countries where rooms and food can cost one-third as much as in northern Europe. The cost analysis is shown in Table 2-4.

Table 2-4
1983 Travel Cost Analysis

Room, daily average	$22.68	Note 6
Food, daily average	$22.82	Note 7.
Transportation (daily pro rata)	$19.40	Note 8.
Sub Total	$64.90	
Thirty Miscellaneous Items	$33.30	
Daily TOTAL	$98.20	Note 9

NOTES to Table 2-4:

6.) Hotel prices for a three star single with toilet and tub (or shower) ranged from $35-$50 throughout Scandinavia to $7-$30 in Greece and Iberia. Single rooms ran from $20 to $40 in France, Germany, Ireland, Switzerland, Austria, and Holland. Overall, I stayed in slightly better rooms on this trip than I did in 1980, but thanks to the strong dollar, the average daily cost was almost identical.

7.) Dinner prices for the complete stuffing ranged from about $15-$30 in Scandinavia to $5-$20 in Greece and Iberia. The high end prices in Greece included a floor show and live music. I don't think that I ate any better on the 1983/84 trip, but my costs were significantly higher despite the fact that the dollar was worth much more than in 1980 — 50% more in Germany to 100% more in Italy.

8.) The transportation figure is based on two one-way flights plus a two month Eurailpass. The breakdown is shown in Table 2-5.

9.) Thus, at $98.20 per day my 71 day trip cost $6,972.

Table 2-5
1983 Transportation Costs

Air Fare (LA to Düsseldorf on LTU)	$373
Eurailpass (two months)	$560
Air (Amsterdam to Los Angeles on KLM)	$444
TOTAL transportation cost	$1,377
Averaged over 71 days, cost per day	$19

The importance of eating and sleeping in off-the-trail places can never be over emphasized. Front row center always costs more because you get a better view. But when eating or sleeping what you see is your plate or pillow. So get off the main boulevards for real value. And you will usually have a more interesting time to boot. To help get costs under control in northern Europe, seek out Greek and Italian restaurants. They generally offer the best value for low budget travelers, not to mention that it often tastes better than local fare, especially in Britain but not so in France.

1986 at $36 per Day

My 1986 sortie was for five months and was spent mostly in Paris. I rented a small furnished apartment on the left bank near Metro Maubert Mutualité for about $500 a month. I shopped for groceries at the Place Maubert farmer's market and cooked most of my own meals. Getting over there was a bargain. I flew Los Angeles to Amsterdam for $400 round trip after finding a short-lived special deal. Not only that, KLM bumped me up to business class on both flights at no cost. April is a good month to cross the Atlantic and May is a beautiful month to be in Paris. Amsterdam to and from Paris was on a purchased train ticket. My Paris transportation costs were mainly for metro tickets though I lived close enough to the Alliance Française that I preferred to walk to school, usually taking the short cut through the Jardine Luxembourg. I stayed mainly in the city, with occasional day trips out to nearby villages.

Living like this is certainly one of the most economical ways to see Europe, albeit a small part but a very good part. My costs were actually much less than if I had stayed home in Newport Beach.

1990-2000 at a Profit

I spent about half of the 1990s in Europe, but can't give much in the way of cost details that would be relevant for travelers. For over 2 years we lived in Germany. The company I worked for provided a free home, utilities, car, insurance, and maintenance. I had frequent fully paid business trips throughout Germany and eastern Europe. We also enjoyed annual home leaves on the company. As mentioned later in the book, taking a company-paid transfer has got to be one of the best ways to see Europe.

We made a one-month expedition to Istanbul in 1993 using the company car. Traveling through southern and eastern Europe was inexpensive, to say the least. Those who want a low cost vacation, hie thee south and to the former Evil Empire to spend about 1/3 of what you will spend in Germany and France.

A one-month Eurailpass journey in 1997 was also very low on cash expenditures. For that month, I stayed mainly with family and friends in Italy, Austria, Germany, France, and Holland. I used hotels for only five days that May, in Biarritz and Aix-en-Provence where I was one of the few early season visitors. You'll have a hard time finding a room in these cities in July unless you book early. Make sure you read chapter 14, "Hotel, Hostel, B&B, or Private Home; Sleep Options for Travel in Europe." to learn how to get a discount every night in European hotels.

One of the ridiculous ways I wasted money, time, and calm nerves was to rent a car in Amsterdam and make a round trip to Milan to pick up Stephanie in July 1998. I got caught in the herd going south through France, got utterly lost in Switzerland on top of a 9,000 foot mountain on Saturday night at 2:00 am, and lost myself twice again trying to get out of Milan and then around Antwerp. I spent about $1,000 renting a midget of a vehicle, filling it with gas too often, and paying highway and tunnel tolls, meals on the road, and a hotel on the way back north. I could have flown Stephanie to Amsterdam first class for less than that.

2002-2003

My three week trip to The Netherlands and Belgium in December and January was a particularly low cost venture. I used frequent flyer miles for my air ticket and stayed with a good friend in Haarlem. I looked in on 5 of the hotels in Haarlem to see about room rates. The lowest cost, even of those mentioned in the budget guide books, was about $60 per night for a single with toilet and shower. The low cost rooms measured about 6' by 9' and had a single bed. Dinner cost $40 for the two of us at our favorite budget restaurant, including a bottle of wine and a couple shots of jenever. The average price of a 33 cl (11 oz) beer was $2. Round trip train tickets to Amsterdam cost $6 and a round trip "Super Day Return" train to Brussels cost about $35. My major expense category was film and processing, partial results of which you see throughout the book in your hands.

Here is the main hall of the Amsterdam train station. The train is a handy and cheap way to travel back and forth to Haarlem. There are 5 or 6 trains per hour and it takes 15 to 18 minutes. Eating and sleeping can cost you much less in Haarlem than in Amsterdam. [0203]

Chapter 3
Passport and Visas for Europe
Identity and Travel Documents

Advance to Go.

THE PASSPORT

What Is It?

The passport is the pretty little blue book wherein the Secretary of State "hereby requests all whom it may concern to permit the citizen/national of the United States named herein to pass without delay or hindrance and in case of need to give all lawful aid and protection." It's written in English, *et en français* (and in French).

It is about 3" by 5" (9 cm by 12 cm) with a flex cover. Your passport has 24 pages. The inside front cover has your photo and your vital statistics. The first six pages contain information essential for successful trouble free foreign travel — read it. The remaining 18 pages are blank except for headers and anti-forgery color patterns. The blank pages are for visas, entry stamps, and exit stamps issued by foreign governments. The customs agents of some countries also make notations in these pages regarding money and valuables you are carrying with you.

You need a valid United States passport to enter Europe and to come home. Consequently, no airline will accept you on board if you don't have yours in hand. Each individual must have a passport.

How To Get It

To allow time for the mails and processing of your form, get going on getting your passport no less than eight weeks before you plan to depart. In fact, do it now if you don't already have a passport. Look in the white pages under "United States Government," subheadings "State Department" and/or "Passport Agency." Call them up, listen to the recorded message, follow the directions, have your picture taken, fill out the form, pay up, and soon you'll have it.

Though the normal time for getting a passport is measured in weeks, expedited service is available. I once had to get a renewed passport for an unexpected trip on short notice. I applied in person at the Passport Agency in Los Angeles with my tickets in hand to prove my need for speed. My new passport was ready the next afternoon.

A detailed explanation of the costs, requirements, and procedures is not given here because it would fill several pages and may change before you read this. You can pick up the necessary forms at your local post office.

Is Yours Still Valid?

If you already have a passport, check to see that it won't expire while you are traveling or living over there, and that you still look like the person in the picture.

This advice might seem rather rudimentary, but one very intelligent friend of mine recently had an interesting experience at the Seattle airport. With her ticket and passport she checked in to fly over to Amsterdam. Excuse me, but her passport had expired a few months earlier. The airline would not let her on board. She had it fixed the next day and then went on her way.

Children

It used to be that children could be included on a parent's passport, but no more. Everybody needs a separate passport, even infants.

Stamps

In Europe, border police don't often stamp passports these days. In fact, with the inauguration of the European Union, all of the passport control points on common borders of the members (which is most of western Europe) are eliminated.

Even before this, we would often drive through some borders without stopping. As far back as 1976 I drove over the Belgium Netherlands border at 100 mph. I can't even recall seeing the border sign post of Luxembourg though I have been through it a number of times.

On the other hand, police in eastern European countries normally take a long look at your photo and make their mark in your book.

Switzerland maintains strict passport control at all border crossings. Swiss police also have road side check points within the country where you will be required to show your car papers and passport, and answer the question "What are you doing in Switzerland?" Heck, I just came over to taste the chocolate.

On entering most other countries in Europe the police will wave you in as soon as they see the cover of your blue book. You won't even be able to get it out of your pocket before they look at the next customer.

No Fat Books

You might wonder whether or not to get a passport with extra pages for a major trip to Europe. After a few hundred or so border crossings, entry stamps and visas have soiled less than half the pages in the five successive passports I have used over the past 28 years. The USA is responsible for a good share of these, residence visas in various countries cover 7 pages, and entries to countries in the Middle East, Southeast Asia, and Africa occupy more than all else combined. So, since there are 18 blank pages in a 24 page passport, one of those extra-page heavy-duty passports is not necessary for your big tour of Europe. Get the standard thin passport for an easy pocket fit. If you need extra pages you can have them added at any American consulate. I had to do that while in Al Khobar because entry and exit stamps for a round trip from Saudi Arabia to Bahrain covered a full page, and I made a lot of those trips over the causeway connecting the two countries.

We spent six hours parked right here trying to get out of Bulgaria and into Romania, listening to excuses why we couldn't leave, and finally returning back into Bulgaria for another night when it became too late. The next day it looked like the same rigmarole but Elizabeth got mad and walked up to the border guard with a statement: "We're Americans and we want to get out of your country, now!" He let us pass immediately and within an hour we had our visa to travel about in Romania. Some Moldavian travelers at this border told us that the way to get across borders in eastern Europe is to put a small bottle of cheap perfume on your steering column, making it convenient for the guard to reach in and collect his "toll." [0306]

Don't Lose It

Your passport is the property of the United States government. It is an extremely important and valuable piece, the I.D. recognized by everyone, everywhere.

If you lose your passport, or if it is stolen, your travels will hit a very sour note. The finder or thief will have scored big with a readily marketable item, the envy of many people, good and not so. Guard it closely and report its disappearance immediately to the local police and to the nearest US embassy. You will then have to detour to the embassy to get a replacement. There goes a day or a few, big extra cash expense, maybe missed plane connections, and probably temporary starvation since your money, traveler's checks, and credit cards were in the same wallet or purse. With no passport you are nobody, nada, zilch.

See the section "Avoiding Jesse James" in chapter 8 for detailed and firsthand descriptions of the modi operandi of pickpockets and baggage thieves, and how to defend yourself against calamity. It may be the most important thing you will learn in *How To Europe*

If your passport winds up missing try to remember where you used it last. Did you leave it at a hotel desk, airline check-in counter, or did you use it for I.D. when cashing a traveler's check, using a credit card, or picking up mail? Several times waiters have "forgotten" to return my passport after having demanded it as I.D. when I used a credit card to pay for dinner. Keep it in your pocket. I just heard the story of a student who left hers on the plane. Incidentally, do not keep money, your airline ticket, or other valuable papers in your passport.

Hotels

Very few hotel keepers still ask to see your passport. Of those who do request it, most will return it immediately, except in Spain and Portugal where they sometimes keep it half a day or overnight. Be sure to retrieve it as soon as possible. I have seen mine nonchalantly laid on the counter or in a message pigeonhole within easy reach of passers-by.

In eastern Europe the hotel may insist on keeping it until you pay or leave. I pay in advance just to keep my mitts on my passport. Remember that while your hotel keeper holds your passport, you will not be able to cash traveler's checks, pick up mail, rent a car, enter a casino, etc. Think of *YOUR* passport as the last ticket on the last plane from Casablanca, and keep it in *YOUR* pocket.

Aliases

The passport usually has other names in Europe. Be alert for the words *pahs, pahz, paspoort, passaporte, pass, passporto,* and similar sounds.

Copy It

Make a few copies of the first page of your passport, the page with your mug shot and passport number on it. Have the copies laminated, or do it yourself with a couple passes of wide clear package wrapping tape. Keep one laminated copy in your handkerchief pocket, one in your toilet kit, and leave the other with a friend or relative back home.

By the way, I read on a copy machine in a library that it is illegal to copy your passport. *Au contraire, mon ami.* My passport specifically advises that you make two copies to facilitate replacement if it is lost or stolen.

VISA

What Is It?

A visa is an official authorization for a traveler to enter a foreign country. It is issued by the foreign government after you fill out their application form. A nominal fee is usually required. Sometimes the fee is more than nominal.

Visas are entered in your passport by some countries, and are a separate document for other countries. The USA does not give you visas to visit other countries. It is your responsibility to find out if the country you are planning to visit requires you to have a visa. If so, it is your responsibility to apply to that country's embassy for the visa. Uncle Sam will not hold your hand.

Generally Not Needed

Americans do not need a visa to enter most of the countries of Europe, even most of the former communist countries. Stays of up to 90 days are generally allowed without a visa. And when you do need a visa it's usually not too difficult to get it. I drove up to the Ukraine border from Poland, bought a visa, and was speeding east into the former "Evil Empire" within 15 minutes. I applied for my visa to the Baltic countries (Lithuania, Estonia, and Latvia) in Berlin and had it within a couple of hours. Elizabeth and I drove up to the border, bought our visas to enter Romania, and were on our way within an hour, though we had been delayed for 6 hours by the Bulgarian border police.

Before the Fall of the Wall, we applied for visas to Hungary at their consulate in Paris and received them within 24 hours. The same year the French had a mighty cow over the USA about something or another and were requiring Americans to visa up before entering France. I have one of those souvenir visas. Turkey did the same thing in retaliation for a similarly imprudent impudence by the US government, and then hiked the fee to the same exorbitant amount charged to Turks for a visa to the USA. It's just time and money.

Russia remains a difficult place for foreign travelers. It requires Americans to apply for a visa before entering. Not only a visa but an itinerary approved by Russia is required. These stupid regulations just keep many of us out of the country. There are plenty of other countries welcoming us without those overbearing restrictions.

You don't need a visa to enter The Netherlands or most other European countries. In fact you'll normally have to ask just to get entry and exit stamps in your passport. Here is a page from my passport showing a few stamps. Dates are in the European system, dd.mm.yy. [0309]

When Required

Citizens of countries other than the USA should check the visa requirements for all the countries that they might visit. Look at a map — you can't take the train from Italy to Spain without going through France. This fact was discovered too late by a Colombian fellow I met along the way. Apply for multiple entry visas. Failing that, request a couple extra entry permits just in case your itinerary is upset by strikes, natural disasters, or true love. In his case it was *amour.* Another alternative for citizens of countries other than the USA is to obtain a Schengen Visa.

Schengen Visa

In the old days of visa free 90 day travel the 90 days applied to an individual country. On the 89th day you could hop across the border, get an entry stamp in the country next door, and then go back for another 89 days. It's not so convenient since the Schengen visa was invented.

The Schengen Agreement of 1985 was inaugurated between the Netherlands, Belgium, Luxembourg, Germany, and France as a framework to make it easier for free movement of people and goods across their respective borders. In 1990 this became more concrete with another agreement on establishing a Schengen visa for foreigners wishing to travel in these countries. One visa could serve for all five countries making it much easier for travelers to move about. There are now 14 countries in the Schengen Zone. The notable exceptions are Switzerland, Britain, and Ireland.

This sounds good for travelers, but there is a drawback for Americans planning to travel for more than three months. Now the 90 days applies to all the members of the Schengen Zone, and the 90 days is valid for a six month period. Thus you cannot stay more than 90 days in the Schengen Zone before you must take a 90 day exit from the Schengen Zone. Maybe take a three month layover in Bulgaria or Turkey, and enjoy great food and economy rates.

If you plan a long visit to one country it would probably be easy to stay under radar on this regulation. The fact that passport entry and exit stamps are usually not done anymore would make it difficult for Authority to enforce the regulation. Besides, the police are not out on the streets checking identity papers. I've gone over the 90 day limit in Holland and France without a problem, so far, despite the fact that I ask for entry and exit stamps when I fly in and out.

Invalid Visa

If you have a visa and it is expired, well, just don't go. One of the most startling things seen in my travels occurred when a business associate and I arrived in Kiev at the invitation of an official Ukraine government bureau. My partner's visa had been issued when we were first informed of the trip, but then the visit had been delayed a month. We landed the day after his visa expired. On arrival, he was escorted upstairs in the terminal building amongst expressions of *nyet problemsky* (no problem). But an hour later he was brought back into the terminal by a couple of big guys, one on each arm. They marched him straight back to the plane on which we had just arrived. The lesson, don't even think of violating the exit date. Border police are about the most hard-case people you are going to meet in Europe or anywhere. My partner had his visa renewed within a day at the Soviet embassy in Vienna, but that was an expensive affair. So, no visa, no go.

Residence Visa

If you plan to spend a year or so in one country you do need to obtain a visa and explain why you are lolling about over there. I've obtained residence visas twice for purposes of working in Europe. These were obtained at my employers' request and with their cash, patience, and time for the paperwork. These visas must be renewed annually. If you are being transferred to work in a foreign country, the company you are working for will most certainly go through the exertions of facilitating the visa process for you, and will also be required to obtain a work permit for you from the foreign government. That's another story. See chapter 21, "Working in Europe."

Before the fall of the wall I probably couldn't have gone to Leipzig because it was in communist East Germany. But I went a couple of years later and posed in front of the now defunct hammer and sickle. [0307a]

Obtaining a Visitor's Visa

There are few European countries which require Americans to obtain a visa. If you are going to one which has this requirement it would be best to get the visa before you go to Europe. When you are traveling by train you cannot obtain a visa at the border. If you are driving into a country visas are often available at major border points. It may also be possible to obtain a visa as you arrive by plane, but don't count on it, and you will not want to encounter the delay and bother after an international flight. Actually, the airline may not allow you to board the flight if you don't have a visa for the country you are landing in, if a visa is required there.

To obtain an application for a visa contact a consulate or the embassy of the country of your choice. Each country has an embassy in Washington, DC, and many countries maintain consulates in major American cities. Look in your phone book yellow pages under the heading "Consulates and Other Foreign Government Representatives." If there is no listing for the country you are interested in, contact their embassy in Washington. Offices of many foreign consulates are provided in the "Prime Travel Data" section of *www.enjoy-europe.com*.

Obtaining a visa may take a week or more, plus post office delays. It is possible to expedite the process by presenting yourself at the proper office or by paying a specialized visa service to do the legwork for you. Ask your travel agent. If you are going to more than one country which requires a visa, you can only apply for them one at a time since you must send in your passport with your visa application.

FURTHER REGULATIONS

No Freeloaders

When entering some countries, you will be asked to explain why you are there, where you are staying, and how long you will be hanging around. Furthermore, you may be required to show your return ticket and tell the border police how much money you have. The reason for these questions is to make sure you don't settle down and start living off the local taxpayers. If you do not satisfy the requirements, you can be escorted onto the next plane or train out of the country.

When communism still ruled in the east we saw a group of Russians taken off the train as we entered Yugoslavia from Hungary. Yugoslavia at the time had a requirement that all visitors must have at least $200 in United States currency. These Russians were carrying rubles to pay for their vacation, but the Yugoslavs did not care much for rubles, or Russians either for that matter. The Hungarian trainmen had the same opinion of the Russians and enjoyed a good laugh over their fate. This part of former Yugoslavia is now Croatia.

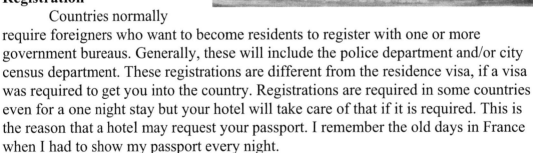

The passport and customs police welcome you to Poland. [0302]

Customs

Customs police are usually on hand to greet you at each border crossing, except at European Union member interface borders. See chapter 25, "Passing Customs," for important information on these welcoming formalities.

Registration

Countries normally require foreigners who want to become residents to register with one or more government bureaus. Generally, these will include the police department and/or city census department. These registrations are different from the residence visa, if a visa was required to get you into the country. Registrations are required in some countries even for a one night stay but your hotel will take care of that if it is required. This is the reason that a hotel may request your passport. I remember the old days in France when I had to show my passport every night.

If you are living in a foreign country you must register and renew annually, in person at the proper city office. Make sure that the process is complete. In some cases your first visit is simply to fill out the forms, and a second visit is required to receive the police approval stamp in your passport. Failure to have the proper OKs in your passport can lead to detention.

These procedures had not been adequately explained to me and I did not get the approval stamp from the police when I first moved to Holland. It mattered not until late one Sunday night when I drove up to the Dutch border from a weekend visit in Germany. I was stopped, and after a half hour of questions from the Dutch border police I was finally allowed to drive on. It's best to avoid the potential for such problems by double checking to see that you have met all the requirements.

Paperwork at the Bottom of the Pile Gathers No Dust

Figure on leaving your passport behind for up to a few weeks while they are "working" on your official registration stamps. I have speeded up the process to an hour or so by telling officials that I must make an important business trip out of the country in the next few days. Let's face it — they're government bureaucrats and they're just sitting on all that paper till it hatches. But you have to be courteous and give Authority its due, or boy are you in deep stuff.

If you have trouble understanding the local officials, discuss the rules and regulations with other Americans living in the city. More on this is presented in chapter 22, "Living in Europe."

Illegals

Some travelers get very comfortable where they are at the moment and just decide to stay. If you stay more than 90 days without becoming registered and are later found out the consequences can be a quick eviction from the country and a multi-year prohibition from entering again. If this happens to you in one of the countries in the Schengen Zone you will have difficulty entering any one of them in the future. Keep your trap shut about your situation if you are over the limit because you never know who will report you. Some citizens are uptight about "rich" Americans and American foreign policy so they may wish to make a statement. Or it may simply be a case of *amour* gone sour.

You might call this a floating craps game, literally. At this boat casino in the Duna (Donau in German and Danube in English) River in Budapest, Hungary you must show your passport to be admitted. Do you feel lucky tonight? [0305]

Chapter 4
Flying to Europe
Travel Starts at the Airport

To travel agent or not to travel agent is your first question.

AIR FARES

The Bazaar

Unless you're going the old fashioned way by steam ship, you need an airline ticket to get to Europe. There are a number of ways to buy one. You can use a travel agency convenient and close to your home, call an airline, or call a flight consolidator, a.k.a. "bucket shop." You can also shop the internet, either through a discount travel services vendor or directly on an airline's web site.

The myriad of fares and conditions, varying from airline to airline and day to day, is a bizarre bazaar. Searching for the lowest cost fare is a tedious job, but can save you hundreds of dollars.

When shopping for the lowest fares for international travel, it is best to fly Monday through Thursday, stay no more than 30 days, and purchase at least 14 days prior to departure. These strategies offer dramatic savings over the normal fares. And fares during late winter and early spring are normally the lowest of the year. Travel in July can cost three times as much as in April and five times as much as in March. The airlines are almost begging people to fly to Europe in late winter.

Then again, if you have enough miles in a frequent flyer program you don't need to buy a ticket — you can have one for free.

Connections

The cheapest fares between North America and Europe often require a connection unless you are in New York or another major gateway city near the east coast. A connection is a change of planes in a city between your home and your destination. There are standard minimum times allowed for connections, depending on the connection city, to allow you and your luggage to make the connection. If your first flight is delayed, you, and more likely your checked luggage, may miss the next flight.

Within Europe

If you plan to fly within Europe, expect to pay high fares. The only bargain is with round-trip tickets. You might have to pay $200 for a one-way flight, but just $215 for a round-trip ticket.

Besides crossing waters in a hurry, there may be other times when you want to use a plane. For example, trying to go from Geneva to Amsterdam by train is a 12 hour ordeal with at least two changes. After some diligent searching I found a 90 minute direct flight on KLM for the same price as the train. Europe is starting to relax air price controls so that it won't cost more to fly from Frankfurt to Berlin than it costs to go from Frankfurt to New York. Also, there are a number of upstart airlines in Europe which are offering excellent fares compared to the national carriers. Some of these budget airlines are low on frills and fly to secondary airports in metropolitan areas.

TRAVEL AGENTS

What is a Travel Agent?

Travel agents make reservations and sell tickets for air travel, package tours, auto rental, hotels, rail passes, and related services. The travel agent normally receives a commission from the airline or tour operator so the cost to you is the same as if you purchased the ticket direct. Travel agents are a very convenient source for tickets, saving you the time and anxiety that you would otherwise spend standing in line at the airport, browsing the internet, or scouring through big city newspapers. If you know what you want, usually one call is all it takes.

Limitations

Finding a really good travel agent is a really big challenge. All of them make mistakes once in a while, and a few are incompetent. I have heard of some atrocious blunders. Remember, it's your time, your money, and your dream trip — so select an agent with care. Ask friends who have traveled overseas for recommendations. Discuss your plans with agents to see if they seem to know what they are talking about. See if they will take time to offer advice and if they will shop around for you for the lowest cost tickets. Unfortunately most agents are overworked and can't volunteer much time for anything.

Travel agents are not required to be experienced travelers and few have the ability or time to provide you with personal trip planning. If an agent has been where you are going, he/she probably traveled at the partial or full expense of a tour operator. The agents I have met in my travels who were on one of these "fam trips" (familiarization trips) were more interested in enjoying the entertainment than in scrounging around for ideas and information that would help their customers. Lucky you if your travel agent is one of the exceptions.

Commissions

Travel agents do not receive a salary from the airlines. Travel agents make their living from commissions on the services and products they sell. However some airlines have eliminated travel agent commissions. Commissions are typically 10%, but some tours offer 20% or more, plus bonuses and freebees for the agent. So, when you go into a travel agency asking for the cheapest ticket, don't expect jet speed service. But if you get it, tell your friends.

At some airports there aren't enough berths at the terminal so a bus takes the passengers to the plane which is parked out on the tarmac. These passengers board at Athens, Greece, and have a long climb up to the door of a Boeing 747 jumbo jet. [0401]

DO IT YOURSELF

Call the Airlines

I'd rather do at least part of the work myself. I phone a half dozen airlines before I talk to my agent so I have some information about special deals currently available. Airline personnel take more time with you and may have more immediate information on fares and routes than a travel agent. Of course, you must call up several airlines to see which has the best schedule and fares to suit your plans. This can be a very worthwhile endeavor, though very time consuming. You may find that slight changes in your plans can give you more direct flights or save you money. You can save hundreds of dollars by phoning around. Then put your shoes on and go out to an agent whom you can challenge to come up with a better deal, or just ask the agent to purchase the flights that you found on your own. You can reserve the flight with the airline and then buy the ticket from your agent.

Airline Web Sites

All airlines have web sites providing schedules and ticket purchase capabilities. See the category "Airlines for Travel to Europe" in the TRAVELERS YELLOW PAGES section of *www.enjoy-europe.com*. Special deals are always popping up in your email inbox if you put yourself on their email alert lists. Many airlines send out a weekly newsletter by email touting their bargains, new routes, and special offers for earning frequent flyer miles, many of which do not require a flight.

On Line Do-Alls

There are several internet services which offer sort of a "universal" reservation and ticketing service. Major companies in this bargain air fare business are linked in the category "Discount Travel Vendors" of the TRAVELERS YELLOW PAGES. These services are very good, but none is totally complete. Try several and you'll see the differences. Before purchasing, check with the airline or your travel agent to see if a better deal is available.

Flight Consolidators

A profitable pastime would be a visit to your local library to check the travel sections in Sunday editions of the *New York Times*, *Los Angeles Times*, *Chicago Tribune*, or major papers near your home town. You'll find really cheap fares advertised in tiny tiny print. Call up the advertiser and find out what the terms and conditions might be, i.e., nonrefundable and no changes.

We saved a lot on Stephanie's 2002 trip to Italy by buying through a shop called Traveling Traveler in Los Angeles. They and others quoted us prices on regular flights of major European carriers like KLM, Lufthansa, and Swiss at prices 1/3 less than the carriers themselves. These shops seem to have different deals with different airlines. Some say they can book you from anyplace in the USA so you don't need to live in Los Angeles or New York City for special deals.

Flight consolidators within Europe also offer very good prices on scheduled flights. My favorite travel agency lately had been NBBS in Holland, until they closed shop, another casualty of 9/11. My Christmas 1999 round trip from Amsterdam to Los Angeles and Chicago was only $350 plus tax. On top of that United Airlines bumped me up to business class for free, and allowed me into the Red Carpet Lounge at Dulles Washington Airport where I find myself writing this in the comfort of plush chairs and carpeting with free espresso, juices, and cookies, plus magazines, a football game on TV, and a bar. You don't mind a long connection in these surroundings. It sure beats the chrome and plastic corral where I usually find myself.

FREQUENT FLYER PROGRAMS

Fly for Free

Many people can by-pass the travel agent and the need for opening up their checkbook altogether. The airlines' frequent flyer programs have put zillions of free miles at the disposal of the public over the years. This must be a good deal for the air carriers also because the foreign airlines have followed suit. If you travel on business, you're probably already enrolled in half a dozen of these programs, and you're always trying to maximize your credits with one particular airline. It doesn't do you any good to have 10,000 miles with each of five different airlines. You need 50,000 miles with only one airline to be awarded a free ticket to Europe. Award levels vary and depend on the airline, time of year, and class of service. People with these miles seldom have time to use them, but can let family members do so. I've flown my wife, daughter, and father-in-law several times overseas but have only used the miles personally a couple of times. If you have a relative who flies a lot, call him/her and see if you can borrow some mileage, maybe repayable in picture postcards from Istanbul?

Blackout Dates

In using your miles you will normally find a few inconveniences. Many airlines have blackout dates during which they will not allow you to fly with the FF miles. Other airlines without blackout dates will require you to use more of your frequent flyer miles to get a ticket during high season. High season is usually the entire summer plus the Christmas holidays, and maybe other busy periods.

Availability of Frequent Flyer Seats

Most airlines have a fixed maximum number of seats for free flyers. When these seats are taken they will not accept you. If you fall into this predicament and can't get a confirmation on the day you want to go, call up your reserve of patience and persistence. Just keep calling, like every week or twice a week and, as the day approaches, every day. It is likely that someone will cancel or change their reservation. Persistence pays.

It's also likely that the airline will open up more seats for frequent flyers. At the moment of writing this I am on a KLM flight from Detroit to Amsterdam. It has been an ordeal getting this flight. Northwest WorldPerks offers flights to Europe for 50,000 miles. Until the summer of 2002 it was 40,000 miles. After spending hours on Northwest's web site trying different possibilities for a flight I gave up and phoned the office. It was a snap to get a seat, but it cost me another 5,000 miles. The only seats available on line were at a mileage requirement of 60,000 to 100,000 miles. Northwest is playing a game with customers trying to get them to use 100,000 miles for what Northwest advertises for 50,000 miles. There will probably be a lawsuit.

FF Flexibility

A very nice feature of using frequent flyer miles to go to Europe is that flights can be changed without penalty. If you buy a super discount ticket and want to change your return date it will cost $100 to $150 on most carriers. With FF miles, call the reservation center and see if a flight is available for the day you wish to change to. If you change return flights after you have a ticket you may be required to get your ticket reissued. Allow time for that.

Sign Up

If you don't regularly fly or belong to a frequent flyer plan, sign up for one anyway. On your flight to Europe, make sure the miles are logged into your account. For the number of miles logged on four round trips between Europe and North America, most airlines' programs will award you a free flight.

And you don't even need to fly to gather up frequent flyer miles. Our daughter Stephanie flew to Italy using miles accumulated on Elizabeth's British Airways VISA card. True, she had to fly on British Air which meant changing planes in London, but it a was a free flight. I met a woman who charges her new cars to her VISA card so she can rack up more miles.

I use my American Express card at every instance when I buy anything from groceries to telephone service to airline tickets because I'm enrolled in their frequent flyer plan. For a nominal annual charge (getting to be not-so-nominal), every dollar I spend with the Amex card counts as a "mile," and can be transferred to several different frequent flyer programs. This company and others offer double miles and even quintuple miles during special promotions.

The long distance telephone companies give out miles, rental car companies donate, some grocery stores, and even some cereal boxes give them away. I picked up 5,000 miles from cereal box coupons last year. Do not pass up opportunities for free travel. It is beautiful!

AIRLINES

Services

Which one should you do business with? Commercial air carriers all provide certain minimum standards of safety and service as dictated by law. If you are afraid of flying, have faith — the pilot wants to get home and watch his favorite TV show just like you. For US domestic carriers, statistics indicate that there are about three times as many who die on the planes during normal flight as who die in crashes. A heart attack on board is more likely to end your days than an airplane uh-oh. You probably have a better chance of having an auto accident on the way to the airport than of having your plane go down.

Actually, there are differences in the caliber of in-flight service, food, and on-time arrival between airlines. These differences are variable since they depend on the weather, the size of the plane, length of flight, and other factors.

Charter

Charter air carriers normally offer the lowest published fares. Tickets for these flights are available through travel agents, and the charter carrier itself, e.g. Martinair, LTU, and others. There are conditions that you must suffer if you are going to take a charter, especially rules about refunds in case you cancel. These charter carriers normally fly only during the summer season, and only to a very select group of cities.

Specials

New routes by new carriers usually mean good cheap fares. Some junior European airlines are trying to start up international service and offer very good rates. Some major American carriers are also trying for a foothold in certain European cities, probably the reason that I had that beautiful round-trip on United from Amsterdam to Los Angeles for less than you would pay for a flight from Chicago to Detroit.

SCHEDULES

Official Airline Guide, OAG
Which airline is flying from Yourville to your destination, or nearby? In the old days, any travel agent with his Official Airline Guide, Worldwide Edition, could thumb up the right page and read off any schedule on the planet. The OAG monthly could also be found in most American business offices in the custody of the secretary of the highest ranking person, or lying among the phone books. Many business travelers would rather spend an hour or two figuring out their itinerary with this book than leave it in the hands of a travel agent.

Internet
Another way to check things out is to use the latest technology offered by computers and modems. If you're plugged in to the internet, you are probably already aware that you can sign on with almost any airline reservation system. Your travel agent uses basically the same system. With this service, you can check flight schedules to and from almost anywhere. An on-line connection also gives you all the conditions for ticket purchase, refund, changes, and etc.

However most internet services are still pretty weak when it comes to multi city reservations. If you want a three day layover in Amsterdam on your way to Warsaw it is easier to phone your travel agent. By the way, a layover like this is usually no extra cost so if you have a business trip to Europe ask about stuffing in a pleasure stop at one end of your business. Sit by a pool somewhere and write your trip report before heading back to the turmoil of the home office.

Timetables
As you are planning your flight, call the airlines which fly on your route and ask for a flight schedule booklet. If you're near the airport, go over and pick up a copy from the ticket counter. It will be handy to have in case you start thinking about changing plans. These schedules may also tell you about food services, stops and connections, seating plans, equipment, and include airport site plans. Travel agents will rarely volunteer this information, though it could have an influence on your flight selection.

Delays
Getting there on time with all your wits and belongings in tact depends on a lot of people and things working together. Sometimes they don't.

Every once in a while the TV evening news features a story about a bunch of whiners who had to wait an hour or so for their flight. So what? Bring a book. Have a beer. Meet somebody new.

A key part of the flying equation is the pilot. There is probably no other cause of delay and frustration more profound and/or devastating than pilot strikes.

Connection times on international flights are designed to allow you to change planes and possibly clear Customs and Passport Control in your connecting city. Meanwhile the airline is finding your luggage and transferring it to your next flight. Nice theory. You'll see in chapter 5 that I advocate packing light and not checking any luggage. Nevertheless, I have been in the check luggage situation on several of my extended business trips. And for those few flights where I made an overseas connection, my bags usually do not make it. Air France left my bags in Paris on one occasion even though I had an overnight layover. I had time to take the R.E.R train to the city, have a beautiful dinner in Montparnasse, take a long stroll through the Left Bank, and return to my airport hotel for a good night of sleep before continuing the next day. My luggage which had been checked through to my final destination missed the flight. In another case, British Air didn't have time to transfer my bags at Heathrow due to a late start from Amsterdam. When I arrived in Detroit my luggage didn't. BA gave me an allowance of up to $75.00 per bag to spend as I needed. My bags showed up at the house two days later, but the money I spent for clothes and other necessities was repaid by the airline. New rags for free — I should have spent the whole allotment. Northwest missed my connection in Detroit on my last return from Amsterdam. If you ask they will give you a shave kit which includes a T-shirt.

AIRPORT PROCEDURES

Parking

Most airports have short term and long term parking. Short term is closer to the terminal, and is more expensive.

Entering the parking lot may be your first encounter with airport security. There may be armed National Guard troops or police on duty to check the trunk of your car and give you a cursory look-over. More about security below.

Check-In

The first thing you do at the airport is check in at a departure counter. Locate your airline and the check-in position for your class of service — tourist, business, or first class. When you check in you are given a boarding pass with a seat assignment. A claim ticket(s) for your checked bag(s) is glued or stapled to your travel ticket envelope. The gate number for your flight will be on your boarding pass and the check-in agent will wave his/her arm in the general direction. The agent will probably write the gate number on your ticket envelope and circle it. The boarding gate is somewhere back in the caverns of the airport. You will get there, eventually.

On your way to the gate you will encounter the security metal detector and the x-ray belt for your carry-on items. So, it is a good idea to get moving toward your gate without delay.

Overbooked

Airlines typically overbook their flights, if they can. If they have 200 seats on a plane they sell maybe 220. They do this because some people will not arrive for the flight and the airlines want to fly as full as possible. This can create opportunity if the number of people who show up exceeds the number of seats. Volunteers are sought out who will give up their seat and take the next flight in exchange for discounts or free flight vouchers.

Due to an error at Northwest Airlines there was no information in the computer about me when I showed up to fly to Detroit from Amsterdam in January 2003. They finally found my record and told me that I was supposed to have been on the flight yesterday. Today's flight was 40 seats overbooked with not a fat chance of getting on board. But I went through all the security stuff anyway - it took over an hour. At the gate the NW folks gave me a seat right off even though there were still dozens of people behind me. My seat was at one of the doors, where they like to put big people. These seats have advantages of plenty of leg room, but have no seat in front of you under which to stash any carry on items like this computer I'm working on at the moment. It has to go in the overhead bin for take-off and landing.

The Bar Europa at Barcelona airport serves snacks and drinks. Yes, you may smoke. [0402]

Bumping Up

Sometimes at check-in you are given the rude surprise that your reserved seat has been reassigned and there is no seat available. Or you might be told to wait a little bit, which could turn out to be 15 to 30 minutes. Several airlines have put me "on hold" at the counter in the last few years. While I waited the airline agent was poking around on his computer terminal, or would disappear for a while through one of those doors behind the baggage belt. I can wait here or at the gate I figure, so I wait here. Apparently what the agent does in each of these instances is find a seat for me in business class or first class. I've been bumped up a few times flying trans-Atlantic, on United, Air France, and KLM, and within Europe on Lufthansa. On one of my KLM round trips Los Angeles - Amsterdam I was bumped up to business class each way, and with a ticket that only cost me $400! That's flying. Besides being treated like a prince on the plane you also have privileges to the airline's VIP lounge at both airports.

If you think that I was given privileges because I wrote a travel book, it can't be. The author of this book, "John Bermont," is just a pen name. I travel under my real name.

Even after boarding a British Airlines flight in London with an assigned seat on one flight I was told by the stewardess that someone else had the same seat. I didn't want that window seat anyway, and after some diplomacy with another stewardess I was given an aisle seat with nobody in the seat next to it. This transpired after having been told three times that the plane was completely full without a single seat available. So, be polite but resolute. It can help to ask other flight attendants or the purser. Once anyone in charge of anything digs in his/her heels there is no turning back or mind changing allowed in this life, especially with Europeans.

SECURITY

The New War

Thanks to deviates who try to hijack or bomb planes, everybody and everything going on the plane is subject to several checks. This is nothing to fool around with, so just follow instructions and do as you are told. Your life and the lives of many others depends on it. Fooling around with security can be a Federal felony with prison time plus 5 figure fines.

It has become war since September 11, 2001. The attack on the United States and on civilization has brought mass murder to a monstrous new level. While hundreds of innocent people were killed on the planes, thousands more were killed at their desks on that unbelievable morning. My personal experience with terrorist murder is in the dedication to this book, with additional notes in the first chapter. The security measures are designed to prevent another event, and so far millions of passengers have flown without another successful attack. But there are plenty of devils still out there, hiding and planning their next move. Be vigilant and call authority when you see something out of the ordinary.

As you read this section you should realize that security checks take time. There are hundreds of people on your plane and perhaps a dozen planes taking off within a short period of time. Expect a line at each check point. Do not arrive at the last minute. For international flights, airlines recommend that you arrive 2 to 3 hours before flight time. I recommend that you bring a book, a sandwich, and a beverage.

First Check

Your first security check happens when you walk up to the counter with your ticket. You must show a photo ID. Either before or after the airline accepts your checked luggage, it is subject to x-ray examination and/or hand search, either in your presence or behind the wall. The x-ray equipment is very strong and will damage undeveloped photo film. In some airports and with some airlines you must wait near the check-in counter until your bags are x-rayed.

For many years the check-in attendant would also ask you if you packed your own bags and if you are carrying anything for anybody. This procedure was discontinued, at least for domestic flights, in 2002. I think that this procedure should have been retained. It is virtually innocuous and may trigger a reaction in one person which one day will save a flight full of people. The questions make you think and cost nothing compared to the massive security which is in every airport.

Second Check
        After leaving the check-in counter you proceed to your gate and encounter the security check point. The usual practice at security check is to lay your carry-on items on a belt which runs everything through an x-ray machine. Experts look at everything on their screen. If there is something they don't recognize you are then requested to open your bags for a hand search. They also direct you to remove your laptop computer from its case and lay it on the belt. There will be a small poster there advising you what cannot be brought on board the plane, either in your carry-on luggage or in your pockets. The signs also direct you to put all metal items in your carry-on bag. It would be more convenient to do this at home to save time at the security check point.
        Meanwhile, as your goods are going through the x-ray machine, you walk through an open door device which checks you for metallic objects. This is not an x-ray machine so don't worry about being zapped. Before you go through, you should have emptied your pockets of coins, keys, and anything else made of steel, copper, silver, etc.. Some of these door devices are so sensitive that they will buzz for a dime. I have been asked to go through as many as three times before passing without sounding the alarm.

After your carry-on bag is checked you'll get a tag like this. It is still subject to search after approval. [0414]

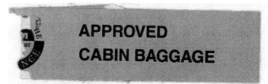

Third Check
        Even after going through without setting off the alarm, I have been searched a number of times with a hand-held metal detector. I am usually given a police-type frisking in Amsterdam's Schiphol Airport — arms up and a complete pat down. They started doing that with me years before 9/11, and it happened again in January 2003.
        Your jacket must usually be removed and some people are asked to put their shoes on the x-ray belt. I was asked to put my Birkenstock sandals on the x-ray belt in the backwoods MBS airport serving Midland, Bay City, and Saginaw, Michigan. This USA airport security business is serious business, since the horse got out of the barn.

Fourth Check
        After passing through the metal detector, you retrieve your pocket change, eyeglasses, calculator, and other stuff you may have given to the attendant. Then you retrieve your belongings which went on the belt under the x-ray eye. If you passed a camera through the belt, you may be asked to open it and let the security guard look through it. If you passed a laptop computer through, the security guard may wipe parts of it and put the wipe cloth in a device which can detect certain substances.

Fifth Check

At the gate during boarding there is another check. Randomly selected people are called aside and requested to go through a personal search of their carry-on bag and their pockets. Some are asked to remove their shoes for further inspection.

Special Checks

At times of national emergencies, other measures may be enforced. During the 1991 Gulf War we had to take all the batteries out of our cameras, video recorders, computers, and other devices and pack the batteries separately.

Questions

Amsterdam has always had tight security, with a final check at the boarding gate. Now, just before you board the plane, they have an additional procedure. There are a dozen security officers in front of the gate. They interview everyone for about 5 minutes with plenty of questions and redundant questions to trip up the liars. They jump on anything out of the ordinary, like my changed ticket.

Self Defense

For personal security, always seal your checked bags. I use a black wire tie to secure the zipper to another zipper or strap ring. This prevents free-lance shopping by airport personnel. A wire tie works better than any suitcase lock I've seen, and it is inconspicuous. You have to cut it to get it off. Nail clippers work well, and are allowed on the aircraft in your pocket.

Emergency Contact

Your airline may or may not give you a card before you board on which you can write the name, address, and phone number of someone to contact in case of an emergency or accident. You have the option of declining. This was in effect for a few years but seems to have disappeared as of 2003.

Schiphol Airport Amsterdam makes it easy to get oriented with user friendly signs in English. [0412]

ON THE PLANE

Seat Assignment

Seating on the plane is by assignment only. Your seat number is shown on your boarding pass. If, after takeoff, you want to move to another seat just get up and do it. If you see a seat that you particularly like, make your move as soon as the doors are closed. I made the mistake of asking the stewardess for an OK to move to another seat on a KLM flight. Dutch solid heads told me to wait until the doors were locked, and later told me to wait until the fasten seat belt sign was turned off. On other flights I just got up and changed seats with no problem. On this KLM flight someone else did the same before the control freak stewardess came back to me. Never again mister nice guy for me. Get up and change seats and don't budge unless you are asked by the steward.

Seats are numbered starting with row 1 in the very front of the plane. That is in either first or business class. Across the plane, seats are lettered starting with A at the port side window. If there are 8 seats across, as on many 747s, seat H is at the starboard side window. If there are 10 across K would be the window seat because they normally don't use the letter I. Some airline timetables show the seat configuration for their aircraft.

You can normally get a seat assignment when you pay for your ticket rather than waiting until you check-in. Since I suffer from acrophobia, I prefer the aisle. If you want to look out the window, and control the window shade, request a window seat. With a window seat you have to ask the person on the aisle to let you out when you need to use the toilet. Conversely, on the aisle you are likely to have an occasional nudge and an "excuse me" from your row mate. Teenagers sitting by the window like to pole vault out to the aisle and are less likely to disturb you than if an older person was sitting over there.

If you are a big person and want extra leg room, request a bulkhead seat or a seat at an emergency exit door. Then you won't have a person in front of you leaning his seat back and crushing your kneecaps. You won't have any problems getting out for the pottie, or being disturbed by someone else wishing to go.

Seats at the emergency exit doors are usually assigned to larger people who can help with plane evacuation if that becomes necessary. This practice probably enabled me to get a seat on that flight from Amsterdam to Detroit after I was told that it was 40 seats overbooked. At the gate they gave me a beautiful seat at the exit door with yards of leg room.

Boarding

After getting to the departure gate, you will have to wait for your row to be called before boarding. Planes are normally boarded in a standard order -- disabled people, people with toddlers, first class, business class, and then tourist class. Tourist class is boarded by rows, starting with the highest numbers which are in the back of the plane. When the batch of rows including yours is called, snap to and get right up to the attendant who is taking boarding passes and allowing people on the plane. KLM seems to let everybody board at once. Queues are apparently disallowed in the Netherlands.

It's a good idea to be early on the plane. If you are first on for your row you can put your carry-on luggage in the overhead bin. If the others get there first and fill it up with their stuff, you will have to hunt around for a place to put your bag. You might even be asked to check it in the luggage hold.

Safety Instructions

After everybody is seated and the doors are closed the flight attendants begin the safety instruction. They show you how to buckle and unbuckle your seat belt. They demonstrate the use of the emergency oxygen masks. They demonstrate the manner of putting on, strapping down, and inflating the emergency flotation vest. They point out the emergency exits. Sometimes the safety instruction is given over the video screens. Most people seemingly have something more important to do than pay attention to the safety lesson. Sad.

Bus 300 takes you directly to the Haarlem train station from Amsterdam's airport. You can also use a taxi or the train. [0413]

Eating

Most flights provide meals, anything from a mini baggie of sugared peanuts to a full dinner and a breakfast depending on flight duration, time of day, and class of service. Chances are that your eastbound trans-Atlantic flight will include dinner and/or lunch and/or breakfast. Meals on international flights are not as bad as those on domestic flights, except that I've never had a breakfast worth eating on any flight. Just before writing this paragraph I had a nice lasagna for dinner, courtesy of KLM. Food and soft drinks are free. Alcoholic beverages are free on trans-Atlantic flights, with seemingly no limit. It is reported that some American carriers are now charging $4 for beer, wine, and spirits. My last trans-Atlantic flight on Northwest from Amsterdam to Detroit provided gratis drinks.

Flights within Europe are short and there is little time for regular service. Sometimes there is a bin of bagged food in the gate area. It's self service. On a morning flight from London to Amsterdam the flight attendants zipped through the plane literally throwing a covered styrofoam plate in everybody's lap. Who wants British food anyway?

European business class is a necessary sop for upper level employees, and a joke. I have enjoyed it but for the short flights under two hours it is of dubious value. During dinner on a Sabena flight from Brussels to Edinburgh, I turned around and noticed that the tourist class was also sitting in six-across seats and appeared to be enjoying a nice meal like us in business class. I asked the stewardess what the difference was between business class and tourist class. She was taken aback for a moment, then replied that we had a hot meal and theirs was cold. I asked if that was it and she said that we also got champagne! That was a surprise because no champagne was offered.

When making airline reservations, inquire about the availability of special meals. There is no extra charge for this service. For medical and religious reasons, all airlines will provide special meals to passengers. They also offer a selection of plates besides the normal chicken and beef. Children's meals are also available. I sat next to a fellow from India who requested a Hindu meal. The stewardess should have had his seat number on a list of special meals, but didn't mention it. So if it doesn't come out, ask. The flight attendant probably has it but it may have the wrong seat number on it.

On one flight to Europe the only meats on board were ham and pork. Several people sitting near me asked for something different, but the flight attendant had nothing else to offer. So, if there is something you'd rather not eat, let them know before the plane is up above the clouds.

You must reserve special meals at the time you buy your ticket. It's too late when you see the passenger next to you dive into a chilled seafood plate. He has the only one on the plane.

Smoking

Fortunately, most airlines are flying smoke free these days. But there is a chance that you'll be on a flight with smoking allowed if you fly within Europe.

If you are sensitive to smoke, request a seat in the middle of the no smoking section. Europeans smoke a lot and there may be a lot of Europeans on board, especially if you are flying on one of their airlines. On one overseas flight I was in the first no smoking row and the smoke wafted back for eleven hours. I and everybody around me suffered from coughs and sneezes for the last half of the flight.

Headsets

If you want to listen to the recorded music or the sound track of the on-board movie, use a headset provided by the airline. Headsets are normally free on trans-Atlantic flights.

Electronic Gizmos

During take-off and landing all electronic devices must be turned off. In the air, laptop computers and game devices may be operated. Using mobile phones and other communications devices is prohibited during flight.

Entertainment

Tourist class passengers are treated to a recent release from Hollywood. I just watched an old Christmas episode from "Cheers" with San Malone and his merry gang. You might also see a rebroadcast of the BBC or CNN news, plane route maps and information, and a video clip describing the country you are about to land in. The absolute worst video clip I ever saw was on a KLM flight from Amsterdam to

Manama, Bahrain. The flight was on New Years Eve and the video showed celebrations around the world. While the video was showing all that champagne bubbling down the gullets of happy folks everywhere on the planet, our plane was sitting on the tarmac in Kuwait. We were dry because Kuwait is a "dry" country. It was a New Years Eve not to be forgotten, like my last bug in the eye. Another thing I didn't like about that flight was the part where we flew along the southern border of Iraq, very low and very slow on the Saudi Arabian side of the line in the sand.

Business and First Class passengers are normally provided with an individual video screen on their arm rest. You can watch any of several movies or rock concerts or whatever else, and switch channels just as if you were at home.

Climate on Board

International flights pass through air that is about 60 below zero and extremely dry. Sometimes the inside air can feel almost as cold. Bring a sweater on board if you have thin blood. Ask for an extra blanket if you need it.

To avoid dehydration drink plenty of your favorite beverage. I don't go along with those people who say drink juices and water, and avoid alcoholic drinks. I don't drink fruit juices unless they have been fermented first. Fruit juices are full of fructose and I'm sweet enough already. Alcoholic beverages, especially red wine, help you warm up, are excellent relaxants, and have been found to benefit your heart.

On Board Magazine

In the pocket attached to the back of the seat in front of you is the current issue of the airline's on board magazine. These magazines normally have a few good articles, schedules of movies on board, maps of the carrier's system, a duty free shopping catalog, crossword puzzles, plenty beaucoup advertisements, and a coupon for joining the airline's frequent flyer program. Join. It's free and you can get free flights.

What's Down Below

If you want to know what you are flying over check out the maps in the on board magazine. You might be able to figure it out. These maps show big arcs from city to city, not straight lines. To understand why, use a globe and a piece of string to locate the shortest route between your departure and arrival cities. You'll see that a flight from Los Angeles to Amsterdam flies further north than one from New York to Amsterdam.

Landing

On the plane, keep a note of the expected landing time. If you have an alarm watch (see chapter 6, "A Packing List for Europe"), set it for about one hour before arrival. When the alarm rings, get in line at the toilets for a pit stop. Toilets get awfully busy just before landing, and the bumps start as the plane descends through the clouds.

POTPOURRI

Baggage

Please see chapter 24, "Shipping from Europe," for regulations about checked and carry-on baggage. One potentially important point is that baggage allowances within Europe are less than they are for trans-Atlantic flights.

Caveat Emptor

Regardless of which airline you choose, check your ticket immediately and thoroughly on receipt. Everything on it means something, and if you do not understand it, ASK! It's YOUR trip and mistakes are against YOUR good times for which you cannot be refunded, even if you do get all of your money back, which you probably won't. Consider yourself fallible and the one you are dealing with as fallible and get slightly, temporarily, paranoid. Mistakes are especially likely when you are making changes. Make sure that not less and not more than you intended was changed. Check and recheck. And when dealing overseas with someone who does not speak American English or speaks it with an accent, write down your intentions. This will reduce the chance of an error, but it will not eliminate it. On my last flight from Amsterdam I changed my reservation but the lady in Northwest's Minneapolis office changed the day on me, a fact that I did not discover until I showed up at the airport a day late, according to them.

If you decide to go by way of a package tour, know what you are buying. Read all the terms and conditions to make sure that you and the tour are in harmony. Compare with what you will need to spend. See chapter 2, "On Budget in Europe," for a list and descriptions of expense items. Ask for clarification in writing for all generalizations, maybes, and obfuscations. Good luck.

Flight Number

Every "flight" is assigned a flight number by the airline. This includes two letters designating the name of the airline company and 2 to 4 numbers for their flight number, for example, XY1234.

A flight may be non-stop or it may stop along the way in various cities. For best use of your time select a non-stop flight. Multiple stop itineraries usually offer more economical travel. You may have more than one flight number and ticket. This would normally mean that you get off and board another flight in a city along the way.

Code Share

Sometimes a single flight can have two flight numbers when it is on a route served by partner airlines. For example, over the years one of my favorite flights to Europe is on KL602, non-stop Los Angeles to Amsterdam on KLM Royal Dutch Airlines. This is also flight NW8602 in the Northwest Airlines schedule. Same plane, different name. In fact, all NW flights with four digits beginning with 8 are actually

KLM flights. Tonight I'm on NW8618 from Detroit to Amsterdam, but it's actually KL618. Nice flight.

The most unusual code sharing I have seen is with American Airlines and the Thalys. Thalys is the premium high speed train between Amsterdam and Paris. Actually it only enjoys high speed track between Brussels and Paris and it is no faster than a regular train between Amsterdam and Brussels, until the high speed track is completed. American Airlines does not fly to Brussels, but has a code share with the Thalys between Paris and Brussels. Thus, if you book an AA flight to Brussels you'll be flying into Paris and then taking the high speed train to Brussels, designated as AA7395 with aircraft type TGV. This is the French designation for high speed train. The Brussels airport city code is a strange one, ZYR for the Brussels Midi train station. You probably want to go to the Brussels Central station so hop on the next local train to the center of the city.

Equipment

"Equipment" is airline jargon for the type of airplane. Most international airlines fly "jumbo jets" — the Boeing 747 or 767, DC-10, or Airbus 300 series. Formerly they also used the Lockheed TriStar L-1011, which is, in my judgment, the nicest riding plane ever built. But it is a gas guzzler so you don't see this one very often, unless you are flying in Saudi Arabia. If I ever become a billionaire I'll buy a TriStar and learn to drive it. The big birds are definitely more comfortable than the smaller planes on those long overseas flights.

Seats

Some carriers put more seats on a plane than others. I have been on budget domestic flights with five rows of seats jammed in where there were just four windows. There was virtually no room for my knees. It is reported that this is also done on some international charter flights. So if you're a big person you might want to check on this before buying a low cost ticket for a 10 hour flight.

Reconfirmation

On one flight my reservation had been canceled by the airline. I had reconfirmed with their automatic system the day before, but that system did not acknowledge the fact. When I arrived for check-in three hours before flight time my reservation was no longer in the computer. The agent said that all airlines assume that you are not going to fly if you do not reconfirm at least three days before the flight. I was surprised. With all the trouble they go to getting customers you'd think that they would assume the other way, especially for a passenger with a paid-up ticket in hand. Traveling tip: Don't assume anything with airlines — let them do the assuming. This airline has since changed their policy and does not require reconfirmation, at this time. Verify reconfirmation requirements or none when you buy your ticket.

Multiple Terminals

This probably applies to only a few large city airports. In Los Angeles, for example, there is a separate international terminal, yet not all international flights arrive at or depart from the Bradley International Terminal. There is a similar situation in Detroit. Check with your travel agent to determine which terminal your flight departs from and returns to before you head for the airport. Getting lost in a big airport minutes before your flight time is just no fun.

INTERNATIONAL AIRPORT FACILITIES

More Than at Home

International airports offer a number of facilities not normally seen in US domestic airports. Of course, you will always find bars, restaurants, car rentals, gift shops, ATM machines, and newsstands.

Duty Free Shopping

After obtaining a boarding pass you can browse through the "duty free shops." Items featured are usually luxury goods, alcohol, and tobacco. You cannot use the duty free shops when you land. They are only for departing passengers.

Many airlines also offer duty free shopping while you are on board. There will probably be a catalog of items in your seat pocket or there will be a duty free section in the in-flight magazine. If you don't want to buy and don't want to be disturbed ask the flight attendant to skip you before you fall asleep.

Banks

Before there were ATM machines there were banks. Remember those? Most international airports have a bank which primarily serves as a money exchange office. When you land get enough local currency to get you to a bank in town where you will probably receive a better exchange rate for your dollars. If you have an ATM card use it in a machine at the airport and extract the cash you will need for the next few days.

Luggage Storage

Some airports offer baggage check rooms and/or luggage lockers. For example, Amsterdam's Schiphol Airport has short term lockers and long term attended luggage storage on the lowest level of the terminal. It's very convenient.

Observation Deck

If you like to watch the planes taking off and landing, most airports have an outdoor deck or restaurant area to accommodate you.

Train Station

Many European airports are connected to the city center by local or international trains. If you have a Eurailpass you can start using it to get to town right from the airport. If you are staying there for a few days you might want to pay for a ticket to extend the validity of your Eurailpass and not waste a day on a short hop.

Other Ground Transportation

In addition to direct train service in many cities, European airports are served by taxis, metro lines, city buses, hotel buses, and/or airline buses. There is always a way to get to your hotel.

DEEP VEIN THROMBOSIS, DVT

The information in this section is paraphrased from the web site of the Alaska Department of Health. This is not meant to be medical advice, and is surely not complete. Studies continue on DVT. For more information see your doctor. Do not sue me.

What is DVT?

DVT is clotting in the veins of the legs. It has been known for decades that this condition can happen when taking long haul air flights like those you will make in crossing the Atlantic. However, there is no proof that flying per se is a cause of DVT because DVT is fairly common in the general population, affecting approximately one in 2,000 people. DVT is associated primarily with sitting in one position for many hours. There are a number of other contributory factors having to do with advanced age, family history, pregnancy, recent hip or knee operations, and your personal health history regarding blood clotting.

DVT is a life threatening condition. The clots can break loose from the legs and lodge in the lungs causing pulmonary embolus, PE. This can cause the lungs to collapse followed by heart failure. If the floating clot lodges in your heart it can be heart failure pretty quick when your pump muscles quit.

The first symptom of DVT is a pain in one leg. You may have swelling, tenderness, or redness, especially in the upper calf. The condition frequently occurs after the flight, sometimes days later. The symptoms of subsequent PE are breathlessness and chest pain.

Preventing DVT

The obvious and easiest way of reducing the risk of DVT is to get some exercise on the plane. In-your-chair isometrics, deep breathing, bending, and foot massage every hour or so would be good. Many frequent travelers, including me, take a hike around the plane every once in a while. You never know who you will see on board.

Diet and medication can also be considered. Some people advocate aspirin for its reported anti-thrombotic properties. This is held in dispute by others. Some people advocate one or more of the aspirin substitutes. Avoiding excessive alcohol consumption and drinking plenty of water are also suggested. Wearing elastic stockings is reportedly helpful.

There are some public advocacy groups which blame the close seating in tourist class for DVT. There is no room to move around in the seat — you can't even cross your legs unless you are under 10 years of age. A few airlines show in-flight videos discussing DVT and how to prevent it. Most airlines do not mention it.

Here is the schedule of trains from Brussels Nord or Noord train station to the Brussels airport, in French, Dutch, German, and English. Brussels has three main train stations and you can catch the airport train from each, every 20 minutes. [0404]

JET LAG

You may have heard of jet lag as one of those late-night "comedians" interviewed a well-traveled "starlet" on his program. However, it is real.

What's This?

Jet lag is a discomfort caused by your body's attempts to move all of its daily functions ahead or behind in accordance with the number of time zones you have crossed. For example, at 5pm in Los Angeles, it is 8pm in New York, and 1am in London. A nonstop flight departing Los Angeles at noon arrives in London at 11pm Los Angeles time, just about bed time. But it will be 7am in London. Your body wants to sleep. It's certainly not ready for breakfast, much less a British breakfast, and a day at the Tower followed by a night on the town.

AIRPORT CITY EXPRESS →

Liaison Bruxelles-Nord – Bruxelles-National-Aéroport

Verbinding Brussel-Noord – Brussel-Nationaal-Luchthaven

Verbindung Brüssel-Nord – Brüssel-National-Flughafen

Connection North station – Brussels-National-Airport

Heure de départ / Departure	Voie / Platform	Heure de départ / Departure	Voie / Platform	Heure de départ / Departure	Voie / Platform	Heure de départ / Departure	Voie / Platform
5.45	3	10.18	3	15.02	3	20.02	3
6.02	3	10.45	3	15.18	3	20.18	3
6.18	3	11.02	3	15.45	3	20.45	3
6.45	3	11.18	3	16.02	3	20.45	3
7.02	3	11.45	3	16.18	3	21.02	3
7.18	3	12.02	3	16.45	3	21.18	3
7.45	3	12.18	3	17.02	3	21.45	3
8.02	3	12.45	3	17.18	3	22.02	6
8.23	5	13.02	3	17.45	3	22.18	3
8.18	3	13.18	6	18.04	3	22.45	3
8.45	3	13.18	3	18.18	3	23.02	3
9.02	3	13.45	3	18.45	3	23.18	3
9.18	3	14.02	3	19.02	3		
9.45	3	14.18	3	19.18	3		
10.02	3	14.45	3	19.45	3		

Prevention

For flights to Europe it is a big help if you are able to sleep on the eastbound flight. Sleep will be difficult if you are crammed into an undersized seat with oversized persons jammed in on both sides and pigging the armrests. It can be getting uncomfortable in six hours, but you may have four more to go. And when you can't get your mind off your discomfort, you can't relax and sleep.

In going to Europe I have found it helpful to get on a plane after having had only a couple hours of sleep the night before. Bring a pocket book on board, and maybe take a mild relaxant like aspirin or a glass of wine to help you doze off. These work for me when flying to Europe.

It is also helpful, especially when flying from the eastern time zone, to fly as late in evening as possible. Flying from Detroit, for example, you can depart at about 4pm and arrive in Amsterdam at 6am. That corresponds to midnight in Detroit where your body clock is still residing. You are past your bedtime but the world around you is just waking up. Instead, you can take a later flight at about 11pm from Detroit which arrives in Amsterdam at about 1pm the next afternoon. You are pretty sure of getting at least a few hours of good sleep on the late plane because it is flying during your normal sleep time. You'll arrive much more refreshed than if you take the afternoon departure.

Adding to your discomfort when arriving early morning in Europe is the probability that you will not be able to check into your hotel until noon. One way to shake off the initial effects of jet lag is to take a good hot shower and change your clothes. If you are scheduling an early arrival then also schedule an early check-in.

Cure

No quick fix has yet been found. The only cure for jet lag is time. The common rule of thumb is that it takes approximately one day to cure each time zone traversed. I would say that this is for a complete cure. You will be almost normal in one third of this time, depending on how you behave and on the direction in which you are traveling.

There is some dispute among sufferers whether it is easier to recuperate when going east or when going west. I find the adjustment easier when traveling from Europe to America. The entire flight westbound is during daylight and you arrive only a few hours later than you departed, by local clock time, even though the actual flight time can be half a day. It's equivalent to staying up way past your normal bedtime though you have a whole night to catch up on your sleep.

There is a "drug" which reportedly can reduce the effects of jet lag. It is widely available on the internet. Please consult your doctor before using this substance.

Surviving Jet Lag

On arrival after a six to ten hour flight, you can expect to be a bit edgy and hypersensitive, but not necessarily tired. You'll be just blah blah and feeling like you have a mild flu. Struggle through the day to stay awake until the right local sleeping time. This forces your body to begin getting in step with local time. You will awaken often during the first night, and probably won't sleep at all if you dozed off during the first day. Falling asleep during your first day will prolong your jet lag by at least a day.

On the second day, you will feel OK in the morning, but become extremely drowsy in the middle of the afternoon. You will be sleepy that evening, but get only a restless sleep, probably waking several times. Have a big pasta dinner to help you sleep through the night.

After your first two brutal days in Europe, the third day will feature a marked increase in your comfort. Tiredness will set in during the afternoon. Stay up until at least 10pm so that you won't wake up before 4am.

By the fourth day you will have forgotten that you had jet lag. Keep moving and have a wild night. That's all.

UNACCOMPANIED MINOR, UM

What is UM?

Children from about 5 years and up can travel alone. The minimum age depends on the airline. It's called Unaccompanied Minor status, UM for short. We have flown Stephanie unaccompanied to Italy almost every year since she was 7. She has made 12 trans-Atlantic flights on her own, plus a number of additional legs within Europe and the USA. Initially we flew her on non-stop flights from Los Angeles to Milan where her aunt lives. Starting when she was 10 she began making connections with the assistance of airline personnel. Alitalia has discontinued its non-stop LAX-MXP service forcing her to make connections for the future.

Procedures for UM are rather simple. The airlines need to know certain information about the identity of the person who is bringing the child to the airport and the person who is picking him/her up. Names, address, relationships, and telephone numbers are needed. To pick up the child, the receiving adult must present a passport or other official identification.

Services

Airline personnel help with boarding at airports. Non-passengers are prohibited beyond the first control point which is still a mile from the security and passport check points. The boarding area makes up most of the airport. Therefore you have to leave your kid in the hands of the airline for over an hour before flight time. Amsterdam's Schiphol Airport has a kid play zone so they won't get bored. I've flown Stephanie from Schiphol to Malpensa in Milan and to Heathrow in London, each time signing her away long before flight time.

Connections

Though non-stop service is certainly better, faster, and safer, you can not tell the airline where to land. The child may need to make a connection. Stephanie has connected in Chicago with United Airlines, London with British Air, in Paris with Air France, and in Frankfurt with Lufthansa. Everything normally went OK, except she mentioned that the fellow from Air France was not too well informed or prepared for his assignment. He left Stephanie and three other kids waiting alone while he returned somewhere to get a key for a locked door, whereupon a couple of stewardesses started asking the kids some questions, in French. Duh? The fellow came back and all went OK for her continuing flight to Geneva where I was living at the time. On her most recent connection, Lufthansa lost her bag in Frankfurt but got it to her in Milan the next day. Nothing unusual about that. But she was very upset that the stewardess did not wake her up for breakfast on the leg to Milan. Even though Stephanie woke up during the food service she was not given any breakfast. In my experience, Lufthansa crew are the second least helpful of any airline except Iberia.

Unaccompanied Minors wear a small tag like this one issued by Air France. [0411]

No Last Flight

Scheduling a child for UM status is slightly more difficult than for making adult reservations. Generally, airlines will not allow a child to make a connection if the flight they are connecting to is the last flight of the day from a connecting city. Some airlines will allow this if the child is at least 12, or 15, or some other minimum age and flying UM. Some airlines with only one flight a day from an American gateway city will allow a UM to make the connection to Europe because international flights are rarely canceled.

Kids Meal

Make sure you order the "kids meal" for the UM flight, or you will discover that Air France does not serve French fries and that kids don't necessarily like French food. But, Stephanie says, the deserts are superb.

Cost

The international airlines charge extra for UM status if there is a connection. It is generally priced per flight leg. Making a connection means two legs. It was $50 on Lufthansa in 2002.

Chapter 5
What To Wear in Europe
Travel Clothes for All Occasions

Do not wear the emperor's clothes. Put on something a little more modest.

CLOTHING GUIDELINES

What will you wear to Europe? This is a major concern, but it is secondary. The real question is — how much to bring? You are infinitely better off going with nothing but an umbrella and a toothbrush than with the load you would typically bring on a vacation in the United States.

Pack Light

As every traveler and chronicler of the subject relates, pack light. Seldom does anyone define "pack light" except to present a list of clothes and accessories to bring, no such list ever being universally practical. To enjoy travel, you must pack light. To define pack light, travel with your chosen load and see for yourself if it is convenient and gives you the freedom you need.

Dress Sharp

It pays to be well presented, with a European flavor. Europeans are clothes conscious. Northern European clothing looks rather somber, while brighter colors are more common as you go south. Clothes represent personality and social status. People wear their better clothes almost all the time.

Europeans seeing you for the first time and only briefly will judge you completely by your appearance, and will behave accordingly. Unfortunately for the traveler, most of your personal contact in Europe will be with hotel clerks and café waiters. To secure a good room, good table, and good service, dress as if you deserve it. In fact, you will be stopped at the door of many places if you are not properly dressed.

Be Comfortable

In addition, you must keep yourself comfortable. Northern European weather is generally cooler, wetter, and more variable than in the United States. South of the

Alps and Pyrenees it can be warm and stuffy just about any time of the year. Walking in and out of museums, restaurants, and stores may force you to off and on your coat. In stores the heat from those little halogen lamps can be very uncomfortable. Be ready for rain or shine, hot or cold.

Pack Light Field Test

I propose the following test, preferably taken in a light rain.

Pack everything, put on your hat and coat, open your umbrella, (raining or not), check the time, and walk one mile away from home with everything you have. Then, pretending you are trying to catch a train or trying to get to the tourist office before it closes, run or walk home. If you can make the round trip comfortably within 45 minutes, you have packed light. It is best if your test course includes a short, steep hill or several flights of stairs, upwards on the return leg.

Also make sure that all of your traveling companions can pass the pack light field test. If not, old friends may become lifetime enemies. Failure to obey the pack light rule will doom you in so many ways that you will be better off to stay home and water your tomatoes. Those taking a cruise or tour may think that they can escape this rule, but be aware that porters and taxis are usually scarce and/or expensive.

RECOMMENDED CLOTHING

Rules for the easy traveler, then, are rather formidable:
1. Pack light
2. Dress sharp
3. Be comfortable

Typical Tourist Clothing

The clothes worn by most American tourists announce them as Americans better than any trilingual poster ever could. From the ground up you're wearing: jogger or tennis shoes, worn Levi's, collared tee shirt, and ski jacket, with a backpack. If you are past the age of backpacks, your oversized plastic suitcase will even more effectively identify you as an American.

Go Like a Local

For a number of reasons you are better off looking like a local citizen rather than a standard American tourist. The primary reason is to avoid being a target of pickpockets, a breed endemic in Europe.

For many years my personal preference was a pair of black slip-on shoes, wool/polyester blend slacks, turtleneck shirt, and sport coat. This ensemble will get you through almost any door in Europe with reasonable respect, keep you comfortable under most weather conditions, and allow you to blend in without being instantly identified as "the American."

The wool/polyester blend slacks look more like wool than plastic, but they wash drip dry. You shouldn't need to iron these if you care for them according to the label. Turtleneck shirts are not easy to find in America, but you should be able to find them in the better department stores, in ski clothing shops, or in the Lands End catalog. An open collar dress shirt is a good substitute for the turtleneck in warmer weather. In very few restaurants is a tie required, though you'll see them often in better establishments. For off-season travel, I also bring a lightweight turtleneck sweater. My sport coat has a herringbone pattern and travels very well without showing wrinkles or minor stains.

Levi's

Levis and other brands of denim jeans became fashionable in Europe in the 1990's. Levis are now tolerated in many cafés and restaurants during the day. However, regular slacks are much more common as street wear in major cities throughout Europe. Based on my observations of people walking through the central train stations of Amsterdam and Brussels in 2003 less than 20% were wearing denim jeans. The preference for the vast majority, men and women, young and old, was black slacks.

Slacks are also much more in harmony with packing light. Levis are heavy and bulky, and take a day to dry out when they get rained on. If you do wear denim, select a lightweight pair with a bit of fashion. You might want to consider wearing Levi slacks rather than Levi jeans. Levi Strauss makes a good looking line called "Action Slacks." These are 100% Dacron and travel very well. Wash them off in the shower at night and hang them to drip dry by morning. I have a couple pairs in black.

When strolling in major cities in the summer a lightweight pair of black slacks or a skirt plus a white top will serve you well. This is standard attire for a large percentage of the native populations, and tourists from other European countries.

I have no ambition of being a clothing cop so accept this chapter as you will. The advice is based on my personal experience in Europe. Yeah sure, you can wear your back yard jeans or shorts, t-shirt or no shirt, sneakers or flip-flops, and that is the way you will viewed and treated in the cosmopolitan cities throughout Europe. Expect no respect.

Layers

Other writers suggest that travelers dress in "layers." This is explained as dressing in items that can be added to or removed individually without changing everything when the weather changes. This requires that all of your clothes be complementary and mixable. Dark, neutral, and earth colors tend to avoid fashion clashes, and do not need cleaning as often as lighter colors. A heavy coat for winter travel can be replaced by a lightweight windbreaker and a good sweater. But if you're going to Finland in January you might consider taking the heavy coat.

Shoes

In Europe you'll notice all sorts of footwear — boots, clogs, tennis, joggers, sandals, army issue, and Italian fashion. Many people will see and examine your shoes before their eyes come up to meet yours, if they ever do.

Appearance is important. Wear a good looking, durable, broken-in pair of shoes. Your average American department store shoes will probably be mistaken for Italian fashion. Perfect. An average pair of polished black slip-ons will get you in anywhere. Also, rubber soles will survive far better than leather soles on the rain soaked sidewalks of Europe.

Instead of shoes, I have become a convert to sandals, more specifically Birkenstocks, a German brand. Once you break in a pair of Birkenstocks you will never go back to shoes again, except for during stormy weather. Birkenstocks have a half inch of cork between the hard rubber bottom and the leather part you rest your feet in. Cork is very easy to walk on and you can go all day in these things. You won't even want to go barefoot again. I recommend black socks with the Birkenstocks, unless you are at the beach.

This is a very old picture, but the only one I could find to illustrate the point — my typical travel apparel in the major cities of Europe. On a brisk May day in Paris I start out with a sweater and sport coat. As it warms up in the afternoon I take off the sweater and carry it in a shopping bag. Dressed like this you will never be recognized as an American, and you will be given better treatment than the frumpy Yanks who walk around Paris in tennis shoes, then come home complaining that the French don't like Americans. Yes, that is the front door of Notre Dame Cathedral behind me. After 182 years of construction they finished it in 1363 AD. Photo by ?[0512]

Carry an extra pair of shoes since it is likely that your shoes will get soaked occasionally. If you invest in a pair with natural leather uppers, you can oil them to the point that they resist water like wax paper. Use mink oil or equivalent once a week.

Again, do not wear any kind of sports shoes, e.g. tennis, jogging, or whatever else they call them these days. I was with some business associates in The Hague a few years ago and we decided to make a pub crawl. Two of them had just bought new jogger shoes and wore these out for the evening stroll. Several places would not allow my friends in the door. These places were just your average Dutch cafés and bars, not fancy or up-scale. And these guys were businessmen in their 50s, certainly good potential customers. Those doormen want to keep their jobs so they keep the off-spec people outside. Nothing looks clunkier than fresh white tennies. In my Amsterdam and Brussels train station observations, jogger shoes were worn by less than 5% of those passing through, usually by young people with backpacks.

An alternative for those who like tennies is the Florsheim line of shoes called "Comfortech." These are black slip-ons with a cushion bottom. They look great at a distance and will get you past any maitre d' or doorman.

Rain Gear

Weather protection is essential. Bring a telescoping umbrella. A lightweight hooded mackintosh is very handy for those frequent all day rains. A light pair of leather gloves and a hat are helpful for off-season travel, and can even be useful in northern Europe in the summer.

WOMEN'S WEAR

My typists and friends who have read this book all say that it is overly male oriented. A major reason is my discussion of clothing, but the attitude probably surfaces in other areas as well. Girls claim that they simply can't travel with only a carry-on bag, and some bring everything but the kitchen sink on a weekend sortie.

Here's How

I used to travel like that but learned the hard way how to do it the easy way. For a weekend trip to Paris with my Dutch girl friend years ago I packed two suitcases with six days worth of clothes and other just-in-case stuff and drove over to pick her up. I was amazed. She wore a black jumpsuit, colorful scarf, a fashionable raincoat, and carried a slightly oversized purse with everything she needed. Although our room was a nice one in an above average hotel, there was hardly enough space to hang my things or stash the suitcases. My precious Paris time was wasted putting things away, deciding what to wear, and repacking everything.

Women writers can give you plenty of tips for advice on how to pack light. Consult the books of Mesdames Kaye, Hesse, Zobel, Bereny, and Baxel. Pack light. Yes, you can do it.

Friendly Helpers

In fact it is more important for women to pack light than for men. Remember — if you pack it you carry it, you burro you. And if you have too much and some helpful stranger offers to give you a hand in a train station or airport, chances are nine out of ten that he is helping himself. You might have nothing left to carry when he is done with you. You wonder why a guy would steal a woman's suitcase? He probably has a girl friend who would be overjoyed with some American clothes and toiletries. If your suitcase takes a walk, I hope that you didn't hide your money and passport in it; cash, I.D., and clothes — what a score!

By the way, when the friendly helper is done with your suitcase, you might look to see if you still have a purse. One of his buddies standing nearby probably picked that off as the first cavalier distracted you with his charming accented English. This scenario sounds a little harsh, but this is the real world, not the fantasy feely-good world created by most travel writers. See chapter 8, "Money," for advice on avoiding Jesse James and the bandit gangs. They're everywhere you want to be because they just love tourists.

BUSINESS WEAR

No Dockers
Casual is not cool. Americans traveling to Europe on business must wear their best. Impression is critical in doing business overseas. If you have started wearing Dockers to work because they are so comfortable, put them aside for your trip.

The Tie Is the Thing
A dark plain lightweight wool suit will be accepted for all occasions. Use it for after work social events as well. White shirts are OK, though you'll see many people wearing colors. Ties from the top fashion names are the order of the day.

Women
Ladies, please please leave your Madeline Albright suits at home. Better yet just throw them in the trash. Those tight pastel skirts and jackets look horrible. Invest in a neutral dark pants suit, a few white and/or splashy blouses, and scarves. Don't bring your scarves - buy them when you get there, especially if you are going to France.

Coin operated laundromats are common in French cities. La Savonnerie in Marseille is open from 6:30am to 8:00pm every day. Those small sparkling stainless steel washers will cost you about $3.00 for a load (prices are in francs because this photo was taken before the euro was introduced). Allow plenty of time for a wash so bring your travel record book and get it up to date while you wait. [0505]

LAUNDRY

Unfortunately you do have to wash your clothes while traveling. There are several ways to get it done.

Hotel Service

In standard tourist class hotels you rarely see a laundry bag, a normal item in American motels. When I have found the laundry bag in Europe I almost used it for something else after reading the prices. It would be cheaper to buy new clothes at American prices, but you won't find American prices in Europe. If the hotel does not have a cleaning or laundry service, the desk clerk will be able to direct you to a dry cleaner or laundromat.

If you are on an extended business trip you probably must use the hotel service because you don't have time to do it yourself. Some miserly Dilbert managers will single out this item on your expense report and try to disallow it. Stand your ground.

When having dry cleaning done, make sure that cleaning is done and not just pressing. Write down the native word for cleaning because attendants rarely speak English. If there are spots or stains, point them out to the attendant. Spot removal can't be guaranteed because the spot may be due to loss of dye rather than some misdirected spaghetti sauce or red wine.

As every child in Osnabrück, Germany knows, Waschbär (literally and phonetically - "wash bear") is a raccoon. The sign further announces Sofortdienst *(Immediate Service) for sweaters, women's skirts, trousers, jackets, dresses, and overcoats. At the bottom the sign advises "First class cleaning, repairs, special spot removal, hand ironed." [0509]*

Waschbär

Sofortdienst

Pullover	.....	1.⁷⁵
D.-Rock	.....	4.²⁵
Hose	....	4.²⁵
Jacke	....	4.⁹⁵
Kleid	....	5.⁹⁵
Mantel	......	7.⁹⁵

erstklassig gereinigt, appretiert, speziel entfleckt, handgebügelt

Laundromats

Laundromats are usually attended, sometimes are coin operated, normally have restricted hours, and are typically closed one or two days a week. European machines are smaller than American machines and take one hour or more per load. Part way through the wash cycle the machine pauses for an extended soak.

If you allow the laundromat to do the wash for you the attendant will set the temperature depending on the color of your clothes. Attendants follow the rules on the machine, period. Your permanent press white shirts will probably be boiled and returned as permanently wrinkled. I suggest that you do it yourself in a coin machine. If you can't read the directions, ask around to see if someone speaks English. If that fails, watch the others. Temperatures are in Celsius, a.k.a. centigrade. For information on Celsius see chapter 27, "Weights and Measures in Europe."

The price of one load of wash can be three dollars or more. Detergent will be available, either in single load sizes from a coin automat or free from a soap tub.

Dryers are similar to ours, and you should have no difficulty. Dryers normally run on a ten minute cycle, and the cost is reasonable.

Lonely Planet is the only guide book series which locates laundromats in the major cities. Use their maps and legend to find a place to wash your clothes.

Wash Basin or Bidet

It's the old fashioned way. If you do not want to go to a laundromat then you scrub, soak, rinse, wring, and hang to dry.

Almost every hotel room in France is posted, "Don't wash your clothes in the room, and don't eat in the room" — free translation from *le français* (French). My theory is that if no drip marks or crumbs are left on the floor, the spirit of the hotel keeper's request is honored. Hand washing clothes in your room will certainly save you money, will probably occupy less of your time, and will relieve you of the uncertainty of delay due to sometimes service.

No, you don't get two thrones. Throughout Europe bathrooms of better hotels have a bidet next to the potty. The bidet is designed for washing your private parts. Washing those privates in a bidet is a European tradition, while a daily shower (known as a douche *in most of Europe) or tubbing of the whole body is the American way. Lesser hotels may have only a bidet in the room and then the main throne will be in a separate room down the hall. Bidet is pronounced like bee-day with emphasis on the bee. You'll find much more on European hotels in chapter 14, "Hotel, Hostel, B&B;, or Private Home."[0506]*

After washing all of my identical black socks I hang them to dry in front of the ajar French window in my Nice hotel room. My clothesline is a length of nylon reinforced strapping tape. Strapping tape is an essential traveler's friend. [0507]

Instead of doing your laundry in the wash basin, use the bidet. The bidet is clean so why not? You can let your laundry soak for a while and still be able to use the wash basin to brush your teeth.

One challenge will be in hanging your clothes while they are dripping. If you have no bathtub or shower in the room, use a newspaper to catch the drips. Sometimes a bit of ingenuity will be needed to figure out what to tie your line on. Some rooms are almost impossible. Take your wash down in the morning, even if it is still damp, so that the chambermaid doesn't observe. You don't need a confrontation with the hotel keeper. Wring out your underwear and hang it over the usually present radiator. It will be warm and dry by morning. But dust off the radiator first. And do the wash early in the evening since the heat is often turned off at night and then comes back on for a few hours in the morning.

BUYING EUROPEAN CLOTHES

Buying clothes in Europe can be a challenge. Clothing is cut differently, partly for style and partly to fit the build of the average citizen. This varies considerably from country to country. Getting items refitted is another challenge. Store clerks in Paris can make promises but delivery is another story, as I learned.

Size Conversion Tables

Take care in using the clothing size conversion tables presented in travel books. Tables differ. Sales clerks are seldom knowledgeable or helpful on this. They know less about American sizes than you can learn about European sizes. Size tables are posted in some of the large department stores, though in some stores I have seen conflicting conversion tables for American to European sizes on the wall and on garment packages. I have bought the same size under shorts with the same brand name in two different European countries; one was loose and one was tight.

At a department store in Munich, this poster converts American to German sizes for men's slacks. Don't necessarily believe it. Try them on and sit in them before you buy. [0510]

The True Test

If you buy clothes in Europe, try them on or have yourself measured by a competent salesperson. Measurements and sizes will normally be in centimeters (2.5 cm = one inch). Men's shirt sleeves are measured from the shoulders, not the spine. Ascertain whether or not it will shrink when washed. Cotton items purchased in Europe will probably shrink.

Original Amerikanische Inch-Maße

Waist (Bundweite)	Inseam Length (Schrittlänge)	entspricht ca. dt. Größe
27	32	
27	34	40
27	36	84
28	32	84L
28	34	42
28	36	86
29	32	86L
29	34	43
29	36	88
30	32	88 extra lang
30	34	44
30	36	44L
31	32	X
31	34	46
31	36	90
32	32	90L
32	34	X
32	36	94
33	32	94 extra lang
33	34	23
33	36	48
33	38	96
33	38	96 extra lang

HAIR

Although it is not something that most of us pack for a trip, hair is an important part of your wardrobe in the context of your appearance.

Men

The long grizzly look is characteristic of laborers and dopey students, just as it is in the United States. Before you go, get a haircut. Short hair is much easier to take care of, an important consideration while traveling. But, don't get a military trim. That's too short.

The morning shave is probably the one thing most men wish they could do without, but it would be better to continue shaving. Beards invoke suspicion in many people (e.g., customs agents and bank tellers), fear in some (e.g., young women), and instant dislike in most of the rest (e.g., hotel clerks and maitres d'). You don't need hassles and rejections from these folks while you are traveling.

Women

Traditionally, European women do not shave their legs. But they seldom show much leg (except at the beach) since their dresses overlap their boots. An American woman traveling in Europe could easily escape the regular leg shaving. In addition, many European women do not shave under their arms. The traditions are crumbling and younger women are more likely to shave these days. Whether or not to go native is a matter of personal taste.

Have you been noticing that your traveling companions are keeping their distance? Maybe you should visit the Active Laundry and suds your duds this week? This is in Istanbul, Turkey. [0502]

Chapter 6
A Packing List for Europe
Travel Accessories

You are the burro of your bureau.

The previous chapter gave a rundown on your clothing requirements. That is only half of your load. Your suitcase must also be a miniature bathroom closet, laundry room, library, drugstore, office, tool box, and photo supply headquarters. All this is in addition to your clothes. Good luck!

PERSONAL CARE ITEMS

You will need your toothbrush and a few other things while you travel. Check your medicine cabinet and the top of your bedroom dresser for those things that you use on a regular basis. You know what you use in the bathroom every morning so you are the best list maker for these little things.

If you are traveling with a companion, save some donkey duty by splitting your list and sharing the use of normal necessities like toothpaste. If you are traveling for a long period, don't bother bringing along enough of everything for the whole trip. You can stop in any grocery, drug, or department store for your consumables. Your hotel will probably provide enough of the basics, or you can pack a midget size bottle of the things you need just as a starter for the first few days. Leave the big bottles at home, especially if it means the difference between checking or not checking a bag on the plane. Not only are they heavy and bulky but they pose the risk of leakage in your luggage. That's a mess you don't need on arrival. On the other hand, when you buy products in Europe you will be lucky to find your favorite brand unless it is one of the majors.

Electrical Gadgets

Intelligence on the use of electricity in Europe is presented in chapter 11, "Electricity in Europe." The voltage and frequency are not the same as in the USA, and the plugs are different. Many items used in the home are not suitable for travel, and some will not work in Europe. If you use an electric razor, hair blower, or any other electro-mechanical device check it over before you pack it for your trip.

Here are notes on the personal care electrical gadgets that many travelers are inclined to pack. You'll have to think for yourself on this to decide what you want to bring. There are as many packing lists as there are travelers, multiplied by the number of destinations and seasons.

Electric Razor

An electric razor with rechargeable batteries and dual voltage charger (110/220) is quite handy. With this baby you can shave anytime and anyplace in minutes as long as you keep your batteries charged. It will present only an occasional nuisance because special outlets for electric razors in many newer or refurbished hotels will not supply enough power to operate the charger. In such cases, use a regular outlet in the room.

A standard electric razor will operate in Europe if the voltage is transformed to 110 volts. Fortunately, the special razor outlets in most hotels typically have two outlets. One is at 110 volts (yours) and one is at 220 volts. But the bad news is that both outlets often require the round-prong European plug, and you can't use your razor unless you have a plug adapter. The better hotels use an American receptacle for the 110 volt outlet.

I gave up on electric razors after several of them gave up on me. I'm back to the safety razor on which great improvements have been made over the years. Blades last for weeks. The razor and blades are lighter and smaller than an electric razor, though you'll also need something to soften up the whiskers. I use vinegar as described below.

Hair blower

Hair blowers are more or less a standard American appliance. If you use one, it is best to leave it home. Your sink-size blower will require a five pound transformer. You'd rather carry around a watermelon. If you feel you really need a hair blower, purchase a compact dual voltage model designed for travelers. You can buy this in most department stores in Europe, or at a duty free shop before boarding.

Maybe you don't need to carry one. Most upscale hotels, even some standard tourist hotels, now have a hair blower permanently wired in. If you make advance reservations ask your hotel(s) if the room has a hair blower.

A hair blower can be used for more than one thing. Occasionally it will come in handy for drying your clothes, whether rained on or washed in your room. I used it one night to furnish heat in a freezing German hotel room.

If you notice that the lights in your room start to dim or flicker when you turn on your hair blower, turn off everything but the one light you really need. Dimming lights means that the hotel wiring is old. You may blow a fuse if you keep everything turned on. Yes, I've done that.

As with electric razors, I gave up on hair blowers years ago. Now I simply comb my hair straight back after showering. It dries in about half an hour.

Travel Iron

This is something that most travelers will not need. If you are doing your own laundry in your room, hang it up above the tub and let it drip dry. It won't look perfect when you put it on, but nothing does after an hour of wear anyway.

For a quick touch up, ask your hotel if they have an iron to loan or if there is a nearby pressing shop. Test the hotel's iron on a towel to make sure it is clean before laying it on your clothes.

If you do carry an iron, buy a compact travel iron in a department store after you arrive in Europe. It will be rated for 220 volts and give you little trouble, except for the possibility of dimming light syndrome.

Other Options for Personal Care

Just because you use something every day does not mean that you must bring it with you. When you start packing your suitcase or backpack it's time to think - "Do I really need that?" And if so - "Do I really need to bring it?" Here are some thoughts on products that you probably use on a regular basis.

Shampoo

I've come to the conclusion that shampoo is one of the most worthless substances known to man. Right next to it is hair conditioner. Why wash all the natural oils out of your hair just to put back a mixture of overpriced perfumed chemicals from a fancy bottle? Try washing your hair in water for a week and see if you find yourself presentable. If so you can scratch two bottles of chemicals from your packing list. You'll also be saving some environmental damage that went into making the stuff and extra expense at the wastewater treatment plant getting rid of the excess chemicals before they reach our beautiful fish. I haven't used shampoo for years.

Mouthwash

Inspection of the labels of some of those green and blue bottles in the drugstores reveals the fact that they are full of many ingredients, including alcohol at a concentration of up to 26%. Some of the ingredients are poisons so you won't want to drink the stuff. There is another form of alcohol which will kill most of those germs causing bad breath, but won't kill you unless you really try. It will just make you feel warm and comfortable. It's called vodka, normally about 40% alcohol. I sometimes use vodka as mouthwash before bed. It has other uses as described in the next section of this chapter, "Traveler's Supplies."

Deodorant

Body odor is the stink put out by bacterial action on your body oils and perspiration. Vodka also snuffs these bacteria. High strength isopropyl alcohol (91% or 96% IPA) is more effective than vodka, and cheaper. One thing to be aware of is that many deodorants contain aluminum. A high level of aluminum in the brains of deceased Alzheimer's persons is a common factor of the disease. The cause of Alzheimer's disease is not known, but it would be prudent to avoid putting more aluminum in or on your body until the medical investigators find out what is happening here. Those deodorants also contain a brew of other chemicals. The sprays usually contain butane and other flammable gases with appropriate warnings against using the product near an open flame.

TRAVELER'S SUPPLIES

Not everybody will need all the things in these lists. Look them over and consider the accompanying explanations.

Two Dozen Little Things

There are a couple dozen items to consider bringing with you in order to make your travels comfortable and enjoyable. This looks like a lot of gadgets and stuff, but most of it is small and light. All of it, including 2 ounce starter bottles of the liquids but excluding the bags, fits into one of those 8½"x6"x3" nylon net travel sacks. This is about the size of your travel guide book plus a Thomas Cook Timetable.

Alarm chronograph: A digital "alarm chronograph" is a wristwatch of ultimate utility to the traveler. Most of them feature at least a half dozen functions, including: time, time in another time zone, chronograph (a.k.a. stopwatch or elapsed time meter), date, day of the week, alarm clock, and night light. Some include miniature calculators. When buying an alarm chronograph, go through all the motions with the experienced sales clerk so that you know how to use it. Instruction books with these watches are notoriously difficult to follow. The battery will last 6 to 12 months. It may not be possible to find equivalent batteries overseas and it's very difficult to change the battery yourself. If in doubt about whether the battery will last through your trip, waste the few dollars and have a jeweler change it before departure. If it's water resistant you can wear one of these watches while swimming and showering.

Calculator: If you are traveling through a lot of countries, a credit card size electronic calculator is very handy for converting the cost of goods and services into American dollars so you know how much you are spending. It is easy to get confused when you are in a different country every other day. Even though a dozen countries of central Europe have adopted the *euro* as their common currency, many others including Britain, Switzerland, and Denmark have not.

The calculator is also a powerful tool when you are negotiating for a lower price in hotels and shops. In Europe, almost everything is negotiable. Your calculator is a strategic assistant and it shows the hotel keeper or merchant that you are a formidable shopper.

Coffee beans: Chew on a bean for a quick perk up when it's not convenient to get a cup of coffee. If you don't like grit in your mouth, swallow the bean whole. Dark chocolate is also an alkaloid source if you don't like coffee. Caffeine is a handy cure for mild headaches.

Coin purse: When traveling around a lot, you need something to keep the coins of each country separate. A coin purse with several pockets would do. Or use a disposable latex glove and slip coins of different countries in different fingers.

Compass: Since you won't often be able to see the North Star, one of these guys comes in very handy very often. It saves a lot of steps walking to corners and checking street signs, which are always missing when you need them the most, just like cops and cabs. Make sure that a big chunk of metal does not interfere when making a reading.

Condoms: Besides the obvious, use these to hold your toothbrush, soap, coins, and other odds and ends. They also come in handy as water balloons during civil disturbances.

Dictionaries/guidebooks: A detailed discussion of recommended literature for the road is in chapter 10.

Earplugs: Sometimes you don't know you have a disputatious room until midnight. Carry a few packets of foam rubber roll-up earplugs for those noisy nights.

Electrical devices: A list of electrical devices and intelligence on European electricity is in chapter 11.

Flashlight: Bring a mini light operating on AA cells. A penlight is slightly bigger than a felt tip marker and throws a good beam. If traveling by auto, carry a big heavy duty flashlight. Test it now and then to make sure the batteries are always good. Replacement batteries are available throughout Europe. British use the word "torch" for flashlight.

Mirror: Slip a CD in your toilet kit. The underside makes a handy, good-enough, safe, and very lightweight mirror. If you don't have a few CDs offering 1,025 hours of AOL laying around the house you don't have an address in America.

Paper bags: Nab a few bags when you see them. Paper bags preserve fruit much better than plastic bags, the common bagging material in Europe. I assume that you will want an orange or a lemon (as in lemonade) in the morning and you will not want to pay the hotel price.

Paper towels: Take a few extra towels from the restroom on your plane or train, fold them up, and keep them in your hip pocket or purse. Washrooms in Europe are not always supplied and these will come in very handy. The last time I was in Antwerp I gave mine to a couple of women who had fallen down an escalator in the train station. One of the women had blood streaming down all over her face.

Photo equipment: A discussion of travel photography and equipment is presented in chapter 12.

If you forget to pack something, make a trip to one of the large department stores in Europe. This is the Stockmann in Helsinki. Save yourself the trouble of looking all around for what you want. Go to the information desk over there on the ground floor with a large i and ask in straight-away English for whatever you need. [0604]

Plastic bags: Bring a dozen Ziploc baggies, in the sandwich, quart, and gallon sizes. They can be used for dirty clothes, soap, lotions, and miscellaneous small items. Squeeze out the excess air just before sealing so they don't waste too much room in your suitcase. Budget travelers can use bread wrappers or grab a few bags from the roll in the produce section of your home supermarket.

Another good use for baggies takes advantage of their ability to hold air. I used them once to pad a suitcase chuck full of champagne. Simply give them a couple lungs of air, zip them up, and tuck them in the voids.

The two gallon size Ziploc bags are great for packing clothes. Each will hold a couple pairs of slacks, a few shirts, or a suit. Fold your clothes neatly. After putting your clothes in the bag, zip it almost closed, lay it on the bed or a soft chair, then sit on it to squeeze out the air. Then zip up the last inch. Your clothes become "vacuum packed" and easy to arrange in your luggage. Sometimes you have to show the contents of your suitcase or backpack to a customs officer. If everything is in Ziplocs, just turn your bag upside down and dump everything out in front of him. The look on the guy's face is a travel moment.

Plastic utensils: A few plastic spoons, forks, and knives will help you picnic. I haven't found a way to carry plastic cups without breaking them. Most hotel rooms have a glass or two anyway.

Portable radio: A miniature AM/FM radio is nice company. Most of the budget hotels now have TV in the rooms, but very few have radios. In Britain you can understand everything. On the Continent, tune in to one of the BBC stations (excellent humor) or American Armed Forces Network (football, top forty, etc.). Unfortunately, Radio Luxembourg (rock and roll with English disk jockeys) has been silent for about ten years; it was the greatest and could be heard throughout northern Europe. On local radio in France and Germany, you are likely to hear the original version of American popular music, mixed in with politics and classical compositions. Programming is rather helter-skelter. On the trains the AM band is all static but the FM stations come in clear as a bell. It's so nice to hear the Beatles or the Stones instead of the steel wheels on steel track. My radio is smaller than a deck of cards and has a stereo head phone jack but no speaker. Perfect.

Snack bag: To avoid the high prices and horrible food in most American airports pack a sandwich and a drink to tide you over the couple of hours that you will be waiting for your plane to depart. Your airline will request that you arrive 2 to 3 hours before departure. Most of this time will be wasted, but it is necessary for security clearance.

In Europe carry a chocolate or granola bar for emergencies. A can of tuna or sardines might come in handy now and then. Always carry something with you in case everything is closed when your train arrives. It happens.

Sun screen a/o tanning lotion: If you are going to southern Europe during the summer you might want to pack a bottle of your favorite sun screen. If you are going to do some beach time maybe you want tanning lotion. Olive oil works for me. All of these can be purchased in Europe.

Swiss army knife: Don't leave home without it. This is a superbly engineered and manufactured item. Get one with the scissors, corkscrew, and can opener blades as a minimum. Practice using the can opener. Be careful and have patience.

There are two brands of "official" Swiss army knives — Wenger and Victorinox. Each brand has scores of models.

Airline regulations now prohibit knives in carry-on luggage so you will have to put this in your checked luggage (if any) or buy a knife as soon as you land. If your first stop is Switzerland, you are in luck. You will have a much greater selection and will save some cash. You might also buy your alarm chronograph over there. The Swiss are known for precision watches.

Tape measure: When shopping for something to fit, a small tape measure will help. A cloth tape from a sewing shop is fine, or grab one of the freebees in Ikea.

Telescope/binoculars: A telescope or binoculars can be very useful in examining gargoyles on cathedrals and bullet marks on the sides of castles. There are some good quality small glasses available at camera shops.

Toilet paper: Public restrooms in most of Europe are usually supplied, but not often in Spain and Portugal, and rarely in the eastern countries. Even when supplied in the pottie stall you may fail to recognize it as TP, though its location will tell you what it is. Sometimes, especially in bars, there isn't even a pottie — just a hole in a ceramic floor basin bracketed by two little mesas for your feet. Carry a pocket package of Kleenex tissues or real butt paper in your day bag.

Toothpicks: In some countries, toothpicks are everywhere and in others they are nowhere. Fill a cigar tube with toothpicks if you use them. Or carry the matchbook size Johnson & Johnson Stim-u-Dent to clean your teeth after dinner. Stim-u-Dent is readily available in Europe wherever you find toothpaste.

Vinegar: For dry hands, a vinegar rub works better, quicker, and lasts longer than the fancy expensive á-la-gooey products. Just don't get vinegar in your eyes. It stings real good in an open wound, also, but is good in calming down minor skin irritations and in relieving itchy scalp.

You can shave without the foamy stuff using vinegar instead of shaving cream. It softens your whiskers so well that you won't feel them being cut. Rub the vinegar onto your face, take your shower, and shave while you're still in the shower stall, assuming that you have the CD "mirror" mentioned above. Some readers of the on-line edition of this chapter doubt that this works and some are afraid of the vinegar sting if they get a nick. Yes, it does work and I shave this way every day. No, you won't get a stinging nick if you give your face a quick rinse just before shaving. And most likely you will be surprised that there are no whiskers left because there was no tug on your razor or sandpaper sound as you shaved. People who are queasy about putting vinegar on their face should look at the ingredients list of any popular shaving foam. It's an incredible brew of chemicals plus flammable butane and propane gases to get it out of the can.

Buy a small bottle of vinegar in a grocery store after you arrive. I would advise transferring it to a plastic bottle if it isn't already packaged that way. Do not buy the high strength 25% acid variety sold in Germany; get the normal 5% solution.

Vitamins: If you're in the habit of popping a few alphabet pills every morning, don't forget to pack a supply. If you are traveling east of the old Iron Curtain, you may have difficulty finding vitamins.

I buy a tube of 1000 mg vitamin C tablets at a pharmacy after arrival and then walk into any pharmacy when I'm running low and simply show them the tube to buy more. That way you only have to translate it once. Tip: write it down, "Vitamin C," and show it to the clerk. It's spelled the same all over Europe but pronounced so much differently that nobody will understand you. Store clerks got their jobs because they flunked English and most other subjects in school. Some vitamin C tablets look and act like "Alka-Selzer." Drop them in a glass of water or juice and they fizz up and dissolve.

Vodka: Vodka is the diminutive Russian and Polish word for water. Vodka is distilled grain alcohol, though it is also made from potatoes in Poland, my favorite. There are many types of alcohol and most of them are poisons. Vodka is ethyl alcohol, also known as ethanol and/or grain alcohol. It is normally 40% alcohol, 80 proof. Some brands are a higher concentration.
Alcohol has quite a few worthwhile uses.

- Vodka can disinfect cuts and scratches. This is painful, but extremely effective in preventing infection and helping the healing process.

- It can knock out a cold better than any cold medicine on the market. In the evening, down a pint of vodka or brandy, bundle up with more on than you would wear in an Arctic howl, and sweat it out. You might still be drunk in the morning, but voila! — no cold. Use a good quality (triple distilled) product to avoid a hangover and a splitting headache the next morning. My preference for this application is Hennessy cognac, with or without fresh squeezed lemon juice.

- If you are beset with crabs or other body lice, soak a handkerchief in vodka and sponge around the infested areas. The vodka will dehydrate the little buggers and get rid of them surer and safer than those other products. Wash out your clothes in very hot water to get the strays.

- As mentioned in a previous section, alcohol can also be used as a mouthwash, disinfectant, and deodorant. You see it on the ingredients lists of many of those products, though it is usually listed as an "inactive" ingredient. It's also a nice refreshing aftershave, without the perfumes.

So, if only for medicinal purposes, carry a bottle of firewater. You can buy it in the duty free shop before you leave, or duty free on the plane, though these are usually liter bottles and pretty heavy. Ask your stewardess for a couple extra 50 ml airline bottles while the in-flight bar is still open. These are free on most international flights, though the stewardess is not likely to give them to you if she knows that you are taking them with you off the plane.

Wash cloth: Budget hotels are not likely to have them. You can buy one of the European pocket style cloths and keep your soap in it, and keep both in a Zip-loc bag.

Water cup heater: If you like to have a cup of tea, instant coffee, or Turkish coffee in your room before you venture out in the morning, carry a one cup water heater. Morning java in the room is very nice. Making unfiltered Turkish coffee is a snap. Add a spoonful of espresso type ground coffee to your cup of hot water, stir it up, and let it settle. Therefore half of the cup is grounds, making it less than easy to drink. It is best to buy the heater in a European department store after you arrive so you won't have to use electrical voltage and plug adapters. Use the glass which you find in virtually every hotel room, except that the newer "motel 6" type sleepers usually have only plastic drinking cups.

Wire ties: Wire ties are small strips of high strength plastic which are made to hold electrical wires in place. They are also called cable ties. Buy them in hardware stores, the electrical section. Use a wire tie instead of a lock to secure your luggage, and hold anything securely. To remove them, snip with your nail clippers.

Medical Bag
For the time being, your rudimentary first aid bag should include at a minimum:
  Band-Aids
  Antiseptic cream
  Aspirin
Other products to consider are discussed later in chapter 20, "Health and Safety.".

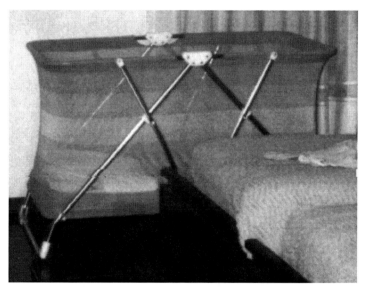

It's not on the lists in this chapter but one of the things to bring if you are traveling with child is a folding portable crib. This was one of the most thoughtful gifts we ever received. With a toddler you also need a barrel of diapers, baby food, nipples, bottle and liners, balls, noisy toys, crayons, coloring books, and other kid stuff. It's more work traveling with a child but it is worth it. [0601]

Repair Kit
  Things made by human beings break sooner or later. The sole exception might be refrigerators made during the early 1950's. Most appliances were made for use at home with a life expectancy of several years. Traveling with them will increase their breakdown probability by a factor of ten. Even things made for the road don't stand up as you expect.

  The fix-it kit described here can probably be assembled from the tools and things you have around the house. Most of it fits into one of those zippered carrying cases used for pocket size electronic calculators.

There are limits to being a repairman on the road of course — if you are not handy at home, you certainly won't be any better at it while traveling.

Glue: Bring Duco cement or something like that, and carry it inside a plastic or metal cigar tube so that it doesn't squeeze out early. A tiny tube of Krazy or Super glue could also find a place in your bag.

Needles and threads: Make up a little sewing kit with needles and a few yards of thread to match your clothes. Check your buttons and reinforce those danglers before leaving home. Keep your pins and needles in a plastic 35mm film canister.

Latex gloves: Disposable latex or vinyl gloves are handy when you get into some dirty work, like putting the chain back on your bicycle or hand washing your clothes. A package weighs almost nothing and can be stuffed in anywhere.

Oil: A squirt will get some things moving and stop some things from squeaking. A drop of oil can help obstinate zippers, but be careful not to get any on your clothes. Miniature oilers the size of felt tip markers with hypodermic type nozzles are available at hardware stores and sportsman shops. Carry this in a cigar tube or Ziploc sandwich bag. If you don't want to carry oil and need a drop or two, ask for a bit of olive oil in a restaurant or use a dab of hand soap.

Leatherman Tool: This is one of the handiest multi-tools you'll ever find. It's a rugged stainless steel item made in the USA (don't buy a cheap Chinese knock-off) and can cut, screw, saw, file, etc. Since September 11 you won't be able to carry this on the plane so it will have to go in checked luggage.

Pliers: A small pair of needle nose pliers with wire cutter can be handy. The Leatherman includes a pair of needle nose pliers.

Scissors: Your Swiss Army knife probably includes a pair of scissors. Scissors are not allowed in carry on luggage so you'll have to put these in checked luggage.

Screwdrivers: Bring a skinny small blade, a stubby handle wide blade, and a small Phillips. A jeweler's screwdriver set can be handy, especially if you wear eyeglasses. The Leatherman includes several styles of screwdriver and your Swiss Army knife has at least one screwdriver.

String: A small roll of 140 lb. nylon test line can be purchased at your local hardware or sporting goods store. This makes a great clothesline if you need to hang your clothes up to dry.

Tape: Nylon filament tape, also known as package wrapping tape and strapping tape, sticks great and doesn't break. Fixes suitcases, wraps parcels, etc. Tape is also a good lint remover. Brush a piece over your clothes and grab up all the loose dust.

Tweezers: They come in handy once in a while, especially for people with fat fingers, like me. Many Swiss Army knives include a small pair of tweezers.

Wrench: A good quality, miniature 4" adjustable wrench can come in handy. Another that is very helpful is the 8mm x 13mm open end wrench from an old VW tool kit. This little piece of steel once saved my bladder from certain eruption by getting me into a locked toilet on an overnight Swedish train.

Laundry Supplies

If you plan on doing your own cleaning and spiffing up, some of the following items will be helpful:
- Woolite or dish detergent
- Clothesline
- Clothespins
- Shoe polish
- Shoe brush

The first three items, Woolite, line, and pins, are sold in convenient traveler's kits available in some luggage and travel supply stores. The Woolite package contains 10 individually sealed packets with a quarter fluid ounce in each, just right for a bidet-sized load. The line and pins kit leaves a lot to be desired with the clothesline, but the hooks and pins hit the spot. For a good clothesline, use the 140 pound nylon test line mentioned above. A piece of strapping tape is also good. It is strong and you can attach it in odd places.

Since Woolite is pretty rough on your hands, use your latex gloves when washing. Dish detergent is also very good for cleaning clothes. It is easy on the hands, but rough on some colors. Your shampoo, if you use the stuff, can also be used for washing clothes but may leave a strong aroma due to the fragrances they put in it.

A mini shoe brush and miniature can of polish should suffice. Many of the better hotels have electric shoe shine machines on each floor so you could skip the brush. Or wipe off the excess with a paper towel and buff your shoes with a sock.

FORBIDDEN ITEMS

High Altitude Conditions

There are a few things that you can't bring on a plane, and/or pack in your luggage. Airplane temperature and pressure, especially in the baggage hold, are lower than ground conditions. Liquids can leak and/or freeze and present the potential for serious consequences in an airplane.

Traditional Flammables

Examples of prohibitions by airlines are: no matches or lighters in your checked luggage, no flammable liquids like fuel or solvents on board, no fireworks, and no harsh household or industrial chemicals. If you have a question about the propriety of any unusual material you wish to bring on board, ask the airline. If you need any of these for traveling, buy them after you land in Europe.

Weapons

The rules have changed since the terror of September 11. Nothing that can be used as a weapon can be brought on board. I've carried a Swiss Army knife in my pocket on planes all over the world for over 35 years. It's always in my pocket. No more on planes. Now I must put it in checked baggage, if any, or budget the price of a new one for every flight. Even knitting needles are prohibited on board.

DOCUMENTS AND VALUABLES

To conclude this chapter, the table below lists the items to carry on your person, not in your luggage. Again, you won't need to bring all of these items. For example, if you have a Eurailpass you probably won't need train tickets. If you need train tickets it is probably better to buy them in Europe. These subjects are discussed in detail in separate chapters as noted in the third column.

Item	Description	Chapters
Money	cash, traveler's checks, personal checks, credit cards, ATM card, telephone card	8, 19
Identification	passport, visas, driver's license, international driving permit	3, 18, 20
Tickets	airline ticket, hotel confirmation, Eurailpass, train tickets, train reservations, car rental reservation	4, 14, 17
Travel records	notebook, camera, video recorder	8, 9, 12
Miscellaneous	Customs registration certificates, international certificates of vaccination, frequent flyer cards	24, 20, 4

Here is the main departure board at Gare du Nord *(North Train Station) in Paris, France. Doesn't this scene just get your juices running? Travel with a* Eurailpass *and be the master of your own destiny. Train stations harbor dens of thieves so be extremely cautious. Just recently a Dutch friend had his wallet stolen in this station as he was returning to Holland. While he was doing the pro forma police report he met an American who had just arrived. The American was in the police station to report his bag stolen. It contained an expensive camera and his passport. That is a bad way to start a European vacation. Never, never, never put anything of value in your luggage. Keep your wallet in a tight front pants pocket. Never let go of your luggage. See chapter 8 to learn about defenses against the bandits of Europe. They are everywhere, and they don't need no stinking badges. [0605]*

Chapter 7
Luggage for Europe
Travel Light

Be a happy traveler. Fly to Europe with nothing but a carry on bag.

LUGGAGE VERSUS THE AIRLINES

Check-In
    The first stop for you and your luggage is going to be the airline check-in counter. Here you will see the first rewards of packing light. It eliminates the hassle of standing in line at baggage check-in or finding and tipping a skycap. However, if you don't already have a boarding pass you will be required to stand in line to get one because you cannot go into the boarding area without it.
    If you have luggage to check things have become much worse since September 11. Airlines are installing new and time consuming procedures for your checked luggage. On my flight out of Los Angeles in June 2002 all passengers with checked luggage had to wait in the check-in area while the bags went through a large x-ray machine in the lobby. Bags containing items which the security personnel could not identify were diverted. The owner was then paged and requested to open it up for a hand inspection. Therefore you could not go to the departure gate until your bag went through the x-ray monster. There was only one machine, a very slow machine, and there were hundreds of bags.
    More recently, departing from Detroit to Amsterdam in December 2002, I had no bag to check. I flew with only my carry-on and laptop. These went through security check points as described in chapter 4. Returning from Amsterdam in January 2003 I had an extra bag which I checked in. Before I reached the check in counter it was hand inspected and then x-rayed.

Landing
    Your disposition at the other end of your flight is even more dependent on whether or not you have checked luggage. If you do not check any luggage, you don't have a half hour wait for the carrousel to deliver your bag on arrival. Your bag does not get mutilated by man and machine, or get lost (funny how baggage often takes free rides all over the world, or no ride at all). You don't want to wait a day or two on

arrival for your bag to be found and delivered, interrupting plans and forcing you to change reservations. Sure enough, KLM lost my checked bag before I landed in Detroit on that last flight. I made my connecting flight and they gave me a shave kit at my final destination. Northwest delivered my bag the next morning.

These things have all happened to gazillions of travelers and have cumulatively caused untold centuries of grief. Even though it might sound like it, don't think that airline people are bad — they're just human.

Pack Light Bonuses

Other pack light advantages are to be pronto in line at customs, first out of the terminal, and at the head of the queue for taxis, buses, car rental, hotel space, ATMs, and other amenities. When 300 passengers get off a jumbo there are lines everywhere.

Here is all you need for months of solo care-free rail travel in Europe. My suitcase is 13" high by 18" wide by 9" thick (2,100"³ or 34 liters), and flexible. The umbrella handle is hooked over my jacket armpit so I always have it handy. In my pockets go the wallet, travel record book, miniature camera, and tape recorder. I keep my SLR camera with telephoto lens on a strap around my neck. My ever growing collection of books and maps is another story, solved by frequent trips to post offices. A short fat man in an Amsterdam bar some years ago went ballistic when he saw my hardware, rudimentary essentials for a travel writer. He went stomping around the back of the café screaming to everybody that I was a CIA spy. What a scene. [0710]

Carry On Bag

When following the rule of pack light, all that a traveler has is one carry-on bag. The maximum dimensions are 21" x 16" x 8", or maybe 23" x 13" x 9". Check with your airline for their exact dimensions. The general rule is that the total linear dimensions may not exceed 45". The fundamental requirement is that it must fit in the overhead bin or under the seat in front of you. In addition to the carry-on bag you are also allowed a purse, briefcase, or laptop computer.

Many airlines have installed bins at the check-in counters and/or cutouts on the security belt machines. If your bag doesn't fit in the bin or through the cutout you must check it. If you happen to get an oversized bag on board, you could find that the overhead bin has a 9" opening, whereupon you do have a problem. And if you try to sneak past the check-in counter with an extra bag you will probably be stopped at the gate and requested to check one of them.

Airlines have various limits on the maximum weight allowed for a carry on bag. This is not much of a concern when flying across the Atlantic but if you have a connection within Europe it could be a problem because the limits are lower and your carry on is likely to be weighed. Check with your travel agent or airline.

You won't always have an assist getting on the train so make sure you can carry your own bag. Platforms at some stations are at train level, but most often you must climb a few steep steps, as on this lin *(platform) at Constanta, Romania.* [0701]

Checked Baggage

If you must carry more with you than you can fit in a carry-on, you can check baggage. Most people check as much baggage as is allowed. I think that if the limits were ten times as much, many people would take the limit. Please see chapter 24, "Shipping Your Treasures Home," for more complete information on airline baggage allowances.

RECOMMENDED LUGGAGE

Carry-on size: The maximum linear dimensions must be less than 45" (114 cm) and one dimension must be no more than 9" (23 cm).

Soft case with zippered openings: You can stuff this into odd shaped tight places. It won't break your kneecap when walking, and it is lighter than a hard case.

At least three separate compartments: Each compartment must be accessible from the outside. Pack separately:
- clothes
- toiletries and hardware
- maps and guidebooks.

Organize well and you'll be able to get at anything in seconds.

Handle and shoulder strap: Shoulder strap is the key word. Carry more with less fatigue and have two hands free at all times.

Wheels: This is something I wouldn't have suggested 20 years ago, but it is certainly worth considering. If you are marginal on the pack light field test (see chapter 5, "What to Wear in Europe") a wheeled suitcase can be a big aid to your comfort. Wheels and handle take up space so select a good one.

Heavy duty hardware: Selecting durable lightweight luggage is a challenge. There are few suitcases with strong enough handles and strap attachments. Even the most expensive leather cases often have handle attachments that are hardly more than tinfoil, or are sewn onto areas that are not adequately reinforced and seem to be designed to fall off under moderate use in a short time. Inspect carefully before buying anything. A nylon strap handle encircling the bag is one of the best designs. You'll find these in sports shops, usually emblazoned with the name of a certain Greek goddess.

At Victoria Railroad Station in London, passengers wait in line to board. On the Continent there is rarely a line since tickets are checked on the train. Notice the small suitcases carried by these astute travelers. [0708]

A Good Choice

After looking over the luggage in department stores and luggage shops, pay a visit to a well-stocked office supply store, for example, Staples, Office Max, or Office Depot. Examine the array of carry-on bags designed for frequent business travelers. These bags can hold a laptop computer, a clean shirt, a couple changes of underwear, and a few pounds of bananas. They are made of tough nylon, have a shoulder strap and/or wheels, and have more pockets than a hunter's jacket. Some, like the one I use, have an expansion zipper so one compartment can be enlarged by a couple of inches, after you get to Europe. These rugged nylon bags are great and cost a fraction of similar bags sporting famous brand names.

A Day Bag

Besides a carry-on bag travelers should have a day bag. This can be used in Europe to carry things like your guide book, city map, extra film, a snack, water bottle, roll of toilet paper, and other daily odds and ends that won't fit in your pockets.

On arrival in most cities you can stash most of your things in a train station locker or luggage check room. Use your day bag while you are out looking for your hotel or while making an afternoon stopover in a city along the way.

Your day bag can be a light weight nylon bag with a shoulder strap. It should fold up to no bigger than a pocket book. You can buy one in any of the thousands of shops located in tourist areas in Europe.

Large, medium, and small luggage lockers are available in the Brussels Central Station. Large is 36"x36"x20" and costs €3.30 per 24 hours. Medium is 36"x24"x15" and costs €2.80. Small is 36"x15"x12" and costs €2.00. [0712]

ALTERNATE LUGGAGE

Other forms of luggage commonly used by travelers are the full size suitcase and the backpack.

Full Size Suitcase

A large suitcase is a definite mistake. It must be checked for air travel. It does not fit in overhead luggage racks on trains. It will not fit in most of the train station lock boxes. You might even have trouble getting it in the trunk of your rental car or taxi. It will be difficult to get on the elevator or up the stairs at many hotels. It will weigh a ton after two blocks and you will be the beast of burden. Poor burro.

If you absolutely must bring too much stuff, a large suitcase with rollers or one of the fold-up luggage carts would help, but would still leave severe disadvantages. It would be better to carry two smaller cases. But think about it — are you going to Europe to enjoy some time off or do you want to hurt yourself struggling with and sweating over a stupid plastic box of stuff all over the place?

Backpack

The backpack is very popular with young travelers, and is even used by a few grandmothers. A great load can be carried with relative ease, at least without pulling your arms out of their sockets.

A few problems should be mentioned. To get at things like maps and guidebooks, you have to sling it off your back. Many people overload themselves to the point that they need someone to help them get the pack mounted on their back. Also, some rigid frame packs are so large that they do not fit in the train station lock boxes. When mounted, the big backpacks make it nearly impossible for you to get on an elevator or up the steps of a train.

A backpack can also be a temptation for street thieves. A beautiful little leather backpack that Elizabeth bought at the bazaar in Istanbul quickly attracted some gypsies. They staged a cute rouse and nearly had their mitts inside it as we were walking on the street in broad daylight. More about these gypsy thieves can be found in chapter 8.

Airline baggage men can shake the tar out of a loosely packed backpack. I've seen them coming down the ramp at baggage claim, followed by pots and pans, toothbrush, guidebooks, shoes, etc. You can and should request a box or plastic bag from the airline in which to place your backpack before the airline starts to mangle it. Then make sure to pick up the right one at baggage claim since there may be other backpacks traveling in similar bags.

These girls help each other get into their backpacks. Do they really need all that stuff? Is this a vacation? [0709]

PACKING

Gravity Rules
Heavy stuff likes to settle to the bottom. Put it there in the first place so it doesn't mess things up as it goes down. The bottom of your bag as you carry it is not necessarily the bottom as you pack it. Put the heavy stuff on the side opposite the handle.

Roll 'em or Fold 'em
I've done it both ways and have concluded that folding works best. Fold your outer garments, shirts and slacks especially. It's OK to roll your underwear, though I don't find any advantage it doing that with soft sided luggage. If you have a hard case rolling your underwear would allow you to stuff those items in the corners.

Vacuum Pack
I learned one of the best travel tips from a friend in Holland years ago. Use 2 gallon Ziploc bags to pack your clothing. Each bag holds a couple of shirts or slacks. After neatly folding your clothes put them in the Ziploc and zip it up except for the last inch. Lay it on your bed, sit on it, and zip it up. The result is like vacuum packed cheese. This keeps your clothes reasonably well pressed, and clean and dry no matter what. Unfortunately the newer Ziploc bags do not hold a vacuum, apparently because they are made in two pieces and then assembled, imperfectly. Try to find bags without seams between the zip lock and the baggie.

Trial Packing
Do a trial packing a few days before you depart. If you do the pack light field test as described in chapter 5 you will have done this. If you don't do the field test

then at least do the trial packing. My trial packing usually turns up the fact that my luggage needs repair work, something I conveniently forgot to do after my last trip.

They don't want you parking your stuff for more than three days in the Geneva, Switzerland train station lock boxes. This is typical for train stations throughout Europe. If you need more time for a hike up to Mont Blanc use the attended luggage check room. The open hours here are from 4:00am to 12:45am. The h stands for heure, the *French word for hour. [0703]*

BUSTED BAGS

Stuff Happens

The men and machines of the airlines handling your bag behind the wall can easily inflict severe damage. If your bag is damaged you must complain immediately, not tomorrow.

Free Replacement

The worst harm that I experienced was on a KLM flight from Los Angeles to Amsterdam. The zipper had been ripped and destroyed. I went to KLM's service desk in Schiphol airport where the young lady told me to see the luggage repair shop and KLM would pay for repairs, or she would give me a flat $25. I went to the luggage repair but it was a Sunday and it was closed. So I looked in the luggage shop and was surprised to find the exact same bag available for $75. Only then did I remember having bought my bag there the year before. So I bought a new one and went back to KLM's service desk with both bags and the receipt. They paid the full $75, but were not especially happy about it.

LOCK IT UP

It is a good idea to secure your bags against casual snooping and pilferage.

Locks

Small locks designed to hold the zippers of soft sided bags can be purchased in most stores selling luggage or travelers supplies. I use one of these on my carry-on bag. My favorite is the combination style. It is stronger than those flimsy things with tin foil keys. But I don't trust those bright brass locks on checked luggage, and I think that they make a statement — "there must be valuable stuff in this locked bag."

Passengers visit and chat on a EuroCity express train from Paris. Notice the abbreviated luggage space above your seat. In some cars there is space for one jumbo bag between back-to-back seats and in others there is a luggage bin near the door. It is a good idea to keep your luggage within eyesight, especially when the train is in a station. Thieves work the rail cars. They stroll through and pick up what they will, then jump off with their new clothes just before the train leaves the station. [0702]

Wire Ties

For checked luggage, when I have it, I prefer to seal the zippers with a wire tie, also called a cable tie. Wire ties are strong. The black ones are inconspicuous and don't advertise the fact that you have locked your bag. To use a wire tie, you insert the small end in the eye and pull it through to lock it with the ribbed side on the inside of the loop. Snip off the tail with nail clippers. To remove these you must cut them off so bring nail clippers in your carry-on bag or a pocket. Leave a little slack in the wire tie to make it easier to cut open.

Wire ties can also be used to tie your luggage to the rack in a train. This gives you additional security when you go to the toilet or to the café car. Loop the wire tie through the handle of your bag and around a sturdy member of the rack. Wire ties can be joined together if you need more length.

Strapping Tape

Another security and identification measure is to wrap your checked bag with nylon reinforced strapping tape. This helps keep the contents inside if the bag is ripped open by airline personnel or equipment, and discourages free-lance operators. It also makes your bag easily identifiable at baggage claim. So many bags look alike nowadays that this tape will help you find, and help prevent others from accidentally grabbing, yours. The tape also makes your bag look rather shabby in transit. That's good. You do not want your goods traveling in a fancy bag shouting "steal me." I have seen other travelers use duct tape, also called duck tape by those who cannot pronounce duct.

THE INVENTION OF THE WHEEL

Rolling Luggage

I used to scoff at people who used those little luggage dollies or luggage with wheels. Not any more. Even when packing light a set of wheels can be a tremendous help. One of the biggest backaches for travelers in Europe is lugging your luggage around town if there are no luggage lockers available in the train station. The French have a habit of sealing train station luggage lockers when terror is in the air. Spain did this long ago, and permanently, thanks to some malcontents who put bombs in a few lockers. The over reaction of security functionaires is to prevent anyone from using the lockers. For independent travelers wheels can make a big difference in comfort and convenience these days, especially on a hot afternoon in Rome. You might as well put your bag on wheels as on your back.

If you violated the rule of pack light and there is no elevator in the train station, look for a luggage mover device like this one in the main train station of Nürnberg, Germany. [0704]

Buy It Over There

Consider buying a luggage dolly when you arrive in Europe. This way it will not be in your luggage allowance on the plane. Wheels add volume and weight, and may be considered as an extra piece of luggage. Your airline may require that you bring it as checked baggage instead of bringing it in the cabin as carry-on.

Whereas American airports charge $3 for temporary use of a luggage cart, European airports generally give you free use of one, all the way from baggage claim through customs and to the curb. Wheel your luggage out to the shopping zone after you clear customs. There is almost always an airport store where you can buy a luggage dolly.

Train stations in smaller cities of Italy normally have baggage check rooms instead of self-serve lockers. This Deposito Bagagli a Mano *(baggage check room) is at Ventimiglia near the French border.* [0706]

Chapter 8
Cash, Check, and Credit Card
Travel with Some of Each in Europe

Since the days of Marco Polo the double-edged problem facing travelers is:
>	Carry money that can't be lost or stolen.
>	Carry money that is accepted everywhere.

AVOIDING JESSE JAMES

There are many things to know about money, about exchanging your US dollars for European currencies, and about the money instruments available to travelers. The most important thing to know is how to protect your money, passport, and belongings against thieves.

Pickpockets
Pickpockets thrive in the train stations, airports, post offices, museums, amusement parks, and crowded city tourist offices. Thieves also make a good living in the subways and on the streets. Nearly every traveler I have met in Europe has a story to tell about an attempted theft on themselves or on someone they know. I've had five brushes with these devils and they are batting 20% on me, actually on Elizabeth but I was with her. The loss was relatively minor. In too many cases, it is a sad story because the thief was very successful. It is a frustrating calamity when it happens because the police can do virtually nothing except to hear your story and then file it. You are left with the burden of canceling credit cards, getting more cash, and replacing documents.

You Probably Haven't Seen This on TV
What follows might sound funny, even dumbfounding. Some human looking creatures will try almost anything to steal a buck. They are brazen and audacious and cunning. They prefer to pick on the weak and helpless, but, as I learned by firsthand experience, they'll go after a 6'1" 190-pounder also, at least in the off-season.

Ketchup: A Chinese businessman on a train from Paris to Cologne told me an interesting story. He was in a Paris *Metro* station and some people started shouting at him and pointing at the back of his coat. He took it off to have a look and found ketchup on it. Just then someone came over to help him clean it off. The businessman appreciated that, but felt something inside his breast pocket as the friendly helper was wiping off the ketchup. He grabbed the thief by the wrist as he was extracting the businessman's wallet. I found that story hard to believe, but the businessman went back to his compartment and returned with an expensive fur coat. It had a two-inch wide river of ketchup right down the middle of the back.

This fellow with his thumbs in his pockets will be trying to pick your pockets when you get to Madrid. He tried it on me with the hand cream trick described in the text. I went back the next day to take this picture with a telephoto lens. "Thumbs" can usually be found gambling at a three-pods-and-a-pea game operated by a woman with short rust colored hair . These crooks do know where to hang out; this is at the Metro stop Banco de Espana *(Bank of Spain). [0815]*

Hand cream: Three weeks later I was in Madrid. Walking back to my hotel from the post office on a major boulevard at sunny noontime, an older couple started shouting at me and pointing at the sky and at the back of my jacket. After a moment, I put my hand around in the back and felt something slippery. My hand came back smeared with hand cream. Immediately a younger fellow appeared out of nowhere and approached me with some napkins to help wipe it off. Such a friendly good Samaritan! Wrong. Remembering the story of the Chinese businessman, and recognizing my helper as a fellow I had seen gambling on the sidewalk with US $20 bills the day before, I became alarmed. I pulled my jacket together and backed up, shouting "No! No!" The helper with the napkins became slightly disoriented. He walked out into the *Calle de Alcala* (Alcala Street), a major boulevard in Madrid, and was nearly run over before he got his wits together and went back the way he came. The man and woman who shouted at me, and who were obviously part of the heist play, kept walking up the boulevard as if nothing had happened. During the ten minute walk back to my hotel, not another soul mentioned anything about the white streak on the back of my coat.

Mustard: I heard a similar story in Portugal, except that it was mustard over there.

Cardboard: Another modus operandi involves the use of a piece of cardboard and some teenage girls in worn dresses. The girls approach you holding the cardboard outstretched as if they were beggars. They put the cardboard up close to your chin with one hand, thus concealing the other hand which is busy grabbing your wallet down below. A friend told me that a group of girls had tried this on him in Rome. Two days later a solo pre-teen girl tried it on me near the Rome train station.

"Stop dem Diebstahl" means guard yourself against thieves by not leaving anything in your car when you park it on a street in Germany. [0817]

On the Train: When Elizabeth and I found a compartment on the Venice to Vienna overnight train, we quickly chucked our stuff in the overhead rack and settled in. Though she put her purse up there, I was sure it was temporary. To make a toilet trip during the night I reached under the seat for my shoes and found her purse there. Good enough, I thought. But the next morning she said she hadn't put it there. Then we discovered that some money and credit cards were missing. Telephone calls from Vienna to cancel the cards were time consuming and expensive, using most of the time we had available before catching our train to Budapest. For some reason the thief was selective in rifling her purse and took only two credit cards and the cash, leaving behind the American Express card — a discerning thief. The thief must have been someone in the compartment since I was sleeping next to the door and am easily awakened when train doors are opened.

Tragic Success: I've talked with many people who were hit hard, even before landing in Europe. A girl I met while traveling had flown from San Francisco to Los Angeles to catch a flight to Europe. While she was waiting for the boarding call at Los Angeles airport someone stole her purse with her passport and money — only a half hour before departure. A friend of mine had his watch stripped off his wrist in the Louvre Museum in Paris. An Australian girl I met had her purse stolen while she sat in a Barcelona café with five other people. The passport of an American girl disappeared in Basel on the day her tour group was to depart for Paris and fly home. I met two others from the group who stayed behind to help her out. They wasted at least a day and additional expense going to Zurich to get a replacement passport. A Dutch guy I met on a train was on his way home after one day of a one month vacation. Somebody stole his wallet.

I could fill a book with details of these and other stories. So, "Let's be careful out there."

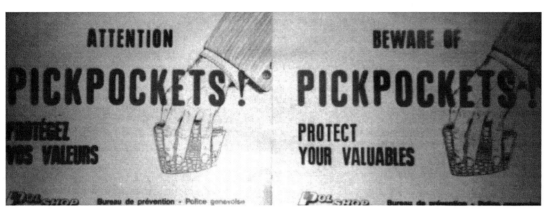

The Geneva, Switzerland police warn you. Every train station should be posted with this advisory, especially those where the problem is much worse. [0808]

Baggage Thieves

Many travelers "hide" their passport and money in their suitcase. Baggage thieves know this — that's why they are thriving in the tax free baggage-stealing business. Baggage thieves also know that there are clothes, toiletries, a camera, razor, and other goodies inside which would make a nice present to their girl friend or earn a little money at the flea market. The one thing that baggage thieves do not think or care about is the disaster they wreak on the dream vacations of those whose suitcases disappear. That's not their department.

Baggage thieves operate primarily in airports, train stations, and on trains. They prosper in and around the confusion of tourist information offices and hotel booking offices. They also examine parked cars and open the trunks of those with out-of-town license plates.

Friends of mine have had their cars broken into in Paris and a thief rifled the suitcase of another friend on a French train. Gone were his money and traveler's checks. An American bicyclist I met had his luggage stolen from under his legs while he was sleeping in a French train station. I have met other travelers, bitter and frustrated, who had their belongings stolen on trains, in train stations, and from their cars.

SELF DEFENSE

On Guard

Armed robbery and mugging seem to be less prevalent in Europe than in the United States. But you have to be careful not to display yourself as a tempting target for quick fingers on fast feet. Be alert at all times in public places. Look around in train stations and post offices. Study the faces and the actions of loiterers and strollers. Most people are going somewhere or doing something. But you'll see some who seem to be planted there, just watching and waiting.

Gypsies

Some people will consider this paragraph as "profiling" but it is just the way things are. I only report it for your self defense. The message is be alert for gypsies. They usually work in groups and act like a pack of hyenas on the street. I'll never forget the fright I once had in Milan. When traveling with Elizabeth and our two-year old Stephanie we had to cross a major boulevard near the train station. With a toddler you carry an unbelievable amount of stuff and we had to cross in shifts. As I was beginning to come over with the second load I saw a half dozen gypsy women slowly approaching Elizabeth as she was yelling at me in alarm. Boy did I move, and the gypsies cleared out.

Though they hang out more frequently in southern and eastern Europe, gypsies can be anywhere. Major cities such as Paris and Rome have large numbers. When you see the women, dressed in characteristic flower print dresses and skirts, go on red alert because they are likely to have a close encounter with your wallet, wristwatch, passport, or whatever else you have of value. Be especially wary of the children. They are trained in the art of theft from an early age.

Camcorder

I have discovered a great defense against gypsies, no matter how many are circling. Start filming them with your video recorder. It is simply amazing how fast they scatter. They sometimes make abusive threats as they flee. An old woman in Warsaw started hitting me but she couldn't kill a fly with those jabs.

When we stayed in Milan for a week visiting Elizabeth's sister, I used to stroll over to the train station with my camcorder nonchalantly hanging in my right hand, set on pause and ready to roll. When the gypsies approached, I would raise it and start filming. You'd think I had an Uzi machine gun by the way they ran. One fellow, about 25, was so mad or disgusted that he stopped and turned toward me, pulled his pants down, grabbed his joint, and shouted "Here, take a picture of this!" Even his girl friend partner was shocked.

I have a half hour video of another gypsy girl trying the beggar scam in Warsaw solo while her tribe stood across the street. It's a very well rehearsed procedure. She would not approach couples, only single walkers unless there was someone walking within 20 feet or so. If you are traveling alone you are particularly vulnerable. If you are approached for a handout anywhere in Europe never give a penny.

If you don't carry a camcorder, an ordinary camera will suffice as your imitation Uzi.

Keep It Close

No matter how you carry it, keep money out of sight and close to your body. Since the Madrid incident, I always keep my wallet and passport in a tight front pants pocket in crowded areas. When I come over from Haarlem and the train enters the

Amsterdam train station I instinctively move my wallet from my rear pocket to the front. The Amsterdam train station is a rat hole of beggars and thieves.

On the Kalverstraat in Amsterdam large banners like this warn you in four languages "Beware of pickpockets!" Nuf said? [0824]

Money Belt

Many travelers use a money belt. A money belt is a pocket on a belt which should be worn under your shirt or blouse. Many wear it on the outside so they can get to it in a hurry, a habit which razor toting thieves really do appreciate. Keep your passport and a two day supply of local cash on your person at all times. If your hotel has a safe, you can use it to keep your traveler's checks, other foreign money, airline ticket, etc. Do not forget to retrieve them from the hotel safe when you check out.

Circle Your Wagons

Defense against baggage thieves is rather simple — just hang on to your stuff. Do not *EVER* accept a gratis offer from a stranger to watch your bags while you buy a ticket or powder your nose. On the train, sit in a compartment already occupied by one or two people who have so much luggage that they couldn't carry yours if they did steal it. Get a conversation going and each can be the watchdog while others go to the toilet or dining car. But again, do not leave any valuables in your bag. I normally loop my luggage shoulder strap through one of the iron bars on the luggage rack. That would at least slow down anyone trying to steal it. Use a cable tie to seal your bag whenever it is out of your sight. I think this saved me on a flight from Los Angeles to Geneva, connecting through New York and Barcelona.

Secure Parking

Always park your rental car on a busy, well-lighted street. Never leave anything visible in the car, and never leave anything in the trunk overnight. Lock your car if it will be unattended for more than ten seconds. I have seen camper vans parked in the big cities with long chains around the girth to prevent anyone from opening the doors.

Street Wise

On the street, hang onto your stuff. In Dublin, a traveling friend and I were saying goodbyes and exchanging addresses at an intersection. Though we had put our bags down for just a moment, a policeman came over to warn us to hang onto them or they would be stolen. In both Barcelona and Naples, hotel clerks warned me that thieves would pull my camera off the neck strap. Nobody did because I always have one hand on my camera when I'm out around town.

When sitting in a café, secure your purse or camera to your chair by putting the strap around the arm or a rung, and putting your purse or camera through the loop. Pull the loop tight, and keep your seat!

Team Sport

Pickpockets and baggage thieves often work in small groups. One or two are there to distract you in some way, another one makes the grab, (s)he quickly passes it off to another, and the runner makes his getaway in the confusion. You don't know what to do. There is not a heck of a lot that you can do, during or after the fact.

Prevention works best. Try to not look like a tourist, especially not like a wealthy American tourist. If you want to keep your nice jewelry and purse, leave them home. With the costume that I wear (see chapter 5, "What To Wear in Europe"), many people mistake me for a European over there, at least until I pull out my city map and camera.

Also, never give money to a beggar, no matter how destitute they appear. That is part of their ruse. When they determine where you keep your cash they'll be back to help themselves when you least expect it.

MONEY

Now that you know how to protect yourself, here is a rundown on the money used in Europe.

Each country formerly had its own currency. This has changed as of 2002 and now the euro is the currency of a dozen countries in central Europe, and is accepted by many businesses in Eastern Europe.

Greenbacks

United States dollars are legal tender in the United States for goods and services and taxes. You normally cannot use dollars in Europe. In most countries of Europe, the only thing you can legally buy with United States dollars is the currency of the country in which you are present. These currencies are sold by banks and other businesses in accordance with national laws. Each bank or place of exchange posts buying and selling rates for major currencies, although the eight digit decimal rates in the computers are actually used in calculating the transaction.

WHERE TO CHANGE MONEY

One of the first things you need to do in Europe, or before you go, is obtain some local currency. There are several ways to do this.

Your Home Town

Ask your bank about buying some *euros* or *kroner* and don't be surprised if you get a blank stare. If they can help you, they will probably need to order the money for you a week in advance, and charge a ridiculous fee for the service.

You can buy it at the exchange office in your USA departure airport. This will also be expensive. The exchange office in the Los Angeles airport was selling euros in June 2002 at a price approximately 20% higher than the published rate. That spells ripoff to me.

If you are a fool with money and don't want to stand in line at an airport, try to change at a large hotel near your departure airport. World class hotels usually change major currencies for their guests. This can cost you 20% to 30% more than at the airport.

Do not accept the old national currencies of the countries which have switched to the euro. These are examples of the old banknotes which were retired in 2002: 1,000 Greek Drachmas, 100 German Deutschemark, and 200 French francs. The design of the euro is disgusting in comparison. [0812]

In Europe

The traditional place to change money is at just about any bank in Europe. The exchange rates are reasonable and are usually posted in a window or at the door. Another alternative is to use your ATM card when you arrive in Europe. This is one of the handiest and best deals you will find. Cash machines are ubiquitous in Europe. With virtually any American ATM card or credit card you can obtain local currency at cash machines in European airports, and throughout the countryside.

There are also numerous money exchange offices in major cities. These places can be tricky as pointed out later in this chapter. Finally, never change money with anyone on the street. You will be approached fairly often in some cities. Here are some details on the options available in Europe.

Many post offices in Europe also act as banks and will exchange your greenbacks for local currency. This post office in Prague, Czech Republic also offers fax service, telephones, and stamps for collectors. [0803]

Banks

It used to be that virtually all banks in Europe exchanged foreign money, and they usually offered the best exchange rates. They all knew what each other was doing so it was hard to find any real bargains.

Most banks in western Europe are no longer in the currency exchange business. The reasons are that the euro is the common currency of 12 nations, and ATM machines are becoming more common than dog poop on the sidewalks. There is very little business in currency exchange and ATM machines can do it 24/7. However, there are still a few countries which are not in the Euro Zone, notably Britain, Switzerland, Sweden, and Denmark. You will probably find banks in these countries which will exchange currencies.

Since banks pay rent, salaries, and interest on their inventory, and expect to make a profit, a spread exists between buying and selling rates. They buy low and sell high. Thus, when arriving in Copenhagen and buying *kroner* you might receive seven *kroner* per dollar, but the next person in line returning home will have to pay eight *kroner* for each dollar when he cashes in his excess. It's like buying a new car — immediate depreciation. So, don't buy more money than you think you will be using in any one country.

In addition to the buy/sell spread, there is usually a transaction fee, normally called a "commission." This is sometimes a flat amount (so it is better to make large transactions to reduce the relative amount) or it can be a percentage of the transaction.

Procedures

When exchanging money in some banks, you give your cash or traveler's checks to a clerk at one window who calculates the transaction. He gives you a plastic or metal token with a number on it, and passes the paperwork to another window, the cashier. Shortly, the cashier will call out your number, in the native language of course, and pay you the money. If you can't understand the local language, you won't know when it's your turn. It's a good idea to keep your eyes on your paperwork behind the counter so you know when it's your cash being dished out. In a bank in Holland they once tried to give me somebody else's money.

You'll see plenty of store front windows offering to exchange your dollars for local money. This one is on the Damrak in Amsterdam. Watch out when you see "0% commission" advertised. [0820]

When

It's best to do your banking in the morning. Lines are longer at noon (if the banks are open during lunch) and in the afternoons.

Airports

International air terminals in Europe have an exchange window, bank, and/or ATM machine. On arrival it would be a good idea to get about $100 in foreign currency right at the airport. This should more than cover your expenses in getting to town and checking in at your hotel.

The exchange rate is not as good at airports in the USA as it is in Europe because the European currencies have little demand in our country. On the other hand, US $100 bills are the *monnaie du monde* (money of the world) by my observations on four continents. Use the new ones with the big picture of Benjamin Franklin. I call them Bennies.

Arriving at Schiphol Airport in Holland a few years ago I swapped $100 at the ABN-AMRO bank window in the entry hall. Later that day I exchanged more at the ABN-AMRO bank branch in Haarlem. Not only did I get a slightly better exchange rate in Haarlem but the commission was also less. The difference was about a 1% benefit in using the Haarlem branch for exchanging money.

Here is a Citibank ATM sign in Athens, Greece. ATMs are almost everywhere. [0818]

Train Stations

Most major train stations have an exchange office with extended hours. Usually it costs you more to buy foreign currency at these offices. You pay for the convenience. I have seen buy/sell spreads at some train station exchange offices of 8% to 9%. The spread should be about 2% with a strong dollar. Look for a cash machine in the train station.

The keypad of this ATM in Athens is unusual in that it also has the alpha characters, including the Greek version. You are better off to convert your PIN to a numeric code of four characters prior to departure. [0819]

Ships

Ships and ferries crossing international borders have exchange windows which operate more or less like banks. Usually exchange windows on ships are only open during part of the journey. Open hours will normally be posted at the exchange window and/or announced over the public address system. If you cannot find an exchange office ask the purser if he will make an exchange for you. Ports do not have convenient exchange windows.

Wechsel is the German word for money exchange, so this office in Prague, Czech Republic will get the attention of visitors from over the border. [0801]

American Express

Many Americans use American Express offices to exchange money. The Paris office is a very busy place. You could easily spend an hour in there, so bring a book or make a new friend. Holders of Amex cards receive expedited treatment.

Money Changers

Exchange rates for small amounts are sometimes not as good as for larger amounts.

In Paris a few years ago I was seduced by what appeared to be an excellent rate for *Deutschemarks* with no commission charge. Instead I was shorted by about 10% because the small print said that the exchange rate was only for amounts over $1,000. I didn't read the small print. Heck, I didn't even see that tiny print at the bottom of his poster after reading the good exchange rate in big letters at the top. I asked for my money back and the teller refused. Whereupon I took his picture, told him he was a thief and that I would put his picture in my next edition. Whereupon he bounced out of his booth and tried to take the camera out of my hand. The scuffle didn't last long and I kept my camera. His face isn't worth the ink so a picture of the shop on rue de Rivoli is adjacent. Watch out.

Probably the only time I felt cheated in changing money was at this window on rue de Rivoli in Paris, France. If you want to do business with street front swaps do not give them your money until they write down the amount you are going to receive. "No commission" is a come-on for a lousy exchange rate. [0809]

Last Resort

When I was living in Geneva, Switzerland I would often make day trips over to France on weekends. Usually I had enough French *francs* with me but one Sunday I was short. I was stymied everywhere in town trying to change Swiss *Franks* for French *francs*. Banks were closed and hotels would only make change for their guests. Finally, I went into the casino at Aix-les-Bains and bought casino tokens with my *CHF*. At another cash window I traded all the tokens for *FF* and received as good an exchange rate as at a bank, had one been open.

ATM MACHINES

Your Bank Card

One of the really amazing developments over the past 20 years has been the introduction of automatic teller machines, ATMs. You can use most of the American ATM cards throughout Europe. These cards are usually identified on the reverse with names like Cirrus, Star, Plus, and others. These names are also used in Europe and where you see them you can usually use your matching ATM card. Your bank will probably charge a fee of up to $3 for each transaction, and the foreign bank might also dip his fingers in. This suggests that you draw large amounts infrequently rather than take small doses. The money you receive is local currency, and is deducted from your home bank account after the banks make the conversion calculation and tack on their fees.

Bank systems have regularly scheduled maintenance periods when you may not be able to access cash. Ask you bank about this before going to Europe. The off period is probably the wee hours of the day at home, which can be mid day in Europe.

In Germany we lived near a US Army base which had an ATM machine dishing out US dollars, US dollars being the coin of the base. I used the machine several times before they put up a notice warning that it was to be used only by military personnel. The machine was outside the fence so anybody could draw dollars without paying commissions to a German bank. Dollars came in handy for my trips to the eastern countries. The former communist countries love American dollars.

Geldautomat is the German word for automatic teller machine, ATM.. In most of these you can use your bank card if it has the logos of Cirrus or Plus on the back. Many of these machines also accept credit cards for cash advances. [0810]

Credit Cards

You can also use your credit card with personal identification number (PIN) to take cash advances according to the terms and credit limits of your account. Check the reverse of your card to see which systems they belong to and look over the section on credit cards later in this chapter.

PIN

Make sure that you remember your PIN as a number and not as a word. The reason is that most European ATMs do not have alpha characters and the number pads do not have the same pattern as ours at home. For example, if your password/PIN is "cash" remember it as 2274 or you may have trouble accessing your account.

Four digit PINs are the norm in Europe. If you use a 5 or 6 digit PIN change it before your trip or you will not be able to use your card in most cash machines.

Fraud

Where there is cash there are criminals. Try to use ATMs which are attached to banks, not those in stores. ATMs are not regulated as banks are and anybody can buy an ATM and install it anywhere. Some of these, in New York and California so far, have been modified by the ATM owner (not necessarily the store owner) to harvest account and PIN numbers. Thereafter the crooks cleaned out the bank accounts of many people.

CASH

The Mighty Dollar

In the eastern countries, there are unusual things going on with money. In most of them you can use dollars to pay for many things. For instance, in Budapest some hotels post their rates in *forints* and dollars. In Kiev my hotel would only accept dollars. In Istanbul, rates were posted only in dollars. The reason is that inflation is atrocious in some countries and the local currencies are depreciating at unbelievable rates. As an extreme example, in October 1994 the Russian *ruble* plunged by about 25% in one day, triggering a national crisis. It happened again about four years later, triggering an international crisis.

Many people would rather have dollars. The situation has spawned street trader businesses in dollars throughout the eastern and southern European countries. A colleague used a street trader in Budapest and got an excellent exchange rate, which she discovered later was for cut up newspapers sandwiched between two legitimate *forint* banknotes. If it's too good to be true it's probably a scam.

Not knowing what to expect when we ventured off through the east, I carried about $1,500 in my shoes. But here in Istanbul, Turkey you can use almost all the plastic known to man to obtain local cash. [0806]

The Euro, €

The new kid in the bank is the *euro*, using a symbol that looks like a C bisected by an equals sign. The euro is probably unique in centuries as the single currency of a multitude of free countries.

The European Union, EU, consists of 15 independent countries. The EU has had a parliament in Strasbourg and administrative offices in Brussels for many years. As a next step toward complete unification of Europe, a common currency has been issued. Most of the EU countries have decided to use the *euro* and abandon their historical currencies.

The *Euro Zone* consists of Austria, Belgium, Finland, France, Germany, Greece, Ireland, Italy, Luxembourg, The Netherlands, Portugal, and Spain. For these countries there will no longer be a need to scramble to change money every time we cross a border. Three members of the European Union are not in the *Euro Zone* and will therefore continue using their own currencies. Britain and Denmark chose not to join the *Euro Zone* and Sweden did not meet the requirements.

Countries which are not in the European Union do not use the *euro*. Notable among these is Switzerland, along with all of the countries of the former Warsaw Pact, i.e. eastern Europe. Many of them are trying to join and some are on the short list for the EU, though the formality will not happen until 2004 and that won't automatically put them in the Euro Zone anyway. In the meantime the euro and the dollar are the de facto currencies in many of the eastern countries, much like the

Deutschemark was in prior years.

My Dutch bank statements began showing transactions in *euro* in 1999. My grocery store in France was showing *euro* equivalent prices in mid-1999. This was done in many countries to start getting the population accustomed to the new currency. Many people remain confused even a year after the official change. Count your change. Be especially wary of money changers and know whether the *euro* is worth more or less than a dollar when you make your trip.

One of the nice things about the *euro* is that it is worth about a dollar. It started out being worth $1.18 on 1 January 1999 (three years before it became official), but unraveled quite a bit down to 80¢ at one time, and then bounced back up to $1.19 in the spring of 2003. It's about $1.10 as of late summer 2003. You won't be bouncing around between 2 German *Deutschemarks*, 7 French *francs*, and 2,000 Italian *lira* week by week anymore. But you will still have to put up with widely different exchange rates in Switzerland, Poland, Britain, and many other countries.

Hold the 100 euro note up to the light and notice the watermark on the left. All European bank notes have been watermarked for decades to guard against forgery. This picture shows about half of the bill. [0821]

Caveats

Do not flash a fist full of greenbacks and ask, jokingly or insultingly, "How much is that in real money?" They'll tell you, all right. In exchange for the insult, you will probably be tapped for another 25% to 50%.

Coins

Coins are not exchangeable outside the country of origin. This often presents a problem because coins are what you often need immediately on entering any country. Luggage lockers normally require coins, and change is not as easy to get in Europe as it is at home. Merchants do not like to give it out. The easiest way to get change is to go to the foreign exchange window in the airport or train station and get about three times as much as you think you will need.

Coin telephones, if available, are often out of order and/or steal your money. Instead of using a coin phone, buy a telephone card. In fact, the currency exchange office in the Antwerp train station (that's a picture of it on the front cover of *How To Europe*) would not give me change but gladly sold me a telephone card. That is far handier than putting a bunch of coins in the slot for a call. The card phones are usually in operating order. However most phone cards have an expiration date so if you don't use it up donate it to someone before you leave the country. For much more information on using the phones in Europe see chapter 19, "Communicating as You Travel."

TRAVELER'S CHECKS

Many Americans arrive on foreign shores with a booklet full of traveler's checks. I've seen them standing in one hour lines and then spend ten minutes signing enough to get them through the next few days. This is not an ideal way to spend your time.

Traveler's checks do solve the problem of carrying money securely, and money that is usually accepted in western Europe. Be aware though, that they are usually worthless without your I.D., i.e. your passport. Don't be surprised if your change comes back with no passport. Demand its immediate return. It is better to show your passport to the waiter at the table and let him copy whatever he wants, but do not let it out of your control. Remember that "your" passport is the property of the US government, even though you paid for it.

If you are planning extensive travel within one country and can stick to your budget, buy traveler's checks denominated in the currency of that country. They will be more readily accepted in restaurants, though acceptance is never guaranteed.

Most of the countries of Europe are not in the Euro Zone. Here are a few old samples from the eastern countries, Romania, Poland, and Russia. Many countries retire their banknotes every 5 or 10 years and redesign everything. [0816]

Buying Fee

Travelers checks are normally sold with a fee of 1%. Some traveler's checks are issued with no service charge. Contact your bank, credit union, automobile club, or employer to see if traveler's checks are available with no service charge.

Cashing Fee

The user of US dollar traveler's checks will often be short-changed. Most places of exchange charge a fee for cashing traveler's checks. After all, if you gave them greenbacks they could immediately turn around and give them to the next customer. With traveler's checks, they have to wait to be paid in local currency by the issuer. Normally you can avoid the fee by cashing traveler's checks at an office of the issuer of the traveler's checks. But that's where the long lines are. Or, if the fee is per transaction and not per traveler's check, cash a bunch to get the fee down to half a percent or so.

Expect to be really short-changed when cashing US dollar traveler's checks at hotels. Their exchange rates may be steeply discounted costing you up to another 25% for your room. At restaurants it can be worse. US dollar traveler's checks are worth less than paper napkins in some establishments. Though they are normally accepted, I have seen waiters scream at the mention of the words "traveler's check."

Name Brands

Use only internationally recognized traveler's checks. Do follow the directions and stash the receipt with serial numbers in a place where you won't lose it if your checks are lost or stolen.

Refunds for lost or stolen traveler's checks are available throughout Europe at branch offices of the issuer. American Express, Thomas Cook (Wagon-Lits Cook in some countries), and the other major companies can replace checks within 24 hours. Get explicit refund information before buying any traveler's check. That's why you are buying them in the first place. Read that small print in your check envelope and follow directions.

Dinosaurs

With the large number of ATM cash machines throughout Europe, travelers checks are history. Don't bother bringing any, unless you need them for peace of mind.

PERSONAL CHECKS

Personal checks drawn on a United States bank account can be used in Europe under certain circumstances. One program is highly promoted by American Express to its card holders, and I made extensive use of it during my travels in the past. If you have an American Express card, their offices or associates in Europe will cash your personal checks up to US $1,000 every 20 days or so. This is a pretty good service. You must accept local currency (which can be converted to other currencies at an additional premium), and generally you must take some of the funds in traveler's checks for which there is an additional charge. American Express card holders get preferential treatment at Amex offices, and rightly so. The annual membership fee is rather high.

CREDIT CARDS

Acceptability

It's getting so that you can almost live on plastic in western Europe. Credit cards are accepted in the bigger and/or better establishments to an only slightly lesser degree than at home. They can also be used in some telephones, when buying train tickets and reservations, in some taxis, and in virtually all hotels over one star.

Commonly accepted cards are Carte Blanche, Visa, Diner's Club, American Express, MasterCard, and several European cards. MasterCard and Visa are each affiliated with major credit card systems in different countries.

As a general rule, prices are higher in restaurants, hotels, and shops honoring these cards. The low budget traveler can use this generalization and avoid those establishments whose front doors are covered by certain "welcome" emblems.

Shop For a Card

It really pays to shop around before signing up for a credit card. Visa and MasterCard are issued by different banks at different costs to you. Small banks and S&Ls usually have the lowest costs. Big banks which have done their best to bankrupt themselves making loans to corrupt or inept foreign governments are more likely to scalp Americans with high annual fees, interest, and late payment charges. One thing for travelers to keep in mind is that some airlines issue Visa or MasterCard cards in their name. Not only do you get mileage credit for charges on the card, but the card issuer may also give extra discounts or extra mileage when using their card to purchase airline tickets. These cards usually require an annual fee and carry higher interest rates than most cards.

Cash Advance

A convenient source of funds throughout western Europe and Istanbul is a cash advance from your Visa or MasterCard. I sometimes use one of these cards to draw local currency. When you do this, keep the receipt for the transaction and compare it with your monthly statement. The exchange rate will be calculated by the credit card company and may not be shown on your monthly statement.

Hazards

There are some important points to consider when using credit cards, especially in Europe.

Never sign a charge receipt if the total is not shown in the proper place at the bottom. European sales clerks, waiters, and hotel clerks always leave this space blank. Fill it in before you sign.

Write the name of the currency in front of the total amount. Sales clerks never fill this in, since they are accustomed to *euro, pounds, kroner*, etc.. Use an abbreviation such as *BP* for *British pound*. Most likely your credit card account is carried and billed in US dollars, though it can be in another currency.

Never sign a blank charge receipt. This may be obvious, but you will occasionally be pressed by a hotel desk clerk to sign a blank receipt to assure them that the bill will be paid. Don't even think of signing. If they insist on this, just run a new credit card charge each day and sign nothing except a completed receipt. Do not pay in advance ("to make it simple"). Once they have your money, the negotiating is over. If you arrive on the weekend and a construction site starts up next to your window on Monday morning your options will be limited.

Check your credit card when it is returned by a waiter or sales clerk. Make sure that the card of someone else was not returned by mistake. And make sure that your passport is returned if it was requested for identification. Several times they "forgot" to return my passport. I really don't believe they forgot it at all. They didn't "forget" to ask me for it in the first place. I seriously doubt that they would make you wash the dishes just because you "forgot to bring it tonight." As mentioned above in discussing travelers checks, just show your passport to the waiter but do not let it walk.

Advantages

The advantages of credit cards to the traveler are several:

They are widely accepted for travel necessities at hotels and restaurants, for air fare, rail passes, car rental, taxis, clothing, gifts, and even groceries

They are fairly safe. Your liability is generally limited to $50 for unauthorized use. If you notify the issuer immediately when it is lost or stolen, your liability is zero. Check the fine print in the agreement for the rules of your card. If it disappears look at your receipts to see where you used it last. The sales clerk probably forgot to return it.

A record of your purchases is sent with the bill. This helps your personal accounting so you won't be wondering where all that money went. However, charge slips and receipts often have the wrong date on them. Usually the year is wrong. And the date is written in the European system — day/month/year. If you need this information, get into the habit of writing it on your receipt when you sign it. Also, write down the name and city of the establishment. The imprints are too often impossible to read.

Payment is not due until about 20 days after the statement is dated. This may give you up to 50 days to pay without becoming liable for interest fees and late charges. Additionally, some European establishments are rather slow in sending in charge slips so you might easily get 80 days grace before payment is due. I was billed once for a credit charge made in Stockholm 18 months previously!

The exchange rate is usually better than the rate used when buying bank notes, and no commission is charged. This can save you a percent or so on all credit card purchases. The exchange rate used is that in effect on the day that the charge was processed by the credit card central office, not that in effect at the time you made the transaction. However, different cards use different exchange rates. My cursory examination of bills shows that American Express gives a better exchange rate, and provides excellent back-up documentation for all charges. Some cards, including American Express, have begun adding an international surcharge on all foreign charges. This is 2% of the amount charged and is probably meant to cover fraud rather than any direct expense borne by the company. A credit card can be used to buy gasoline almost anywhere, and without a signature.

Paying

You must make arrangements for receiving the credit card statement and mailing the payment on time. If you are traveling for only a month or so, this is no problem. You will be home before the bill is due. If you are on a heavy duty trip, there are several ways to handle this.

One way is to keep a log of all credit purchases in your travel record book. Devote a page to each credit card and include the payment address. Then airmail your payment for all current charges about 10 days before the due date.

Another way is to set up an automatic payment plan with the bank which issued the card. At the same bank, maintain a checking or saving account which will be debited each month to pay your Visa or MasterCard bill. This leaves you with little control over misuse of your account, and arguments with bank computers are usually frustrating.

You can be billed at a European address. This works well with some credit cards, but not with others. For instance, some credit card companies send bills by surface mail (the boat takes three to four weeks) and the statement arrives several days after payment is due. The next month you will be socked with interest at usury rates and a late fee higher than most parking tickets.

Having your bill sent to a foreign address also presents a problem with proper addressing. When I submitted a change of address to Visa for our move to Germany the bills stopped coming. A few months later a collection agency called. The bills had been sent to someplace in Africa thanks to a nitwit at Bank of America.

Lately, in living in Switzerland and in The Netherlands from 1997 to 1999, American Express statements have been incorrectly addressed. Statements supposedly sent to Geneva, Switzerland never arrived. Somehow one of them arrived in Switzerland addressed to Geneva, WI. Despite half a dozen phone calls to their billing office this went on for months. It seems that these big companies hire from the bottom of the barrel. For Holland, American Express addressed my bills to Haarlem ET. As I recall ET was a movie, not a country. Maybe they can't spell big words. Repeated phone calls have brought either arrogance or helplessness on the part of the American Express "customer service" people. Repeated submittal of change of address notices has not worked.

For American Express I discovered that you can go into any office, generously scattered throughout Europe, and get a statement of your account. Anyone who steals your card can also go in to see your statement, and get a printout with a bunch of your personal data. I did this in Geneva and was not asked for any identification, a password, or anything. The Swiss are so trusting, but they should at least ask for a photo ID before they pass out confidential information.

American Express now has a great way of paying bills by phone. You can phone in and have an electronic debit of your bank account made payable to your American Express account. This saves time and postage.

You can have a trusted friend or relative handle your financial affairs at home, though mistakes can lead to loss of friendship or disharmony. Most people have a full life already and have little time for or interest in handling the affairs of a relative gallivanting around Europe. Choose with care and keep up good communication.

CASH

There is always that old standby — cash. You can buy enough *Franks, euro, pounds, rubles,* or whatever to pay for your entire trip. They will be accepted in the country which issues them, and you won't have to worry about fluctuating exchange rates. But you might have to worry about banking laws on the import and export of their currencies. In fact, some currencies are not available outside their homeland. In those countries you are normally better off carrying dollars anyway.

Cash in Hand

I recommend that you have a days supply of local currency before you depart for any country. It's true that exchange windows are generally available at entry points, but you have good reasons for not standing in that line on arrival. If the train or plane is late, there may be no line because the frontier exchange office is closed. You may be stuck with no local currency until the following day. At virtually all auto crossing borders there is an exchange office for local money, though they do not have 24/7 service. Try to cross borders during daylight hours to make it easier on yourself.

Last Minute Needs

On leaving a country by train, plane, or ship don't trade in all your local currency before boarding. You may want to buy a last minute apple or newspaper, or you may be charged a reservation fee or departure tax. Refreshments on board can be purchased with departure country currency, and often at a lower equivalent price than if you use arrival country currency. Keep ten or twenty dollars worth of your departure country currency until you are well over the border.

Coins

They don't use silver either. European countries have debased their coinage like the USA. Copper, nickel, and aluminum alloy coins are in circulation. While in America the largest coin in general circulation is a quarter, some coins in Europe are worth two dollars. Coins from different countries are very similar to each other and are easily mistaken by Americans who haven't used them before. The natives know the difference and will promptly correct you if you try to use money from the country next door.

When driving, unload all your money at the border, if you can. On leaving Romania we had a problem with this. Even though it was illegal to leave with any of the local cash, and we had receipts for all that we had bought, the bank refused to take our Romanian *lei* and give us Hungarian *forints*. They know the value of their own stuff. At our motel over the border in Makó we were able to unload it at a steep discount for Hungarian *forints*, but then had to pay for the room with German *Marks*. The motel keeper didn't like his native *forints* either.

Emergency Greenbacks

Lastly, always carry some greenbacks wherever you are, and use them only in emergencies. If you have no need, just bring them home. I would recommend carrying five each of $1, $5, and $20 as a minimum. A couple of $50s or $100s would also be a good idea. Bring these from home, of course. Make sure you bring new crisp bills. Europeans do not like dirty old money. And bring the new style "big face." These are the only US bills which are water-marked, among other anti-counterfeiting measures.

MONEY POTPOURRI

Identification

When exchanging money in some countries your passport is required as I.D.

Interbank Transfers

There are other ways to get your money overseas. One is to have your bank transfer funds by mail or wire from your account to an account you have established with a foreign bank. This can be risky if your bank does not normally do this kind of thing. An officer or bank manager should be able to offer competent assistance. Make arrangements for transfers before departure. This service could cost you $25 to $50 per transfer. After arrival in Europe, open a nonresident bank account and write or wire your home bank with your instructions. Banking and money laws vary from country to country so check out all the rules before jumping to this course of action. It would be practical for someone making a long journey or many frequent trips.

Resident Bank Account

Those planning to live overseas for work or study would probably be better off with a resident bank account. But this usually presents at least one other problem. You may be prohibited from maintaining a bank account at home. For example, Dutch authorities will be quick to request an interview if they notice money flowing between your Dutch account and another account under your name outside Holland. Tax evasion is a practiced art in Holland, and few people miss a chance to hide some *zwart gelt* (black money) from the confiscatory tax man. If you complain about American taxes you ain't seen nothing till you see the tax laws of Europe.

Many countries regulate the amount of money that anyone, resident or not, may take over the border. Even US citizens are required to report large transfers, those exceeding $10,000. This regulation is supposed to help stop the illegal drug industry. Fat chance. At the other end of the spectrum, banking is a big business in

Luxembourg due to lack of regulations and complete privacy of account holders.

Letter of Credit

Another way to carry money overseas is to obtain a letter of credit from your home bank. These are usually used by commercial establishments in paying for goods to be exported. In practice, a letter of credit could be likened to a certified check with the added wrinkle that it may be partially debited. It's reported that letters of credit are not held in the highest esteem because of the ease of forgery. Don't play with this unless you know what you are doing.

Caveat Cash

Be careful that you don't receive some funny money as change from storekeepers. This has happened to me several times in Holland. The Dutch retired their old bank notes and substituted new bank notes in various pastel colors. No Dutchman would accept the old currency, but it was passed to American tourists in the 1980s. Germany introduced new banknotes in 1993 and obsoleted the old ones. These countries now use the *euro* so you shouldn't be seeing any Dutch *gulden* anymore, period. It is worthless.

Also, beware of counterfeit money. Several times I have seen French storekeepers hold a 100 or 500 *franc* note up to the light to make sure that it was good. Bank notes in Europe are watermarked. Usually the watermark is the portrait of a national hero found in a blank oval on the note. Sometimes it is a geometric pattern. The new *euro* is also watermarked. Make yourself familiar with the characteristics of the local currency to help avoid the sting.

Regulations

Many of the eastern countries prohibit import of their currencies. That assumes that you could buy them someplace. When you do buy currencies in the east, make sure that you obtain and keep the receipt. These countries are extremely upset by black-market dealing in their currencies. As mentioned above, even with the receipt I was not able to reconvert my Romanian *lei*.

Before returning to the United States, it is best to trade all your excess foreign money back to US dollars. At home, banks charge a fee per transaction per currency, in addition to their high spread. You would probably be better off if you framed the money you brought home.

Barter

If you're out of cash and credit, try the oldest means of exchange — barter. I met an Australian traveler who claimed to have traded a pair of Levis for three nights of room and food for himself and his wife in Yugoslavia. Barter is not very effective in western Europe, even though the price of Levi's is about triple what we pay in the USA. Levi Strauss is pretending to be Calvin Klein in Europe.

Currency buying and selling rates are prominently posted at this money exchange store in Amsterdam, but read the small print and get a <u>net</u> amount written down before giving your money to the guy behind the bullet proof window. [0825]

Chapter 9
A Travel Diary of Europe
Notes Supplement Your Photos

If Marco Polo had not written it down, nobody would know that he had gone to China.

TRAVEL DIARY

Why?

A well kept diary can be more interesting than a load of photographs, reversing the cliché. Your friends will want to know all about your trip, and your record book will be your authoritative reference. Use your travel record as a supplement to your photography. Next winter you can assemble your photos and notes and the other junque you pick up. Ten years from now, or fifty, you'll be glad you did. Maybe you can publish your travel memoirs.

In addition to serving as a diary, your travel record should also serve as your personal data book.

The Book

My favorite type of diary is a 180 page "record book" with numbered pages, sewn binding, and a flex cover. This is a bit bigger than a passport, and fits in a hip or breast pocket. Look through the rack of little black books in a large stationery or office supply store and select one that suits you. Browse through the section next to the accountants ledgers. Don't buy one with the dates already in place. You want to do this yourself because you will write several pages for some days and almost nothing for others.

Before You Go

Start by writing your name, home address, European address (if any), email address, and phone number inside the front cover. Also, you might state that you will pay the postage and/or a reward if a finder will mail it back to you.

Record your passport number and place and date of issue and/or glue a copy of your passport ID page inside the front cover of your travel book.

Record addresses, phone numbers, and email addresses of all of your family and friends in a few pages so you won't need to tote along a separate address book.

Note all of your flight information. This includes your flight record number (reservation number), ticket number, flight numbers, departure and arrival times, and cities of course. Record the phone number of your travel agent or whoever it was that you bought your plane ticket from.

Record the name, address, and phone number of your bank, insurance company, employer, boss's home, doctor, dentist, landlord, clubs, church, lodge, and whomever else you may want to send a card to or who you might want to contact in an emergency. Include account numbers, I.D. numbers, due dates, and etc.

Record the name, address, phone number, monthly payment date, and account number for each of your credit cards. Keep the PIN numbers out of your book.

If needed, record your ISP's URL, DNS numbers, mail and news servers, and dial up number. If you have roaming access get the details from your ISP. This would be a good time to sign on for a free email account from one of the major internet service providers. These allow you to keep in touch using any internet connection.

Record the brand name and serial number of each of your traveler's checks (but do not throw away the receipt).

Go through your checkbook for the last year to see who you do business with. Write down names, addresses, phone numbers, account numbers, and due dates. You may not need the information while in Europe, but if you do, getting it will be expensive and a peck of trouble from the other side of the Atlantic.

On a separate small piece of paper or business card record a clue word or phrase to your PINs and passwords, but not the actual PINs or passwords. Secret this away in your toilet kit or whatever. The general rule in Europe is that PINs must be 4 digits. If yours is not 4 digits change it before you go. Use numbers not alphabetic characters because most keypads only have numbers.

Write in your expected itinerary, must-sees, must-dos, and shopping list.

Tape a calendar inside the back cover. I prefer one like those in the back of the small desk calendars.

Where and When

After all of the above, the book is ready to serve as your daily journal. Start each day with an entry of the date, day of the week (you can easily forget while traveling), and city you're in at the moment. Make notes while waiting for service in restaurants, waiting for trains to depart (writing in a moving train is usually difficult), on ships, and before you start counting sheep. It's interesting to write in restaurants. Service seems to speed up when the waiter sees you writing. Maybe he thinks you are writing a review of the restaurant. Why not?

What

Chronologically record names, addresses, and phone/fax numbers of hotels and restaurants, room numbers, menu items, and prices you paid. Mention sights, letters and cards sent, and miscellaneous info that might prove useful later. Make a note on anything that strikes your fancy or that you might want to recommend to others later. Even make a note of the weather. Many people want to know about the weather over there. Write in contact information for people you meet on your trip with whom you plan to keep in touch.

How Much

Also, keep detailed records of your expenses and currency exchange transactions. This will help you in checking your credit card bills, and in completing your expense report. Many times you do not receive receipts for small items that add up over the weeks. If you have any thoughts about becoming a travel writer, even an article for your local newspaper, this record will be valuable in establishing your expenses when calculating your taxes.

Take the time to write out what the expense was for. My records become so cryptic when I'm in a hurry that it's difficult later to figure out what some things are.

We met this Croatian soldier at an outdoor café in Zagreb during the fighting in 1993. Robert sat alone and enjoyed his days of liberty in a muse, with thumbs up. War - who needs it? [0901]

AUDIO TAPE RECORDERS

Convenient

A cassette tape recorder is a handy way of making notes of your travels. I have found this to be an especially worthwhile endeavor while driving alone through Europe. You see a lot of unusual things and don't have time to stop and write it down or take a picture. I used a tape recorder on drives through France, Sweden, Germany, Poland, Hungary, Ukraine, and Czechoslovakia. The recordings made on the spot jiggle the memory better than photos. In addition to being interesting and amusing when you play it back later, the background sounds of radio and street noise bring back more of the experience. Just imagine yourself as Howard Cosell, turn on the machine, and start talking about what you see, what you're doing, and what you're thinking (within reason).

Microcassette

Microcassette recorders are much smaller, lighter, and more convenient to carry than ordinary recorders if you are traveling by train or other public transportation. I carry one in a pocket of my jacket in all my travels.

Tapes

Bring some cassette or microcassette tapes to fit your recorder. Tapes can also be purchased in Europe.

Letters

Tapes can also be convenient way to correspond. It is much easier to sit back and talk into a microphone than to write as much on paper. Tell the person to whom you are sending the tape to save it for you. You would like it back so you can relive some of your travels in future years. Punch out the record protect tabs before you send it so someone does not inadvertently erase your tape.

Make a note of a few of these sights to see in Haarlem.[0903]

Miscellaneous

Your tape recorder can provide you with entertainment. Buy or record your own tapes and bring along a few hours of home town radio. It's very nice to have after a few weeks or months on the road. The quality on these little recorders is pretty good with a set of earphones. If you make copies for the road from tapes, CDs, or the radio you need a recorder which allows you to disable the automatic recording level feature. Otherwise the music will sound rather bland.

VIDEO RECORDER

Advantages

A hand-size camcorder is an outstanding way to record your travels in Europe. I have used an 8 mm video recorder for a number of years throughout Europe. Not only do you get the sights and sounds, but you get the motion, of course. A big advantage of most camcorders is that you can record in much less light than you need for a camera. The equivalent cost is much lower also since a two hour tape costs about the same as a roll of high speed film, and you don't have developing and printing costs. The cost of camcorders is coming down significantly, and is now down to the cost of a good 35 mm single lens reflex camera and set of lenses.

Battery

A disadvantage of camcorders is that they require a battery. They come with rechargeable batteries, but these deteriorate in a year or so. It is a good idea to have a couple of spares and put the used one in the charger overnight. The instructions say that you must recharge a battery only when it is fully discharged. That is difficult to do if you are going to keep them charged. I have tried shorting them out to drain them, but they get pretty hot doing this and I would not recommend it. Just leave your camera turned on until the battery exhausts.

When you buy a camcorder, make sure that the battery charger is rated for both 110 and 220 volts and 50 and 60 Hertz so it will operate in Europe as well as at home.

NTSC, SECAM, PAL

With the proper connections, you might think that you can watch your videos using the televisions in your European hotel rooms. Sorry. Television systems are different in Europe, as explained in chapter 11, "Electricity in Europe." The USA uses a television broadcast system called NTSC. There are several systems in use in Europe, including SECAM and PAL. If your hotel TV is multi-system and includes NTSC you will be able to watch your videos if you have the video and audio cables with you, maybe. The audio jacks on European and American TVs are compatible, but the video jacks are different.

Don't buy a camcorder in Europe unless you have a multi-system television. Multi-system televisions can be purchased in major department stores and electronic stores in Europe and from a few stores in the USA. See chapter 22 "Living in Europe" for a dialogue on appliances for those planning to live in Europe.

Here I am on the job in Buda, overlooking Pest. The famous Danube River is below, known in Hungary as the Duma. It starts in Germany and flows east to empty into its delta on the Black Sea. The video camcorder in my right hand has become my most trusted note taker, and defense against gypsies. Back in chapter 5 I advised against wearing a beard and long hair, and Levis. I sin now and then. Photo by Elizabeth. [0902]

Chapter 10
Guidebooks, Maps, Dictionaries
Travel in Europe with a Good Guidebook

You are not Lewis and Clark. Somebody has been there before, marked the trail, and left a record. Get a copy.

PUBLICATIONS FOR TRAVELERS

To see Europe through a window on somebody's tour bus is so ridiculous that it should be unimaginable, except that it happens. Let me assure the meek and timid that Europe is at least as civilized as the USA, and more so in many respects. You don't need a jungle guide to show you around.

The logical approach to budget travel is to travel independently, on your own. Study up a little. Then you can go where and when and how it pleases you. Like the song from the 60s — "go where you want to go, do what you want to do." Just go, you mammas and pappas. Here is a rundown on the many publications that empower you to do just that.

This Year's Crop

Travelers face a significant challenge in finding the right information from among the hundreds of publications listing hotels, restaurants, and sights to see in Europe. Bookstores are loaded with titles like Europe, Ireland, France, Holland, and Germany, followed by this year's date and either the author's or publisher's name in the title. How do you know which to choose?

The traditional Frommer's, Fielding's, and Fodor's of travel publishing have been going strong for decades. They have been joined by editions from many other authors and publishers over the past 20 years. Many European publishers, e.g. Baedeker and Michelin, have been going for over a century. Though these books are published in English, they are not as well known in the USA.

Pounds of Fluff

Guidebooks provide information on the sights to see — museums, castles, ancient artifacts, and natural wonders. Most also include listings of hotels and restaurants. Some provide information on other subjects of interest to travelers, e.g., local transportation, night life, and significant events during the year. Costs of hotels and other services are sometimes included, but these figures are usually off because most books are written a year before the date on the cover. Many books with a date on the cover are in the bookstores months before the year actually starts.

When purchasing travel guides, keep the rule of pack light in mind. Many travel writers aspire to be novelists. Writers often include plenty of extraneous information, for example, the name of the "charming" owner of the "marvelous" hotel. Patronizing exaggerations, possibly written under the influence of a free bottle of wine or a free room, will lead you astray. The best known guide books can be the worst on this score.

If you are going to visit only one or two countries then do not buy one of the really fat *Europe* books. Buy a guide(s) that is specific for the country, region, or city you will visit. These will be easier to carry and will be far more detailed on the places of interest to you.

Kudos and Knocks

The first edition of *How To Europe* in 1982 included an "Annotated Bibliography" appendix with a short review of some 110 travel titles. In the second edition in 1985 over 140 travel books were reviewed. Nowadays the number of titles is an order of magnitude higher. At one point in the late 1980s or early 1990s a book was published which consisted entirely of travel book reviews. They have probably given up in frustration with the tsunami of books now coming out every year.

I have used and examined a number of guides and herewith offer a critique of most of the better known books. My comments focus on the section of each book which covers the Netherlands, a.k.a Holland, and more specifically Haarlem. I know it well since I've lived in Haarlem for about four years in various stints since 1975. Some might consider this too narrow a focus, but Holland is a popular destination for travelers and it's a small country. Most of the people speak excellent English so there is no communications barrier. If a writer can't get it right on this country (s)he has no business being in the travel book authoring business. Sometimes they don't get it right. You even wonder if the writer actually went there as you'll see in some of the hoi polloi examples below. Don't waste your money on incompetent writers, no matter how famous the name on the cover.

THE CREAM OF THE CROP

Herewith is a paragraph or a few on specific guide books, authors, and/or publishers giving a general description of the product and/or a critique. I haven't written a guide book, yet, so I can be objective in judging many of those available from the consumer's point of view. The books described here are those you are likely to find in your library or local bookstore. See the sections near the end of this chapter for sources of these publications.

Michelin

The Michelin Tire Company of France has been publishing road maps for a century. More about their maps later. They also publish their "Red" guides to hotels and restaurants yearly, and their "Green" guides to the sights with updates every 5 years or so. Michelin has logically chosen to publish two books, one with the frequently changing information on hotels and restaurants and one with the fixed site information.

Michelin Red: For guidebooks describing where to sleep and eat, the Michelin Red Guides are excellent. Annual updates are published for France, Germany, Benelux (Belgium, Netherlands, Luxembourg), and other countries. Instructions for using the guides are printed in French and in English and in the language(s) of the country covered in the book. The book is set up as a directory, alphabetical by city, so it is a snap to find yourself. Addresses, phone numbers, and fax numbers for hotels and restaurants are given, with locations indicated by grid coordinates which are keyed to adjacent maps for many cities. Icons indicate which credit cards are accepted, if off-street parking is provided, or if the establishment has a particularly pleasant ambiance. Michelin Red books are published in the spring so the price information is more accurate than other guides which start showing up in the bookstores in October of the year before the date on the cover.

The Red Guide for Benelux lists hotels and restaurants in every city and village. The hotel selection for Haarlem lists only two hotels within the city, two of the more upscale establishments. It rates each of them as two star, with five stars as tops. The hotels themselves say they are four star. Each is a three star in my judgement. Backpackers would feel a little out of place in the lobbies. Michelin does include less expensive rooms in nearby villages. The restaurant selection is much wider, listing 15 eateries from one spoon to three spoons, pizzerias to coat and tie places. Having eaten in several of those listed I think that their selection is very representative of the city.

Michelin Green: For guidebooks describing what to see and when, the Michelin Green Guides are superb. These books are convenient to carry and are crammed with maps, sketches, historical background, data, suggested itineraries, and general commentary on the countries covered. There is nothing even in tenth place behind these books.

The Michelin Green Guide for the Netherlands includes a generous few pages on Haarlem. Paragraphs describing the monuments and sights are coded to an excellent map of the city center pinpointing each place. Probably everything worth seeing is described. Even details of hangings at the Frans Hals Museum are included.

One of the most interesting sights in Europe, in my humble opinion as an engineer, is the Cruquius Expo. Michelin is probably the only book which describes it and shows you how to get there. The Cruquius is one of three huge steam engines built around 1850 to pump the water out of the Haarlemmermeer (Lake Haarlem). When you land at Schiphol Airport you are in the middle of the former lake, about 15 feet below sea level.

Michelin books rate five stars in my book. Michelin also has a beautiful web site with maps, hotels, restaurants, and listings of sights to see on line. See the "Maps" section of *www.enjoy-europe.com*.

You can buy local and long distance maps as you travel. This display in the Boghallen bookstore on Radhuspladsen in Copenhagen is typical of many in bookstores and department stores throughout Europe. They even have a street map of Brooklyn up there. You'll find shelves of guide books, including many in English, in another part of the store. [1013]

Fodor's

A very good travel series is published by Fodor's. In addition to descriptions of the things to see, these guides recommend selected hotels and restaurants. Rather than put in specific prices, this series wisely indicates the general cost of things by $, $$, and $$$ signs. They don't need to update this kind of data every year. Hotels and restaurants listed are usually between two and four star. Budget travelers should see the description of Lonely Planet in the next section, below.

Fodor's Europe is nicely organized. Chapters cover individual countries and each gives a good introduction, including a map with north arrow and distance scale. The sights are well covered. The page discussing Haarlem is right on. This is one of the few guide books which mentions the Café Brinkman, one of the best situated in Holland. Café Brinkman serves good food, including a great burger and fries, though the service is even slower than the typical Dutch slow service. If you are sitting on the terrace overlooking the Grote Markt on a busy day, order your second beverage when your first one arrives.

Fodor's book on Holland titled *The Netherlands, Belgium, Luxembourg* goes into far more detail on the Low Countries. If you are planning a visit to this area only, skip the *Europe* book and get this one. However the Holland book doesn't mention the Café Brinkman, but now you know anyway. It does include a trio of good restaurants and two of the better hotels, neither of which are mentioned in most of the other books. One of these is the Hotel Lion d'Or, a Golden Tulip Hotel, which is also recommended by Michelin. The Lion d'Or is a long established hotel designed for business travelers, and is only a stone's throw from the train station. A newer upscale hotel on the south side of the city is the Carlton Square. Fodor's books do not include a map of Haarlem so pick one up at the tourist office.

Fodor's employs good writers. This series is arguably the best written of any on the American market and a pleasure to read. You're on the right road with Fodor's.

Lonely Planet

The first thing you notice with Lonely Planet's *Europe on a Shoestring* is that it has no date on the cover. That's a good sign. Geared to the budget traveler vis-à-vis eats and sleeps, this series of books also contains excellent advice on sights to see and things to do.

This book appears to be independently written — it is not a knock-off from another guide which is the impression I get from many guide books. Thus you get a fresh perspective on the lay of the land, and you won't be breathing the exhaust fumes of other travelers using the hoi polloi (see below) guide books with nearly identical hotel and restaurant listings. I give it an extra star because it mentions one of my favorite cafes in Amsterdam, the Hoppe. The Hoppe is especially active after office hours till mid evening.

Each chapter begins with a map and general introduction to the country at hand. Major cities are illustrated with good maps keyed to excellent tables listing eats, sleeps, museums, laundromats, and all manner of other establishments of interest to the traveler, especially the younger traveler on a tight budget. Lonely Planet covers more countries and cities in more detail in one book than any other guide. The appendices include weather data and essential phrases for many languages.

Lonely Planet's *Europe on a Shoestring* is unquestionably the best of the budget guide books, and one of the best for any budget.

Baedeker

Baedeker is almost synonymous with travel guide book. This publisher has been at it for going on two centuries, and does it right. This brief review covers the Netherlands book, edition 2000.

The first thing you notice about Baedeker is the color photographs. I was thumbing through and getting slightly homesick with all those beautiful images of The Netherlands. Then I was pleasantly surprised to find a photo of the Gravenstenerbrug, an old style counter-weighted lift bridge which is right in front of the house I lived in when I first moved to Holland. Check it out on page 209 for a "Typical view of Haarlem," according to Baedeker. Actually it's not very typical since old bridges like this are hard to find these days. Chapter 1 and 22 of *How To Europe* also show the Gravenstenerbrug. The oft photographed Magere Brug in Amsterdam is similar.

The book also includes a photo of the magnificent Basilica (the other St. Bavo Kerk in Haarlem), a decent city map, the floor plan of the Frans Hals Museum, and details on many other things never reported on by most travel guide writers. Baedeker might be criticized by some for having no hotel or restaurant listings. It's a guide to the sights, and what a good one.

AAA Europe TravelBook

The AAA has produced a book on Europe that might best be called an overview reference book. Every country is covered. Each chapter includes a small road map and a table of reference information. A short history of the country is followed by basic information on food and drink, transportation, accommodation, language, and other topics. Principal touring areas are discussed by city, with maps of the major cities. Weather information and useful expressions in the local language are also provided.

The section on Haarlem mentions the four major museums, along with a brief description of the city. The book covers 30 cities in Holland in similar fashion. The section on Amsterdam includes a map highlighting the major tourist sights with single paragraph descriptions of each.

Though it doesn't go into much detail, it is to the point. The AAA *Europe TravelBook* is a very handy guide to have in your bag.

Eyewitness Travel Guides

This series is published by Dorling Kindersley, abbreviated DK, in London. DK publishes guides to a number of countries in addition to one book on Europe which is commented on here, the First American Edition 2001.

DK's *Eyewitness Europe* covers a number of countries in individual chapters. All of former Western Europe is covered, except Iceland, plus Poland, Czech Republic, and Hungary. Each chapter begins with a brief article on the history and culture, and an overview map of the country. Main features of this book are the selection of outstanding photos and the excellent maps of major cities.

Considering the chapter on Holland I have just a few complaints. It left out Maastricht, certainly a slight to this fun loving capital of Limburg, the southernmost province of The Netherlands. On Haarlem, it left out the Tylers Museum, the oldest in Holland, but did include the Amsterdamse Poort which is omitted from most books. The Amsterdamse Poort is the only remaining piece of the 14th century city walls. As you stand inside this miniature fortress you can just picture the city's defenders shooting their arrows through the slits.

DK's selection of hotels and restaurants is set aside in a section at the end of each chapter. The selection is not very large. It is geared to business travelers, certainly not to budget travelers.

THE HOI POLLOI

There are hundreds if not thousands of other guide books available. Spend a few hours at a good bookstore or at your library thumbing, reading, and comparing before you buy. In fact, you might borrow several older editions from your library to get a feel for the coverage before buying a current edition.

Some of these books were written by people who obviously did not go to the places they write about. Most readers won't know that until they get to Europe with a book of errors and bull. Examples of many uh-ohs are described below. Also, the same few restaurants and hotels show up in several of the more popular books. In general these are the hotels to avoid. But since they are recommended, many travelers suffer anxiety trying to get one of these cheap sleeps, not realizing that no book lists but a small fraction of the hotels in any city.

How do you know which author or publisher to trust? That's a good question. It's a fact that many travel writers are provided with free meals and rooms in exchange for whatever good words the writer can give them in print. The writers never reveal this. Michelin, Lonely Planet, and a few other publishers are known for sending out anonymous researchers. They actually pay for their dinners and rooms so they have the privilege of speaking candidly and objectively. Me too. Here goes.

Look for offices like this one in Sintra, Portugal to pick up full color maps, guide booklets, and calendars of events, along with hotel and restaurant information. This is where you get the best information, and the free information! [1014]

Frommer's

People usually associate travel guide book with Frommer's *Europe on $5 a Day*, now up to $70 a Day.

There are some problems with this book. The 2000 edition of Frommer's *Europe From $60 a Day* stated "Haarlem is only an hour away from Amsterdam by train, and one leaves every hour from Centraal Station." By 2002 Frommer's *Europe From $70 a Day* had reduced the time to 20 minutes, but still had only one train per hour. Another Frommer's *Europe 2002* book says that there is a train every half hour. What's going on? Actually there are six trains an hour from A'dam to Haarlem, taking from 15 to 18 minutes each. Did the writers really go to Haarlem? Look back at Frommer's *Europe on $20 a Day* published in 1982. This one says that the train from Amsterdam to Haarlem leaves "every 15 minutes" and takes "15 minutes for the trip." That is much closer to the facts of 2002 than either of the current books. Those were the days when the cover said "by Arthur Frommer."

Another issue with this book is the disingenuous title. On the second page the editor says that the price on the cover is for *"accommodation and meals only"* (emphasis Frommer's). When you add in the cost of a trans-Atlantic ticket and a rail pass or rental car the $70 goes way up. Besides transportation, you still have to pay for entrance fees, postcards, film, afternoon espresso, evening beverages, and 30 or so other items (see chapter 2 of *How To Europe*, "On Budget in Europe; Travel Expenses.") When you add it all up your cost will be at least double the figure on the cover. Frommer's would have been better off to keep the original title of *Europe on $5 a Day* as a trademark. Then we would just recognize it as a budget guide book, and the mamma of them all.

Europe on $20 a Day was getting very stale as far back as the early 1980s. I regularly used it in the mid-1970s but by 1982 or so the updating was falling way behind. Frommer's still puts a new date on the cover every year and boasts about the improvements. Hard to find those improvements, but the errors sure do pop up. One of the most experienced travel book publishers in the business should be able to get it right after all these years. If you use this book, or one of the other popular budget books, be aware that thousands of other travelers are using the same book, and trying to get a room in the same cheap hotels. Good luck.

Let's Go

This is the Harvard students' project. It looks like they hired the sophomores for the 2000 edition of *Let's Go Europe*. It says "The Netherlands is 6hr. ahead of Greenwich Mean Time." I don't know their definition of "ahead" but here's a secret for you Harvard student writers — at high noon GMT it's 13:00 (that's 1:00 pm) in Holland, except during "summer time" when it is 14:00 in Holland at noon GMT. Harvard students have fixed the error in 2002 by omitting any mention of the time zone in Holland.

Haarlem is covered in a page, recommending the Carillon hotel but no eateries. You can pretty much ignore these books so I won't waste more space on them, and don't waste your money and good times. Get a better book from among those mentioned above.

The maps are an exception. Inside the front and back covers, *Let's Go Europe* has great color maps of many major cities and metro systems. It is one of the best collections of maps I have seen in any guide book. Buy a used edition and tear out the maps for your trip. One of the Paris maps even shows the petite street I lived on, the 100 yard long rue de Trois Portes.

Steves

The *Best of Europe 2002* by Rick Steves has no mention of Greece, Portugal, Norway, Sweden, Finland, Hungary, Czech Republik, or a score of other countries. There are about four dozen countries in Europe but Steves mentions only 12. Duh?

He leaves out many significant cities in the countries he pretends to cover. For example, his 35 page section on Holland includes 8 pages on Haarlem but only half a page on The Hague, 4 lines on Rotterdam, and nothing at all on Maastricht or Utrecht. Buyers of Steves' book are likely to be disappointed by these omissions and many others. This is certainly a skewed selection of the "best," even if Haarlem is a great town, and my home town in Europe. He left Rotterdam out of his 2003 book, but that's OK.

The book starts with Vienna. The next chapter is Bruges, his only mention of Belgium. How about Brussels and Antwerp? They must have failed Steves' "best" test, or he hasn't been there. Either way he has left out two of the best.

Hotel and restaurant selections are basically the same as those in most of the other hoi polloi guides. Unless you want to bump into plenty of Americans and/or fully booked hotels avoid these places. I stayed at the Carillon years ago and found it remarkably seedy by Dutch standards. Steves recommends the Carillon though he does say that many of the rooms are "well-worn." I made a quick re-visit in January 2003. The rooms are clean but aged, and they are pricey at about $60 for a single with plumbing. This is the minimum you can expect to pay in Haarlem for a hotel. Others in this price range include the Amadeus ("smoking cannibis is not permitted in the rooms due to fire regulations" per a sign in the stairwell), Raeckse, and Joops.

Steves includes a full page map of Haarlem. It is rubbish. However, new in the 2003 edition are 16 pages of good color maps of Europe.

Much of Steves' Amsterdam and Haarlem 2002 material is simply reworded from his 1999 book. The limited information on the rest of the country is copied 95% from another of his books, three years old. Steves says that he spends 100 days a year in Europe and that his book is therefore the most up to date available. Laugh, unless you already paid for this paste-up. He probably spends most of those 100 days leading his sheep on three week packaged bus tours. How's that for a guy who preaches independent travel.

Steves mentions the "Lover's Train" service between Amsterdam and Haarlem in his 2002 book and says it is "a misnamed private train that runs hrly." His 2003 book has exactly the same line in it. Actually he misnamed it himself and it hasn't run in this century. The real name was "Lovers Rail." Service stopped in September 1999. Steves' 1999 book did not mention the "Lovers Rail" even though it had been in operation since 1996. The train came and went before he knew it. He did get it right with the regular train — 6 per hour and a 15 minute trip.

In his introduction to *Best of Europe 2002*, Steves says that most publishers update their guidebooks only every two to three years. Then he crows "my research partners and I update it in person every year." That is horse droppings as you can see from the foregoing. He goes on — "If you're packing an old book, you'll learn the seriousness of your mistake .. in Europe." Oops, if you're packing a Rick Steves book you have already learned the seriousness of your mistake by the foregoing, and I could go on but this is far enough. Do yourself a favor and forget Rick Steves.

Rough Guides

The *Rough Guide to Europe* 2002 edition reports that there are four trains per hour from Amsterdam to Haarlem. Haven't these travel writers been there? The hotel, eating, and drinking establishments are pretty much the same as the other budget books. There is no map for Haarlem. The Amsterdam map is OK for a general layout but using it to find anything would be a challenge. The rest of their material on Holland, and more, can be found in one of the better books.

Cadogan

The Cadogan series includes about 50 guides to countries, regions, and major cities in Europe. This brief review is focused on the Holland book, 2000.

The author includes a section on Haarlem but it appears that he didn't spend much time in the city. He says that most visitors to Haarlem stay in Amsterdam or Zandvoort, and then he lists two hotels in Haarlem. These, including the aforementioned Carillon, are the most frequently mentioned in every other guide. The author selects only a few restaurants and cafés, but these are some of the better ones. There is no map for Haarlem. The map of Amsterdam is difficult to follow.

The author has dug up some historical footnotes which make for interesting reading. But there are better, and worse, guides to Holland.

Dummies

Well, this book can't get it right about the train schedule between Amsterdam and Haarlem either. "Every half hour or so a train makes the 20-minute jaunt from Amsterdam," says *Europe for Dummies* 1st Edition. They got that dummies part of it right. One new but not especially popular café is listed. The Carillon is the only hotel mentioned. If nearly every book is recommending the same old hotel do you think you are going to find a room available? If you did would you want to stay in the same place as every Californian, New Yorker, and Texan who went to Europe this summer? This is a book you wouldn't want to be seen with.

Summing It Up for the Hoi Polloi

It is obvious that many travel books have some utterly inexcusable errors. This is really disconcerting. If you are buying a guide book to plan your dream trip to Europe you expect the book to be accurate — especially with the rudimentary information that any fool can read from a poster in a train station. If the book is wrong you are better off with no book.

GUIDES FOR DRIVERS

AA Motoring in Europe

Someone about to begin an automobile vacation should begin by reading the AA *Motoring In Europe* book. This is published by the Automobile Association, Hampshire, England, the equivalent of our AAA. Of course, British drive on the wrong side of the road so what do they know about driving in Europe? Plenty.

Chapter 18 of *How To Europe*

If you can't get the AA book make sure to read chapter 18 of *How To Europe*, "On the Roads of Europe; Travel by Car, Van, or Motorcycle." Photos of many of the road signs are there. The all important Do Not Enter sign is illustrated in chapter 1, also. Know your European road signs or you may loose your life. American road signs are not used in Europe, except for occasional sightings of our red octagon.

MAPS

Before buying maps, look at several. Make sure that the information is presented clearly. Make sure you can read the title block. And make sure it is relatively new.

Map Scales

European maps rarely have a distance bar in the legend. Instead, the scale is stated on the cover as 1:10,000 for city maps, for instance, and maybe 1:500,000 for country maps. Here is the metric system put to good use. Simply multiply a distance measured on the map by the scale factor to find the actual distance. On a map with a scale of 1:100,000, one centimeter on the map is one kilometer on the ground. Here's how you figure that:

There are 100 centimeters per meter, expressed as 100 cm/m. If this is hard to remember, picture the fact that there are 100 cents in a dollar.

Multiply the one centimeter by the scale factor 100,000 to get 100,000 centimeters.

Divide the 100,000 centimeters by 100 cm/m and you get 1,000 meters.

1,000 meters is one kilometer, abbreviated as 1 km. Bingo.

If that's too much math for you, use the approximations in the following table:

Map Scale	Meters per Centimeter	Miles per Inch	Typical Map on which you find this scale
1:10,000	100	0.16	City Map
1:20,000	200	0.3	City Map
1:100,000	1,000 meters, = 1 kilometer	1.6	Regional or Country Map
1:500,000	5 km	8	Country Map
1:10,000,000	100 km	160	Map of Europe

This table begs you to bring a small tape measure as recommended in chapter 6. If you didn't pack it, use your finger. The first digit on your forefinger is approximately one inch, which equals 2½ centimeters.

COUNTRY MAPS

Michelin

Michelin publishes a large map of Europe, individual country maps, regional maps, and some city maps. These are among the finest maps available for travel in Europe. Roads, rails, and ship lines are indicated. Interesting sights and particular cities are highlighted. Some detailed regional maps, e.g. the yellow maps, have a scale of 1:200,000, about 3 miles to the inch. These show every farmhouse and ditch, plus train stations, boulevards, and through routes in the major cities.

National Geographic

For the big picture in a small format, a great map for making travel plans is the *National Geographic* map "Europe." *National Geographic Magazine* publishes beautiful maps which are included in the magazine pretty regularly. Every few years or so they include an updated map of Europe. The reverse side contains a wealth of information, which might include population and language maps, a satellite image, and other information. Those editions of *National Geographic* which contain maps indicate that fact on the spine with the name of the country or region in red. Garage sales and used book sales in your home town usually include hundreds of old copies of *National Geographic* so shopping is easy and cheap. Make sure that the magazine still has the map before you pay 10¢ for it. Also be on the lookout for maps of Italy, Spain, and other countries in old editions of *National Geographic*.

European Map Makers

Besides Michelin, prominent map makers in Europe are Mair, Kümmerly+Frey, Hallwag, and Falk. Except through specialized travel book stores, these maps are not very easily obtained in the USA. Look in the TRAVELERS YELLOW PAGES category Guidebooks on the *www.enjoy-europe.com* web site for sources.

Falk Plans have a variable distance scale showing the center of cities larger than the fringes. Some Falk Plans have a special cut and fold which makes them difficult to use when crossing the cut. But they fit in your pocket and are very handy.

Official National Tourist Offices

Pretty decent maps are given away free by many of the official European government tourist offices in the USA. Look in the TRAVELERS YELLOW PAGES section of *www.enjoy-europe.com* for direct URL links to several dozen of these offices.

The Auto Club

The AAA *Planning Map Of Europe* has seriously deteriorated over the years. Editions published years ago showed traffic signs, including the all-important "Do Not Enter" sign. I can't imagine why they would erase such critical information. Parts of this map are so cluttered that it is nearly worthless. AAA should trash it and start over.

CITY MAPS

Heavy Duty City Maps

City maps published in Europe are bulky. They often include a small booklet with a street index and addresses for police, hospitals, museums, libraries, theaters, camping places, and other public sites. All of this is in the local language and often in two to six additional languages. In some cases it's almost as if they have drawn a map and then written a city guide book around it.

There's Santa Claus getting his bearings at Sindagma Square in Athens. The Greeks make it easy for us foreigners to get around town and out of town. Each sign is in the Greek and in the Latin alphabet or in English, except the sign to Thesaloniki (also spelled Thessaloniki) and Patra (also spelled Patras). But it's a good idea to learn some of that Greek alphabet before you get too far from Athens. [1010]

Maps from City Tourist Offices

"Official" maps issued by city tourist offices are not quite so comprehensive as the ones you can buy in the stores, but they are easier to stuff in your pocket. Many of these maps list and locate hotels, museums, and other establishments of interest to the traveler. Another nice feature is that they are usually free, or at most only a fraction of the cost of the name brand maps.

It is better to request city tourist information by mail or via internet web sites prior to going over. Do this a couple of months prior to departure by writing to the tourist office of the city you plan to visit. The information is free and you will have time to study it before arriving in the city. Internet addresses for many city and regional tourist offices are given in the TRAVELERS YELLOW PAGES of *www.enjoy-europe.com.*

City Public Transit Maps

If the city tourist office levies a charge for their map and you want a freebee, go to a bus or metro station and request a route map. These maps are even less detailed, but may be all that you need, especially if you are using the public transports to get around town. You are doing that, aren't you?

City Map Challenges

Using maps in Europe isn't exactly like it is at home. When looking for a street address, have patience. Here are some examples.

In some French cities the buildings are numbered, but not all store fronts get a different number. One building may occupy a whole block and each store will have the same street address.

In Amsterdam, there is just no correspondence between the addresses on opposite sides of the canals. If you are looking for an odd numbered address, you'd better be on the odd numbered side of the canal.

In Geneva I found odd and even numbers on the same side of the street.

In map street indexes in Germany, remember the interchangeability of umlaut *ä, ö,* and *ü* with *ae, oe,* and *ue,* respectively. The street index may put *ärk* in front of *ajax,* and then again, it might not. The same problem may exist in Austria and Switzerland. There are alphabet aberrations in other European countries, as well. See chapter 26, "Languages, Numbers, Alphabets" for more on this.

When looking for a street in Greece, you'll be confronted by the dual alphabet problem. The city maps I could find only had the Latin alphabet. This is no problem in Athens where the street signs are in both alphabets. But outside Athens, usually only the Greek alphabet is to be found on the street and road signs.

The maps I found in Kiev, Ukraine show the street names and public places using the western alphabet. The street signs are only in Cyrillic - so good luck finding anything.

TRANSLATING BOOKS

There are two generic types of translating books to help us through the foreign languages of Europe. You can use the small phrase books specifically designed for travelers. And/or you can use a paperback pocket-size two language dictionary. I like to carry one of each. The phrase books sometimes include a dictionary, though it is barely adequate. A real dictionary is much better.

Challenge your food translation book to get you through this typical matsedel (menu) in Stockholm. [1012]

Berlitz

Reading menus will be your most frequent need for a translating helper. My favorites are the pocket size books published by Berlitz. Most of the languages of Europe are covered in this series of books. The books include many common phrases, but also contain a great deal of other information. For example the Berlitz *Swedish for Travelers* includes phrases for greetings, directions, menus, shopping, and other situations. It also includes the common road signs, essential for driving in Europe. An oversight in the Berlitz publications is that the pronunciation guide is given for the British accent and not for the American. But you can survive with it. Simply point to the phrase in the book if all else fails.

Berlitz publishes titles for the individual languages of western Europe, plus their *Eastern European Phrase Book*. A typical title is the Berlitz *French Phrase Book and Dictionary*. Put Berlitz in your pocket unless you know the local language.

Barron's

Barron's Educational Series publishes excellent phrase books for many languages. Typical titles are *French at a Glance* and *German at a Glance*. Because they are published in the USA the pronunciation guide is closer to the American accent. These books also include a tremendous amount of basic information and a mini dictionary as do the Berlitz books, plus a few maps.

Dictionaries

Except in England and Ireland you will probably need some form of translating dictionary. A good reason to carry a Foreign/English & English/Foreign dictionary is that you will often get into conversations with foreigners who are nearly fluent but don't know the English word for, say, smuggler. The dictionary helps to keep the conversation going. If you are out shopping it's also handy.

But if you are on one of those tours where you are stuffed into a bus with 20 or 50 other bovine Americans you'll never talk to a European so you won't need a dictionary. Pity, you went to Europe to look through a bus window.

Dictionaries for a few popular languages are available in the USA. If you are going to Italy, France, Germany, Austria, or Switzerland you should have little trouble in finding a pocket dictionary in a large bookstore at home. For other languages you will probably need to go on line and order a book by mail. Check the TRAVELERS YELLOW PAGES section of *www.enjoy-europe.com* and go to the category Guidebooks for sources of dictionaries and phrase books.

Irregular Verbs and Sexual Nouns

Pocket-size translating dictionaries are very helpful. However many words on signs and posters are not in these books. Conjugated forms of verbs are usually not included, and the most common verbs are the most irregular, giving no hint to the root. English is similar, e.g., the verb *to be* becomes *am, are, is, were, was* and others depending on case, number, and tense.

Nouns are generally easy to find, though not always easy to use. Many foreign languages assign a gender to each noun, masculine or feminine, and some use neuter. French, Dutch, and some other languages use special feminine endings to denote female persons. Adjectives may have different endings depending on gender, number, and on the function of the noun. In the extreme case, German has 16 versions of the simple pronoun *the*, starting with *der, die, das* for subject singular masculine, feminine, neuter, and *die* for all subject plurals. Not all forms are unique. It can get confusing, mighty confusing.

Greek

Greek dictionaries present a couple of problems for the user that you won't appreciate until you try to use the things. The Greek, as opposed to the Latin, alphabet is used in all of them of course. All entries are in lower case letters. Most signs in Greece are in upper case letters, which are something else again. Then you have to know the order of the alphabet in order to find a word in there. Would you expect *z* to come before *i* in a dictionary?

Fortunately, learning the phonic Greek alphabet is not especially difficult, and pronunciation is feasible after that. Double fortunately, so many people in Athens speak English that you don't have to worry about any of this. But outside Athens you can find as many people who speak English as you would find speaking Greek in Kansas.

Cyrillic

Turn it up a notch in the Ukraine and Bulgaria — talk about alphabets! These folks have a couple that are similar to Greek, but different. The Bulgarian alphabet was invented by a couple of monks, Saints Cyril and Methodius, who are consequently national heroes. Bulgaria is probably the only country which so honors its cryptographers.

Much more on the subject of alphabets can be found later in chapter 26, "Languages, Numbers, Alphabets; Encounter the Tower of Babel in Europe."

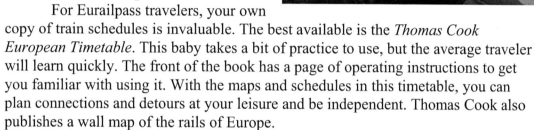

If you forgot to bring your Thomas Cook European Timetable use one of these touch screen terminals to locate your train in Milano, Italy. Service is available in six languages. [1008]

RAILROAD SCHEDULES

Rail travelers will find a schedule of all arrivals and departures posted at each station. This is OK as far as it goes, but most travelers need more.

Thomas Cook European Timetable

For Eurailpass travelers, your own copy of train schedules is invaluable. The best available is the *Thomas Cook European Timetable*. This baby takes a bit of practice to use, but the average traveler will learn quickly. The front of the book has a page of operating instructions to get you familiar with using it. With the maps and schedules in this timetable, you can plan connections and detours at your leisure and be independent. Thomas Cook also publishes a wall map of the rails of Europe.

The *Thomas Cook European Timetable* eliminates the need to wait in line for a bureaucrat at a train station to get you on the right train, which they don't always do very effectively. Sometimes the office is not open when you need it. If you are planning tight connections, ask the conductor on board for advice long before your train arrives. They are always very helpful and more accurate than the train station information offices.

Another advantage of carrying the *Thomas Cook European Timetable* is that pulling it out of your bag usually finds you with new friends wanting to take a look at the schedule or asking about the next train to Dijon.

Train numbers shown in the Timetable are not always the same as the official train number, so don't use these numbers to get you on the right train. Use destination and departure time as a guide and always check the information on the departure platform. Platforms for scheduled trains can be changed at the last minute if a train is running behind schedule.

Do not fail to study the legend in the front of the *Thomas Cook European Timetable* and the small print notes following each schedule. These notes are keyed to symbols at the top of each column.

There is a city index in the front of the book, along with city graphics showing the locations of the various train stations in those cities with more than one station or dock, and a wealth of other information. The *Thomas Cook European Timetable* is published monthly but the only major difference in train service is between summer and the rest of the year. More trains are available in the summer.

Eurail Timetable

A timetable definitely worth getting (it's free to those who purchase a *Eurailpass*) is the *Eurail Timetable*. This synoptic map codes the major cities in Europe and then presents timetables from each city to a number of other major cities. It is very easy to use and makes a handy supplement to the *Thomas Cook European Timetable*, which is not so easy to use because it is so complete. Pick up the *Eurail Timetable* at any Eurail Aid Office in Europe. These offices are indicated on the Eurail Map which comes with your Eurailpass.

Every station in The Netherlands has back lighted maps of the country, accompanied by departure schedules of all trains for the station you are in. How can you get lost? [1017]

National Railroad Timetables

All of the national railroads of Europe publish timetables of various sorts. Some are tables showing all the trains between two cities, as in the French *Horaire* which can be picked up at train stations at no cost. Notes regarding fare supplements, days when the train does not run, and other special conditions are in French, and you'd better read those notes.

At stations in Holland, you can pick up a small booklet called *Intercity: Belangrijkste Treinverbindingen in Nederland* (Important Train Connections in The Netherlands). Notes are in Dutch, and you'd better read those notes. A complete schedule of all Dutch trains can be purchased at many stations for a nominal cost. Explanation of the symbols is in English, but those dangerous footnotes are in Dutch.

The *DB* (German Rail) publishes a booklet titled *Städteverbindungen* (City Connections) showing timetables for selected major city routes. On named trains in Germany the conductor passes out a guide to the train named *Ihr Zug-Begleiter* (Your Train Guide). This shows arrival and departure times and trains connecting from each stop. The symbol translation table is in German and in English.

There is plenty of other literature put out by the various national railroads of Europe showing schedules, routes, and special deals. All of it is in the local language.

So unless you can read it you will not know that a train might only run on weekdays, on Friday only goes halfway, and on Tuesday and Thursday it starts an hour earlier.

Chapter 17 of *How To Europe*

There is much more about trains in chapter 17 of *How To Europe*, "Riding the Rails and Waves." Over the years I've traveled the rails from the north of Norway to southern Portugal and to the eastern end of the Ukraine. It's the best way to go.

PERIODICALS

National Geographic Traveler

The *National Geographic* has arguably the best travel photography published and has an article on a European destination in virtually every issue. It's companion, the *National Geographic Traveler*, is also extremely valuable for travel planning. There is usually one article on Europe in every issue, supplemented with sidebars providing information on travel arrangements and sources for further information.

Condé Nast Traveler

Condé Nast Traveler is probably the best of the travel magazines available at most magazine racks. It's a monthly and regularly features articles on Europe. It also has very good information on general travel topics, e.g. credit cards, jet lag, and other news bits.

Transitions Abroad

Another of my favorites is *Transitions Abroad*, a bimonthly targeting the university oriented audience with extensive information on study abroad programs, working overseas, and general travel information.

International Travel News

Saving the best for nearly last, the *International Travel News* is unquestionably the one journal every traveler should read. The *ITN* is a monthly and features extensive letters, articles, and photos by the readers, probably the most traveled group of any journal's readership in the world. You'll get more first-hand, inside, and upright information about every place on the planet than you'll find anyplace else on the planet.

Weekend Travel Sections in Major Newspapers

Major metropolitan newspapers feature a large travel section every Sunday. You usually see a full color picture of a tropical beach on page one. Inside there is usually one article on a European destination, along with scores of adverts for airfares, package deals, hotels, and other travel services. The best deals are in the smallest advertisements.

AUTHORS NOT TO MISS

Georgia Hesse and Ed Buryn

There are very few books by people who have traveled and who know how to write about it. Two that stand out are: *Going My Way*, by Georgia Hesse (1975, Chronicle Books, San Francisco), and *Vagabonding In Europe And North Africa*, by Ed Buryn (1971, 1973, The Bookworks, Berkeley). What these books have in common and what most books do not have is personal experience, straightforward presentation, and a wealth of information in a small volume. While I take issue with a few points in each book, I strongly recommend both to every traveler. These are certainly out of print. You can search used book stores or the web for an old copy. It will be effort well spent.

Ernest Hemingway and Peter Mayle

These are two of my favorite authors because of the way they write and what they write about. *A Moveable Feast* by Ernest Hemingway recounts some of his life in Paris decades ago. *A Year in Provence* by Peter Mayle describes his life in the south of France. These are two first hand accounts of living in Europe that will entertain and enlighten every traveler. Both authors have a number of other books of interest to those who love faraway places and peoples.

TYPICAL SOURCES

Bookstores, libraries, tourist offices, commercial travel businesses, and our own federal government all provide information of value to travelers. Much of the best and most important information is absolutely free.

Bookstores

Regular bookstores in your home town usually have a section with this year's selection of travel guides. Certain publishers seem to hog much of the shelf space. In my town, the local outlet of a national chain has reduced its inventory to only four publishers of Europe guide books. The regional manager told me that these are the best sellers and corporate headquarters has scratched the others off the list. Unfortunately, the best guide books were among those scratched off and the hoi polloi is about all that is offered. Hype sells.

Travel books are sorted alphabetically by country or by continent or by whatever, depending on the store manager. A few Michelin books are often placed on a nearby rack, if they are stocked at all. There is sometimes a haphazard assemblage of foreign maps in the vicinity of the travel books. The foreign language dictionaries and phrase books are usually in the reference section of the store. Rail timetables are nowhere to be found.

Used Guide Books

Notre Dame Cathedral in Paris hasn't moved for 800 years and the Coliseum has been parked at the same place in Rome for 2000. No additional monuments have been discovered in decades. Why do you need a new guidebook with this year's date on the cover? You don't. These "updated" guidebooks are usually reprints of old material in a new cover. The new cover date is simply for selling more books, the primary goal of the travel guidebook industry. The most popular books are the most prone to this scam.

Used books are sold at used book stores, on-line with specialists like Alibris, on-line with Amazon.com and others, at garage sales, church rummage sales, library used book sales, Salvation Army stores, AAUW used book sales, and other events.

Travel Book Specialists

There are a few bookstores which specialize in information and supplies for travelers. The current editions of Michelin, Berlitz, AA publications, and European maps, may be ordered from a number of mail order travel bookstores. These stores also carry many other guidebooks. Amazon.com also has a huge selection for travelers.

European publishers often have their own, and exclusive, retail outlets. Baedeker, a famous name in travel guides, has this store in Essen, Germany. [1002]

European Book Stores

Bookstores in Europe are convenient sources for dictionaries, maps, and for other locally published guides to hotels and restaurants. European department stores usually have a large, well stocked travel bookstore. When traveling light, you might consider packing only the literature for the first country on your itinerary. On entering a country, buy a pocket translating dictionary and anything else that you couldn't get for free from the city tourist office. Now and then, as the load on your back increases, mail home the materials you don't need any longer. See chapter 24, "Shipping Your Treasures Home" for intelligence on using the post offices in Europe.

Thomas Cook European Timetable
        This monthly schedule of the trains throughout Europe is published in
England and is not easily purchased in the USA. I recently ordered my copy direct
through the Thomas Cook Publications web site. It was delivered in less than two
weeks at a cost, including postage, less than the American price. The American
distributor never responded to an email.
        Once over there, Thomas Cook and Wagon-Lits offices in France, Germany,
and England are good sources for the Timetable. I bought a current copy in Paris for
half of the United States list price. I've also bought it in Frankfurt at the Wagon-Lits
office and also ordered it direct from the publisher when I lived in Geneva.

PUBLIC LIBRARY

        A good public library will have most of the popular travel guidebooks, though
they will probably be two to ten years old. No matter.

914 in the Dewey Decimal System
        Books on Europe are in classification 914 and up of the Dewey Decimal
System. Check them out and make notes on subjects of interest. For instance, if you
want to visit all the ship museums, or wine festivals, or war memorials, research the
literature and compose your personal guidebook. Save yourself $20 or $50 and
benefit from using a half dozen guides rather than one.

Reference
        In addition to guidebooks, you will find dozens of other books and references
to Europe and specific countries. Start with the encyclopedias, and then go to the
book and magazine shelves and reference files. Look for history books, geography,
art, and other specific subjects. Personal travelogues in dusty covers can be
fascinating and informative.

Language Training
        Language tapes, videos, and texts are also available in most libraries. If you
don't know any French, Spanish, or Russian before you head for their countries, some
ear acclimatization beforehand would be a good part of your preparation. Also, have a
good look at chapter 26, "Languages, Numbers, Alphabets; Encounter The Tower of
Babel in Europe" for much more about languages.

Telephone Books
        Major libraries also have telephone books for countries of Europe. These
might help you locate a hotel or restaurant that one of your friends has told you about.
However, using European phone books is not easy. They're all so different that I
won't go into this in detail.

Foreign Newspapers

Libraries, especially university libraries, also carry major foreign newspapers. These can help you brush up on your French or German, tell you what's on stage in London this week, or give you some idea of the price of used cars and apartment rental rates. The daily newspapers of many large cities can also be found on the web, along with their classified advertisements.

TOURIST OFFICES

Do not confuse travel agencies with tourist offices. Your home town telephone directory lists travel agencies. Their business is selling tickets for air travel and package tours. For good personal service, instead of telephone menus and/or internet radio buttons, see your travel agent. They have some great brochures, also.

Tourist offices are something else.

Official National Tourist Offices

Official tourist offices are maintained in the United States by each European country to provide information to prospective tourists. Most countries have offices in New York City with additional offices in other major American cities.

Write or phone and request hotel lists, sightseeing information, and maps. Replies will be forthcoming in days to weeks. The information is free. All you have to do is ask for it. Most of the information is surprisingly objective in describing the country and various customs, but do not expect every day of your journey to be filled with the clear, sunny skies that you see in the photos.

Most countries also have a web site where you can get voluminous information. For a full list of current URLs see the category "Official National Tourist Offices" in the TRAVELERS YELLOW PAGES section of *www.enjoy-europe.com*.

Many countries maintain tourist offices in other European capital cities. I was able to get hotel lists, maps, and tourist information on Ireland in Paris, on Italy, Portugal, and France in Madrid, on Germany in Amsterdam, etc. Finding these offices is not always easy because the local name of each country is usually not the American version; e.g. Holland is *Pays-Bas* in French. Check your foreign language dictionary. Some or all of the literature will be in languages other than ours, but the city maps and hotel lists are easy to follow.

The Small Print

The most important information provided by these tourist offices is generally set aside in several pages of small print in the back of the full color brochures. These sections discuss important items of legal and cultural concern to visitors, particular to each country. Typical subjects are: passports, visas, entry requirements, customs duties, currency, driving laws, alcoholic beverage laws, shopping, taxes, holidays, tipping, weather, banks, and addresses for further information.

Major French cities post maps like this in busy areas. This is Marseille, birthplace of bouillabaisse. Find a restaurant in the Vieux Port (Old Port) area and sit down to enjoy a fine bowl of this fish soup.
[1007]

City Tourist Offices

Almost every city in Europe has a city tourist office. These offices provide maps, hotel lists, and calendars of events. This information is free, though there is sometimes a nominal charge for maps, and always a charge for t-shirts and other "Yeah, I've been there stuff." City tourist offices are normally located in or near the main train station, airport, the town square, or on a major boulevard. City tourist offices are also very helpful when you have a misunderstanding with your hotel. The tourist office can act as translator and help you get the problem straightened out or find you another hotel.

When picking up maps and guides in the city tourist offices, get the English version and the local language version. The reason for this is that the English version will usually have an English translation of the names of buildings and sights (e.g. "Weigh House"), but the buildings and sights themselves have only the local language name on the front door (e.g. *Waag* in Holland). With both maps you can figure out what is what. Some guide maps are in six languages in which case you don't have to get two of them.

Prior to going, you can also write directly to the city tourist office of the cities you plan to visit, advise them that you plan on a holiday there in a month or so, and request a map, a hotel list, and sightseeing information. Most cities will send you a two pound packet of full color brochures. Though "tourist office" usually goes under local language names, e.g. *Verkersamt* in Germany, addressing your letter simply to "Tourist Bureau" will probably land your letter in the right place.

COMMERCIAL TRAVEL BUSINESSES

Railroads, hotels, and other businesses sometimes provide gratis information to help you travel.

Railroads

The railroads are to Europe what the airlines are to the United States. Most of them promote vacation packages including accommodations and supplemental transportation. Brochures describing these packages include information helpful to the free-lance traveler. You can also obtain schedules of major routes and connections from the railroad information offices for point to point travel. This service is usually free, though most railroads charge a fee for their printed schedules.

Buses

Metropolitan rail and bus lines issue free route plans and city maps. Pick them up at bus depots, main train stations, or at city tourist offices. The bus route maps can be particularly helpful because bus stops usually have a sign board showing the route numbers and maps for the routes which stop there. If you get lost, the route map and any nearby bus stop should get you found.

Hotels

First class hotels in major cities usually have booklets with city maps, calendars of events, restaurant lists, etc. A typical title is *This Week In Stockholm*. These booklets are freely available in the better hotels. Even if you're not staying there, just go in and browse the registration counter and the brochure rack in the lobby.

There are a number of better quality hotel groups in Europe that are composed of independently owned and/or chain-managed hotels. Examples are Golden Tulip, Etap, and Ibis. To obtain a free directory, ask the national tourist office when you write for information.

In Holland, VVV stands for a six-mile long word that means Tourist Information Office. This one is at the train station in Haarlem, The Netherlands. For more information about Haarlem see chapter 30, "Melding With Europe" and chapter 1, "What's It All About?" Haarlem is my home town in Europe. [1011]

European Department Stores

Even department stores can provide tourists with helpful maps and information. In Paris, the Galeries Lafayette provides a good street map and plan of the *Metro* on the back side of its perfume advertising flyer. The Stockmann department store in Helsinki has an excellent free city map and four language guide on the back of their advertising flyer. Look for others as you travel and shop through Europe.

UNCLE SAMMY

The Federal Government publishes a number of pamphlets of value to travelers. These are primarily concerned with what you are allowed to bring back into the country, but also concern your health and safety while overseas. One of these,

Know Before You Go, is a must read — before packing your bags. Request it from:
Department of the Treasury
U.S. Customs Service
Washington, D.C. 20229

THE WORLD WIDE WEB, WWW

The WWW is now the information source of choice for many people. There are thousands of web sites dedicated to travel in Europe, to individual countries, and to individual cities. *http://www.enjoy-europe.com* is the URL address of my site.

Search Engines

The easiest way to locate information is to use a search engine such as Google.com, Overture.com, Yahoo.com, or any of dozens more. Type a word or set of words into the little box and hit your return key. *Voilà!* -- you'll have hundreds, maybe hundreds of thousands, of hits.

The problem is that you'll probably get too many hits unless you narrow your search to a set of key words. For example, try something like *Europe travel independent* if you're looking for sources of information on independent travel in Europe. Typing just *travel Europe* will give you three million hits.

Notice that some search engines charge a fee for listings. You are less likely to get a representative or valid listing of sites. You will get a listing of those companies which chose to pay the search engine for a top ranking under certain keywords. Other search engines charge the linked web site a fixed amount for every click through. This is indicated by a figure such as $.05 next to the listing. You don't pay the search engine, but the site does when you click it. These sites are listed first in the search results, with the highest paying site listed at the top as you'll see.

TRAVELERS YELLOW PAGES

In an attempt to bring you the information you need without wading through those pages and pages on your screen, my *TRAVELERS YELLOW PAGES* has links to dozens of pages with information directly pertinent to travel in Europe. For example, the airline category includes direct links to the airlines flying to Europe. Other categories currently on site include discount travel, auto rental, official national tourist offices, city and regional tourist offices, and much more. The eclectic sites and personal web pages give you some unique perspectives on Europe. The guidebooks page links you to sources of books and maps for your travels.

Another section of the *www.enjoy-europe.com* home page is titled "Maps." Here you will find a link to Michelin, an excellent site for maps of Europe.

Chapter 11
Electricity in Europe
Travel Voltage Fundamentals

Don't blow their fuses.

THE DIFFERENCE

Converting European electricity so that it can be used in your American appliances is a major nuisance for travelers.

What is Electricity?

Electricity, in the nearly abstract, is a form of energy consisting of a flow of electrons. The flow can be continuous in one direction (direct current, DC), or it can be reversing on a regular period (alternating current, AC).

Electricity is measured in terms of quantity (amperes, amps) and force (voltage, volts). The energy used is power (watts). In DC and single phase AC circuits, power is equal to the product of quantity and force; in other words, volts multiplied by amps is watts.

The quantity (amps) available at any outlet is determined by the size of the wires furnishing it. The fuse or circuit breaker at the source is designed to limit the flow according to the size of the wires. If you try to draw too much power, the fuse blows before the wire gets so hot that it starts a fire.

The Hz you see on electrical appliances indicates the number of times per second that AC current reverses direction. Hz is the abbreviation for Hertz, named after a German physicist.

Electricity in America

In the United States household electricity is supplied by your local power company at 110 or 120 volts and 60 Hz. The quantity available in American homes is generally 15 to 20 amps at a single outlet or for the total of all outlets served by a single fused circuit. Thus, one circuit may provide from 1650 to 2400 watts of power. One circuit usually supplies more than one outlet, and many people put in a doubler plug to use more lights or appliances from a single outlet. This can cause blown fuses or tripped circuit breakers. A circuit breaker is a switch which automatically opens when too much power is being used; opening the switch shuts off the electricity. Instead of fuses, circuit breakers are used in most homes built in the last few decades.

This is the standard European 220 volt electrical outlet. The metal parts at the top and bottom are the ground connections. Most are silent on the matter, but this one in my hotel room in Mariehamn, Finland, says "use is forbidden while bathing and showering." This is in Finnish, but almost everything else on the island of Åland is written in Swedish because the people here only speak Swedish. [1104]

Electricity in Europe

European electricity is supplied at a nominal 220 volts. The official voltage is 230 +/- 10% or so. The frequency is 50 Hz. Some localities have 110 volts, but 50 cycles is the standard frequency regardless of the voltage throughout Europe. The quantity available depends on the hotel or home where you are staying. You might be able to use a 1000 watt hair blower or travel iron. If the lights start to flicker, shut it off immediately. I once blew a fuse in an old French hotel with a 600 watt hair blower.

APPLIANCES

Electrical Hardware

To use American electrical appliances in Europe, some hardware is needed in order to plug in without electrocuting your machine, and maybe yourself. Since the hotel keeper or desk clerk probably knows less about electricity than you do, don't bother asking if you can plug in your appliances — you may scare him. Just make sure to unplug everything after use.

Low Wattage

Small appliances like radios, razors, battery chargers, etc. can normally operate with a 50 watt transformer. This is a heavy little clunk of metal. If your appliance is marked 60 Hz, and not 50/60 Hz, you run the risk of burning up something inside even when using a transformer.

High Power

Heating devices like hair blowers and irons can use the 1000 or 1600 watt "converter." The converter is a small electronic device which can only be used on appliances rated at the same power as the converter.

50/60

Do not bother bringing an electric clock or clock radio to Europe. These devices, which generally operate on AC motors, will run at only 5/6 of the speed for which they were designed because the speed is determined by the electric frequency. If, for instance, you bring your electric alarm clock and set it at 6 pm when you check into the hotel, it will read only 11 pm when it is midnight, and only 4 am when it is 6 am. You will probably miss breakfast.

If your electrical device has a transformer in it, you probably should not bring it to Europe. Lower frequencies require thicker transformers, and transformers designed for 60 Hz operation will overheat and sometimes burn up when used in 50 Hz circuits. Make sure that your stereo receiver is rated for both 50 and 60 cycles before moving it to Europe; we used to have a tape deck which apparently suffered untimely death due to 50 Hz.

Your tape deck and CD player probably also have transformers in them, plus they may suffer from the "clock syndrome" just described. It may be possible to have a dealer change pulleys or gears inside so your music doesn't sound like a drawl. This might look expensive at first, but is probably cheaper than buying a new one in Europe; European prices are about twice ours.

Your electric razor and hair blower will run at a slower speed, but you'll barely notice the difference. Just make sure to use the right device, "transformer" or "converter," or you will soon smell smoke.

TV

Should you be relocating to Europe for an extended period, don't bother bringing a TV. Not only because of the differences in electricity, but because the broadcast signals in Europe are different, an American TV will have a constant roll and static. Radios work fine, provided you transform the voltage. See chapter 22, "Living in Europe," for more information on television.

EXCEPTIONS AND CAUTIONS

110/220

Although European electricity is generally 220 volts, there are a few places where you will find 110 volts. On entering a hotel room, inspect a light bulb; it will be marked with the voltage as at home. Then you know. You can also find the voltage stamped on the back of the radio or TV if your room has one or the other. But there are exceptions. On a recent visit to Stockholm, I found that the hotel room was 220 volts, except for the shaver outlet in the bathroom; it was 110 volts only. It is more common to find both 110 and 220 volts available in bathroom shaver outlets of the better hotels.

Direct Current

DC electricity is produced by batteries. DC is used to power cameras, flashlights, camera flash units, portable radios, portable recorders and CDs, calculators, camcorders, laptop computers, etc.. Each appliance has its own unique requirements for batteries. This is stated in the operating instructions and in the battery housing. Units which operate on a "plug-in adapter" will generally work on that same adapter in Europe if it is equipped with a dual voltage switch (very few are, regrettably), or if it is used with a transformer, and rated for 50 Hz.

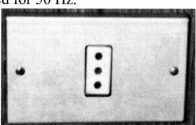

One kind of electrical outlet you might find in Italy is shown here.
[1101]

TRAVELING ELECTRICAL KIT

When bringing electrical appliances to Europe, some or all of the following list must also be carried:

- Plug adapters
- Transformer
- Converter
- Batteries
- Rechargeable batteries
- Battery charger

Plug Adapters

European electrical outlets come in different sizes and shapes. On the Continent, outlets normally require a plug with two round prongs about 0.19 inch in diameter and 0.72 inch apart. Outlets in some older hotels accept a plug with two round holes about 0.15 inch in diameter and 0.72 inch apart. Newer design outlets require a special safety plug, but extenders for the old style can be purchased which will allow you to plug in. The standard safety plug will not fit in the slightly smaller holes of the old hotel outlets; if you run up against that problem, go out to a department store and buy an additional adapter.

The British and Irish use a three prong plug, with two flat prongs in line and one perpendicular.

Newer facilities in Switzerland have another kind of plug. This one has three round prongs in a triangular pattern. You can buy adapters in Switzerland to convert the standard European safety plug to the Swiss outlet. In Eastern Europe it is most likely that you will find the old style European plug.

My recommendation is to buy a Continental plug adapter for each appliance before departure. Carry extras in case they are borrowed or disappear. Plug adapters for the American double flat prongs are virtually impossible to buy in Europe. Or, if you have dual voltage appliances, cut off the American plugs before you go and then install European plugs when you arrive in Europe; I did this for one trip and saved carrying around some extra hardware for a few months.

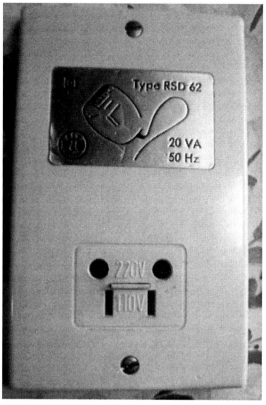

This is a razor outlet as found in many bathrooms in European hotels, though this is a better design than most. With 220 volts at the European round holes and 110 volts at the American outlet, everybody should be able to use this. But it will only deliver 20 VA (equal to 20 watts) so you won't be able to plug in your hair blower. This photo is from my hotel room in Turku (also known as Abo), Finland (also known as Suomi). [1105]

Transformer

A 220/110 volt transformer is a heavy little thing because it is constructed of solid steel plates and copper wire. You will need one if your small appliances are not dual voltage.

Converter

This electronic device reduces 220 volts to 110 volts for use on hair dryers, irons, and other heating devices rated at 1000 watts or more. If your high wattage equipment doesn't have a dual voltage switch, you need one of these converters. It is lighter and smaller than a transformer, and it is not a transformer (see above). If it is used on something like a 400 watt slide projector, the lamp will burn out in a few seconds. I did that.

Batteries

Bring spare batteries for your equipment. If you buy batteries in Europe, do not expect much. Cheap off-brands are widely available, and probably dead on arrival when you get back to your hotel room. Even some Duracell batteries I have bought in Europe were completely dead when I tried to use them a few hours after purchase.

Rechargeable Batteries

Ni-cad rechargeable batteries made by Eveready, General Electric, Panasonic, and others are expensive but pay for themselves in a hurry, especially in Europe.

Battery charger

If you are using rechargeable batteries, you must also carry a charger. These can be bulky since most are designed for a handful of batteries. Shop around for a mini. Check the nameplate input voltage before buying. If it is not a dual voltage model, use a 50 watt transformer to power it in Europe.

Here is electrical hardware for traveling in Europe. The "Archer" brand electrical converter changes 220 volts to 110 volts, only for use on heating appliances rated for the same watts as the converter. Upper left is a 50-watt 220/110 volt transformer for small appliances. On the right, from the bottom up, are two American to European plug adapters, European plug extender, and the British and Irish plug. [1106]

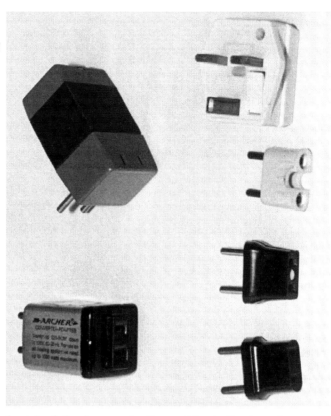

SOURCES

Home Town

Individual plug adapters, transformers, converters, and kits are sold in some department stores (try the wallet section) and by several electrical specialty companies. Radio Shack and similar stores carry these items. Better luggage retailers also carry a selection of electrical devices and other widgets for travelers.

Airports

The duty free shops in international airports carry many electrical appliances. If you didn't have the opportunity to buy what you need before leaving home, browse through the duty free shop before getting on the plane.

In Europe

The American-to-European plug adapters are nearly impossible to find in Europe (reported that it is illegal to sell them in some countries), so you'd better get these before you go. It is possible to buy transformers, but it may be difficult to find a small one suitable for traveling. They are also expensive in Europe. If you really need one, try stores selling hardware, electrical goods, computers, or electronics.

Chapter 12
Photography in Europe
Travel with Your Camera

American and Japanese travelers have at least one thing in common — a camera on a neck strap.

This chapter provides some elementary information on photography, cameras, flash units, and other accessories, and on taking pictures when in Europe. Key points are know your equipment and practice, practice, practice.

EQUIPMENT

What kind of camera, lens, accessories, and film should you use, if any? The bottom line is that your pictures please you. If they don't, all else is for naught. Of course, others might not think that you are the world's greatest photographer, but what do they know? They weren't there.

Do not neglect the rule of pack light. Be comfortable with your equipment. In my early travels, I lugged around entirely too much stuff, cameras and lenses being the heaviest single items in a traveler's bag. Based on years of traveling and personal photography, a suggested photo kit is listed at the end of the chapter.

Camera

If you don't already have a camera, buy a camera buyer's guide and study up on the subject. It will be time well spent for many years to come.

Select a 35mm SLR (single lens reflex) and/or a 35mm range finder of a quality brand name. Off-brands from the discount department stores aren't worth your trouble. A 35mm camera will give much better pictures than the instamatic small film cameras. If you have plenty of cash, go for a top brand automatic camera. You can do a lot more with these and they are less susceptible to breakdown with the rough treatment that travel gives them.

Before leaving, make sure that you are familiar with the camera and that it is in good working order. Change the batteries and shoot a roll of film to make sure that you and it are seeing things the same way. If anything is wrong, take it to a nearby camera shop for a checkup. Allow six weeks for estimates, shipping, repairs and return. A good cleaning may be in order even if nothing is wrong.

If you are taking along a new camera, shoot a few rolls of film before you go to get used to the black box. Results from different cameras differ under some circumstances.

Digital cameras which connect to personal computers are becoming common. This new technology requires several high quality expensive systems, i.e., a computer and a printer, in order to produce good results. I'm still using my trusty old cameras. When I want a digital image I either scan a print or have a CD made when I develop the film. I'm going to stick with my traditional film cameras. Digital cameras have their place but I don't see any advantage in going that route for travel photography.

I came upon this movie shoot on the Champs- Élysées in Paris so I decided to do a shoot of my own. Patrons at Fouquet's got more than a busker that day. Busker is the British word for street entertainer. There are plenty of them in Europe. [1203]

Lens

An important consideration when buying a camera is the focal length of the lens. Focal length is a number expressed in millimeters (mm) which gives an indication of the field of view. A small focal length, e.g. 21mm, gives a very wide view. A high focal length lens, e.g. 200mm, is a telephoto lens. Both of these focal lengths are suitable only for special purposes and are rarely of any value for travel.

SLR cameras have a significant feature in that the lens can be changed. Most SLR cameras are sold with a 50mm lens, also known as the "standard" lens. Skip this lens and select a zoom lens that brackets 50mm. There are a number of lenses available which zoom from about 35mm to about 105mm. One of these lenses will allow you to take pictures of almost anything. Most of the photos you see in this book were shot with a 35/105 zoom lens.

35mm range finder cameras do not have interchangeable lenses. The fixed lens on a 35mm range finder is usually about 40mm. This gives you a wider view than the "standard" lens and is fine for most travel photography. Some of these also have a zoom feature, i.e. one tree instead of three trees on the dummy-proof distance scale.

f-stop

Besides focal length, lenses are sized by aperture, normally talked about as "f-stop." Larger diameter lenses let more light into the camera and are termed "faster." The faster the lens, the lower the f-stop, and the higher the price. Standard 50mm lenses can be f/1.2, f/1.4 or f/1.8. Zoom lenses may be as fast as f/2.8, but most are f/3.5 or f/4.0 depending on the brand name.

A fast lens is nice to have in Europe under poor light conditions. However, accurate focusing is important at low f-stops. At correct focus, all lenses produce the sharpest pictures at about f/5.6. But if you want to make sure that everything from one foot to infinity is in focus, stop it down to f/22, and hope that nothing moves while the shutter is open because you need a longer exposure for higher f-stops.

Filters

The most important camera accessory is a lens filter. The primary purpose of a filter is to keep some unwanted light out of the camera, giving you better pictures. The 1A or UV filters are the most common and practical for outdoor photography, but a polarizing filter can give you strikingly improved shots in many situations. The polarizing filter reduces most reflections, producing more saturated colors, and it blues up the sky when your camera is aimed at right angles to the sun.

Another important benefit of a filter is that it protects your lens from dirt and scratches. Good lenses have a thin surface treatment which you want to protect. If your filter gets scratched it is far less expensive to replace.

I sneaked a peek into the galley through an open portal on the "St. Patrick II" sailing from Le Havre, France, to Rosslare, Ireland. [1207]

Lens Hood

A lens hood reduces the amount of stray light that lands on your lens or filter. This stray light tends to fog your pictures. If direct sunlight hits your lens, you'll have a series of distracting hexagons in your picture. The flexible rubber style that screws into the filter mounting threads is convenient. But they are all bulky and tend to get in your way. Your camera probably won't fit in its case with the lens hood in place.

Flash Unit

A flash unit is not well-suited to travel photography. Most are useless at over 40 feet. For Eiffel Tower pictures at night, you can't use one to reach even the first landing. No museum, public monument, or national cathedral will allow the use of flash inside. Some of these places even charge extra to enter with a camera.

But, for pictures of yourself feasting on the *Noix de Veau Riviera* bring a flash unit. When using the flash with an SLR, make sure that the camera is set at the correct synchronization and the correct speed. Wrong settings can cause half or all of the picture to be black. If you have a built-in automatic flash you should have no problem as long as you give the unit enough time to recharge after each shot. Grainy greeny pictures indicate that you shot the next picture before your flash unit was ready.

Tripod

Leave your standard tripod at home. These are verboten in virtually every museum and they are bulky. For long exposures, press your camera against a wall, or balance it on a chair, window ledge, railing, automobile, or parking meter with the aid of a handkerchief or small bean-bag. Then use the automatic self-timer to trip the shutter so you don't move the camera at the critical moment.

An alternative is a miniature tripod which is about the size of a jumbo felt tip marker. A great device I found in a Swiss camera shop is a camera mount attached to a miniature tripod and 2" C-clamp. The C-clamp holds your camera steady on railings and parking meters which are ubiquitous in Europe.

Camera Batteries

Bring extra batteries for your camera and flash unit. Those small button batteries can be several times as expensive in Europe as in the United States. Some cameras require two or more batteries. Know your camera well since many sales clerks know little about it. The batteries are difficult to find in eastern Europe.

Loupe

A loupe is a small magnifying glass on a mount which is designed specifically for viewing slides and negatives. If you are having your film processed as you travel, a small 8x loupe is a good item to carry. You can review your slides or proof sheets, and go back to reshoot the scene if necessary. Use a fold-up loupe which is about a tenth of the size of the plastic skirt type.

FILM

There are three basic types of film: black and white negative, color negative, and color slide. Prints can be made from each type of film, though prints from slides are not up to the quality of prints from negatives.

Speed

Each type of film is available in several different speeds, ranging from ASA 25 to ASA 1000, and even higher for some films. Film with higher ASA ratings (termed "faster") requires less light, but the picture quality is normally better from film having a lower ASA rating.

The films I use are ASA 400, Kodak black and white Tri-X or Kodak color print Gold. Kodak is always improving its product and you may find different names on their films marketed in Europe. Go to a camera store for expert opinion on the best film for your photography plans.

Quality

Film is made and marketed by several companies in this country, and several more overseas. Kodak is the world leader, and probably the best. Ilford, GAF, and Agfa are also of excellent quality. Noticeably second rate are the cheap films. Think about the total cost of your travels and the relative cost of film and let your conscience be your guide.

Keep your camera loaded and ready to shoot through the windshield as you drive in Switzerland. Scenes like this will greet you as you enter many villages. [1208]

Expiration Date

When buying any film, check the expiration date on the package. Don't buy out of date film, or even film within one year of the date, if you can help it. Faded or dusty boxes in the souvenir shops should warn you that the film is old and has been improperly stored. Do not buy it.

Prices

In general, film is most expensive in souvenir shops, then camera stores, and the least expensive in major department stores. There are some specialty retail chains in central Europe which also offer good prices on film. In Holland go to Capi-Lux; in Germany try Photo Porst; in France shop FNAC. In many stores you'll get a nice discount if you buy in quantity, which can be as little as three rolls. Negotiate. It doesn't cost you anything and you'll usually end up a winner.

Stock Up

Check your film supply on Friday morning to make sure there's enough to get you through the weekend. On Sunday, the only places where you can buy film are the souvenir shops and maybe the train station. Also, stock up before holidays and before trekking through the countryside.

In many countries you'll have trouble finding an English speaking person at the department store film counter. Even in Holland, where almost everybody speaks better English than most Americans, I have been met with blank stares at film counters. Keep the end flap of a film box taped to the back of your camera. When buying film, simply point to the flap to indicate what you want, and poke up some fingers to tell the clerk how many rolls.

My room with a view of the Austrian Alps is in a cloister in Hall-in-Tyrol, a picturesque village just east of Innsbruck. I was on another visit here to see distant relatives on my maternal grandmother's side of the family. [1204]

Processing

Processing costs vary from cheaper to more expensive than in the United States. Color film often comes with a store coupon for free processing, but not free prints, if you return it to the same store. The price of Kodachrome slide film sold in Europe includes processing. The box includes a convenient mailer, and the film can is marked to show that the processing cost is included. Kodak Laboratories in the United States honor the processing statement, even for film from France.

One-hour processing has come to major cities in Europe. You'll see it everywhere. Otherwise, normal processing time can be as short as one day at some camera shops and department stores, but can take a week if mailed to a laboratory.

X-RAYS

Security

Since the dawn of aircraft hijackings, professional and amateur photographers have been concerned about the effects of airport security system X-rays on film. I don't worry about it anymore since I've never noticed any effects on my pictures.

The new security measures introduced in 2002 include a high strength x-ray of your checked luggage. The airlines warm you not to put undeveloped film in your checked luggage.

Do It All Over There

If you are concerned, a sure-fire way to avoid having your film harmed by X-rays is to avoid carrying unprocessed film through airports. Buy your film in Europe and have it developed before you return home. X-rays have no effect on processed slides or negatives.

Lead Lined Bags

Another protection is to use the lead lined film carrying bags which block X-rays and prevent damage to film. I use the Sima brand "Film Shield Pouch" when carrying undeveloped film. This comes with a warning notice that there is "no protection available against high-dose airport X-ray units."

PICTURE TIPS

Read

A book that will boost just about anybody up the photography know-how curve is "The Complete Photographer" by Andreas Feininger. He is a former "Life" magazine photographer. This is an excellent presentation on all aspects of photography.

Open Up

Taking pictures is a very personal subject. Most likely if you are traveling with another person, you will be taking pictures of each other posed in front of the cathedral, arch, painting, etc. Good enough. If you are traveling alone or with another, ask a stranger to take your picture with your camera. You'll have no trouble getting someone to do this, and you may open the door to an interesting conversation or experience.

Turn Around

Don't forget to turn around. Fifty percent of the scenery is behind you.

In the Dark

Many people take pictures of their friends who are standing in shadows or wearing a brimmed hat to shield their eyes from the sun. Automatic exposure cameras use all the light coming in to adjust the aperture. Consequently, the faces of your friends will be rather underexposed. Get them out in the light, or compensate with your backlight feature.

Also have them take off those sun glasses. If the light is too bright, find a completely shaded place so that the camera's automatic exposure will not be fooled by bright backgrounds.

Time Exposure

Shooting in available low light will give you some of your best pictures. Try time exposures inside restaurants, stores, taverns, hotels, and just after sundown. This is especially easy to do with an automatic camera which allows exposures of ten seconds or more. For indoor pictures with incandescent lighting, use tungsten balanced color film. Otherwise everything will look orange and warm. Conversely, pictures taken outdoors with tungsten film will be steel blue.

Time exposures at night make interesting pictures. Place your automatic camera on a secure place, set the shutter release timer, and stand back. This is the Volunteer Fire Department in Faro, Portugal. [1205]

I.D. Shot

It has happened only a few times that my film was lost by a lab. One way to reduce the chance of having film lost is to make the first frame on each roll a shot of your name and address. Print in heavy block letters: "This film is the property of (your name, address, telephone)" on a piece of paper or a handkerchief. Fold it up and carry it with your camera.

An address page large enough to fill out most of a frame at a reasonable focusing distance will be needed. A more convenient alternative is to take a picture of your business card at the start of each roll. The image will not be as big, so shoot with a steady hand.

You might also write on your I.D. card the date and the name of the place where you are. If you take one of those tours whisking you through 10 countries in 15 days you won't have time for processing on the road, and you'll be in such a fog that you won't know where you were by the time your pictures come back.

Verboten

If you want to take a picture inside a store or building, you might want to ask permission first. Outdoors I usually shoot at anything I want, but one time the owner of a German gas station came out to prevent me from taking a picture of his station. My German companion was as surprised as I was.

Cameras are prohibited inside casinos. A guard in a Barcelona Metro stop would not allow me to take pictures inside the station.

Postcards

Don't count on your own camera for all your photos of Europe. When buying postcards, buy a few extras for yourself. The aerial views make especially good keepers. Gather up free tourist pamphlets and literature whenever you're in a tourist office. Even if you can't read Greek, some of it is worth framing.

Stephanie can't hold it in but the mannequin must if he wants any coins in his upturned hat. You see men and women all over France and Europe performing in the street for donations. [1210]

A TRAVELING CAMERA KIT

The List

This is a list of the photography gear I travel with:
- 35mm automatic SLR camera
- 35/105mm zoom lens
- Polarizing filter
- 35mm miniature camera
- Flash unit (sometimes)
- Film
- X-ray film shield bag
- Loupe
- Lens paper and brush
- Bean bag
- Miniature C-clamp/tripod
- Camera instruction manual

Most of these items were discussed above but the 35mm miniature automatic range finder camera was not. There are several brands on the market which are about the size of a cigarette pack and which use 35mm film. This type of camera is exceedingly convenient. I've had an Olympus XA in my pocket for the past 20+ years whenever I am on the road. This thing has taken a beating but keeps on keeping on.

Owners Manual

Are you one of those people who start using gadgets before you read the directions? Part of every manufacturer's job is to make things "idiot proof" to protect you against yourself. Every camera comes with a couple of little booklets, one of which is the operator's manual. The other is promotion for more cameras and lenses. You probably threw both of them in a drawer someplace and couldn't find them in two hours. Now is a good time to dig out the manual and stuff it in a corner of your carry-on bag. Thumb through it first. Your camera will go bad at one time or another. I guarantee it. It might be a simple thing, but you won't know if you don't have the operator's manual handy.

Just wait for a whiff of wind to fill the flag and click. I'm enjoying a cool Dutch beverage while I adjust my tilt for the sunset at Zandvoort. [1202]

Chapter 13
Bring a Smile
Travel Europe in Good Attitude

A sense of humor, prudence, and patience are attributes of a good traveler.

ATTITUDE ADJUSTMENT

Guest Status
While you are in Europe, consider yourself an invited guest. You're not at home and you won't find everything to your liking. Some things will be annoyances, mainly because of your lack of information and understanding of local customs, things, and folklore. Their's isn't always wrong and yours isn't always right, they're just different. That's part of the spice of traveling in Europe.

Beee Cooool
A short temper will discomfort only you, and may raise resentment in whoever or whatever seems to be giving you a problem. At such moments, beaucoup more gremlins are often hatched, temperatures rise, perspiration flows, international relations harden, and your good times start turning rancid.

Take it easy. Laugh it off. It is far better to smile at adversity. If something is wrong, you most likely did it to yourself by acting without enough data or forethought. Mistakes are a part of your education. They should only cost you a little time and/or money.

Ears Are Open
The purpose of this book is to get you up on the learning curve for Europe and thus save you some of these uncomfortable moments, and wasted time and money. Restrain yourself from the temptation to criticize and ridicule. Instead, comment on how interesting or how unusual something may appear. Your conversation could easily be overheard and understood by others around you. Your choice of words may mean the difference between a scowl and a gracious explanation.

NUISANCES

However, there are a few things which can tarnish your good times through no fault of your own. The best defense is some extra care in avoiding these situations, or a quick escape when you find yourself already involved.

This London bobby found it amusing when I asked his permission to shoot him. It's only a camera. Police patrolmen throughout Europe are excellent sources of information and direction finders. [1307]

Politics and Perceptions

Your patience may be tried on occasion by comments about America of a political nature. Younger Europeans love to taunt us about American presidents, social problems, and foreign policy.

Two reasons for this criticism come to mind: one is the complete openness of American society in which all the dirty linen is run up the flagpole, and the other is the Marxist domination of European TV and radio broadcasting. Every American wrongdoing is exaggerated and every virtue is suppressed.

It's been more than a decade since the Iron Curtain came down revealing the treachery and idiocy of communism. But true believers of Marx and Lenin still don't get it. The anti-American disintelligentsia holds sway over public opinion in Europe.

Meanwhile on the other side of the world, the heirs of dictatorship in the mold of Stalin and Hitler continue to rule with brutal force in Beijing. Ironically, five months before the beginning of the end of European communism, the Chinese communists murdered thousands of their own students who were holding a peaceful demonstration in the main square of their capital city. Had the Soviet communists shot the Dresden demonstrators in 1989, as they had in Budapest in 1956 and Prague in 1978, Europe and the world would be a whole different place right now. The difference is beyond description.

Bad Capitalism, Good Communism

A few malcontents have fabricated a straw man which they love to kick around. The USA is maligned around the world, and in Europe. The roots of contempt and envy of Americans may be traceable to European educational systems. It is reported by some to include a far greater study of America than of any other foreign country, with emphasis often placed on treatment of the native American Indians and slavery. This is coupled with a group psychoanalysis of the supposed conformist, naive, moneymaking, arrogant, and aggressive characteristics of the American people. There is nothing we are not guilty of in the eyes of some.

When someone tries to bait you into a political argument, just stand aside. Their mind is so completely fixed that no amount of talk will change it.

As one amusing example, I know a photographer in Holland who claims to be a communist. Yet he is practicing a trade for profit. He once asked for my advice about some Kodak projectors. He wanted to buy two of the latest models. I asked him why he needed two and he replied that he could then show his slides to customers more effectively and sell more photographs. His plan was to invest in better equipment so that he could make more profit. This is simply the essence of capitalism. He denied being a capitalist — he claimed to be a communist, period.

We were strolling on a walk street in Istanbul, Turkey when a police cruiser stopped and offered Elizabeth a bouquet of flowers. Hey, why not? [1302]

INSULTS AND KISSES

Holland

My European life began in 1975 in the Netherlands. The Vietnam War and civil rights abuses and demonstrations were fresh in everyone's mind. The young Dutch people whom I met in cafés knew America by these events. I remember one girl who told me in a very nasty tone "I don't like America." When I told her that I lived in California she beamed from ear to ear and said "I like California!" It's the image that counts.

Meanwhile the older Dutch could not tell me often enough how they helped American flyers escape to Britain during World War Two. Many American bombers crashed in Nazi occupied Holland after being shot up during raids on German factories and military installations. The Dutch underground smuggled the pilots and crews out of Holland. My landlord once told me about two Americans whom they had hidden for a few weeks while they looked for a way to get them out. The servicemen were getting cabin fever so my landlord decided to take them out to dinner. While they were in the restaurant some German soldiers came in. Fortunately none of the Germans noticed the two men who were silently eating with their right hands. Nazis were known to practice summary execution in Haarlem so that meal had the possibility of being my landlord's last supper.

Britain

Envy and ignorance seem to surface where you would expect them the least. British ego is a bore. Some British folks like to put Americans down by referring to us as the "colonists." Their historians must take pride in the role that Britain had in the establishment of the United States. Thomas Jefferson, then 33 years old, penned "A Declaration" on July 4, 1776 in which he and the other 55 members of the Continental Congress accused the British king of "Despotism" and of seeking "the Establishment of an absolute Tyranny over these States." Such management of its colonies must be the reason why Britain is a former colonial master. King George III was not too amused with the comments of Mr. Jefferson and his colleagues. The despot king hired a professional German army to help do his dirty work. Our George and his army whipped them so we can celebrate Independence Day every year. Even the present "royals" believe that George III was correct way back then so it's no surprise that some "commoners" have an attitude toward Americans. Get over it, Brits.

France

Then there's France. Darn near everybody I talk with about France comes up with the statement that the French are nasty to Americans. Very few of these people have actually been to France, but they "heard this" from someone. WRONG! Go with an open attitude and you'll love it. The French love Americans and deeply appreciate the services of the United States Army in the two big wars of the last century.

The main problem in France is the café waiters in Paris. They treat everybody just as bad so don't take it personally. It's just that Americans are not used to insults instead of service. French "diplomacy" is also a stick in the eye.

French like to protest. From farmers to students to air traffic controllers there seems to be a strike a month. Fortunately these are usually one day strikes to get some attention. One day "warning" strikes are used in other countries as well.

Germany

Germans are polite and certainly do like Americans, though there is a subcurrent of discomfort because of WW I and WW II. You'll never notice this as a tourist. But a tiny minority still think that they could have won the second round except for one thing or another, but not blaming their idiot leader.

Eastern Countries

In the eastern countries, Americans are a special lot. This is really amazing because just a few years ago we were all indoctrinated with the idea that the nuclear shoot-out between America and Russia could come any day. When Reagan was President, I loved to show Europeans a Hollywood photo of him in a cowboy outfit wearing a pair of pistols — just to prove that we were ready.

Well, the truth is that the easterners were treated so shabbily by the communist murderers who ruled them that you just can't put it into words. They look up to Americans as their saviors in the times they are going through, and welcome all of us. I am usually not too emotional, but I remember coming home from my first trip to the Ukraine in 1991 and breaking down in tears over the deplorable conditions to which those people had been subjected.

Patience is in order in the eastern countries. They tore down the statues of Marx and Lenin in the early 1990s and jumped into a free economy. Unfortunately they nearly drowned in it. Some countries went back to or stayed with a semblance of the old economic order, with a facade of democracy. It is going to take some time, perhaps a couple of decades, for the eastern countries to reach the standard of living and democracy existing in western Europe. This should be expected. The early history of the United States was not on a fast track either. After those men at Lexington fired the first shots against British law and order in April of 1775, the Declaration of Independence was not signed until July of the following year. Then the Revolutionary War lasted until the Treaty of Paris in 1781. George Washington did not become President until 1789 when the United States adopted the Constitution. That was about 14 years of upheaval until the Founding Fathers got their stuff together and made a nation. So, give the eastern countries a little time to get reorganized. In fact, some are doing quite well already.

APPROPRIATE RESPONSE

There are not very many insulting fools over there who will blame you personally for all of America's perceived sins. But if you bump into a mal-informed jerk, and if you're the kind who can't back out of a tongue fight once the other side gets in a hit, give them the KO punch — just mention that we won't be coming over for their next war. Their cemeteries have enough young Americans.

ANNOYANCES IN THE STREET

Dogs

One common nuisance may trip your patience. You have probably never before seen dogs in hotels, restaurants, trains, and stores. Not until you have been to Europe, especially Amsterdam and Paris.

The dogs don't know any better. Their inconsiderate owners let them crap anywhere — on the sidewalks, in *Metro* stations, and several times on my doorstep.

The authorities are posting more signs to the effect that owners should curb their animals, but there is still plenty of poop around. Watch your step.

Bohemians are flocking back to the Czech Republic. Here is a typical summer scene in Prague. Peruvian bands like this one can be seen and enjoyed throughout Europe. [1301]

Public Drunks

Public drunkenness is common in Scandinavia, and can be seen now and again in other northern European cities. Swedish boys are the worse. These characters often get foul and verbally abusive, but can barely stand up so they are relatively harmless. If confronted by one or a group, do like the locals — totally ignore him or them. The slightest acknowledgment will only bring you problems.

The streets of Paris have little "wine clubs" on a number of public benches, in the streets and in the *Metro* stations. These homeless and hopeless men and women are usually laying next to a half full bottle of wine, often with their colleagues and/or a German shepherd. Local citizens steer clear, and there's no reason for you to stop for a chat.

Beggars and Thieves

Begging seems to be institutionalized in some cities. Dublin has more than they need, and you are accosted often in the Mediterranean countries.

On crossing into Spain at Irun, I saw a sullen shabbily dressed young woman with a crying infant awkwardly slung over her arm. The other arm was outstretched as she went begging around the train station. It was a pathetic sight. Fifteen minutes later I was on the train and looked out the window. There on the platform she had the baby in a bright new stroller and was cheerily waving good-bye to her friends on the train. So much for that act.

In Rome, I saw fathers training their children in the art of begging. In the Milan station, I had to shake off one old woman four times. You do start to question your judgment at times, but I noticed that this woman was avoiding the Italians and kept picking on me. Her judgment was wrong. She didn't get a cent for her effort.

Many beggars are actually thieves. From my hotel window in Warsaw, I watched and videoed a young Gypsy woman as she approached people on the street. She only went up to people walking alone. Those who had a companion were not approached. Also, she would never approach a single walker when there was someone walking behind. She was obviously up to no good.

One of my favorite Sherlock Holmes stories is "The Man with the Twisted Lip." This will give you an insight into the begging profession. How profitable it can be is illustrated by the story from two newspaper reporters who stood on a street corner in New York in the 1960s for two weeks. They made the equivalent of $14,000 per year, more than I was making as a young engineer at the time, and theirs was tax free.

Street Hustlers

Athens has a lot of smooth talking hustlers working the Sindagma (a.k.a. Syntagma) Square area. They approached me a half dozen times a day offering to help me find something or another (I looked like an easy mark with a city map and a camera). Then they tried to get me into a conversation and go to their bar "around the corner." It takes more than "I'm not interested" to get rid of these insistent pests. Several times I had to resort to an abrupt "Get lost." After a few days, I started telling them immediately when they approached "I don't want to go to your bar." That usually worked, but sometimes I got the reply "What, you don't like our country?"

Amsterdam has more street hustlers than any city on the planet. I am approached at least twice every time I walk from the train station to the Dam, a 10 minute walk. When you are approached, don't smile, just laugh. If you do business with him he will be laughing. The old racket was dope, hash and cocaine. Nowadays the street hustlers are not doing so well since "coffie shop" businesses are selling mary jane all over town. At least one of the hustlers found a new product — he asked me if I wanted to buy some viagra.

Smooth talking characters like these are always walking on the other side of the law. If it wasn't a scam, they would be advertising on television. Don't let yourself become the next victim.

The eastern style potty is fairly common in public facilities in eastern and southern Europe. BYOTP (bring your own toilet paper). This hammam *is in a train station somewhere in Germany. There are two important things I learned when I lived in Arabia. One was how to make my own wine and the other was how to squat. You'll be able to buy wine all over Europe, but learn to squat and be prepared for these facilities in many cafés. If you want a clean throne and white TP go to a McDonalds.* [1303]

Chapter 14
Hotel, Hostel, B&B, or Private Home
Sleep Options for Travel in Europe

Finding a cozy place to dream is a challenge.

YOU WON'T FIND IT HERE

Faux Monde

On hotels, a lot of what is written in magazines and travel guide books is nauseous nonsense. Descriptions of charming owners, settings, furniture, cheap prices, and/or (in)famous clientele are not what you need. Much of this is fanciful gross fiction. It's meant to sell perfume as advertised in adjoining pages, or to get repeated free rooms for the writer. Have you ever read one of these reviews with the least bit of criticism?

The Real World

What follows here is the beautiful nuts-and-bolts of what it's really like in Europe. You can sleep better for less no matter what your budget if you don't sleep through this chapter. I'm talking half price, clean rooms, firm beds, good plumbing, and no noise. If you do not appreciate that, you have not been to Europe.

Hotel Lists

There are no hotel lists in this book. Go back to chapter 2 to learn how to get excellent current hotel lists, and how to avoid getting bummers. Some of the best hotel lists are free. Some of the others are in the 2" thick travel guidebooks. See chapter 10.

HOTELS

Ratings by the Stars

There is a greater variety of hotel quality in Europe than in America. In the large cities, major chains operate first class hotels on a par with their hotels in America, though at double the price. At the bottom end of hotel quality are decrepit, dirty hotels which could pass no fire or health department inspection in America. I have stayed in places at both ends of the scale. My comfort and budget dictate the mid-range "standard" European hotel which is described and illustrated below.

Hotels are rated by some government bureaus and given "stars," one star being the lowest and five stars followed by an "L" being the tops. This is reversed in Italy where a "category four" is the lowest and a "category one de luxe" is the best. In some countries, it appears that these ratings are not official, but are whatever the hotel wants to classify itself as. If there is an official rating, as there is in some of the countries with high tourist traffic, it will be posted in the lobby or in the room.

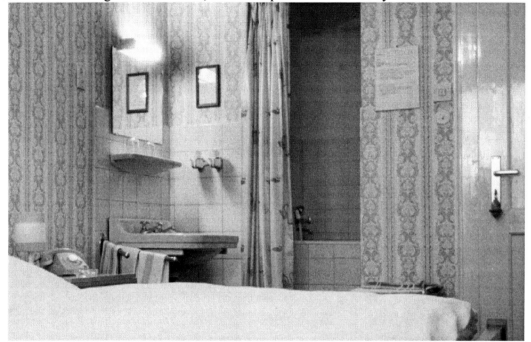

Here is a typical room in a standard European hotel. This one happens to be in Munich. Virtually all hotel rooms have a wash basin and mirror, as in the far corner. This one also has a shower and tub, but no toilet. The toilet is down the hall. Note the bob on the room key in the door. That's typical. The down cover on the bed will keep you amazingly warm despite the frugal use of heat in most hotels like this one. [1419]

Some hotels in France also have an "N" or "NN" in addition to the official stars. These letters seem to mean that the lobby or breakfast room has been remodeled or an elevator installed, but the rooms have been left as they were. I avoid "N" ("never") and "NN" ("never never") hotels because they do not provide extra comfort in proportion to the extra cost. My observations lead me to conclude that the outside of the building will give you a better idea of the room quality than the lobby decor. The lobby is almost always the best looking part of any hotel. That is where the owner spends his day.

First Class

First class hotels, whether part of an American chain or of local luxury vintage, are known by the lobbies they keep and the prices charged. However, a high price does not guarantee a comfortable room. Look for a rating of 4 or 5 in the Michelin Red Book for an objective opinion. Treat with suspicion any self-anointed stars that hotels sometimes like to give themselves.

The clientele of 4 and 5 star hotels are generally European, American, and Japanese business executives and well-to-do tourists. There is a certain loftiness, perhaps arrogance, in the European guests and employees in these places. If you arrive in worn Levi's with a backpack, be prepared to be ignored. Most of these hotels accept the major credit cards.

This my 4 star room in Buda. I've also been on the other side of the Danube and stayed in clean tourist quality hotels in Pest. Hungary is a friendly and very inexpensive country, especially outside of Budapest. The food is great and it often comes with live entertainment. [1407]

Standard Hotels

The "standard" European hotel is nearly as comfortable as any of the above for sleeping, but lacks some amenities which are common and expected in America. In many of these hotels, some of the single rooms have no *douche* (shower) or *W.C.* (toilet). These facilities are located in separate little rooms down the hall. While the room without a shower or toilet is considerably cheaper than one with, some hotels make a small charge to use the shower room. Standard hotels are generally old, relatively small, and are operated by a family or individual with a few employees. The desk closes at midnight and the door is locked, but a ring of the night bell will rouse the keeper to let you in. The Michelin rating for the standard hotel is 2 or 3. Most of the hotels in Europe fit this category. This is the kind of hotel I seek out every night.

This "grand hotel" can't keep it's sign in order. After seeing that feature I wasn't curious enough to look inside. Don't expect any better maintenance in the rooms. [1409]

Not So Good

At the bottom of the barrel are the substandard cheap hotels. You will probably be able to sleep after turning off the lights so that you can't see the grime, worn carpets, and broken blinds. Heat and hot water may be nonexistent, though are usually available for part of the day. Door locks may be a joke that any hair pin could open. The Michelin rating for cheap hotels is one or none. Budget guidebooks frequently list and recommend them. This type of hotel is plentiful in Europe, especially in eastern Europe.

HOW TO FIND A GOOD VALUE ROOM

It is very easy to pay a lot for a lousy room. It is a memorable occasion when you find a good <u>and</u> cheap room.

Overview

On a comfort per price scale of 1 to 10, American basis, there are many hotels at negative 5 and very few equal to plus 5 in Europe. And the hotel desk clerk will notice that you are an American before you get to the desk (about as difficult to do as pointing out a horse in a chicken coop), and he or she will always quote you a price for the most expensive room available, though probably not the most comfortable.

Rather than present a listing of supposedly cheap hotels with charming owners in a few major cities (the popular guidebooks already pretend to do that), my intention here is to tell you how to find a comfortable, inexpensive hotel room in about any city in Europe, on your own. Note that the words "comfortable" and "inexpensive" are relative and subjective, and vary significantly. Prices are higher in the larger cities and resorts, and in the northern part of western Europe. This hotel shopping method doesn't work well during wine festivals, trade fairs, and sports spectacles. There may be no rooms available at any price during these popular events.

Here is the well plumbed bathroom of my 2 star Pisa, Italy hotel room. There's a wash basin, bidet, toilet, and shower. It even has a shower curtain, not always found in standard hotels. [1421]

The Method

First, lay your hands on a hotel list and city map. Both are available at the city tourist office, either free or for a nominal charge. Park your luggage in a train station locker or leave it the trunk of your car if you are driving. Select the section of the city in which you wish to stay, based on your means of travel and *objet de voyage*. Start walking around your chosen neighborhood examining the hotels. For train travelers, this is easy since there is a high concentration of hotels within a five minute walk of the station. Auto travelers might just as well drive around and double park while making inquiries. For each hotel, check the tourist office brochure for prices of singles or doubles, as your case may be. If the hotel is not listed in the tourist office brochure, beware.

Target those hotels whose listed prices are above what you want to pay. Note that some of the better hotels do not list their least expensive rooms with the tourist office. And conversely, hotels listing very cheap rooms usually rent them first, though they try to put Americans in the expensive rooms. One big advantage of the cheapest room in a more expensive hotel is that a better breakfast is provided. This is especially true in Holland, Germany, and Scandinavia where breakfast can almost get you through to dinner. Help yourself again to that table full of eggs, cheese, meat, bread, milk, corn flakes, juices, fruits, etc., etc., but don't abuse the system by packing a lunch from the table unless the owner gives you the OK.

Here is the entry to the CKM Hotel, a tourist class hotel in Prague, Czech Republik. We stayed a few nights. The nightclub features disco music. [1401]

The Action

On entering the hotel to inquire for a room, let the clerk know what you want — double or single, one night or many, toilet and tub or not — in straight-away English. If you know the local language, use it. If you are communicating, good. If not, switch over to your Berlitz Phrase Book or sign language. When he/she gives you a price, pull out your pocket calculator and punch up some keys to find out what it costs in dollars. Announce that the price is too high (it's *ALWAYS* too high) and ask for a less expensive room. Generally you will then be given a lower price for another room with the apologetic explanation that it has no *W.C.* and/or no *douche*, i.e. no bathroom. Here you go through the calculator routine again. This offer will probably be a good deal. If not, excuse yourself, tell them that it is still beyond your budget, wish them a good day, and turn for the door — but don't be too abrupt. Especially if you have been talking to the junior member of a two man staff, you may hear some hurried words of the native tongue followed by an announcement that another room is available at a still lower price. They blinked. You won. If the price is right, take it. If not, make a gracious exit.

If the hotel was only half full last night and it's not looking any better so far today, you may be very pleasantly surprised. At all times, be clean and presentable, courteous and respectful.

Continue prowling the neighborhood practicing your pitch. Within an hour you'll know what the traffic is expected to bear so go back to the hotel offering the best deal. Chances are that the lowest cost room is still available.

If the hotel is full (*complete* in France, *besetzt* in Germany), inquire about a room for the following night if you are planning to stay for a few days or more. On a late arrival your bargaining position may be weak, or if you're in luck the owner has one room left and wants to go to sleep so he'll strike a good deal right off.

Room rate information at the 2 star Hôtel de l'Europe in Toul, France is posted on the door of my room. Below that (not in this picture) is posted the fire escape directions. It's all in French. France is now using the euro so this room would have cost about €30, plus petit déjeuner *(breakfast).* [1408]

Why Not?

Bargaining may seem more appropriate at a flea market, but it can be fun and very profitable when shopping for a hotel room as well. I've received significant discounts from the posted list prices of rooms. Owners figure that it's better to let a $50 room go for $30 than to allow a vacancy for a night. Remember that a hotel room is more perishable than fresh fish on a hot day. The room is worth nothing in the morning if it wasn't rented, but you can always use the rotten fish as fertilizer.

Bargaining is not just for the smaller inexpensive hotels. One New Year's Eve in Amsterdam I was enjoying a drink at a major international hotel and stopped by the reception desk just to see what a room would cost. I was quoted a "rack rate" for a princely sum and promptly told the clerk that it was too much. He immediately lowered the price and I said still too much. Then came his third offer, approaching half price.

On one stay in Stockholm at an upper class hotel my bargaining produced a room without a shower. I had to ride the elevator to take my shower on another floor. Other guests on the lift were wearing their finery to a luncheon banquet, and there I was in bath robe and flip-flops. We exchanged greetings. *Pourquoi pas?* (Why not?)

Using the Tourist Hotel Reservation Office

If the weather is bad, or if you don't want to take the time to shop for a hotel room, most city tourist offices will locate a room and reserve it for a small fee and a deposit. Bargain with the tourist office also. They often try to place you in an overpriced room that just happens to be available because it is shunned by knowledgeable travelers. Carefully review the hotel price list before agreeing to any reservation. Again, go for the cheapest room in a better quality hotel, rather than the cheapest room in town. If you are not satisfied when you arrive at the hotel, go back to the tourist office and start over. If you are not satisfied the next morning go back and start over.

The Carlton Square Hotel in Haarlem is set in a quiet neighborhood and is only a 10 minute walk to the Frans Hals Museum. Every south facing room has a balcony. This is one of the better hotels in Haarlem. The fish stand across the street has the highest prices although not the best haring in town. Budget travelers should head for the Hotel Joops in the center of Haarlem or the Hotel Raeckse which is on the west side. Real budget travelers should go to the B&B Paula, about 2 miles west of the city center, an easy bus ride from the train station. [1425]

HOTEL POTPOURRI

Here follows a catalog of observations on the characteristics of "standard" European hotels, plus some information on higher and lower category hotels.

Good Rooms

Outside influences may very likely affect your comfort, no matter the classification of the hotel. Within an individual hotel, there are good rooms and bad rooms. The good rooms are the quiet rooms. The bad rooms are the ones overlooking a busy street (at less than ten stories), those facing a bus or train station, those next to the elevator, those next to the toilet and shower rooms, those with a church bell tower across the street, those over or near the kitchen, bar, or disco, and all of them if there is no carpet in the hallway.

Avoid taking a room near a construction site, which can be identified by fences, tower cranes, dumpsters, equipment, and supplies. Those guys get up early to start the air hammers. I met a traveler in Valencia who couldn't sleep because the street crews were running a generator and air compressor all night long, painting fresh stripes on the boulevard. I got a good quiet sleep in the same hotel because I had a room facing the side street.

Fight Back

Thin walls were not born in America. There are the occasional noisy and/or weird neighbors and even shouting, bucket-banging maids. Change rooms. Move to another hotel. Don't put up with less than you are entitled to.

I complain and change rooms fairly often. Hotel keepers must figure that people like to sit in the window and listen to the horn-blowing traffic echo between the stone buildings. If you find yourself in a noisy room and it's not convenient to change rooms, look for French door type shutters or a roll down shutter on the outside of your window. These are very effective at blocking noise and keeping the sun out of your eyes in the morning. Earplugs are my last resort to stop noise.

Inspection

Inspecting the room before agreeing to it is a good idea, but a quick inspection can miss some important points. When looking at the room, test the bed to see if it is firm enough, and look out the window to see what nuisances might interfere with your comfort. Test the plumbing to see if the toilet works, if there is hot water, and if there is heat. And look for the electrical outlet if you will need one.

Years ago my Dad checked into a top hotel in Amsterdam and took the room key without checking the room. He came back to the front desk a few minutes later to ask for clean linens because the maid had not done the room. The desk clerk replied that "you Americans are always complaining."

Translating

If the desk clerk does not speak English and if you are not satisfied with something, go to the city tourist office and complain. I have used tourist offices a couple of times to get misunderstandings ironed out. Once in Milan, there was no heat or hot water in the morning. Nobody downstairs could speak enough English to tell me what was wrong so I went to the tourist office over in the train station. They called the hotel and found out for me that the boiler had broken down. Then I asked for a discount on the room and the tourist office obtained a 20% reduction in the room price. Not enough I thought, but I was in a hurry to catch a train so I accepted.

Helpful Strangers

Local citizens may notice you in train stations or airports and ask you if you need a hotel. They appear to want to help you get situated, but what they really want is a commission from the hotel they are going to guide you to. Some new-found traveling companions and I were worn out from a long slow train ride and let ourselves get nabbed by one of these operators in Athens. He led us to one of the worst hotels I have ever had anywhere — no heat, broken toilet (I fixed it), sink leaking on the floor, paint or gas smell in the halls, lukewarm water, and then attempts to rip us off the next morning for an extra 50% because we did not check out by 11:30, and another 7% for tax. I refused to pay either extra and found a better hotel on the next street for half the price.

Triskaidekaphobia

Chances are that you'll never see a hotel with a 13th floor. This is due to the worldwide epidemic of triskaidekaphobia. Triskaidekaphobia is fear of number 13.

Payment

If advance payment is required, and it often is, give the room a complete inspection as described above. You must stay in a good bargaining position, so never pay for more than one night in advance. If you pay for several days in advance, the playing field tilts against you. Problems will probably not be resolved

We stopped at the Motel Nine Crosses while driving through the Czech Republic. Advertising itself in Czech, German, and English, it features a restaurant, bar, and money changing. [1402]

Breakfast

Breakfast is normally served in a special breakfast room, usually on the first floor above the ground floor. Breakfast can also be served in your room.

The price of breakfast is almost always optional. In some countries it is a good value, but in many countries it is not. In France for example, only a cup of coffee, milk, some bread, butter, and jam is usually served. You might find a better deal at a nearby café. Or if you want to supplement the hotel breakfast with some protein, buy a ham and cheese sandwich in a café the night before and save it until morning.

On the other hand, breakfast is a real stuffing in Germany, Holland, Britain, Ireland, and Scandinavia. Bread, cheese, eggs, yogurt, meats, milk, cereal, and more is usually provided. A smorgasbord breakfast in Scandinavia will also include several types of fish. I love herring for breakfast. Eggs are usually soft boiled, still in the shell, and standing in a little egg cup. Knock the top off with the knife and eat the egg from the shell with the miniature spoon provided.

Doubles

Double rooms are more pleasant than single rooms. Single rooms are less likely to have a shower or toilet. For less than twice the price of a single, double rooms usually come fully-plumbed. In many hotels singles and doubles are the same price.

Holidays

Some hotels are closed during part of the year. The owners go on vacation, quite often when you are on vacation, and take holidays when everybody else takes holidays. Many hotels are closed for extended Christmas holidays. The Michelin Red Books are very valuable in that they indicate periods when hotels are closed. It can be rather startling. I was staying in a small hotel in Blois, France for a few days and a public holiday came up. The owner and staff just disappeared for a day and a half.

In the seaside resort village of Zandvoort you'll find very reasonable rates at the "Zimmer Frei" signs on virtually every street. I have used several of these in my visits to Holland. Zandvoort is overrun by German tourists every summer. Thus, one of the signs in German reads "ROOM with breakfast and TV, priced from €17." The beach runs for miles and there is plenty of nightlife. [1426]

Reservations

Normally I only make hotel reservations for business travel. For leisure travel it is best not to arrive in a small town late at night without a reservation. You may have to drive on and on before you find a vacancy. It's better to stop and look for a room late in the afternoon, say no later than 18:00 (6:00 pm). If you haven't found a vacancy after checking with three or four hotels ask for a recommendation from a desk clerk. They probably know which nearby hotel is likely to have vacancies and will call them to make a reservation for you.

If you are going on your first trip, reserve a room for your first few nights in Europe. Continuation of your travels with or without hotel reservations is a matter of personal choice. Without reservations, you may be disappointed as I have been on occasion in Paris, especially in the fall. While the autumn may be off-season for tourists, you will more easily find a hotel room in Paris during August than in September or October. The reason for this is that when the summer is over everybody gets back to work. There is a sudden surge in business trips to meetings and exhibits, *fairs*, in the major cities.

On one trip, I was driving around Poland and scooted over to L'vov in The Ukraine without a reservation. It was hard to find any hotel. I stopped to ask a cop and he asked for my personal and car papers, holding me up for 20 minutes while probably trying to hold me up for some cigarettes. Finally, after nearly knocking my teeth out driving on those cobblestones, I found a hotel but it was full. The desk clerk phoned around and found a room for me at the Hotel Sputnik on the outskirts of the city. The concierge jumped in his car and guided me out there or I never would have found it, for which I tipped him a couple of dollars.

Parking

Small hotels in the cities don't always have parking on the premises, and when they have it there are normally not enough spaces for all the guests. Early arrivals have the advantage. Also you normally pay extra for it.

In resort areas in the eastern countries, select a hotel which has a guard in the parking lot. These hotels will cost more, but the cost of rooms is much less than in western Europe, and there is a good reason for having the a guard. We used one of those steel bars which lock the steering wheel to the brake pedal plus a fake dashboard alarm blinker on all our eastern travels. You can buy these items in European department stores.

If you don't have a parking space on the hotel property, park under a street light on a busy street. Don't hide your car in a back alley because that is where the smashers hang out.

No matter where you park, never leave any valuables in your car overnight.

The owner consented to pose in front of his hotel in Nice, France. I came upon this little place by chance and then discovered that it is recommended in several of the budget guide books. Being named the Petite Louvre, its walls are covered with art reproductions. It had one star when I stayed for a night five years ago. [1415]

Checkout

Checkout time is almost universally 12 noon in Europe. If it is not posted it would be a good idea to ask on the day before your departure. It is also a good courtesy to confirm your departure on the day before you are going to leave.

If you change plans and decide to stay an extra day or so, check with the desk clerk to see if the room is available. Hotels in Europe accept you for the period you said you would stay and may have reserved your room for another guest starting immediately after your departure. I have been asked to change rooms on a number of occasions because my room had been pre-booked. Do not assume that you can keep the room for an extra day. Ask in advance.

Before leaving, check everything in the room to make sure you did not forget anything. I lose a shirt or something about once a month. Riding a taxi to the harbor in Lisbon I suddenly remembered that I had left my money and traveler's checks in the hotel safe. Fortunately there was time to go back and retrieve it all without missing the boat.

Receipt

Carry your hotel receipt or a card from the hotel desk. You may forget where you are staying, or need to phone the hotel while you are out. Good luck finding a phone book, and then finding your hotel in it if you do.

Make sure you get a receipt. A couple years ago I stayed in a small hotel in Düsseldorf. It occupied the 8th floor of an office building. On checking out I paid cash because they did not accept credit cards. But, their "computer was down" and they said they couldn't print a receipt. I nearly left with that explanation, but asked for a hand receipt which they wrote out for me. A few months later I received a bill for the three days I stayed there. Mistake or attempted fraud, I don't know but I have the receipt and they have my money.

The Hotel 'la Madeleine in Brussels occupies a store front window with rooms up above. This is more or less typical of newer city center budget hotels in Europe. Brussels is a city not to miss if you like mussels. [1427]

Taxes

Hotels charge tax. This is usually the national sales tax, which can be over 20%. Tax is almost universally included in the quoted price of the room.

Prices

Many hotels post prices of all rooms on a large board at the desk, or sometimes on the front door or in a window visible from the street. Prices are also normally posted in the room. If there are seasonal rates, the high season rate is shown. Some cities and countries have rules regulating room prices, and the rate card in the room might be an official government notice stating maximum room prices.

As discussed above, prices are flexible. Tour groups and corporations always get discounts, so why shouldn't you? Just ask. Rates for extended stays are particularly flexible.

Lights

Hallway lights usually have only an "on" switch. This switch turns on a timer which automatically turns off the lights after a minute or so. If the lights are already on, move quickly to your door or the stairway since the timer was probably switched on by another guest and could go off at any moment.

If you can't find the light switch in the toilet, look outside in the hallway. Or sometimes it is concealed in the door jamb. Lock the door and the light will come on. The door lock switch is also used on some Paris café toilets.

Keys and Locks

European hotel keys are a pain. They are usually attached to bobs as big as a baseball and are almost impossible to put in your pocket — which is the idea. When you are leaving the hotel at any time, the hotel keeper usually wants the key left at the front desk. It always bothers me that someone can walk up to the desk, ask for my key, and burgle my room. But after having stayed at hundreds of rooms all over Europe, this has never happened. Additional security measures have recently been introduced at a couple of my favorite hotels, so I assume that there have been some problems.

You must check your door lock at each hotel to see how it works. Some lock automatically when you close the door, and others require you to push a button or turn the key. If you have a balcony in Portugal, Spain, Greece, Bulgaria, or Romania, make sure that the window/door has an operating lock. If not, keep the shutters rolled down when you are out of the room.

It was so late that I don't remember which Dorf we were in. This Gasthaus has Fremdenzimmer *(visitor's rooms) but if you see a "besetzt" sign on the door it means "no vacancy." Little hotels like this are all over Germany. They are clean and reasonably priced, and almost always have a restaurant with good home cooking. [1410]*

Safe

Most hotels maintain a safe for the use of guests. Check in your money and jewels, and carry your passport and camera. The safe is normally free, but hotels in resort areas sometimes charge an extra fee for their use. The fee can be for a week's use, so if you are staying for only a night or two it seems rather expensive. Get a receipt or a key to the box. There is usually a deposit required for the key. On check out, the desk clerk will not ask you if you have anything in the hotel safe. You have to remember that for yourself.

Furnishings

TV: It is becoming more common to find a television in a standard hotel. A radio is less common. If your room does have a TV, turn it on and see what's available. Most countries have two government owned channels and often broadcast some pretty off-the-wall stuff, along with a few of your American favorites.

Movies are broadcast in the original language with local subtitles in some countries. In others the local language is dubbed in. Italy has a large number of private commercial TV stations, though TV in other countries is not so well endowed.

You find CNN in the pricey hotels, though the bouffant anchor desk personalities have problems reading their lines. CNN should print the news on screen. Better, tune in the more professional BBC which is also available almost everywhere. They have better news and travel features, and their British accents are not as bad as the London mumblers on CNBC, son or daughter of NBC, the American network.

Phone: Except in the major hotels, you will seldom find a dial phone in the room. Most have a handset connected only to the front desk. Before using the phone, get specifics about the cost, and read chapter 19, "Communicating as You Travel Europe." The phone is a major profit center for hotels and $100 phone bills are not uncommon. There are some easy tricks you can use to keep this under control so make sure you read chapter 19. It can save you many times the cost of this book.

Electrical Outlet: One very well concealed electrical outlet is normal. See chapter 11, "Electricity in Europe," for information on how to use it.

Wash Basin: All rooms have a wash basin with running water. Sometimes the hot and cold water are reversed with the hot on the right. Look for the red handle for hot and the blue handle for cold. Sometimes there is no hot water.

Bidet: Right next to the basin is almost always a bidet. This piece of plumbing, looking somewhat like a toilet, is for washing your private parts. I use the bidet for washing my clothes.

Beds: Beds are generally too short to be comfortable for my 6'1" body, except in Scandinavia where I'm about average size. Beds in cheaper hotels are usually very soft and bad on your back. I have slept on the floor occasionally to get a better sleep.

Hang Ups: Most rooms have a small stand-up wardrobe or hooks on the wall for your clothes.

Mini Fridge: Small refrigerators stocked with drinks and snacks are starting to be seen in the tourist class hotels, in addition to the better hotels where they have been profit centers for years. Take what you please and it will be added to your hotel bill. These usually operate on the honor system, though some are automated. This is very convenient — and you pay dearly for the convenience. I usually buy some beer and cheese at a market and store them in the mini-fridge. It's not written that you can't put your own groceries in there.

Bathroom?

Do not call it a bathroom in Europe. In America, the tub and the potty are in the same room, called the bathroom. In Europe these facilities are often in separate rooms.

Toilet

For the potty, asking for the toilet or W.C. is appropriate. Brits call it the *water closet* or the *loo*. French might call it the *cabinet*.

When getting a room, specify whether or not you want a toilet in the room. Many rooms in Europe do not have a toilet. If there is no toilet in the room, there will be one in the hallway or on another floor.

Toilets in the hallways of many French hotels seem to have been installed in a broom closet as an afterthought. They are never heated and always feature an open window. Toilet paper has a texture somewhere between newsprint and crepe paper. Many travelers carry their own TP which guarantees that they'll have it when the facilities don't.

Shower

Since toilets and tubs are often found in separate rooms in Europe, you must specify whether you want a shower or bathtub when you book your room. Just because you have a toilet does not mean that you have a shower or tub, and vice versa. Many rooms have neither.

There will always be a shower or bathing room on your floor, or someplace else in the hotel. Smaller hotels sometimes charge extra to use the shower room.

Showers often have no shower curtain. In fact, the shower might be only a shower head on the wall of the toilet room with a drain in the middle of the floor. This guarantees that the whole room takes a bath.

Even if there is a shower in your room, there is no guarantee of hot water. In the eastern countries which grew up under the peoples' proletarian dictatorships, hot water can be shut off for a month or more. The reason is that all of the hot water in many towns is supplied from a central heating plant which burns brown coal, the fumes of which are readily and obnoxiously noticed in the air. Once a year the hot water plant must be shut down for routine maintenance. During that period there is no hot water. I stayed in a private home in Leipzig in former East Germany. To make sure he had hot water, the owner had a coal fired hot water heater installed in his bathroom. He had to load it with little bricks of charcoal and fire it up before I could jump in the tub.

Soap

Sometimes the hotel has it, and sometimes it does not. It is a good idea to carry a small bar of soap in your bag just in case. Don't buy it though. Pick up a bar from one of the hotels which leave extras in your bathroom. Bring your own soap to the eastern countries for sure. Their soap reminds you of something we had in the USA about fifty years ago. In fact, many things in the eastern countries are that way.

Elevators

Elevators under assumed names and camouflage are generally found in all hotels which are ranked above one star. A common name for elevator is lift because that is what the British call it and British English is what most people on the Continent learned in school. Some elevators remind you of bird cages, and others are ominously the size of coffins. If an elevator is present, it usually works. If you have a lot of luggage it probably knew you were coming and decided to take the week off.

Small hotel elevators normally have a heavy door that must be pulled open. These are designed to be locked until the elevator arrives, but not always. There is sometimes a second door which is part of the elevator cabin, and this is often a manual door also. Getting in and out with bulky luggage can be an annoyance.

For your own safety, get into the habit of using the stairs when going down. If you always descend by the stairs, you'll know where they are in case of fire. Chances are that if there is a fire, all of the electricity will be out, or soon will be right after you get on the elevator. Keep your flashlight handy on the night stand.

The elevator in this hotel in Naples (known in Italy as Napoli) is installed in the stairwell. You can see it coming. [1416]

Crime

Do not leave valuables laying around visible in your room. Maids sometimes take a break while the door is open. They usually do their work in mid morning and few people are in hotels at that time, but don't risk it. Small valuables can find swift feet. Once your camera or passport disappears there is little chance that you'll ever see it again.

Don't be a criminal yourself. Leave the towels. They are not included in the room price.

Bellhops

There are no bellhops in standard European hotels. Carry your own luggage. There are bellhops in the better quality hotels, especially in the Mediterranean countries and resort areas. Keep some tip money handy.

Forward Reservations

Hotels will normally phone ahead for you and reserve a room in your next city if you ask. In Finland, a desk clerk once made several long distance calls for me before she could find a hotel with an available room, and didn't charge me for the calls.

ALTERNATES TO HOTELS

Pensions

What is a pension? First, it's not pronounced "pen shun," but "pen cee ohn." A pension is usually a small rooming house owned and operated by a retired woman, often a widow.

Three meals per day can be included in the basic rate, though one or two meal "demi pensions" are usually offered. Don't expect to be in gourmet heaven. In small pensions it's just your normal home cooked meal, depending on the country and the owner.

Pension owners prefer that you stay for a few days. The prices are significantly lower than for hotels, partly because they don't have to change the sheets for a new customer every day and they don't have a corporate bean counter telling them how to run their business.

In resort areas on the Mediterranean, pensions can be sprawling complexes of bungalows. You'll find a lot of European families there on vacation.

This is self service. At a motel somewhere out in Bourgogne (Burgundy) the clerk locked up and went home at 23h00 (11 pm), but you can still get a room if there is a vacancy. Put your credit card in the "location automatic" and you'll get a key. France is probably the most tourist friendly country for auto travelers with low cost motels springing up everywhere. Oh how I love Burgundy. [1411]

Bed & Breakfast

The common acronym for this is B&B. You get a bed and breakfast in a private home which has been adapted for accommodating tourists. Though I have never used B&Bs in Britain or Ireland where they are most famous, I have slept in the Dutch equivalent many times. The Dutch equivalent can be identified by a sign in the window or yard of private homes in resort areas. The sign says "*Zimmer Frei.*" This is German for "Room Available." It is normally written in German because most of the visitors are from Germany. Some signs also have English or French translations, but when it says "Room Free," the literal translation of "*Zimmer Frei,*" do not expect to get gratis lodgings. Breakfast is normally not included unless the sign says "*Zimmer und/mit Frühstück*" ("Room and/with Breakfast"). *Zimmer Frei* is normally very cozy and comfortable, with warm welcomes for Americans from the Dutch owners.

Similar establishments are to be found in Scandinavia, Germany, and eastern Europe. On one of my visits to Prague I stayed in a *Zimmer Frei* on the outskirts of the city. I had to hitchhike back to my room that night because the buses had gone to bed before I finished my night on the town.

Hostels

First, notice that *hostel* is not spelled the same as hotel. The French changed hostel to *hôtel* some centuries ago, and in time we just forgot about the little roof over the o. They also changed hospital to *hôpital* but we didn't go along with that change.

Traditional hostels provide bunk house type accommodation and washing and toilet facilities. They are designed primarily for young travelers, though most have no age limit for visitors. At many hostels, facilities are provided for guests to cook their own meals. Each hostel is supervised by house parents. They provide economical meals in some cases. Guests share in the domestic duties as directed by the house parents.

Membership: In order to use most hostels, you must be a member of the hostel association. Write to or phone the American Youth Hostels (AYH) in Washington, DC or look them up on the internet.

It is not necessary to be a youth to be a member, but preference is given to members under 30 when space in the hostel is tight.

Rules: General rules of hostels:
- you must rent or bring your own sheet-type sleeping bag
- no smoking
- doors are usually locked at about 10 pm, and sometimes during midday
- duration of stay is limited to three consecutive nights.

There are variations to these generalities so verify the rules before you check in and unpack all your stuff.

Locations: The AYH publishes directories of hostels in the United States and overseas. Locations and recommendations are also given in the popular budget guidebooks. When using these books, read the directions carefully. A hostel listed for Seville may be quite a distance from the center of town. You may have to catch a bus and travel ten or fifteen miles out to a nearby suburb to get there. This won't be too pleasant if you arrive late at night and/or the clouds are dumping.

Security

Because hostels offer only a communal area for sleeping, security is something to keep in mind. Never leave valuables in an unattended bag. A money belt should also be considered. I've never owned one, but if I ever planned to stay in a hostel I would use a money belt. A padlock to anchor your backpack to something would also be a good idea.

Private Homes

It is sometimes possible to obtain a room in a private home. City tourist offices in Germanic language countries can make the arrangements for you, especially during very busy periods when all of the hotels are full. Rooms in private homes are much less expensive than comparable comfort in a hotel. Most homeowners prefer that you pay in advance. The homeowner gives you a key and then seems to disappear. Usually no breakfast is provided, and kitchen privileges are not granted. But I have been handsomely fed in private homes and treated very well on every occasion. The owners make a little extra money during the travel season, and you have a chance to see the kinds of homes and apartments they live in over there.

I showed up for *Oktoberfest* in München one fine September afternoon and couldn't find a room for less than twice my budget. After partaking of a ritual meal at the *Hofbrauhaus* and a few more *Massen* (huge mugs of beer) at the *Oktoberfest* fair grounds, I boarded an overnight train. I had several hours of sleep in my seat and got off somewhere at about 5 in the morning. I caught a return train (Eurailpass is great!) and slept on that until arriving back in Munich at about 10am. Then the tourist office landed me a great cheap room in a private home. I had a week of *Oktoberfest* — *wunderbar!*

Holland is a particularly hospitable place. One night in Amsterdam, instead of locating a hotel room I went out on the town. I met an interesting girl in a brown bar and enjoyed some drinks and chat. Then she introduced me to her husband talking at another table, and they invited me home to sleep on their couch. They made coffee for me in the morning and I left, giving them my best *Tot ziens!* (See you later!)

*This typical little Dutch hotel in Enkhuizen is also a café, restaurant, and pool hall. But, the sign in the window says "*Du Passage *is away on vacation. Closed from March 3 through 16. Brown bar* Het Ankertoe *is normally open after 4 o'clock." Small hotels scattered throughout the country make Holland an ideal place for an extended vacation by bicycle. If you are unsure of a room for the next night, ask your hotel keeper to phone ahead to hold a room in a town you're likely to reach by dinner time.*

[1423]

Here is a pair of two star hotels in Paris, France. There are about 1,500 hotels in and around the city.
[1413]

Chapter 15
Eating Your Way through Europe
Travel on Your Belly

Man cannot live by Maxims alone.

HOW TO FIND A GOOD RESTAURANT

It's a constant question — "Where do we eat?" Being as how we're not birds who pick their dinner from the ground, we must seek out and decide between hundreds of places on a trip to Europe. The search can be fun, or a gruel, as you decide between menus, prices, and locations.

You have probably brought along a guidebook or two. These looked worthwhile when you bought them but often turn into waste paper and extra weight when you go to use them.

This chapter will explain how to find your own unique eating discoveries. It also provides a general overview of the features of eating out in Europe which you'll find to be slightly different than dining out in your home town.

Streetwise Info

There is an easy way to find a good restaurant anywhere in Europe. Rather than use the guidebooks and lists you bought or were given, just stop someone on the street and ask for a recommendation.

The recommendation will depend on whom you ask. Select someone of approximately your own taste, determined by their age, clothing, and general appearance. If you are looking for specific items, e.g. fish, steak, pizza, vegetarian, etc., mention that. Be ready with a pen and paper to write down the name of the restaurant, or ask them to do it since you probably won't know how to spell steak house in their language. Directions will be confusing, so be ready with the city street map that you picked up at the tourist office when you arrived.

It may easily take 10 minutes to get the message and several more passers-by may stop to offer assistance and comment during the intercourse. Europeans are not in such a hurry as Americans, and they are generally happy to take a few minutes to help you out. Don't be too surprised if someone goes 10 minutes out of his way to escort you to his favorite restaurant. And if the person to whom you have made inquiry happens to have a car nearby, he might insist on driving you there.

This works everywhere. You might be amazed at the enthusiastic assistance you receive. But just imagine that if someone with a foreign accent stopped you on the street in Chicago and asked for a recommendation, you would help them out also, wouldn't you?

Upscale

For the better places, ask owners of shops when you are making other purchases. People in trade and business eat out often and probably know the owner of their favorite restaurant. They can recommend restaurants of good value, off the beaten tourist trail. And if you mention to the owner or head waiter that it was recommended by Monsieur Shopkeeper, you may receive a better table, portion, and service. Of course you can always ask your hotel keeper, though he would be inclined to have you eat in the hotel restaurant if there is one.

Pick Your Neighborhood

Restaurants on high rent boulevards are not likely to provide a good value meal. In major cities, you'll often find good restaurants in the financial district. If you see a few banks on a street, look around for a place to have lunch. Conversely, palatable food at cheap prices is likely to be found in the neighborhood of a university. For really cheap food walk right into the university cafeteria.

Look and Ask

You can window shop the menus of restaurants before sitting down. Virtually every restaurant posts its menu in the window or on a stand out on the sidewalk. Then open the door and look inside to see what fish or meat is fresh today.

In Brussels, the seafood is prominently exhibited in front of the restaurants. In other cities ask to see what they have in the kitchen if it is not displayed. I remember with a smile the time that three new-found fellow travelers from South America and I were given a tour of the kitchen in a Patras, Greece restaurant.

After I go in a restaurant and take a seat, I usually take a stroll. I cruise around the place and discretely look at tables to see what people are having. If I see something that looks appetizing I might ask the customer. It is fun and worthwhile to look at the plates and ask the eaters what they are having and how it tastes. Honest — just do it. I do this in the USA also. If someone asked you, you would tell them, wouldn't you?

I also ask the waitress about any item with which I am unfamiliar. In only a few countries will a waitress know the American name for something. However, there are always other diners within earshot who are only too eager to help. I became familiar with ostrich this way in a Düsseldorf restaurant a few years ago. If you like steak you will love ostrich.

A variation of my restaurant modus operandi is to keep an eye on the plates that the waiter is bringing out. When I see something interesting I ask what it is.

On the Road

Out on the highway, you'll probably pull over whenever you're hungry and can find a place to slip the car in. The best country to drive around is France. Small to large country restaurants all over the country serve the best every day of the year. In the hills of Slovenia and Croatia, just about every roadside eatery has a couple of lambs roasting on the charcoal out in front. I love roasted lamb. On the tollways in Italy and France, restaurants are provided for travelers. The food is not bad and the prices are reasonable. Similarly, rest stops on the *Autobahnen* in Germany usually have a restaurant with respectable food and prices. You can also pull off the highway and find a *Stube* in a nearby town.

Out on the road from Athens to Istanbul, we pulled into a roadside place where not a word of our lingoes were spoken. The owner escorted us into the kitchen where the meats on the menu were described as "moooo", "baaaa," and "oink." The chicken was obvious. [1521]

On the Train

Most people on trains have packed a lunch because train food can be a bit expensive. Eating in the dining car of a long distance express train is a memorable experience. Learn more about dining on the trains in chapter 17.

Low Budget Cuisine

For the lowest cost eating make yourself a picnic. Go to the butcher, the baker, the wine shop, and the cheese shop and buy a little of each. To save time, go to a supermarket. Take your groceries to a park bench, your hotel room, or your train and make yourself comfortable. Cut the bag open and use it as your tablecloth. Lay out your spread and start fixing your own. Wash down a couple of high protein sandwiches with a few glasses of Chateau Rouge and you're set for the afternoon or evening. Some of my finest meals have been at the table in my hotel room with a baguette, tomatoes, paté, a couple of beautiful smelly French cheeses, plus a bottle of wine, of course. You can do this for a few days to save up enough for a night at Maxims.

To expand your culinary experiences, picnic with some local specialties, raw. Steak tartare (raw ground meat) is on the menu of the best restaurants and sandwich shops. Less the spices, the same thing is found at the butcher shop. In Holland it is called *steak Americaine*. Some raw, pickled, and smoked fishes are delicacies all over northern Europe. My favorite is *nieuw haring* (fresh herring) in Holland. Buy it in a fish shop or fish stand, right ready for your champagne picnic.

The Lijnzaat fish stand at the Botermarkt in Haarlem is a busy place. Here you can buy cooked fish, sandwiches, and herring just like the Dutch. These stands are typical throughout The Netherlands. Raw herring is served with chopped onions and sometimes sliced pickle. The monger will cut the raw fish into bite sized pieces to eat with a toothpick. The traditional way to eat it is to pick it up by the tail, put your head back, and chomp off a mouthful at a time. [1523]

RESTAURANT POTPOURRI

European restaurants are more varied than the hotels, and almost as varied as the people. Generally, restaurants are individually owned and are much smaller than at home. Except for the fast sprouting "golden arches" and similar competitors imported from the USA and England, there are few restaurant chains in Europe.

Starving and can't find a restaurant open? Try a train station for fast food French style. You don't even need to know how to read or speak French — just point to a picture of something that looks appetizing. [1503]

Hours

That Europe does not have 24 hour diners is a gross understatement. Restaurants are closed for a good part of the day, and that part of the day varies from place to place. For instance, it's almost impossible to have dinner in France before 7 pm, but difficult to get it after 6 pm in Norway. Spain and Greece probably have the most unconventional eating hours. Most people in those countries eat lunch between two and four in the afternoon, then have dinner between nine and midnight. In Scandinavia, many better restaurants have a live band and dancing in the evening. They charge a hefty price just to walk in the door. In Germany, most restaurants have a *Ruhetag* (day off) even if they are part of a hotel.

In most countries, virtually all restaurants are closed on local holidays. In Holland everything is also closed on New Years Eve, the biggest night out for Americans.

Fixed eating hours generally don't apply to bar food. You can get a snack in most bars and cafes during the day and late at night, and at a reasonable cost.

These cafés in Ljubljana have taken over the sidewalk so the pedestrians take to the street, whatever there is of it. [1505]

Water

After getting a table, the first punishment for Americans in northern European restaurants is: do not pass go, do not collect a glass of water, go directly to eating. Actually there are at least two ways to get a glass of water. One is to order bottled water, and pay for it. Another is to order a cola, beer, tomato juice, or whatever, and a glass of water at the same time. The water usually comes for free, unless it's bottled water. Specify ice if you want it and be happy with the meager cube delivered.

On the other hand, in many restaurants in the Mediterranean countries, a carafe of water is brought to your table with the menu. But it would be a good idea to avoid drinking water other than sealed bottle in southern and eastern Europe, especially during the summer. Catching an intestinal bug can be devastating.

Service

Second punishment is the "service." Holland has probably the worst restaurant service in Europe, but no country has service of as good a quality as we are accustomed to in the USA. You might sit helpless for ten minutes while the waiter stands five feet away reading a newspaper. Take it easy! The waiter or waitress gets

15% of the tab which is already included in the price of everything on the menu, or added on before you get the bill. Why move fast if the tips are fixed? A German friend of mine told me that her father finally got tired of waiting for service in one Dutch restaurant so he walked over to the waiter's station and asked the waiter, who was having a cigarette with a friend, when he was going to bring the menu. The waiter replied that it wouldn't be long, and added, "You have to wait in the doctor's office too, don't you?"

At a two star restaurant in Paris, there were more penguins than customers, but most of them posed discreetly out of earshot. It was impossible to get anything until they determined that it was our turn. "Penguin" is my term for a waiter in a tuxedo because that is what they look like.

This Metzgerei (butcher) in Frankfurt a/M (am Main) also serves great sandwiches, salads, and beverages — cheap, fast, and good. [1504]

Fast Service

There are exceptions to every rule, and the best exception to the surly café service in Paris is at the Triadou Haussmann near the *Gare St. Lazare* (St. Lazare Train Station). I had the funniest, fastest waiter in my life there. Ask for the *service rapide* if it is still advertised on the front window. By the way, the bad reputation of France is due, in my opinion, to the malcontents who serve as café waiters in Paris. The average Frenchman is as hospitable as the average American, and Parisians in general are par with Chicagoans when it comes to the friendly factor.

If you are really in a hurry to eat, tell the head waiter immediately, before sitting down. Otherwise forget it, and forget about going anywhere for the next couple of hours. It's just not right to eat French food in a hurry, and they normally won't let you do it.

Bummer Service

Don't let waiters intimidate you, bring things you didn't order, and jack up the prices. In Madrid, a waiter left a full bottle of wine on my table and I promptly told him to replace it with the half bottle I had ordered. Then I ordered squids at 525 pesetas (this was before the euro) and he brought a plate with a large fish on it. He had already made me wait long enough, so I ate it. Then he gave me a bill for 900 pesetas, the price of the fish I had eaten. I shoved that back at him and reminded him of what I had ordered. A couple more waiters and a few minutes later, they brought me a bill for 525 pesetas which I paid. It was a darn good fish.

In Paris I ordered a *demi* at a café. The waiter brought out a half liter glass of beer. I reminded him that I had ordered a *demi* and asked him to take it back. He stood there playing dumb. I stood up and told him to go fly his kite, well actually I made it a bit more understandable by commenting on his negative IQ and maternal canine ancestry or something to that effect. I walked over to another café.

In Athens I went out to dinner with some doctors from Latin America, fellow travelers I met on the boat from Italy. The service was good, but the waiters pulled some exorbitant stunts. They kept delivering little trays of sauces which we thought were included with the appetizers we had ordered. When the bill came, we found out that those little trays cost two to five dollars each. Watch out in the Plaka section near the Acropolis. The food and entertainment are great, but the bill can bust your budget with the slick "service."

In the gastronomic capital, Brussels, you can also find fast food places like this. One of those big burgers costs 3.20 euros and should keep you going for the afternoon. [1526]

Coffee

There is quite a difference in the types of coffee served in Europe. In England and Ireland it is black or white. "White" is with cream. Expresso, also called espresso, is my addiction. This is a strong, two sip coffee served in France and Italy usually accompanied by a twist of lemon peel. Coffee is very black in Spain and Portugal, but not especially tasty. Greek coffee is a sweet, two sip cup, half of which is fine muddy grounds. Ask for "o-hee sak-reen" if you don't want a pound of sugar in your Greek coffee, and don't stir it up! Turkish coffee also comes with a half cup of grounds which doesn't leave much room for the liquid.

There must be hundreds of little taverns like this one in Madrid. This one has its menu painted on the window. Notice the hams hanging from the ceiling. They cure them up there for 18 months. [1513]

Cocoa

For those who want to stay awake and do not want to take coffee, try chocolate. A few ounces of dark chocolate has about as much of the alkaloid caffeine in it as a cup of coffee, and is a better pick up for me than caffeine. Chocolate can keep me awake for half the night. I carry a bar of dark bitter chocolate with me all the time for a quick afternoon pick up.

On the door of a restaurant in Kiev Pepsi is spelled in Cyrillic. [1519]

Menu

The word *menu* is often used to denote a particular dinner selection, and *card* (*carte* or *karte*) refers to what we think of as the menu. On the card are often several menus of three to seven course meals in addition to the *á la carte* lists. The menus allow substitutions, if stated, and they are less expensive than assembling a meal from the *á la carte* lists. Look for daily specials which can be posted on cards on your table, on a blackboard hanging on the wall, or posted out front on the sidewalk.

Often you will be told, after you order an item, "it is finished." The translation of this is that you won't be eating that one today, probably because they haven't had it available for a week. In the eastern countries, menus list many items, only a few of which have prices next to them. Most of the priced items are available.

For an excellent introduction to European menus, consult the practice menus in the Marling Menu Masters. Reading the menus, even with a translating dictionary, is difficult until you've been in a country for a week or two and know what to expect. Many of the better restaurants provide an English translation menu. Some of these translations are confusing or amusing. Almost every one translates "escargots" to "snails." This sort of spoils the essence of slugs baked in butter and garlic.

With a tankard above the door it is not hard to figure out what is dispensed in this Prague establishment. Some of the best beer in the world is made in the Czech Republic. [1506]

Prices

As a general rule, you can eat much better at a lower cost in a nearby smaller city than in a large city. For instance, from Nice, go over to Antibes for dinner. With a Eurailpass this trip costs you nothing.

In general, it costs less to eat and drink as you go south and east. In northern Europe, the best values are to be had in Greek and Italian restaurants, in small cafes and bars, and at smorgasbords where you can pork out at a reasonable cost. Prices are already low in Spain, but if you want to save a little more, eat at the *barra* ("bar") rather than at a *mesa* ("table").

The champions in low cost eating are in the eastern countries, and the further east you go the lower the cost goes. Devaluation of the currencies of Russia and Ukraine are a major reason for these bargains. With six business colleagues, dinner cost $10 for the whole table in one of the better hotels in Kiev several years ago, including two bottles of vodka and wine. The meal was not great, barely edible.

In the west, fine restaurants can be within everyone's budget if you're not too hungry, or if you know what to order. One of the most magnificent stuffings I ever had cost less than two Big Macs at a top hotel in Stockholm. The *sillbord* was an appetizer of nine assorted types of herring, baked potato, sour cream, and cheeses, and could feed two people plus a doggie bag. One beer and a cup of coffee almost doubled the price.

Tax and Tip

A 15% service fee (call it the tip) is usually included in the price of everything in most restaurants and bars in Europe. Look for a note on the menu. When the 15% service fee is not included in the price, it is always added to your bill and demanded by the waiter. This add-on method seems to be a common practice in Scandinavia, Italy, and Paris.

The service fee notation will be accompanied with a mention of the national sales tax. The tax can be known as *T.V.A., ETC, V.A.T., MOMS., I.V.A,* or some other initials. Consult your Berlitz or Marling for the local name. The tax ranges from 7% to over 20% depending on the country. Tax is always included in the prices.

Menu prices and bills don't always look the same. The prices on the bill may be shown without the tax, and then the tax is added on. The result should be the same as the total using the prices on the menu. If you are in doubt, ask for an explanation. If they made a mistake, give them a wide berth on offering a rationalization.

So as a general rule it is not necessary to tip in Europe — the waiter has already tipped himself. The price on the menu is normally the total you will pay, tax and tip included.

If you are not sure, ask the owner if you can look at a menu before sitting down and ask if those prices include service and tax. Do not ask the waiter after he presents the bill whether or not his tip has been included. That is tacky and will embarrass him, if he knows the meaning of the word tip.

If you find yourself in need of a good steak when you are in Antwerp, Belgium look for an Argentine steak house. Similar establishments are all over northern Europe. [1527]

Extra Costs

In Italy many *ristorante* and *trattoria* menus have a *pane e coperto* (bread and cover) charge stated at the top of the menu. You must ask for butter for the bread, but the butter is often free. The bread charge is a minimum of $1, and is in addition to the 15% service charge.

In Athens, many cafes charge extra at Christmas. A note on one menu said, in English, that the service charge is increased for the period December 16 through January 15 due to the Christmas bonus, from 16% to 28%. Not all of them were doing this.

The interior of the New York Coffee House in Budapest, Hungary is a sight not to be missed. They just don't build them like this anymore. This sign above the door is a severe understatement. [1520]

Tastes Good and Not So

Americans are beef eaters. European beef generally does not taste as good as that in the USA, and/or may be tough. Spain is a possible exception to this statement. In the rest of Europe look for an Argentine steak house for the closest resemblance to American beef.

Pork, lamb, chicken, fish, and cheese in Europe is usually better than that in America. Eat the local products and in-season specialties for better dining and lower prices.

However, the quality varies remarkably within Europe. The British truly deserve their well-earned reputation for consistently bad tasting food. Whenever possible eat in a Greek, Italian, or French restaurant in London. Also, avoid any place on the Continent with a British sounding name. Tip: *Anglais* and *Londres* are French words meaning English and London, respectively.

Our experience in Istanbul was outstanding. The food at a local café near Topkapi Gate was so good that we ate there just about every night, taking "our table" on the balcony to watch the worlds walk by. It was fascinating. Other clients and the owner were good conversationalists.

For the best overall dining in my book, get out into the French countryside. Go to Burgundy (between Dijon and Lyon) and the Loire Valley (between Orleans and Angers) for great groceries, fowl, meat, and wine at a reasonable cost. The triangle formed by Geneva, Orleans, and Strasbourg should have some ebullient epicurean moniker attached to it. When I lived in Holland, a friend told me that for my vacation I should eat my way through France. That is outstandingly good advice.

On my way south from Holland to France, as I discovered years later, I should have been stopping in Brussels. You can become addicted to mussels in this city. Skip Brussels and you have doomed yourself to having passed up some of the best eating on the planet.

I have had memorable and low-cost meals in all of the Mediterranean countries, and great fish in Portugal and Scandinavia. During the fall, wild game is available in many restaurants in Germany, Holland, and France. I love wild rabbit in Holland and deer in Germany. Fall is also the time for real bock beer from the keg and *Beaujolais Nouveau* wine in France. This wine goes great with Thanksgiving turkey.

Food in the eastern countries is generally pretty bad. You might even wish you were over in England. When driving through Poland, I would usually go to the top hotel in any city and order the best steak on the menu. It was always mediocre, but I was on a beef diet at the time so I kept hoping for something better. When Elizabeth and I made our trip through Bulgaria and Romania, we ate in the best places available, which left plenty to be desired by standards in western Europe.

Most travelers still bring along something to eat when going to the east since there is no telling what you are going to be served. The *Chicken Kiev* I was served every night at the hotel in Kiev seemed to contain something different each time. I'm sure the situation will improve, but in the meantime, just accept it as part of the experience. If you see the kind of crustaceans the Parisians consider delicacies (if it's organic eat it), you can probably eat that eastern stuff. Actually one of the worse meals I ever had was the owner's specialty in a small German hotel It was a *hausgemacht* (home made) sausage with blood still dripping out of it. The owner beamed as I ate it — to avoid offending him.

A few years after the Fall of the Wall (that was November 1989), I had dinner in Leipzig (former East Germany) with a couple of business colleagues and the situation can be described as bizarre at best. We were seated at a table with a drunk, a stoned drunk with his cheek on the table and fast asleep. They soon took him out. Our meals came in shifts, at various temperatures and with some semblance of what we though we had ordered. My colleagues were Germans and they were just as shocked as I. It was about the only place in town and we were just short of starvation at the moment, so we suffered it.

Duplicating Home

Trying to find something "just like home" is going to be a grind of time. Unless you were brought up on food by a first generation American and you go back to your mother's homeland you just won't find much of anything resembling American cooking. On a special event during my first years in The Netherlands our host treated us to prime rib. It was a terrible piece of meat. A good local fish would have been far more appetizing.

Surrounded by music and it's not even stereo. We were early at this Istanbul restaurant and had the entertainment to ourselves. It is proper and expected to tip the musicians. [1501]

Seating

In some restaurants, every vacant table displays a "reserved" card. Probably none of these tables is reserved. Ask the head waiter for a table and you will be seated immediately if you are properly dressed, i.e., no Levis and no Nikes.

If you walk in and notice that every table is occupied, ask the head waiter for a seat anyway. He will sometimes seat you at a table partially occupied by other guests, at least one of whom wants to practice English. Don't be bashful. This is an excellent opportunity to meet Europeans. If you don't know the local language, simply say "Hello," and then add that you are a tourist from America and sorry but you only speak English. You'll probably have a pretty good conversation going in seconds.

Sugar & Spice

Sugar and fake sweetener are usually on the tables. Salt and pepper are also present, but in northern Europe it is white pepper, not black pepper.

Eating Procedure

How do you eat? I was taught at home to cut my food, then put the knife down, transfer the fork to my right hand, put my left hand in my lap, fork the food into my mouth, eat the food, put the fork in my left hand, spear some food, pick up the knife, and start again. Europeans laugh when they see this. They keep the fork in the left hand and they keep it busy. They keep the knife in the right hand cutting or scooping food up on the fork and only put the knife down to take a drink of wine or beer.

Europeans normally break off a piece of bread instead of biting off a piece. Sandwiches are usually open face and are eaten with a knife and fork.

When finished with your soup, put the spoon in the saucer that the soup bowl came in. When done with your dinner, put your knife and fork on your plate with the handles on the right side. Waiters understand these positions and are more likely to clear your table when they see them.

At a seafood restaurant in Portugal, instead of knives and forks, the waiter gave most people a mallet and a small square of wood. It was a noisy restaurant, and the people were having a great time bashing open those crab legs.

At a restaurant in Lyon, France, notice the shucker behind his baskets of huitres *(oysters). [1514]*

Alcoholic Beverages

Many Americans start dinner in a restaurant with a cocktail. In Europe people will start with a glass of dry sherry or another wine derivative.

Beer, wine, and locally distilled spirits are part of the way of life in most of Europe. Children are brought up with spirits on the table and consequently it is no big deal to turn 21 for the first legal drink as it is in the USA. Some cafés are posted with a minimum age, 16 or 18, but usually not. I've never seen anybody checking ID in a bar or restaurant.

The exception to liberal drinking laws is Scandinavia. They have a pretty weird attitude on alcohol up there. Official policy is to make it as difficult as possible to have a drink. In Finland, it is against the law to sell gin, vodka, or *akvavit* (a nicely flavored distilled grain alcohol) in a café unless it is mixed in a drink. All alcohol sold in Finland is controlled by the state monopoly *ALKO*. This company imports French wine in bulk and bottles it under its own labels, *OY ALKO*. In Sweden, alcoholic beverages are sold by the state monopoly *Systembolaget*, inconveniently closed on Saturday and Sunday. These unusual laws create aberrations which tourists can take advantage of. For example, wines in Swedish restaurants are not marked up as high as beer. For the price of three beers, you can get a full bottle of French Beaujolais or German Riesling.

Before ordering any distilled spirits, specify what size you want. The menu normally gives prices for 2cl and 4cl. In the Scandinavian and Mediterranean countries, you might get 8cl if you just order the "big one." Specify 4cl if that is what you want.

There are very strict laws regarding drinking and driving in every country. For more details, see chapter 18, "On the Roads of Europe."

On rue des Bouchers also known as Beenhouwerstraat the restaurants display the catch of the day out in front on what was formerly the sidewalk. This is Brussels, Belgium, home of great mussels. [1525]

Toasting

Americans toast by clanking glasses with an appropriate "Cheers!" or some other greeting. In Holland, Germany and some other countries the custom does not include clanking the glasses. But it does include a straight eyeball-to-eyeball stare for a split second as you hold your glass up.

The Bill

After eating, getting attention and getting the bill is often a problem. Wave at the waiter. When he notices you, hold up your left hand and mimic writing squiggles on it with your right. He will understand.

When the waiter presents the bill, check the prices versus the menu, and the addition. In Holland and in Spain I have had a different menu and prices shown to me after I questioned the price of dinner. In Holland the waiter went back to the kitchen after my protest and came back ten minutes later with a menu on which he had taped little squares of paper with higher prices. I couldn't believe it. "Be fair," I said, and paid the amount shown on the table menu. That restaurant is no longer in business.

Mistakes in adding up the bill are common, and most of the time the numbers run a little high. Many restaurants are changing to computerized bill printing. This is nice because now I can read them. Handwriting and numbers are difficult to interpret in Europe. I haven't found any errors in arithmetic on the electronic bills, but have seen cases where the price or quantity of an item was inflated. Also, make sure that something you didn't order is not slipped onto your bill.

This is the way the Dutch go grocery shopping in Amsterdam – on their bicycles with luggage racks and saddle bags. Buy your in-room picnic fixins here to save time and money, not to mention having a better meal than from the sandwich shops. [1524]

Bar Food

For good food at reasonable prices, eat in a bar. At almost any time during the day in Holland and Dutch-speaking parts of Belgium, ask for an *uitsmijter* (white bread topped with ham or cheese and two sunny-side up eggs) or *erwtensoep* (delicious heavy pea soup with sausage) and *roggebrood* (black rye bread) with raw bacon on the side, but only available during the winter). In France and French-speaking parts of Belgium ask for a *croque monsieur* (toasted ham and cheese sandwich) or a *croque madame* (toasted ham, cheese, and egg sandwich). In Greece, the taverns have all kinds of things to eat and you usually get an appetizer with your drink. Over in Italy I found a gourmet cafeteria in the back of a tavern in Milan. For under six bucks I had two large pieces of salmon, a garden of groceries, and a glass of good red wine.

At bars in Italy they do make it a bit difficult to get served. First survey the food on display and then go over to the cashier and pay for what you want. Then go back to the counter with the receipt and order your food. Give the receipt to the waiter/waitress behind the bar as payment. He/she will promptly give it a rip and throw it on the counter next to your selection. It's doubly difficult for those of us who don't speak Italian. How do you tell the cashier what it is that you want when the unknown delicacy is on a counter 30 feet away? Somehow it happens.

Over in Madrid, the tourist office will give you a city map showing where most of the taverns are located. Each one has a selection of things to eat and I spent several days making the rounds trying all the *tapas* possible. In one bar, I ordered *paella* — a heap of saffron rice with a few small clams, crabs, and pieces of chicken. There I was in a public place staring at two little red crabs hiding in my rice, and they were staring back at me! They were about three inches across and too small to break open. What else could I do? They were already cooked, so I ate them, eyeballs, shell, and all. They were crispy like potato chips and tasted pretty good.

If you're starving late at night in Holland, ask for a *tostie* while you have a beer and trade tales with your new-found Dutch friends in a cozy brown bar. A *tostie* is a cheese or ham sandwich popped into the toaster.

Tourists enjoy their caffe espresso *at a sidewalk spot near the Vatican in Rome. These cafes also serve ham and cheese sandwiches and other snacks. [1515]*

Toilets

Toilets in restaurants are usually marked with the symbol of a man or woman, or have the local name for "man" or "woman" on the door. Some may simply have a triangle on one door and a circle on the other. Other obtuse symbols can also be seen. If uncertain, ask, or wait to see who comes out or goes in.

Toilets normally go under other names over there but are never called the "bathroom." Though often labeled *W.C.* (for water closet), local names like *toalet* in Scandinavia, *services* or *aseos* in Spain, or *loo* in Britain are commonly used. Generally you can get what you want by asking for the "toilet" or W.C., but pronounced as "wee cee" (France, Italy, etc.), or "vay say" (Germany, Holland, eastern Europe, etc.).

The eastern countries normally use the *hammam*, a form of toilet that is simply a square ceramic depression in the floor. It has two elevated shoe shaped platforms in it and a hole in the middle. You'll find these in many cafes in France, Italy, and the eastern countries.

Do not expect toilet paper in European toilets. Let yourself be surprised. Tip:

you won't often be surprised in the eastern countries. If you find toilet paper you might not recognize it, except for the fact that it is in the toilet room.

I never eat in MacDonald's "restaurants" but I'm glad they are parked in a few countries with less than standard sanitary standards. MacDonald's toilets have clean thrones and white toilet paper.

A passenger in a first class car to Rome buys a snack from a station vendor. If there is no food service on the train, you are likely to see these carts in the stations. But don't get off the train to buy a sandwich. It's better to starve a little than to see your train moving out with your suitcase while you're waiting for change! [1517]

Emergency Snack

There are few things more uncomfortable than hunger so travel on a full belly and/or with a full meal in your sack. You'll have an unusual timetable, not always of your own making. Arrival times will not be regular, and trains can run late, causing missed connections and late arrivals. On the highways, traffic jams can be worse than anything you've seen at home.

Carry some bread, cheese, and fruit on the train or in your car. Carry a can of sardines or some other durable at all times for those late night emergencies. A chocolate or granola bar can tide you over for a couple hours. A spoonful of peanut butter is another great snack.

Smoking

There are beaucoup more smokers in Europe than at home. It is still fashionable to smoke cigarettes. Also, cigars are common and acceptable for an after dinner smoke in restaurants. Holland has great cigars, and they're cheap. I was amused in Copenhagen to see two women light up cigars after eating. Apparently this is an old tradition of Danish women.

Dessert

The desserts offered after dinner in Europe are beautiful. They are not big but they are beautiful. From cream cakes to fresh fruit to the darkest chocolate creations, you normally have a impossible choice.

I rarely take a dessert. I'm sweet enough. I prefer the cheese platters. There are so many cheeses and so little time.

Doggie Bags

There are no doggie bags in Europe. This should not stop you from rolling up some bread and your leftovers in a paper napkin and taking them back to your hotel. It might be all the breakfast you need tomorrow morning.

At a café in Monza, Italy the appetizers are already laid out on the counter. [1509]

Chapter 16
Getting Around Town
Bus, Streetcar, Subway, Taxi, Bike, and Shoe

Leave your car at the city limits.

PERSONAL AUTO

Don't Even Think About It

Europe's cities are no easier to drive and park in than ours in the USA. Among the drawbacks of using a personal auto in the major cities are the following hazards and headaches: lack of parking spaces, expensive street parking, confusing parking regulations, massive traffic jams, narrow one-way streets, poorly marked streets, streets with new names every few blocks, auto theft and burglary, bus lanes indicated in the local language, fearless law flaunting pedestrians, rule-the-road streetcar drivers, double-parked delivery trucks, radar traps, and the numerous unpredictable and utterly unfamiliar driving habits of the local citizens. If you must for whatever reason take life and liberty into your own hands, read the details on driving in Europe later in chapter 18, "On the Roads of Europe."

You can walk faster than you can drive in Geneva, Switzerland. I twice had pedestrians come over to my car and offer assistance after noticing me jammed in traffic with a map in hand. [1617]

Sane Alternates
Use the indigenous public transportation facilities to enjoy your time, avoid major hassles, and save money. The preferred means of navigating European cities are subways, streetcars, buses, taxis, bicycling, and walking.

One of the major headaches associated with driving a car in virtually any city is finding a place to park it. Here in a municipal lot of Aschaffenburg, Germany all of the rules are written in German under the respective international icons for No Parking and for Parking. Parking is not allowed on Wednesday (abbreviated Mi for Mittwoch) and Saturday from 4am to 2pm because the farmers market uses the lot on those days. Only cars can be parked. Buy a parking permit from a machine on the lot and place it on your dash. Parking is free on evenings and weekends. Don't walk your dog here. My advice: obey the rules whether you can read them or not. German cops go by the book and love to write tickets. I've had a few. Bottom line - leave your car at the city limits. [1602]

PUBLIC TRANSIT

Most cities have excellent public transportation systems. The subways, streetcars, and buses are part of an integrated network that was designed for daily commuters but can be efficiently used by tourists. Routes for city rail systems often extend to the suburbs and airports.

The "strip" is valid on buses and trams throughout Holland, plus the metro in Amsterdam. Use one coupon plus another one for each zone you travel in. The cost of a 15 coupon Nationale Strippen Kaart is 6.20 euro, a big savings over paying for each individual ride. This picture shows only the first five strips. [1641]

Tickets and Passes

Tickets can be purchased at windows or kiosks in the train stations, and sometimes from the driver or from ticket *automats*. Tickets are often interchangeable between buses, *trams* (streetcars), and *metros* (subways) in the major cities.

Passes or blocks of tickets can usually be purchased which give a discount to regular users of the system, and save time standing in ticket lines every time you get on a bus. In Amsterdam, purchase a *strip*, valid for the *Metro*, the *trams*, and the buses throughout Holland. Details on using the system are available at the *Metro-Tram-Bus* Information office outside Centraal Station. In Paris, purchase a *carnet* of ten tickets and save time and money using the *Metro*. Longer term visitors can buy a monthly *Carte Orange*. London, Rome, Stockholm, and other major cities also have specials.

Passes and block ticket discounts are not always designed for tourists. They facilitate use of the systems by commuters going to work every day. So see if the terms suit your sightseeing schedule before buying.

For a flat fee in some cities you can travel as far as you can go in one hour. In other cities you must pay for distance according to zone maps. Since each city has a different manner of doing business, ask for information at the city tourist office about fares, zones, and hours of operation.

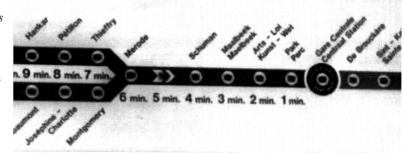

The Brussels metro stations have these boards indicating where the trains are and how long it will be before the next one arrives. [1644]

Routes and Schedules

Request a route map at the city tourist information office or at a ticket window. A route map might be called a *plan* or *plano* or *mappa* or something similar depending on where you are. There are usually route maps posted in the subway stations and itineraries posted at streetcar and bus stops. But the time when you need one is the time that it won't be handy. Be prepared. Route maps are usually free and they are often detailed enough so that you don't need to buy a city map.

Bus and tram routes are numbered. Metro routes are usually identified by the names of the stations at each end of the line and/or by route numbers and letters.

This is the Embankment *tube stop on the* London Underground. *There is a convenient map of the system on the wall. You can understand why they call it "The Tube." [1625]*

If you're new in town and not sure where to get off, it's a good idea to tell the driver of a streetcar or bus where you want to go. The driver probably can't speak English, so point out the place on a city map or in a guidebook, or write it in block letters in your travel record book and show it to the driver. You won't be able to understand the name of the stop he tells you to get off at either, and if you can understand it the windows may be so dirty or fogged that you won't be able to see it anyway. So sit as close to the driver as you can. When your stop comes up, he'll let you know. Keep one eye on the driver.

Schedules are sometimes posted at streetcar and bus stops. Bus drivers often ignore schedules, so you should also. Since you don't know when your ride will show up, allow yourself an extra fifteen minutes when using the public transports. At a remote stop you might wait half an hour and then have two of your number pass within minutes.

Subways, streetcars, and buses have limited, if any, service after midnight. Before you take off for a night of carousing on the other side of town, make sure you can get back to your hotel.

Weekend service is much less frequent than during the week. Public transportation is usually shut down or severely reduced on public holidays. Employee job actions, "strikes," are frequent, but usually last for only a day or so.

A sign above the Paris Metro platform notes the trains going in the direction of Mairie d'Ivry and Villejuif, with connections to line M9. [1638]

Subways

Just outside or in another cavern of the main train station, the *Métropolitain*, *U-bahn*, *Underground*, or otherwise named subway lines originate or intersect.

Boarding usually involves putting your ticket into a turnstile and walking through. If you are carrying a heavy load you might have a slight difficulty getting through. Then you have to find the right platform and get on the right train to go in the right direction. Almost all stations are very well posted, but it sure helps to have that system map in hand just in case.

Making transfers is easy. When you get off, just follow the signs to the rail line going in your direction. Some of those connecting tunnels are pretty long, so have patience and keep walking. Don't bother running because there is a train every few minutes anyway.

"Make your choice!" The metro ticket automat in the Brussels central train station sells individual tickets, and tickets valid for 5 or 10 rides, or a whole day, and other cards. This is in French but pressing the "Other languages" button will give you other languages. [1643]

FAITES VOTRE CHOIX !
08.01.2003   16:02:39
1 VOYAGE   AUTRES CARTES
5 VOYAGES   NEDERLANDS
10 VOYAGES   OTHER LANGUAGES
UN JOUR   AIDE

Getting off is a snap everywhere except in London and in Rome. In most cities, just follow the exit signs, e.g., *sortie* in Paris, *Ausgang* in Munich, and soon you'll see daylight, or city lights. Paris makes it especially easy with those *Plan du Quartier* maps in all the *Metro* stations so you know where you're coming out.

The problem in London is that you have to *queue up* (get in line) and give your ticket to an agent when exiting. Many people on the Continent ride for free, illegally. In London, all tickets are stamped with originating and destination stations so it's tough to cheat. Over in Paris, it is usually easy to get on without a ticket. However, special agents may ask to see your ticket and slap a fine on you if you don't have one. Some *Metro* stations in Paris post names of recently convicted free riders, with the amounts they were fined. It can be expensive.

The Munich system is a relatively new one in Europe. It opened for the 1972 Olympics. The subways in Paris and London are a century old. Amsterdam has a new and very good metro system.

Most *Metro* and *U-bahn* stations have escalators to help you get up out of the tunnels. If the escalator is not running, walk up and step on the metal plate in front of it. It will probably start. If it does not start, you are probably in Rome. Rome also has poorly marked directions and the deepest, deepest tunnels on the Continent.

The big M *means* Metro *which means "Metropolitan Railway." Similar signs are used in all major cities, except it might be a* T *or* U *or some other letter depending on the local name for "subway." This is an entrance in Rome, Italy, adjacent to one of the city's fountains. [1627]*

Streetcars

Many major cities have streetcar systems. Streetcars are usually called *trams*. Since these run on city streets, stop often, and compete for limited space with autos and pedestrians, the traveling is slow compared to the subways. But going slow can have its advantages for sightseers. Armed with a good city map and a day ticket, you can scoot all over town, checking out the people, architecture, parks, and castles in the relaxed position. A "good city map" shows all streets, numbered tram/bus routes and stops, and the major edifices.

We used the trams to get around handily in Budapest, Hungary. [1603]

The tram is the quick, cheap, and easy way to go from Topkapi Gate to the center of Istanbul, Turkey. Trams are not air conditioned and can get steamy inside. [1613]

The main streetcar station is usually right outside the main train station. There are stops every quarter mile or so, and frequent service. If you see a track, you're not far from a ride.

On boarding, show your ticket to the driver or put it in the time stamper machine as the local rules specify. Just because you see a lot of people get on and sit down, apparently without a ticket, does not mean that you can ride for free. Those people might have a monthly pass or a transfer in their pocket, or they might be risking a fine by riding for free.

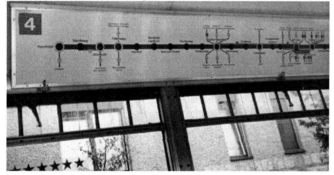

Many buses, streetcars, and subway cars have line maps on the ceiling showing all stops and connections. This is on streetcar line 4 in Zurich, Switzerland. [1628]

The double-decker bus is a moving London monument. Enter at the rear, climb the stairs, and take a seat. The conductor will come around shortly and sell you a ticket, price depending on how far you are going. Or make it easy on yourself and buy a pass to ride all day. [1630]

ATAC is the acronym for the urban bus line system in Rome, Italy. This Fermata *(bus stop) shows which buses stop here and where they go. With a* Roma Pass *and a good city map, you can navigate the city with ease on the two* Metro *and the numerous bus lines.* [1631]

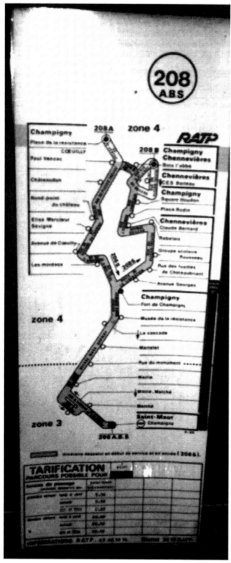

Here is the route for bus 208 in Paris, France. The city could hardly make it easier for you. Buy the carnet of ten tickets to save time, trouble, and money. [1616]

Do not drive, ride a bike, or walk on or between tram rails. The cars are electric and are very quiet, especially with all the other street noise around you. Amsterdam conductors love to wait until they are on your heels and then they *RING THE BELL!!!*

Buses

Buses are sometimes called *autobuses.*

Buses are in use in all of the large cities, most of the small ones, and cross-country. A card valid for unlimited travel for a day or for several days can be purchased which would make for generally good do-it-yourself sightseeing.

Rail travelers who want to get to a small town which has no train service should inquire at the railroad information office in a nearby city about bus service. Intercity service often includes stops at crossroads and in the middle of nowhere. In some countries bus drivers stop for people waving them down along the highway.

A reticulated electric bus jammed with passengers to standing room only leaves the Constanta, Romania train station. [1611]

Sometimes you can pay on the bus, but before you stand in a line waiting to get on, find out whether you will be able to purchase a ticket on board. Tickets are usually more expensive when buying individually or from a driver. When buying a ticket from the driver, try to have the correct change.

Schedules for intercity buses originating at main train stations are followed more closely than those for the in-town buses. I've had pretty good service in Germany, Holland, Greece, Norway, and Portugal on intercity buses. And these buses are very comfortable

Buses typically have stop buttons so you can let the driver know when you want to get off. Since the uscita *light is already lit on this bus it means that a passenger has already signaled the driver so he will stop at the next bus halt in Monza, Italy. [1622]*

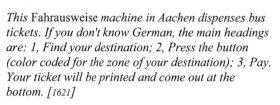

This Fahrausweise *machine in Aachen dispenses bus tickets. If you don't know German, the main headings are: 1, Find your destination; 2, Press the button (color coded for the zone of your destination); 3, Pay. Your ticket will be printed and come out at the bottom. [1621]*

TAXIS

Taxis seem to be everywhere, except when you need them most. Taxis wait at train stations, airports, at large hotels, and outside night clubs.

If you are a fan of the wild rides in amusement parks, you might want to take a taxi ride just for the thrill of it. They're not for the fainthearted. Also, some will rip you off, just like at home. Another thrill.

Before getting in any taxi, find out approximately how much the ride will cost. Ask the hotel concierge or the tourist office for an estimate.

Also ask the taxi driver for his estimate before getting in. Write down the name of your destination and the price you think you heard from him and ask him to agree to what you have written. Compare. If he quotes 59 verbally, it may turn out to be 95 (not necessarily an attempted rip-off; see chapter 26).

If the taxi driver plays dumb and can't speak English, get suspicious in a hurry. Find someone to translate, or take another taxi. In all cases, write down the name of your destination and show it to the driver. Unless you are a fluent native, there is always the possibility that you will be deposited on the wrong side of town.

The average London taxi driver is the most helpful and civilized member of the taxi driver species. But across the Channel, be careful. I found the drivers in Rome to be particularly suited to larceny. On a visit to my client in Aachen, Germany I had been faxed a map and a taxi estimate. The first taxi driver looked at it and agreed. About 15 minutes later the meter was getting close to the amount and the client's factory was nowhere in sight. I asked about it and the taxi driver said that we were going the "fast way" and that my "company was paying for it anyway." Stuff this. I got him to turn off the meter and deliver me for the price he had agreed to.

The Algemene Taxi Centrale provides service for only 5 euros per person anywhere in Haarlem, The Netherlands. This fellow is waiting outside the train station and can whisk you straight to your hotel or the B&B Paula. [1642]

Catching a Taxi

With enough patience, you can get a taxi by waiting in the designated line at the train station or airport. You can wave them down in some cities, though taxis rarely cruise and usually will not stop for you except in London, Madrid, Lisbon, and Athens. Taxis wait at some *Metro* stations in Paris. You can phone them, or tip a hotel bell captain or head waiter to order one around. At the disco there is normally a line of taxis waiting outside late at night. Many people use taxis for going out carousing because of the severe penalties for driving after drinking.

Outside the Cologne, Germany train station, these Mercedes taxis wait for clients. In most cities, there is a line of clients rather than taxis. In the background is the famous Dom. *[1633]*

Taxi drivers do not like to make short runs when there is a line of waiting taxis. If they take you three blocks, they have to go to the back of the taxi line and wait another half hour for their turn again when they return. So they probably won't give you a ride. That's your problem if it's raining.

When taking a taxi to a slightly out of the way place where you won't be staying long, tell the driver to wait. It may be difficult to hail another taxi when you're ready to return. A good example is Athens, Greece. If you take a taxi to the Acropolis and pay him it might take a long time to get another taxi after walking around the ruins for a half hour. In Sintra, Portugal, I had an excellent English speaking taxi driver who drove me from the train station up to the castle, waited 45 minutes while I took the guided tour, and drove me back to the town square, all for about the price of a good lunch.

A taxi at the Geneva, Switzerland train station sports decals for American Express, Diners Club, VISA, and Carte Blue. [1607]

Night Charges

Taxis operating late at night typically charge a higher rate than during the day. Don't be surprised to pay twice as much to get home. Taxis often charge more than the meter on Sundays also. And sometimes they arbitrarily charge 10% to 20% more than the meter. I don't know why, but when they do it I take all the change.

Taxi is spelled a little differently in Varna, Bulgaria, and this sign means don't stand your car in the taxi stand. [1637]

Taxi Fares

    Taxis are expensive in northern Europe and darn cheap in the Mediterranean countries. Have plenty of cash with you in Stockholm, Sweden, even for short trips. In Athens, Greece you can be almost anywhere in the city for about the price of a beer.

    Taxis will take you cross-country also. One driver in Athens quoted $45.00 for the three hour trip to Patras, Greece. I took the bus. And "taxi drivers" can pop up just when you need them most. Thanks to my lack of attention when crossing from Portugal to Spain, I just missed a train to Huelva. The next train would be four hours later. There was a fellow from Brazil and a girl from Australia similarly stuck. I went to the café across the street to use the facilities and have a brandy. While there, one of the good old boys at the bar said he has a "taxi" and would drive me the 50 miles for $14.00. Though neither of us could speak the other's language, I negotiated it down to $10.00 for the three of us. So for about $3.50 each, Ernest, Kathrine, and I got a one hour ride in the oldest limo I've ever seen, arriving at Huelva in plenty of time to make our connection to Seville. (Note: When crossing from Portugal to Spain, advance your watch, and vice versa; they are in different time zones.)

    In the eastern countries taxis are also very cheap. From a beach hotel on the north end of the city a taxi ride into the center of Constanta, Romania was about a dollar. I didn't want to drive too much around there anyway, preferring to leave the car in the guarded parking lot of our hotel.

The Spirka in Varna, Bulgaria is a hybrid bus/taxi, similar in operation to the Domus in Istanbul except that the Domus uses small sedans. After filling up with passengers, the driver goes on his route letting off customers as they request. [1609]

Domus

    In Istanbul, Turkey a type of taxi called a *Domus* is very handy for getting across the city. We stayed near Topkapi Gate and learned about the *Domus* after a couple days. The *Domus* driver waits until his car is full and then takes off for the top of the hill. Passengers can go all the way or get off when they want. Taxis and the *Metro* are already very cheap in Istanbul, but we saved a few more pennies with this very interesting arrangement, stuffed in a little car with the locals.

Treintaxi

　　Treintaxis act like personal mini buses. They load up and drop passengers off at their home or office. If you are traveling with a group this is an excellent way to go from the station to your hotel. The cost is a few dollars per person. In Holland *Treintaxis* are available at most major train stations, except Amsterdam. If there isn't one parked, there will be a telephone handy to call one.

BICYCLES

Holland

　　Bicycles may be the most common form of transportation in Holland. There is some danger in riding a bike, particularly in Amsterdam, and it may take a while to get accustomed to the local rules. An ambulance nearly ran me over. Generally, bicycles have the same right to the road as automobiles, and they take it. Use arm signals to indicate turns, make sure your bell and front and rear lights work, and that it has fenders.

Here you go - go native in Holland. Rent a bike at the Heemstede train station for a very reasonable rate. Get all over town and out of town down to Keukenhof on your own schedule. [1619]

　　In many Dutch cities, and between cities, narrow roads have been constructed for the exclusive use of bicycles and mopeds. These usually have separate traffic signals using the outline of a bicycle. Depending on distance, traffic, and parking conditions, a bicycle may get you there faster than any other vehicle in Holland.

Elsewhere

　　Bicycles are also popular in Denmark, parts of Belgium, and in northwestern Germany.

　　In Aschaffenburg, our German home town, we used our bicycles frequently for short trips to the market and for Sunday rides along the Main River. During the summer it was impossible to ride for half an hour without finding a beer *Fest* of some sort in one of the *Dorfs* (towns) facing the river. For the most part, there is a paved bike path on at least one side of the river. Along the path late in the season we made frequent stops to get off and pick wild raspberries which seemed to be everywhere.

　　Some major cities have free loaner bicycle programs. You'll find free bikes in Geneva, Copenhagen, Amsterdam, and other cities which are trying to cut down on traffic congestion. I had a free bike in Blois, France that enabled me to visit the château at Chambord.

Owners park their bicycles in the street at the Münster, Germany, train station. There was another acre of them around the corner. I guess that they do this every day. [1634]

MOPEDS

Mopeds are probably the second most popular form of transportation in Holland. Moped drivers are allowed to use the bicycle paths. Helmets are required and the maximum size engine for a moped is 50 cc. This is the vehicle of choice for pre-car teenagers.

In the village of Muggio, Italy north of Milan, these signs seem to cover just about everything. [1623]

WALKING

Shoe leather should not be forgotten. The most interesting parts of most major cities are relatively small in area and can be reached within half an hour from a central location.

Sidewalk Hazards

Some sidewalks are very narrow And they are often used for parking cars, café extensions, and glass recycle bins. Additionally, watch out for dog droppings aplenty. Don't worry too much about muggers except in some neighborhoods which are easy to identify. Even after dark the streets are safer than in America. However, do be careful of pickpockets and camera and purse snatchers, especially in the capital cities and in the Mediterranean countries.

There is sometimes a certain lack of courtesy by European pedestrians. In Amsterdam, locals play "sidewalk chicken" to see who will step out of the way first. In the big cities in southern Europe, "sidewalk bumper shoulders" is played by many locals. They seem to want to bump into you, and they succeed.

Crosswalks

Do be careful crossing streets. Crosswalks in some countries are meaningless. Or if they have any meaning, it is simply that they are a target zone for drivers. Look around for traffic, and move quickly when it is clear. Crossing signals vary in appearance, but all will be red for "Don't Walk" and green for "Walk." In some countries the signals also give an audible sound indicating when it is safe to cross and when to wait. These sounds are different in each country.

Before you go up to the street and start walking around lost, look for one of these ever-present maps in the Paris, France Metro stations. This is the area around the Montparnasse railroad station. [1635]

Rome deserves special consideration by pedestrians, and since I lived to tell about it, here goes. Do not start to cross a street if the walk signal, *AVANTI*, is already lighted when you get to the corner. It can change to *ALT* within seconds and give drivers the green light to run you down. Be patient and wait until you see the signal turn to *AVANTI* with your own eyes. Then move quickly. The drivers in Rome don't like to slow down, much less stop. Some of them speed up when they see a red light. The red must drive them mad. In the city they don't like to waste their headlight bulbs either, so they often drive with parking lights or even no lights at night.

"When in Rome, do as the Romans do" is an adage with a great deal of merit. But, when in Athens I would not advise following the locals jaywalking and crossing against the signals. I have seen citizens stranded in the middle of busy boulevards by swarms of speeding drivers hell-bent to take their right to the road. Courtesy? Are you kidding?

On the other hand, the drivers in Sweden and Finland are more courteous than any I have seen anywhere. Crosswalks are honored and pedestrians are given an opportunity to escape when caught in traffic.

Many cities have prohibited autos from central districts or major shopping streets, like this Fußgängerbereich *(pedestrian zone) in Heidelberg, Germany. In addition to native German, the zone is posted in French and English. The small print rules are posted in German only. That's my little Stephanie running toward me, while Elizabeth and her dad Stefan Varga look on[1606]*

Pedestrian Tunnels

In many large cities, underground tunnels are provided for pedestrians to cross the major boulevards. Some of these feature escalators. I have seen some tourists who actually made it running across the *Place Charles de Gaulle* to visit the *Arc de Triomphe*. There are several underground tunnels so you do not have to run like a rabbit.

If you see chains or guard rails along the curb, you can assume that it is illegal to jump over to cross the street. Look for a tunnel or a crosswalk somewhere on the block. Otherwise you might come home as hamburger in a box.

Use the public transport or walk when you are in major cities throughout Europe. Notice the damp street and the umbrellas. The middle name for Holland should be rain. This is a view of the Leidsestraat, not far from the Leidseplein, a busy café and restaurant zone. [1646]

Chapter 17
Riding the Rails and Waves
Travel Europe by Train and Ferry

On the rails is the way to go.

TRAIN SERVICE

Trains are the best way to enjoy travel in Europe, and the most relaxing travel this side of a rocking chair. Train service includes normal trains and the relatively new high speed premium service trains.

First & Second Class

On most trains there are two classes of service, first and second. First class seating is plusher and roomier. Second class is filled up more often than first even though it has far more seats on most trains. First class costs about 50% more than second class, but you get there at the same time.

High Speed Service

In addition to the "normal" trains, there are special high speed trains available in a few countries serving major cities. The first European high speed train was the French *TGV*, or *Train à Grande Vitesse* (High Speed Train). Similar trains include the *Thalys* which runs from Paris to Amsterdam via Brussels and the *Eurostar* which makes the run through the "Chunnel," connecting London with Paris and Brussels. In Germany the premium high speed train is the *InterCity Express* (*ICE*). Italy and Switzerland have the *Cisalpino*, Spain its *AVE* (*Alta Velocidad Española*), and Sweden the *X2000*. There are others.

What do they mean by high speed? This is considered to be anywhere from 200 km/hr to 300 km/hr, or 125 MPH to 185 MPH. That's pretty fast, especially when you consider that the trains go from city center to city center, though not at full speed within the city limits. In addition to the high speed, comfort and amenities on board are much better than on the normal trains.

Trans-Europe Express, (*TEE*) trains of a generation ago were exclusively first class. They were formerly the top of the line but have been phased out by *TGV*, *ICE*, and the other high speed trains. The premium trains of today normally have two classes of service.

The insides look something like a plane and it rides at least as well as one with no air turbulence. But this happens to be a train, the Train à Grande Vitesse. *She cruises at over 130 mph. Luggage racks are above the seats, and additional luggage space is provided near the door. The* TGV, *as it's commonly referred to, is available on a few long distance lines in France and to Geneva, Switzerland. [1722]*

TICKETS

Do not board a train without a ticket. If you do it will be embarrassing and expensive when the conductor comes around. Also, don't try to hide in the toilet. The conductors know all the tricks and have keys to every door.

Ticket Windows

Train tickets are sold at windows in every station. Look for the symbol of two overlapping rectangles with numbers 1 and 2. There is usually a line of people waiting.

Ticket Vending Machines

Machines in many stations dispense tickets for travel within the country. It helps to know some of the local language and rules of travel to use these machines. You are confronted with buttons or a touch screen with selections for one-way or round trip, full or reduced fare, tickets with a date or without, and choice of payment. Maybe your credit card will work and maybe it won't. You might need a card with the chip like the European bank cards.

Stamp Your Ticket

Before boarding a train you must stamp your ticket in some countries. This is not necessary if your ticket already has today's date on it. In the station hall or on the platform are orange, yellow, or red metal boxes with a slot in the side or the front. Put your ticket in the slot and the machine will stamp it with today's date and/or time. If you forget to stamp your ticket you are liable for a severe penalty. It will cost. If you tell the conductor of your error before he discovers it the fine will probably be less.

Surcharges

Supplements to normal fares or special fares are charged on *TGV, Talgo, IC,* EC, *Thalys, ICE,* and other premium trains because they get you there faster, with fewer stops and more comfort. If you are traveling on a rail pass you may or may not need to pay the supplement. Look carefully at the conditions of your pass.

Most of these high speed trains also require a seat reservation. There goes some more cash, even for *Eurailpass* holders. You'll have to pony up for a reservation unless you want to ride a normal train. On the Paris to Brussels route you won't find a normal train, except for the midnight run.

If you pay for a ticket, reservation, or supplement, make sure that all of the information on it is correct. In paying for a supplement on an Italian train, I did not notice that the conductor had put the wrong date on it. An hour later the crew changed and a more attentive conductor noticed that I was traveling on a supplement that was apparently two days old. He tried to charge me again, but I convinced him that the other conductor had made a mistake, or at least he gave up trying to collect after my protests. Notice that dates in Europe are written in dd.mm.yy format, not mm/dd/yy as we do in the USA.

Save time and maybe aggravation at the ticket window. Buy your local train ticket from machines like this throughout Holland. Other countries have similar dispensers. Then look for the ticket stamping machine and stamp your ticket before getting on the train unless your ticket is already dated. [1707]

RAIL PASSES

Better than a pocketful of tickets is one of the rail passes. These take one of several forms. The best known and most useful is the *Eurailpass*.

Eurailpass

Eurailpass is a joint project of the national rail companies of 17 countries. The notable non-participant is the United Kingdom. Britain has its own rail pass program. Hungary is the only former eastern European nation in the program. A regular *Eurailpass* provides unlimited first class travel throughout the member countries. You can travel from Norway to Greece to Portugal, and ferry on over to Ireland and use the rails over there. It's all included. If you are planning a trip for a month or more and want the maximum from your time and money, *Eurailpass* is the way to go.

Additionally, and just as importantly, the *Eurailpass* gives you a freedom which you've never known before. Just go to a station and get on the next train to wherever strikes your fancy. When you get to wherever and if you are not happy with what you found, just hop on another train. You have got a carte blanche pass that you can use 24 hours a day. I've met travelers who have lived on the trains for months. If you can't find a suitable hotel before your bed time, just go to the train station and get on a long distance train. I have often used overnighters to save a hotel expense.

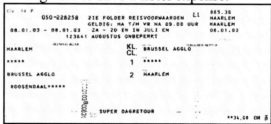

If you don't have a rail pass ask at the station for special fares. This is a Super Dagretour *(Super Day Round Trip) ticket from Haarlem to Brussels. These tickets allow you to travel after 9:00 am and save substantially over normal fares in Holland. This fare is not valid on weekends nor in July and August. [1752]*

There are many different rail passes, varying in length of time covered and other features. Regular *Eurailpass* is available for consecutive first class travel for 15 days, 21 days, one month, two months, and three months. The price goes up as the number of weeks increases, but not proportionally. A three month pass works out to less than $20 per day, while a one month pass is about $30 per day.

Eurailpass Flexi offers lower overall cost but restricted travel, say 10 or 15 days out of a two month period. With this one you don't feel like you're wasting your assets if you hang around in Rome for a few days. But your cost per day on the rails is much higher, about $60 per day for the 15 day deal. You have to start looking at the cost of individual tickets or have some serious travel plans, and that takes much of the fun out of railing around Europe.

Another pass called the *Eurail Selectpass* is a new variety introduced in 2003. This allows unlimited travel in any of 3, 4, or 5 countries that are connected by rail or ship. There are sub-varieties of this pass designed for two or more people traveling together or for people under the age of 26. Another version allows train travel plus a couple days of auto rental.

There are another half dozen types of *Eurailpasses* available. For example, *Eurailpass Saver* is a special arrangement for two or more traveling together. This family plan saves you about 15% over individual passes. *Eurailpass Youth* is for those under 26 years old and is valid for second class travel. The cost can be as low as $13 per day for a three month pass while a 15 day pass will run you $27 per day.

Buying a *Eurailpass*

The *Eurailpass* can only be purchased outside of Europe, or so they say. Your travel agent may say that it takes a week to get the pass. I've used *Eurailpasses* a number of times and my experience is that it takes as little as three days. I even bought one on the spot from an authorized agent in Saudi Arabia. You need to give your passport number to the issuing agent. That number is then typed on your *Eurailpass* along with your name, and you sign it. *Eurailpass* is not transferable and is only valid with your passport. The conductors in Holland always ask to see your passport, but they seldom ask in any other country.

Having given you this information, a slight correction is in order. American *Eurailpass* issuers want you to believe that the *Eurailpass* is only available in the

USA. I guess it's a marketing or business approach. Not only did I buy one in Arabia, I have bought *Eurailpasses* in Paris, and have read that it can be done in other cities in Europe. Visit a Eurail office (listed in the Eurail brochure) with your passport and credit card, or cash, and see what can be done. In Paris, the office is in the *Gare St. Lazare* (St. Lazare Train Station) just off the main hall. A number of other passes are also available there, most of which are less expensive but also less versatile. Many agencies sell *Eurailpasses* over the internet.

Sitting like it is ready to pounce the ICE provides premium service in Germany and to major stations in Holland. Here you see one in The Hague. [1760]

Validating

Eurailpass cannot be used and its period does not start until it is validated. It must be validated in Europe before getting on your first train. To do this, present it at the ticket window in any station and the agent will enter the starting and ending dates (in the European system: day/month/year). Have a calendar with you and check these dates carefully before you leave the window.

This is a sleeping car on the Finnish State Railways at Turku, destined for Joensuu. You can see the edges of the upper bunks in the windows. Much of Finland is bilingual, Finnish and Swedish, thus the word for "sleeping car" is on the car in Finnish, makuuvaunu, *and in Swedish,* sovvagn. *[1723]*

Other Rail Passes

Unlimited mileage passes are also issued by the individual national railroads of Europe. Many countries offer special passes to encourage visitors. Some are valid for everyone and some are designed for families or small groups. Special super deals are available to senior citizens, junior citizens, and students, generally limited to those over 62 or under 26 years old. Britain, excluding itself from the *Eurailpass* plan, offers its own pass which must be purchased outside Britain. Other countries offer special passes which can be purchased after arrival. One excellent pass providing travel throughout all of western Europe and some of eastern Europe is the

Inter-Rail Pass. The *Inter-Rail Pass* is only available to those under 23 who have resided in Europe for at least six months.

This model in the Antwerp, Belgium central station shows the newly remodeled station. It's a beauty. [1763]

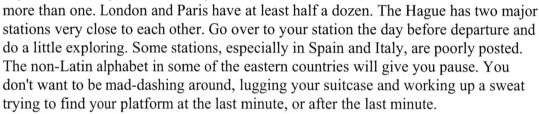

GOING TO THE STATION

Find Your Station

Know which station your train departs from. Major cities usually have more than one. London and Paris have at least half a dozen. The Hague has two major stations very close to each other. Go over to your station the day before departure and do a little exploring. Some stations, especially in Spain and Italy, are poorly posted. The non-Latin alphabet in some of the eastern countries will give you pause. You don't want to be mad-dashing around, lugging your suitcase and working up a sweat trying to find your platform at the last minute, or after the last minute.

Odlazak *at Zagreb's train station is also translated into English/French and German. The yellow posters under the sign have detailed information about each departure, in Croatian. If you are doing serious time on the trains of Europe carry a Thomas Cook European Timetable.* Dolazak *(arrivals) are posted nearby. [1712]*

Find Your Train

As you enter major train stations you will normally see a large airport style departure board hanging about a mile high in the main hall. Scattered around the station on the walls will be poster size schedules of departing trains. Smaller stations usually have only the posters. Locating your train is most easily done by determining departure time and destination, rather than by train number. The track number will be adjacent to the train identification, though you will not see the word "track." It will be the local name, e.g. *voi, spoor,* etc.

Sometimes while you are standing on a platform everybody around you grabs their bags and starts trotting toward the exit stairs. They probably just heard an announcement over the public address system saying that there has been a change and your train will depart from another platform. This announcement will be in the local language only. Quickly find a conductor and ask for help. Failing that, ask one of the local citizens in the migrating herd. You are bound to find a helpful English speaker very quickly.

This photo is about 20 years old but illustrates an important point. The train departs from the Gare de Lyon (Lyon Train Station) in Paris at 9:55 am, is a type Rapide train (actually not very rapid), and is train number 5461 with 1st and 2nd class seating. The key point is that the first ten cars go all the way to Toulouse, while the last four cars are detached in Narbonne. Always make sure that the car you are boarding is going where you want to go.[1727]

Find Your Car

Platforms in major stations of some countries have boards showing the complete assemblage of each train. The train number, departure time, and destination are shown, followed by an outline of the train with engine, first class cars, second class cars, diner, mail, etc., in the same order as on the train. An indicator on the board shows where the board is located relative to the train when it stops. There may also be zones A, B, C, D on the board and posted above the platform to further help you find your car. The car location board also shows the car numbers. If you have a reservation you can be standing next to your car when it stops and not have to haul your luggage through the narrow, crowded passageways of several other cars.

These boards are not evident in some countries. Often, track numbers are not even posted in Spain and Portugal and you must ask at a ticket window where to go to get on your train. In Italy, car locations are stated on the yellow departure posters, *Treni in Partenza*. They tell you where the first class cars are located: *testa* (front), *centro* (middle), *coda* (rear), *verso testa* (toward the front) or *verso coda* (toward the rear) is about as descriptive as it gets. In Belgium and Holland the car position indicator is only used for the premium international trains, i.e., the *Thalys* to France and the *ICE* to Germany.

If the train is originating in your city it will probably be in position long before departure time. Get to the station a half hour early, get on board, and pick a good seat. If the train is passing through, get there early enough to locate the track, eyeball the board giving the *Composition des Trains*, and position yourself near the designated stopping point for a first or second class car (as your case may be) going your way. If there is no board showing car locations, ask a conductor on the platform or at the station master's office before the train arrives.

This is the plush interior of the Thalys premium train which makes its run between Paris and Amsterdam, stopping in Brussels and The Hague. [1756]

Just because a car is sitting on the track from which your train departs does not mean that it is going your way, or that it is going all the way, or that it is going at all. Trains are split and portions are sent in different directions along the way. In some stations, e.g. Antwerp Central with only way one in and out for the trains rather than straight through, the first few cars nearest the main hall may not even be attached to the train. If there are no signs on the cars, go to the head of the train and ask the conductor or engineer. Just point to the train and ask "Madrid?", or whatever city you are bound for.

Double check to make sure you are getting in the right car. Almost all cars, especially on international trains, have a signboard near the door, either outside and/or inside, showing the car number and origin and destination of that particular car. Some will have a sheet of paper with the destination taped to a window visible from the outside.

Find Your Seat

When the train stops, move quickly to a door and scramble on board, not waiting for other travelers hauling six oversized suitcases up the narrow steps. Get a seat, spread out, and don't budge until the train has pulled out of the station and the seat grabbing flurry has settled down.

If it's night and you want to sleep, get in an empty compartment if available, pull the seats down, turn off the lights, and pull the curtains. This discourages other travelers from intruding into "your" compartment and cramping your sleeping style. However, don't hesitate to open the door and pull back the curtains of other compartments at any time. Often you'll find one person comfortably occupying a curtained compartment while five may be stuffed in the next one. Park yourself where you will have the most comfort.

A door of voiture *4 (car 4) on the* SNCF (French National Railroads). *This is a second class car with seat numbers 61 through 108 at this end where smoking is allowed. It is bound for Evian-les-Bains, and stops in the other half dozen cities. This car becomes part of four separate trains in its journey across France. [1726]*

Try to get a seat on the shady side of day trains. On the shady side the sun is not glaring on your window, perhaps giving you a sunburn, and it's much easier to see out and photograph the countryside. Don't immediately sit down on the shady side though. When the train leaves it might toot toot north for a few minutes and then head south. Know your route and which way the train is going. Sit on the north side of east/west trains, the west side of morning trains, and the east side of afternoon trains.

When you get settled, make a note of your car number and seat number so if you forget something it will be much easier to find it or report it. I saw one worried man telling the conductor that his coat and luggage were stolen while he was in the restaurant wagon. He was looking in the wrong car which the conductor pointed out after looking at the passenger's reservation receipt.

This train to Dortmund stops in a number of other German cities along the way, plus the Frankfurt airport. First class is in the front, stopping in zones A&B along the platform. This is an IC (InterCity) mit Zuschlag *(with surcharge). It arrives at 10:12 and departs at 10:14, making the typical two minute stop in Nürnberg. Don't be late because only trains can do that. [1718]*

SLEEPING ON THE TRAIN

Couchettes

Sleeping cars and couchette berths are offered on many long distance trains. This service comes at an extra charge and is not included in regular ticket prices or the rail passes. Couchettes are bunk-style berths. Compartments in first class cars have four single berths, and in second class cars there are six.

Over in the Ukraine I traveled east from Kiev on an overnight train, sharing a cabin with three colleagues. We had a fine time, especially since one fellow traveler had brought along adequate provisions of bread, sausages, and vodka which was shared all around. Our train left about midnight and reached our destination in the eastern Ukraine late in the next evening, a 21 hour ride. The Ukraine is a mighty big wheat field. The toilets were filthy despite the presence of a "maid" in each car. She seemed to be glued to the chair in her cubicle.

Sleep in Your Seat

As a general rule I don't use berths in western Europe since I have always been able to stretch out in a first class compartment for a reasonable night's sleep. Even with six people in the compartment, the seats can be slid out together and the armrests lifted so that the compartment becomes the equivalent of a king size bed. Everybody flops in. It looks like a can of sardines. There is the sometimes inconvenience of people climbing over you, or vice versa, to make for the toilet or a breath of fresh air. Everybody quickly accepts the etiquette of temporary communal living. When sleeping, keep your wallet and passport stuffed in with your private parts, and sleep on your camera.

Overnight trains are becoming less common in Europe. There are a few special overnight trains like the *CityNightLine* trains from Amsterdam to Basel and Zurich and another to Munich. One of these can save you a day of travel and the cost can offset the price of a hotel room.

EATING ON THE TRAIN

Dine Well

At the moment of writing this (which was many years ago) on a *TEE* train from Amsterdam to Paris, the head waiter came through the car, suitably attired with menu in hand, and announced the first sitting, speaking in French. Immediately the stampede to the dining car started. Late arrivals do not get much attention. If you wish to eat, get up and get moving with the locals. American deference, courtesy, and service are pretty rare in Europe. On the successors to the *Trans-Europe Express*, the *InterCity*, *TGV*, *ICE*, and others, dining is a bit formal, and can come at an appropriate price, when available.

Dining on these trains is a nice way to pass the travel hours and presents opportunities to meet others. Most eaters are European businessmen or relatively well-to-do Europeans. Occasionally a few drops of wine may splash out of your glass, thanks to rough tracks.

I looked in the window of the dining car on a Talgo *train ready to depart Barcelona, Spain. Those are real flowers on the table and you are going to get an outstanding meal on this train.* [1724]

Fast Forward

TEE trains don't exist anymore and my nostalgia for a by-gone era will never be cured. However the services and comfort on board their high speed successors have improved significantly. The old European customs, good and not-so, have also survived. For example, expecting a nice meal on a *TGV* train in eastern France one Sunday evening, the conductor said that the dining car only ran on weekdays. Weekenders are served from a small bar and can get a *croque monsieur* (toasted cheese sandwich) or pizza. Severely disappointed was I. Consult the timetable to make sure the train has a diner wagon. Look for a crossed knife and fork at the top of the column in your Thomas Cook European Timetable.

One of my most pleasant European diners was on an *IC* coming down along the Rhine River from Essen en route to Frankfurt. Not only was it a great meal, but the moving scenery along the Rhine River was outstanding. Vineyards covered the slopes and castles capped the crests. It was an utterly relaxing afternoon.

On some trains, the head waiter will accept reservations for a seat in the dining car. Ask as soon as possible. Specify nonsmoking or smoking for your comfort.

Here comes the coffee service on a German IC. Instead of pushing the usual cart the waiter in apron, about to enter the door down the corridor, is carrying a tray from the diner. [1719]

Cart Service

Food and drink are sold on virtually all of the international trains and on most other long distance trains. If there is no diner or snack bar, a waiter pushes a cart through the trains. Selections are normally limited to coffee, milk, beer, wine, soft drinks, yogurt, cold sandwiches, and sausages which resemble hot dogs. Prices are high.

Service is available for only part of a journey, even though the attendant is on board for the duration of the trip. And service can be lousy. On a recent trip from Brussels to The Hague I saw the service cart come in the door of my car and a few minutes later the server answered his cell phone. He stayed right there for over half an hour talking his important stuff. Luckily I had already had dinner and had brought a can of beer on board with me.

Local commuter trains do not have food or beverage service. Bring your own.

A Full Diner at Your Seat

Diner can be served at your seat on some trains. On a *Talgo* in Spain the head waiter came through the car at about noon to see who would like to have lunch. I volunteered. An hour later he put a tray on my seat similar to those on some airplanes. Then followed a delicious fish with pimentos, a pork chop, peas, a half bottle of *vino tinto* (red wine - very good, but the train shook up the sediment), roll, sweet roll, banana, and coffee. Total cost for a great meal was about the same as you would pay in a restaurant at home.

These symbols on train windows mean don't throw anything out the window, and don't stick your head out the window. [1758]

Brown Bag It

Budget travelers, including most Europeans and usually me, bring a sack of bread, cheese, ham, and beer on board and fix dinner at their seat. Do the same. Can your trash.

RESERVATIONS

Just because you have a ticket or a rail pass does not mean that you have a seat, or even that you can ride the train. Seat reservations are required for some trains, and are highly recommended for many others.

You usually buy a reservation at any ticket window and it usually costs a few dollars. You can also reserve seats at travel agencies in Europe. Make reservations at least a day in advance if you really want to go. Your reservation card will show your origin and destination, the train number, the car number, and your seat number. It will also indicate smoking or non-smoking and seat position, i.e., window or aisle.

If you are not happy with the seat which was reserved for you look around for another open seat. Just move yourself. Let the conductor know.

A Meisterwerk of German info art in the Essen station displays the main trains for the Ruhrgebiet (Ruhr River industrial area) from Düsseldorf to Bochum and surroundings. [1706]

Reservation Required

Almost all of the premium trains, such as the *TGV* and *Thalys*, require a reservation. Many Swedish and a few Norwegian trains require a reservation, though if you get on without one, the conductor may find you an empty seat and collect a reservation fee. Reservations are required on all superior trains in Spain, on some in Portugal, and on international trains in Italy and some other countries. Your best bet is to invest in a current copy of the *Thomas Cook European Timetable* to determine reservation requirements. In addition to the premium trains, a capital **R** in a rectangle at the top of the column indicates a train requiring a reservation.

I did not have the task of obtaining the tickets or reservations for our odyssey across the Ukraine. My host took care of that. It is reported that obtaining tickets and reservations is very difficult in Russia and the Ukraine. Our travels into Hungary when it was still under communist rule posed no problems — we just got on the trains with our *Eurailpasses*.

Reservation Recommended

Even though seat reservations are generally not required, there are some trains on which they are highly recommended. I would definitely make a reservation for any train on popular routes during the summer and around the major holidays like Christmas and Easter.

Additionally, I would reserve a seat on international express and higher class trains for travel on Friday afternoons and evenings and on Sunday afternoons and evenings throughout the year. These trains are full of businessmen riding first class, just where your *EurailPass* will seat you.

ON THE TRAIN

Smoke Zone

Train cars are divided into smoking sections and nonsmoking sections. Sometimes the whole car is nonsmoking. Nonsmoking is always posted, and smoking usually is.

In addition to the multilingual notices, look for the cigarette symbol with or without a line through it. A cigarette symbol is usually posted at each door, and again in the car. Cigars and pipes are allowed, and common. If you are in a smoking section, be prepared for beaucoup plenty of smoke. When requesting your reservation, specify nonsmoking or smoking.

You can sit in non-smoking and then go to the smoking area when you want to puff. Even smokers get burning eyes if they sit in that haze for too long. If you want to relocate to another seat after getting on the train, just do it. Let the conductor know so he can indicate your new seat as reserved and the other seat as vacant.

A typical train station tell-you-where-it-is board, courtesy of the Osnabrück station. Straight ahead is your Ausgang *(one of the German words for exit), taxi, bus, and telephone. To the right are baggage checking, baggage lockers, ticket window, hair salon, and train information. The last line shows toilets and a restaurant to the left and another telephone to the right. Pretty easy, huh? [1734]*

Baggage

Baggage can sometimes be checked, but almost everybody carries theirs on board, except for royalty. We rode the *TGV* from Geneva to Paris in a car with a Saudi princess and her 20 servants and escort, plus their own dinner fixins which gave the whole car a certain aroma. In Paris a crew unloaded scores of bags from the luggage car, and blocked our exit for about 10 minutes.

For the rest of us, there are two wire luggage racks above the seats which easily hold any bag that you can carry on a plane, plus a smaller bag. Can you lift your luggage and put it on a narrow ledge six feet above the floor? If not leave it on the floor. If the train is full this can block a seat and cause consternation. Coming back to Haarlem from Amsterdam the other day this happened. A Dutch woman stood in the aisle and eventually "persuaded" another woman whose luggage blocked the only remaining seat that the luggage should be moved so she could sit down.

The newer airline-style coaches on *TGV* trains have luggage compartments near the doors in addition to luggage space above the seats. Some have space for a bag between back-to-back seats. I prefer to keep my goods close at hand.

Additional lower level luggage space is provided on this international train from The Hague to Brussels. You can also rent the padlock and wire to secure your goods. The cost is one euro. [1762]

Windows

On most of the old trains, you can pull the window down for a better look and a breath of fresh air. Newer cars are air conditioned and have sealed windows.

Windows usually have blinds. Some are like curtains, some are like shades, and some cars have manual or electric Venetian blinds between the inner and outer sealed windows. Play with them for a minute to see how they work.

Newspaper

Carry a newspaper or magazine. Put it on your seat while you are in the dining car, the toilet, or just roaming around. This will discourage others from rearranging themselves into your window seat. A newspaper is also handy for relaxing your feet. Put it on the seat opposite and prop up your leathers. Otherwise you must take your shoes off, which could spoil the appetite of others nearby.

Crime

Keep your seat and keep your eye on your luggage while the train is in a station. Professional thieves loiter on some platforms, board trains, walk through the cars, grab what they can, and jump off before departure.

Keep your valuables under your control at all times. Elizabeth had her purse rifled while we slept on an overnight train from Venice to Vienna, probably by a fellow passenger. A friend of mine went to the toilet and had his cash and camera taken out of his bag by a new-found "friend" on a French train. Never leave money or valuables in your bag anytime anywhere anyway.

I have heard reports of other problems, including a bizarre story of a couple who were offered oranges by some other travelers on a train in Portugal. They ate the oranges and the next thing they remember was waking up with no wallets and no luggage. At least twice I have heard the story of a gang which operates on trains from Milan. They open the train compartment door, mace the passengers, and grab their wallets and suitcases.

As discussed in other parts of this book, do not stand out as wealthy or as an American. If you do you are making yourself a tasty target for the vermin. Orientals should be aware that pickpocket professionals know that you are likely to be carrying a large quantity of cash. Less cash and more credit cards would be advisable when traveling.

Please see chapter 8 for more examples of the underworld at work, and sure-fire means of defense against these lowlifes.

The departure board for banlieue (suburban) trains from the Paris Montparnasse railroad station shows all stations on the route and indicates stations at which the train will stop. Toutes Gares *is "All Stations." [1735]*

Plumbing

Rail cars usually have a unisex toilet at each end with a locking door. Floor pedals or levers on the wall activate the flush and basin water. The basin water is not fit for drinking.

Use of the toilets is forbidden while the train is stopped in a station. The reason is that they flush right down onto the tracks and the stations would be smelling like outhouses.

On some trains in Spain, the toilets are locked at the origin until the train is out of the station. When the conductor comes around to check tickets, which could be a half hour later, he unlocks the toilets. Don't drink coffee until the toilets are unlocked.

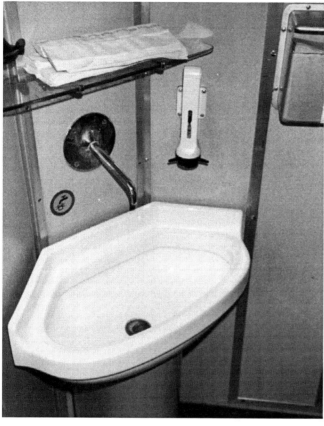

Functioning toilet and hand wash facilities are found on virtually every train. Usually you step on a floor pedal for water, but on a few trains the spigot is pivoted and water flows when you rotate it out over the basin. There is usually an electric shaver outlet; the electricity is at 220 volts. [1736]

Step on the golf ball size chrome button on the floor when you have finished your business. The further east you go the more you should consider bringing a supply of butt wipes. [1716]

This plexiglass bracket is designed to hold reservation cards. You'll see it on the window of train compartments facing the corridor. I reserved seat number 75 to Köln, and that is where the conductor has placed a small card indicating that the seat is reserved. No other seats in this cabin are reserved so anybody with a first class ticket can come in and help themselves. [1715]

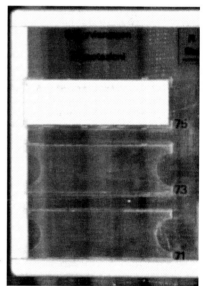

Seat Reservation Card

Never sit in a seat displaying a reservation card, unless it's yours. However if the reservation card indicates that the seat is reserved from say Karlsruhe to Frankfurt, and you are going from Basel to Karlsruhe, just help yourself to the seat. The reservation card will be attached to the seat, or be in a holder on the outside of the compartment. On those reservation only trains in Sweden and Norway reservation cards are not evident. Ask the conductor if there is a seat available. On a train with reservation cards, all seats without a card are available. First come, first served.

If someone claims that you are in their reserved seat (though the seat does not have a reservation card), politely ask to see his/her reservation receipt and make sure to check the car number. The car number will be posted in large numbers on the outside and/or inside of the car near the door and it will be indicated on the reservation receipt. Being in the wrong car is the most common mistake made by people with reservations. The reservation system is computerized, and it works better than you would expect. Request a window seat if you want it.

Boards like this show the position of each car when the train stops in a station. The letters A, B, C, D correspond to signs above the platform and each car is numbered. Position yourself near the stopping point for the car in which you have a reservation. [1721]

Personal Safety

Be careful near train doors which close automatically just before the train departs. I suffered a great deal of pain but no injury when my hand got caught in the closing doors of a Dutch train in Amsterdam. It was the culmination of a bizarre series of events. The train was already 10 minutes late when an announcement came over the loudspeaker, in Dutch, that the train driver and conductor were not on board and the person making the announcement had "no idea where they were." So a group of us got off to hop on a train also going to Haarlem parked on the other side of the platform. As we were walking over, the engines of our train started up so we went back and boarded again. But one woman had only one leg in when the door started closing. I and a couple of other passengers tried to hold the door and/or pull her in. She got in but my hand was stuck as the train started rolling. Fortunately someone pulled the emergency stop and then the doors could be opened. The long haired conductor had no comment when he reset the emergency stop. If he had been on the job none of this would have happened. There was a story in the Dutch newspapers in 2003 that a 19 year old woman was awarded about $900,000 in damages when she was caught in the doors of a train and lost both of her legs in the ensuing disaster.

Many commuter trains in The Netherlands are double decker models. Reservations are not available and there is normally no food or beverage service on these short haul trains. [1755]

Seat Numbers

Seat numbers in compartments vary from country to country. The numbers may be in sequence from the door or from the window and may have odds and evens on opposite sides. Numbers normally start with 11, 21, 31, etc. in each compartment, but you can find some like 1, 2, 4 opposite 5, 6, 8 and other combinations around Europe.

Back and Forth

Train cars travel in both directions, and within a car some of the seats face in each direction. With a reserved seat, you are just as likely to be traveling forward as backward. The train will reverse in some stations, a new engine will be attached to the rear, and the train will take off. On one train in Spain when it reversed in a station, the passengers got up, pushed a lever at the base of each seat, and rotated all the seats so they faced forward. This feature was unique. I've never seen it on any other train.

If you need help at a Portuguese train station, inquire at the Chefs da Estação *(Station Master) office. Even if you aren't using the trains, many stations in Portugal are worth a visit just to see the beautiful* azulejos *(tiles) on the walls. This is at Marvão. [1732]*

OFFICIALDOM

Don't believe or obey anyone except the conductor, passport police, and customs police. And you'd better believe these folks.

Conductor
The conductor is present on the platform before the train departs and then walks through the train checking all tickets shortly after departure. He is the law on board, and he is the best source of information for arrival times and connections. Conductors are invariably courteous and helpful. They usually speak English. Crews change on long distance trains, so you may be asked for your ticket several times on a long trip.

Passport Police
For the most part, passport police have become people of the past with the open borders of the European Union. However, many countries are not members of the EU so you may encounter passport controls. Switzerland has the most rigorous controls you will experience anywhere.

Passport police walk through the train at some border crossings. They work in pairs and are armed. They ask to see your passport and perhaps ask where you are coming from, going to, and why. These guys and gals are gruff because they have a job that can get a bit testy. Don't take it personally. Just show them the little blue book with your smiling mug shot on the first page.

Customs
Customs police are also becoming extinct in the European Union. They are usually right behind the passport police, if any. These gentlemen and sometimes ladies are in uniform or in business suits. Expect no problems in first class, but they'll normally ask a few questions of second class passengers. They will conduct a search if they are suspicious.

ARRIVING

Getting Off
Know your route. Just after the train pulls out of the last station before your destination or connection, start getting ready to get off. Take a pit stop. Shave. Brush your hair. Powder your nose. Whatever. Gather up your belongings. Recheck around your seat and in the luggage rack.

Train stops are announced in some countries, but usually in the local language. On international express class trains in Germany and Spain, train stops are also announced in French and English a few minutes before arrival. On *InterCity* trains in Germany, the conductors pass out a complete schedule, *Ihr Zug-Begleiter* (Your Guide to the Train). This shows every stop and connection. The symbol translation table is in German and in English.

To open the door on a train, you usually push a latch lever down and push the door outward. I found that the doors of trains in Spain open inward, the opposite of most countries. Sometimes a small section of the floor in front of the door folds up, revealing the steps. You cannot open the door on some Irish trains from the inside. You must reach out the window to grab the door latch, or find a door that is already open. Many trains in Holland have push buttons for opening the door.

Passengers wait for the international train to Brussels on platform 4a in The Hague, The Netherlands. The flag number 15 indicates the stop position for car 15 on the Thalys. [1759]

Short Stops

Be at the door before the train comes to a stop. Train stops are typically two minutes. If the train is running late, the stops are abbreviated. Be quick and bully your way off just like the locals. There may be a crowd trying to board. If you don't get off before the first passenger pushes on, you could find yourself riding that train to the next station.

Longer Stops

Though trains normally make two minute stops in major cities they sometimes stop for 15 to 30 minutes to load and unload mail and do some car switching. You may have time to jump off and make a call or buy a paper, but this can be risky.

At a scheduled 15 minute stop in Zagreb, I decided to buy sandwiches because there was no food on the Budapest to Trieste train. There was supposed to have been a diner car, but there wasn't and we were starving. Prior to jumping off, I walked back through the train to a car where I could get a better view of the platform and see if there was a food kiosk convenient on the platform. While looking out the window, the train started moving back toward Budapest, and picking up speed. I looked out the end window and saw the car with Elizabeth in it, but it was still standing! After some panicky shouts to an unconcerned worker on the train the car I was in finally stopped a mile down the track. I jumped out and ran back up the tracks to the station. I still had some time. I found a bank in the station to change money, bought two sandwiches, and scampered back out to the car where Elizabeth was. It was gone! Oh my! Then, from another track on another platform, I heard Elizabeth calling me. They had moved our car to attach some more before continuing on to Italy. It took a while for my heart to resume normal speed.

This is the main hall of the Copenhagen, Denmark train station, the primary entry point for Scandinavia. The baggage check room is on the right, at the far end is a darn good smorgasbord behind the cafeteria, and out the far end is the amazing Tivoli Gardens. The sign Billetter *indicates "tickets," but you should be able to decipher* Tobak, Chokolade, *and* Bank. [1731]*

The Greek trains operate rather informally. Be patient for this type of scene at every stop. This is Corinth. To spend the hours, bring a good book, or a deck of cards if you are traveling with others. [1733]

Where You Are is Where You Are

My worst gaffe in train travel involved a northbound German train when traveling with my daughter Stephanie. We were to get off in Darmstadt at 16:29 (4:29pm; trains use the 24 hour system). As the time approached I heard an announcement which included the word Darmstadt. When the train stopped we got off. This was one of the few times in my European travels when someone was to meet us at the station, however our friend Connie was not there. After a beer I called her home and her husband Uwe told me that she had also called and was waiting at the station for us. I looked again, everywhere, but couldn't find her. Finally I asked the café owner what city we were in. It was Bensheim, about 10 minutes before Darmstadt. We caught the next train to finish the trip. Contributing to my error was the fact that our train had stopped in the middle of nowhere and then proceeded slowly past a red light on the tracks. We lost about ten minutes, and the announcement that I had heard was that the following stop would be Darmstadt. So, check the signs on the platform to make sure you are where you want to be before jumping off.

POTPOURRI

Good Travel Days

Tuesdays are good days to travel. Fridays are busy. It is best to avoid traveling on Sunday since the trains are busy, plus tourist offices and other friends of the traveler may be closed or have limited hours. Also watch out for Easter, Christmas, New Years Day, and local holidays. They are busy traveling periods, though many trains don't operate, schedules may be different, and all businesses are welded shut.

Arrivals and departures are posted on a single poster in the small station at Evian-les-Bains, France. Evian is a ritzy village on scenic Lac Léman. The light over the silver lake has a brilliant glow to it. You have to experience it. [1709]

Modern Mode

Stephanie and I are on an *ICE* train from Basel, Switzerland to Karlsruhe, Germany at the moment that I am writing this paragraph. The car is a beauty. In second class we have our choice of several channels of music using our own stereo headgear and the train's stereo system. She can have her teen stuff and I have some relaxing jazz. The seats are comfortable and recline, and the car is air conditioned on this hot July day. Though not as smooth or quiet as the *TGV* trains I've been on, this car is certainly very nice. Stephanie checked on the first class accommodations and found three across seating instead of four, and more comfortable seats. This second class wagon has open airline type seating plus compartment seating as in the old days. A small area is reserved for heavy luggage to save you the effort of lifting your bags about six feet onto the rack, and a hook in the car lets you hang your coat. There is a telephone booth in the dining car.

As we charge into the new century, European train travel is keeping pace with the other comforts of life. The only disadvantage is the extra cost for reservations and supplements on the superior trains. But it sure isn't as bad as the cost of gasoline, especially in Europe.

TRAIN STATION FACILITIES

In any city, the train station is a hub of activity.

Tourist Office

When arriving in town, don't waste any time getting to the tourist office or hotel information office if you don't already have a hotel reservation, city map, and directory of sights and events. These offices are generally either in or near the train station or center of town. Request a town map and a hotel list. The best time to arrive anyplace is between ten in the morning and noon. It's at this time that the hotel keepers know who is leaving and how many rooms will be available for that night, and the tourist office has not yet closed for the two hour lunch break.

Tourist offices close for the day early in the afternoon in Scandinavia and Ireland. It seems that my train always arrives a half hour too late in these countries. If the tourist office is closed, I ask at the *information* office (see below), a ticket window, or the money exchange window for a town map and hotel list. One of these is usually able to help me. But, failing that, I buy a town map at the newspaper kiosk in the train station and go out on my own to find a hotel room.

i

For connection information and special help, major train stations typically have an office for train information. This is marked with a large lower case **i** or marked *information*. Try pronouncing it "een-for-mah-cee-ohn." You normally cannot get hotel or tourist information in these offices, but they will tell you where the tourist office is located.

Pickpocket Central

At the risk of boring you to death with this warning, train stations are notorious as hangouts for pickpockets and baggage thieves. Some stations have posters to this effect, and some have periodic warnings over the public address system. Most stations do not mention anything. Keep your "American space" around you at all times. When you are in a line, a "queue" to you Brits, be especially wary of those who are trying to cut in.

Pickpockets usually work as a team. One or more distracts you while another makes the lift and passes your goods to another, never to be seen again. Hold on to your luggage at all times and keep your wallet in a tight front pants pocket. Some travelers use "money belts" for security but I don't see the need for these things. I have never been robbed though a number of attempts have been made on me. Stay alert at all times, especially in the stations and within a few blocks.

Also, never give any money to a beggar in a train station. These people are professionals. They dress and behave for the maximum empathy. Some are thieves and just looking to see where you reach for the money that you are donating. They may come back for another dip into your pocket without you knowing it, until you reach for your wallet later in the day.

Reading Timetables

Departures and arrivals are posted in each station, departures normally on a yellow or buff-colored poster and arrivals on a white poster. Timetables use the 24 hour clock. Therefore 16:00 or 16h00 is 4 pm to us Americans.

Codes for the days of the week go from Monday = 1 to Sunday = 7. Codes for the months use Roman numerals; e.g., January = I to December = XII. See chapter 28, "Time and Dates," for more important information on this subject.

*Luggage carts are available at the Karlsruhe HBF (*main train station*). You put a coin in the slot but you get it back when you return the cart. Grocery store carts work the same way. [1708]*

Luggage Lockers

Luggage lockers are almost universally available in train stations in northern Europe. Dimensions and costs vary. In Amsterdam the small lockers are about 12"x18"x36" and cost about $2.50 per 24 hours. Medium lockers are 12"x24"x36" and cost about $4.00 for 24 hours.

After 72 hours, station attendants may remove the contents to the baggage checkroom. You'll pay again to retrieve your belongings. Baggage checkrooms are almost always available in stations if your bag doesn't fit the locker or if all of the lockers are full. Fees vary.

Portuguese train stations are pretty thin on luggage lockers. If you can't find one, look around for the *Deposito de Volumes* window and check your luggage with the fellow on duty. In Italy you are more likely to encounter attended baggage check rooms.

There are plenty of luggage lockers in Spain, but they are all sealed shut, and there are no baggage check rooms either. Some anti-government terrorists found it amusing to plant bombs in their baggage so there is no service for anybody anymore. French security forces also sealed all the lockers in the country for a period in the late 1990s thanks to an isolated bombing. That was when I decided that luggage with wheels is a good investment. With the war on terror underway lockers may be eliminated in other countries, either temporarily or permanently.

Bike Rentals

In Holland and Belgium, bicycle rental offices are generally in or handy to the station. Before renting a bicycle, check it out mechanically. Make sure the lights, bell, and brakes work. Drive it around the block to make sure you are comfortable and secure on it. Bring it back immediately for adjustments if there is anything wrong.

The price for a day's bicycle rental is about what you would pay for lunch. Leave your International Driving Permit as security, not your passport. You'll probably need your passport during the day and you don't want it lying there amongst some oily papers and receipts.

Other Facilities

Banks have foreign exchange offices in the larger train stations, but they usually have a long line waiting. There is probably a bank across the street, and it probably offers a better exchange rate. It is far better to arrive with some local currency so you could be at the head of that hotel office line instead because you will need some local currency to secure a hotel reservation.

Major train stations also have ATMs, a snack bar, drink bar, restaurant, showers, toilets, post office, newsstands, and candy stand. Some have been expanded underground to include large shopping centers. Train stations are good places to do after hours shopping. Stores in western Europe generally close at 6 or 7 pm, earlier on Saturday, and are not open on Sunday. Train station markets selling everything from bananas to birthday cards are often open until midnight, and on Sunday.

FERRIES

Boats and ferries are a convenient way to travel between Ireland and England and the Continent, some of the countries in Scandinavia, between Italy and Greece, and to a few other water-bound places. If you are in a hurry take a plane.

Tickets

Tickets are sold at the port, or straight through train/boat/train tickets can be purchased for, say, Amsterdam to Copenhagen, at the major train stations.

Eurailpass allows free passage or reduced fares on many ferries. Free passage is provided between Ireland and France, Germany and Denmark, Denmark and Sweden, and others. In most cases, regular service is provided by more than one steamship company but *Eurailpass* is only valid for one of the companies. Make sure that you go to the right dock at the right time for a free ride with your rail pass.

Eurailpass does not entitle you to a cabin. Cabin charges are not cheap.

Port taxes are often charged. These are in addition to the price of the ticket, and must be paid before boarding. Have a few extra dollars worth of local currency in your pocket when you go to the port. I have not experienced a fee for getting off.

It is best to buy your ticket or cabin supplement at an office of the shipping company. In Brindisi and in Patras there must be a hundred shops selling tickets for the Greek/Italian ferries.

The Nisikli Turizm agency offers daily ferry service from Varna, Bulgaria to Istanbul, Turkey, and from Varna to Constanta, Romania. "Non stop" in the window means that they answer the phone during the lunch hours. [1710]

Boarding

The ferries carry cars and trucks, and whole trains roll on board. There is sometimes a gang plank for pedestrians, but often you'll walk up the ramp dodging cars and trucks. The ramp can be wet, oily, and slippery so watch your step.

Drive On

I've driven on board a number of times. My first was an overnight ferry from Amsterdam to Gothenburg, from where I made a circuit of Sweden and Denmark, returning on another ferry from Rødbyhavn to Puttgarden, Germany. I made the short crossover from Jutland to Sweden on another trip. In the south, we went from Ancona to Patra on an overnighter. Those Greek truck drivers sure can party. I've driven onto small river ferries several times in Holland.

Bringing your car on an overnight long distance ferry is expensive, but you can't drive a car over open waters. You should inquire about reservations in advance during high traffic seasons.

The ship's crew packs cars and 18-wheelers in together tighter than anything you can imagine. Usually, after you park in the hold under crew directions, you give your keys to the crew master and will not be able to get into your car during the voyage. Do not leave any valuables in your car.

At the dock, early arrivals get better service, but may or may not get off first depending on whether the ship docks bow or stern.

Your car may be moved by the crew to allow others to get off if the ship makes other ports before your destination and your car is in the way. We were the last to drive on in Ancona and had a precarious parking spot at the top of a ramp. The ship made port twice before reaching Patras, our destination. Each time I went to the aft bridge and watched our car to make sure that it made it back on board before the ship steamed out of port. Better to make sure than to be sorry I figured, and it was an interesting show watching the dock side operations.

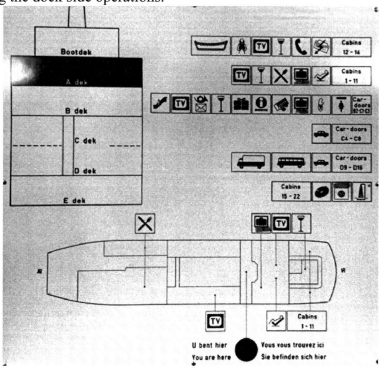

This is the layout of a ferry from Dover, England, to Oostende, Belgium, showing where everything is with icons. Luggage is stowed, self service wise, in baggage rooms with no attendant and no key. Notice the bar aft. This is the preferred place to be because the ride is smoother in the rear, the chairs are more comfortable here, and, of course, you can settle your stomach with a shot of scotch. Crackers or toast can also help. [1737]

Facilities

On board, you'll normally find a large number of theater-style seats, bars and a disco, cafeteria or snack bar, dining room, currency exchange, duty free shop, casino or just a blackjack table, plus the necessary facilities and a lot of "do not enter" doors. Small river crossing ferries have no amenities, but for a five minute ride you can probably do without.

Reservations

Reservations are normally not required. There is enough deck space on most of the big ferries for a medium sized army. If you want a cabin, you should reserve it as soon as possible.

When reserving a bunk in a cabin, specify whether you want an upper or a lower berth. And ask for smoking or nonsmoking as your case may be. I met a honeymoon couple who thought they were getting a private cabin. When they boarded they found out that they had tickets for two berths: him in a cabin with three other fellows and she in with three other girls. And they paid 25% more than they should have at a ticket shop. They complained to the purser and he was kind enough to help their marriage off the rocks by giving them a private cabin at no extra charge.

The Silvia Regina, *and her sister ship the* Finlandia, *had been the two largest ferry boats in Europe. I'll go back to Finland just to ride the magnificent* Finlandia *again, if for nothing else. The ride between Stockholm and Helsinki is included free with* Eurailpass, *and "sleep-in" bunks are free on board. Remember to reset your watch because Finland and Sweden are in different time zones. This ship is approaching port and has begun to open its forward hold for the discharge of cars and trucks. That curved part that makes it look like a shark is the forward door beginning to open. On the ship* Estonia *this forward port is the part which was knocked off by a storm in the Baltic, leading to the immediate sinking of the ship along with over 900 of its passengers in October of 1994. Such a large catastrophe is rare but many lesser ones are more frequent.* [1739]

Dining

If there is a formal dining room, eating on the long distance ferries is even better than on the high speed international trains. First and second seatings are announced before leaving port. It is best to put in your reservation as soon as possible. If you do not hear the announcement, ask the purser. On Scandinavian ferries the smorgasbords   breakfast, lunch, and dinner — are good values for great food. Don't miss a chance for one of these feasts.

Low budget travelers should bring a picnic. The cafeteria and snack bars on board are usually quite expensive, with quality on the order of dog food.

Coin of the Captain's Realm

Usually, money of each country on the route is accepted for food and goods. Change your greenbacks at the purser's office if there is no regular exchange office.

Duty Free Shops

Virtually every ferry which crosses international borders, and that is virtually every ferry, has a duty free shop. Locals stock up on tobacco and alcohol, products which suffer some pretty high taxes in most countries.

In the duty free shops, the clerks expect you to take a shopping basket. Even if you are only buying one bottle, they don't want you to carry it (and maybe slip it under your coat).

On the Espresso Grecia, *a disadvantage of off-season travel is that they put a safety net in the pool instead of water. Ships like this cross between Greece and Italy in 16 to 18 hours, but can have delays due to rough water and wind in the Ionian Sea. Remember to reset your watch because Greece and Italy are in different time zones. [1738]*

Lockers

Luggage lockers are only available on a few ferries. Normally, those who are sleeping on chairs and did not take a cabin stack their luggage in one central area. I haven't met anybody who suffered a theft on board, but remember to leave no cameras or valuables in your bag.

The ship's safe is normally available for storing your valuables. Ask the purser. I slept in a chair and used the safe on the *Espresso Grecia* but they refused to give me a receipt or key as hotels always do. The next morning one of my cameras was missing. After I protested, they finally gave it back, laughing. Nice joke for them.

Time Zone

Ship time is usually the time at the home port of the ship. This is important when crossing between Finland and Sweden, France and Ireland, France and England, and Italy and Greece. In each case the ports are in different time zones. With abbreviated dining hours, I have missed my lunch a couple times on these ferries because of confusing signs and/or my own lack of attention. If in doubt, ask a steward in the dining room and synchronize your watch to his.

The Purser

If you have a problem or question on board, always ask the purser. They invariably speak English, but seem to want to be doing something else than answering questions. So ask your questions clearly and completely. They will never volunteer any information.

Getting Off

Disembarking is usually quite simple. Just walk down the plank or up the ramp with everybody else, flash your passport to the police, and walk through the "Nothing to Declare" gate.

Returning to Italy from Greece, though, was another story. Only two passport police were on duty at Brindisi and they looked at every passport with extra care. It took over half an hour to get off the ship and there were still plenty of people behind me. I knew the port so I started walking toward the exit a few hundred yards away, but two policemen waved me back (waving back in Italian is similar to the "get lost" wave in America, but not as abrupt with the motion) and pointed me toward a building. I walked back to the building, in one door and out the other side without paying any attention to the commotion going on at my left, and then back toward the port exit where I had been several minutes earlier. I was anxious to get out of there so I wouldn't miss the train. Later on the train, some travelers told me that the Italian police made everybody put their bags down on a long counter. Then dogs walked over the bags several times, sniffing for dope. I had walked right past the whole operation. Nobody asked me anything in there!

Potpourri

A few large ferries have telephones. Most of the people in Europe have a phone in their pocket.

The large ferries feature casinos with roulette, blackjack, and slot machines. A live band and dance floor attracts young and old. It reminds you of a wedding party. There might be a movie theater on board.

Ships often have showers in the restrooms, but you must bring your own soap and towels. If you have a cabin, soap and towels are usually provided.

Dress on board is casual in the south and more formal in the north. Between Stockholm and Helsinki many of the locals dress up pretty smartly and party hard. Between Italy and Greece they party hard in dress down.

In rough weather, the ship might heave pretty badly. The Baltic, Adriatic, and Ionian seas, and the English Channel can have some unbelievably huge waves. Ride in the back to reduce the motion. You might want to look around for life vests in really bad conditions so you know where to run if the ship starts to drink quick.

On the ferry from Oostende to Dover, instructions are posted for use of the life jackets in Dutch, French, English, and German. Sorry, no stewardess will demonstrate. [1740]

GEBRUIKSAANWIJZING REDDINGGORDEL 'STANDARD'
MODE D'EMPLOI GILET DE SAUVETAGE 'STANDARD'
INSTRUCTION FOR USE LIFEJACKET 'STANDARD'
GEBRAUCHSANWEISUNG RETTUNGSGURTEL 'STANDARD'

Trek reddinggord l over uw hoofd aan

Passez la brass re par dessus la tête

Place lifejacket over your head

Ziehen Sie den Rettungsgürtel
über Ihren Kopf

Trek banden zijdelings strak aan

Fermez la brassière en tirant
les rubans vers l'extérieur

Tighten both tapes by pulling sideways

Ziehen Sie die Bänder nach der Seite
straff an

Haal banden kruiselings achter uw rug
langs

Croisez les rubans derrière le dos

Cross tapes behind your back

Bänder hinter dem Rücken kreuzen

Bevestig banden aan voorzijde met een
stevige knoop over reddinggordel heen

Nouez les rubans sur le devant
de la brassière

Fasten tapes with a firm knot
in front of lifejacket

Bänder festknoten über die "Front"-
Teile des Gürtels

Chapter 18
On the Roads of Europe
Travel by Car, Van, or Motorcycle

Drive it or park it.

THE DIFFERENCES

Cost
The biggest difference between driving in Europe and driving in America is that driving in Europe costs more. The price of automobiles, insurance, gasoline, and maintenance can be two to three times higher than at home.

Almost Everything Else
Other significant differences include the types of cars in use, roads and road markings, courtesy or lack thereof, speed, and rules of the road, both official and customary. Before venturing out in a car, a thorough reading of "AA Motoring in Europe" would be time well spent. This book is available in many bookstores in the USA and Europe, and from your AAA.

DRIVER'S LICENSE

Home State Driver's License
A valid driver's license is required to operate an automobile, motorcycle, or moped in Europe. Your home state driver's license is sufficient in most cases. In some cases operation of anything other than a normal sedan requires a special license. For example, you may need a special license to ride a motorcycle in Europe.

International Driving Permit
It would be a good idea to have an International Driving Permit (IDP) when driving in Europe. It is required in some countries. Even if you do not plan to drive in Europe, get an IDP. It is a handy additional piece of identification which can sometimes be left as deposit when renting a bicycle or a deck chair. You don't want to leave your passport.

Basically all that the IDP does is translate your driver's license unto umpteen foreign languages showing what class of vehicle you are authorized to operate. If you have language difficulty with the local police the IDP will probably save you some grief. Your home state driver's license is still needed when driving in Europe with the International Driving Permit.

Heading north on Autobahn 1 (shown on maps as the "A1" and as the "E73") near the German town of Remscheid, the sign announces a Rasthof (rest stop) with gas, food, and lodging located 1.1 kilometers (about 3/4 mile) down the road. The next gas station is 50 km (30 miles) further. Being as how there are no speed limits on the German Autobahnen you will be there in short order. [1827]

The IDP is sold at offices of the American Automobile Association. Bring one valid driver's license, two passport photos, and your checkbook to an office of the AAA and you'll have an IDP in about ten minutes. Most AAA offices can take your picture if you don't have extra passport photos available.

I've had about 10 IDPs over the years. They expire in one year. When I had a German drivers license, I bought my IDP from the German authorities. It is basically the same piece of paper as issued in the USA.

European Driver's License

For those planning to live overseas, apply for a local driver's license. It is required in all countries if you stay for more than a year.

VEHICLES

There are a number of ways to have a car available in Europe. These are: rent one, buy a new one, buy a used one, bring one with you, or let your company provide you with one. The choice depends on the length and purpose of your trip, the weight of your wallet, or the attitude of your employer.

European vs. American Cars

European cars are noticeably different, and you don't need an "ultimate driving machine" to experience the differences. Europe has nothing to compare to the standard Detroit Ironmobile with ho-hum automatic transmission and swish-swash suspension.

In Poland it looks like the usual suspects have scratched out the Russian names on this huge traffic sign hanging low over the sidewalk. The wrench sign indicates that there is a mechanic about 300 meters (about 2/10 of a mile) to the right at the intersection. [1805]

The typical European car has a tight manual transmission, sports car type steering, and road-wise suspension. A medium size car, both in physical size and in engine performance, used to be the Volkswagen Beetle. Families of four traveled in what in America was considered the student's car. Even after the end of traditional Bug production, maybe half the cars in Europe are smaller than Volkswagens.

American cars are rare in Europe. Most of them in Europe are owned by American servicemen. The rest belong to the well-to-do, to American businessmen, to Swedish teenagers, and to those engaged in shady businesses. They really appear out of place in the narrow streets and abbreviated parking spaces of Europe.

Here is the convenient Avis rent a car office and a news stand in the train station in Nancy, France. Reserving a rental car is a good idea. You can guarantee availability and price, and have a USA office to complain to if something goes wrong. Be prepared to spend some time getting the paperwork settled. [1811]

Auto Rental

Auto rental and leasing agencies are located throughout Europe. Advice and assistance on renting a car in Europe are areas where a good travel agent can help. Also consult the AAA and the international car rental companies. Hertz, Avis, National, and Budget maintain offices in the major cities and in some surprising out-of-the-way places. These companies operate under their own name or affiliated company names in Europe. Call one of the majors and request a world-wide directory. These directories list agency locations, car types, rates, taxes, insurance requirements, minimum age, and other conditions. Look in the TRAVELERS YELLOW PAGES of *www.enjoy-europe.com* for web site URLs.

Three of the major auto rental firms share an office in the Antwerp, Belgium train station. [1850]

It's possible to save money by renting from one of the local European car rental companies. Inquire at the national tourist office before departure, or at the local tourist office on arrival. European airlines are also a good source for information on local car rental agencies. And even the European railroads, recognizing their natural limitations, can help you rent a car. The French National Railroad, *SNCF*, promotes special combination rail/car packages.

At all rental agencies, the style and price range are more varied than in America. Individual agencies rent autos ranging from the cheap and under-powered midget cars to the most expensive Mercedes.

Standard transmission is standard. You pay more for an automatic. Air conditioning is not standard. Maybe you'll want to get a car cover if you are traveling in the summer. These keep the car much cooler when parked in the sun.

Generally, you must be at least 21 or 25 to rent a car, and for some expensive models, 30 years old. Some companies also have maximum age limits. Prices and/or taxes vary between companies and countries. Special deals exist for weekends. You can get weekly or monthly rates, and rates with unlimited "mileage" (kilometers over there).

Make sure to consider the cost of extras when renting an auto. Gasoline is never included in the rental price. This is generally about three times the cost in the USA.

Renting an auto always involves insurance. The collision damage waiver, CDW, is as high or higher in Europe as it is in the USA. For a small car this can increase the rental charges by 50%. When using major credit cards, this cost is usually paid by the credit card company. However, the cost may be covered for only a limited time, say two weeks, and may not cover anything except a standard sedan. Also, some rental agencies in Europe may want to sell you the insurance so bad that they won't accept your refusal to sign on for CDW. It would be a good idea to bring along a copy of the printed form from your credit card company stating what is covered and under what conditions.

If you have a choice in the matter it would be better to avoid renting a car in Germany and driving it to adjacent countries. The reason is that there is still some bad feeling over WW II, and even though you or your parents may have helped defeat the Nazis, the people in Poland, France, and Holland only see the German auto tags. With German auto tags, I had one bad experience in Holland and a colleague had his windows wantonly busted out in France. I put a USA oval sticker on our car when we made the trip to Istanbul.

Police in Amsterdam boot an illegally parked car. They mean business. [1824]

With German plates you are also more likely to receive the Denver boot for illegal parking in Holland. The Dutch authorities, unhappy that some German drivers ignore parking meters and violation notices, attach a wheel clamp, as it's known in Europe, to German cars in addition to giving a ticket. This is an expensive thing to get removed. My car was clamped in Bratislava, Slovakia. Inadvertently, I had parked overnight in the space reserved for the Chief of Police, right in front of the police station. It would have been an expensive ticket. While the police were removing the clamp, I talked them down to half price, and then kept negotiating and got it down to zero.

Auto Purchase, New Cars

European cars can be purchased through some car dealers and through specialized agencies in the United States for tourist pickup at the factory or at a dealer near your European destination. You can order a car for foreign delivery, pick it up on arrival, drive through Europe on vacation, and have it shipped home. Problems because of the distances become earthshaking. I know of one man who ordered a German sports car for pickup, but delivery was delayed throughout his six week trip. He had to go back to Europe a couple of months later just to pick it up. And I know of another who ended up with the wrong color because he did not double-check the order. You have to really want those oval plates to go through with it.

If you are considering the purchase of a new European auto, talk to a dealer about his tourist delivery program. You might want to make this a part of your European experience. Get references and speak to recent customers to see whether the deals go through smoothly or not. My experience in going to half a dozen auto dealers at home is that tourist delivery is something they don't do very often and something that they are not especially interested in doing. That's what you have to watch out for. Disinterest breeds sloppy paperwork and mistakes.

Here is a typical country road intersection, in Switzerland on the outskirts of Bussigny-pres-Lausanne. Notice the inverted triangle YIELD sign on the pavement. STOP signs are rare in Europe. [1830]

Purchase of a car to return it home requires a significant amount of work and hassle. The cost savings are not as great as they once were. You save the amount of foreign taxes which may easily be consumed by insurance and return freight costs. U.S. Customs will probably have an invoice ready for you. Some states will slap a sales tax on cars which have recently been purchased overseas. But you do save the cost of renting a car while you are in Europe.

Besides the auto companies, some specialized firms offer auto purchase services. Some models are available immediately. Inquire about package deals, possibly including insurance, shipping, taxes, customs, and trip planning.

If you are living in Europe and decide to buy a new car, be ready for surprises. Prices of European cars vary considerably. They are almost always cheaper in the country where they are made, but are usually cheaper in America! For instance, my Porsche was priced 20% higher in Holland than what I had paid for it in California, even though Holland borders Germany where the car was made. The equivalent model for sale in Holland had none of California's engine trashing pollution control equipment and did not sail halfway around the world, but it did have some exorbitant "accessories" — value added tax and a luxury tax.

Cars in dealer showrooms usually have two prices, the price before taxes and the price including taxes. Tax them to death is the rule in Europe, and dodge the taxes is the most rewarding game in town.

Auto Purchase, Used Cars

Purchase of a used car in Europe is no less risky than doing the same in America. As always, it is likely that you are buying someone else's problem. Used car prices are fairly reasonable.

If you are buying a used car with the intention of shipping it back home, know that modifications are going to be required to meet American safety and pollution control requirements. The price on that Mercedes may look pretty sweet until United

States Customs orders you to post bond and have it modified, or else export it or destroy it. Some autos require many more, and more expensive, changes than others. For instance, do not bring a car home that does not have DOT etched on every window. Another big nuisance would be a British car with right hand drive. You can do better. In fact you could hardly do worse. Another problem will probably be insurance. European specification autos may be more expensive to repair and consequently your insurance company may be reluctant to extend coverage. Simple things like tail light covers are often different. Importing a replacement is very expensive and takes time.

Before shipping a used car home, contact the US Customs Service, the EPA, and the Department of Transportation to find out what officialdom will require of you, your bank account, and your vehicle. You should also contact your state motor vehicle department and local pollution control agency to see what standards the car will have to meet in order to be registered in your state.

This used car lot on a street in Haarlem sports a 1993 Alfa Romeo for €1,350 and behind it is a 1991 VW Golf (like a Rabbit) for €2,000. This was in January 2003. For an extended vacation you could buy a used car and resell it when you're ready to go home. [1847]

To determine used car prices in Europe, locate a copy of a major European city newspaper and check the want ads. Large libraries and some news dealers carry these papers. You can also read the major European newspapers and their classified advertisements on the web. Most have an internet site.

STREETS AND ROADS

Flying Low

Probably the best road in the world is an hour stretch of the *E10* through Belgium. It is a straight, flat, wide freeway and completely lighted at night. But, for real excitement, try keeping up with the Fiats on the winding *A7* tollway through the mountains of Northern Italy. Sweaty palms!!

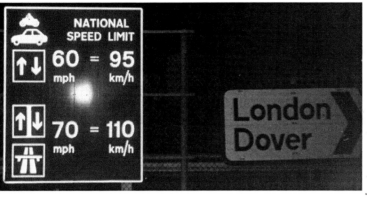

On inter-city roads in England, the speed limit is 60 mph for autos and motorcycles, and on divided highways and expressways it is 70 mph. But notice the direction of the arrows. They drive on the left in Britain and Ireland, with right hand drive cars. On the Continent, they do it the American way. The conversion from mph to km/h is for the benefit of Continentals who use the metric system exclusively. The British still use some of their historic system of weights and measures. The bright spot on the sign is a reflection on my flash unit. Try not to do that with your flash. [1828]

Expressways

The variety of roads in Europe is greater than in America. The superhighway system throughout Europe is equivalent to our Interstate Highway System. Parts of it, particularly in France, Greece, Spain, and Italy, are tolled. Austria, Switzerland, Slovakia, and some other countries charge an annual fee to use the expressways. You will be asked to buy a sticker for your car as you drive in. In all other countries it is generally freeway.

The autoroutes of France have a speed limit of 130 km/hr (80 mph) and are virtually deserted because of the high tolls. Along the way, Stephanie enjoys fast French food overlooking the fast lanes. [1819]

Secondary Roads

Off the superhighways, road quality drops suddenly to winding, two-lane asphalt paving. There is usually little or no shoulder, and the road often narrows to one and a half or even one lane. You sometimes find yourself driving under a haystack. Since most of Europe is agricultural, be prepared for livestock and slowly moving produce wagons. In eastern Europe, horse drawn wagons are common, even on the main highways. Sunday afternoon is walking day in rural areas throughout

Europe. You may run across (not literally, I hope!) whole families walking abreast on the road.

Instead of 200 km/hr (125 mph) and more, sometimes the German Autobahnen *are parking lots. Here is the A3, just east of Frankfurt, on a very busy very typical Sunday summer afternoon. More than one person has stepped out of his car. One guy has his kid on his shoulders. How would you like to be shifting gears in this? [1809]*

The sign in the foreground indicates that the little road is for mopeds and bicycles. In the distance the 70 indicates the speed limit in km/hr and above that is a sign prohibiting entry to tractors, mopeds, and bicycles. The Netherlands is a very well organized country. [1848]

City Streets

In the cities and towns, anything is possible. Surfaces can be concrete, asphalt, brick, or nearly impassable cobblestone. There are very few cities with wide boulevards, and not many with a one mile stretch of straight street. Paris is one of the few exceptions to this statement. Besides having narrow winding streets, names sometimes change at irregular intervals. A good example is a major ring road in Düsseldorf, Germany. The name changes at least eight times within one mile.

Good maps are essential. Because of the narrow streets, there are many which are one-way. If you miss a turn, it is difficult to double back. Gothenburg, Sweden reminds me of a whirlpool. Once I get in the center of town, I find it almost impossible to get out.

A motorist is getting ready to tank up at the Mobil gas station in Patras, Greece. There is a Budget Rent A Car office next door, and other auto rental companies nearby. At the Athens Bus Station, you can catch a modern motorcoach to Athens every half hour. That bus is a good value. [1832]

In Munich, Germany a typical street scene displays some very important information. From the right the signs say "No stopping to the right of this sign," "No parking to the left of this sign, workdays, Monday through Friday, 7 am to 6 pm," "All traffic must turn left," and in the distance the round board with the white band: "Do not enter — wrong way." Similar signs are in use throughout Europe. [1835]

Some streets are posted to allow entry only for busses or taxis. It's easy to miss these because the sign may be in the local language. German cities are almost always in reconstruction with detours galore. These can be extremely frustrating. With the ancient designs of most European cities, it's a near impossibility to drive around the block and double back. Once you're off the path it will take some time to get reoriented.

ROAD MARKINGS

Route Numbers

There is a definite lack of route signs on the roads. Those roads which are numbered on maps seldom have the numbers posted along the roads. Compass directions at exits and intersections, e.g. north and south, are not posted. To get to where you are going, you often need to know the name of every *village* or *Dorf* in between. It's not difficult to get lost.

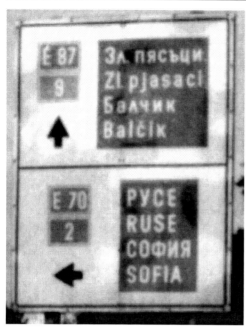

This road sign in Bulgaria gives the spellings of cities in the Bulgarian alphabet and in the Roman alphabet. Don't expect to see this feature on all signs, and don't expect to see the route numbers along the roads. Have a good map, one that includes names in the local spelling. This also applies to the Ukraine, Greece, Russia, and other countries using different alphabets. [1815]

Street Signs

In the cities street names are seldom seen on signposts at intersections. The usual practice is to have the street name posted on the corner of a building just above the ground floor. New buildings and redecorated buildings often have no street names posted. Again, it is not difficult to get lost, especially on a rainy night.

Do Not Enter

European road signs are mainly symbolic due to the large number of languages and the great amount of international traffic. These signs are virtually unknown in America, though a few are coming into use in some areas. It's easy to learn the most important ones. However, modifiers to the posted regulation, e.g. "Sunday only," are always given in the local language.

The most important sign as pointed out in the first chapter is the symbol for DO NOT ENTER — WRONG WAY. It's about 18 inches in diameter with a horizontal white band on a red background.

One Way

One way signs in Europe are usually black and white on a horizontal rectangular plate with a large arrow. Inside the arrow is usually the local word(s) for one way, e.g., *Einbahnstrasse* (German) and *senso unico* (Italian).

This stop sign is in Turkey. [1843]

Stop

Although STOP signs are rare in Europe, they pop up in some unusual places. French speaking locales seem to have the most. Over in Kiev, The Ukraine, I looked up at an intersection and saw a nondescript sign with the word "stop" in Cyrillic next to an American stop sign.

Stop signs may be printed our way, and in Cyrillic as we have here in Kiev, Ukraine. [1841]

Priority and Yield

Another common sign is the yellow diamond, indicating PRIORITY over the intersecting road. The intersecting road will have an inverted triangle sign, white with a red border, meaning YIELD. If neither road has a sign, the vehicle on the right has the right of way.

The PRIORITY yellow diamond stays in effect until you pass another yellow diamond with a diagonal line across it. Unposted intersections are rare in the countryside but common in the cities. Watch out. Europeans, especially taxi drivers, who are making a right turn do not even look for oncoming traffic since they have the right of way at unposted intersections when turning right. If they are going straight through, they only look to the right. If they see that a pump on the accelerator will get them into the intersection before another vehicle gets there, they do it.

Here's a good reason for not driving in Madrid at noon. I thought that being a matador would be dangerous enough for anyone. This cop stands out there all alone without a red sheet or a sword. [1829]

Speed Limits

Speed limit signs are round. These have only a number indicating the speed limit, in kilometers per hour. Speed limits within cities are generally 50 km/h (30 mph). Speed limits between cities are normally 90 to 110 km per hour (approximately 65 mph) on the major roads.

Speed limits on most expressways are 130 kph (80 mph). In some countries the citizens obey absolutely and in others they sing and laugh as they put the pedal to the floor.

Speed limit signs on the *Autobahnen* (expressways) in Germany are for the most part merely advisory, as you will learn soon after driving on. The legal limit is no limit. My daily drive to work was normally at 105 mph (170 kilometers per hour) and I was passed often. In the frequent construction zones, speeds are severely regulated. Some speed limit signs in Germany add the words *bei Nässe* to indicate that the limit applies when the road is wet.

NO

Also round are signs indicating that ENTRY IS PROHIBITED for certain types of vehicles. A silhouette of a car, motorcycle, truck, or horse drawn wagon in the white circle is specific for that vehicle. A round sign with two cars, the one on the left being red, means NO PASSING. A round plaque with no picture means NO VEHICLES of any kind may enter.

NO LEFT TURN, NO RIGHT TURN, and NO U TURN signs are round with an arrow indicating the direction and a diagonal band across it meaning that it is prohibited.

A round blue sign with the silhouette of an adult holding a child's hand means that the road or path may be used by PEDESTRIANS ONLY.

City Limits

A rectangular sign with the city name typically indicates the city limit as you enter every city or village throughout Europe. City speed limits are generally 50 km/hr whether posted or not. Slow down. As you exit the city you'll see a sign with the city name and a diagonal line through it. Speed up.

Hazard

Triangles pointing up warn of SPECIAL ROAD CONDITIONS. They usually show a silhouette of the condition such as curves, skidding auto, running children, crosswalk, or just a large exclamation mark!

Mamaia is the Black Sea resort hotel district of Constanta, Romania. Centrum is the direction to the center of the city. You also see crosswalk and parking signs similar to those used throughout Europe. [1816]

Signals

Traffic signals are the same as in America, green for go and red for stop. Signals are normally turned off at night, or changed to blinking yellows or blinking reds. Pedestrians in some cities are treated to audio versions of walk and don't walk.

The Full Story

There are many other signs. The AA book *Motoring in Europe* and the book *Enjoy Europe by Car* show most of the common icons. The Berlitz

Phrase Books for Travelers also show many of the signs. The popular guide books do not provide this information.

DRIVING HABITS AND LAWS

City Driving

There is a myth prevalent in America regarding the difficulty of driving in Paris. *Au contraire, mon ami.* Driving in Paris is actually sane, almost easy, except for the problem of blocked intersections during rush hours.

Amsterdam, though, is a city that will test your command of sailor's English. You must bully and bluff your way through narrow streets jammed with unruly drivers, streetcars, buses, mopeds, bicycles, dogs, and double-parked trucks. And pedestrians should be aware that painted crosswalks in Amsterdam are not safe. Drivers stop for dogs, but humans receive an insulting blast on the horn. The Dutch joke is that a driver turns on his wipers if a pedestrian is crossing the street. That's to wipe the blood off the windshield -- typical Dutch humor, and not far off the mark.

A few cities where it might even be worse than Amsterdam are Lisbon, Rome, Madrid, and Athens. In these cities you'll find massive horn-honking traffic jams as citizens go home for the afternoon lunch and siesta. At times when there is no traffic jam, every driver seems to be racing for the checkered flag. Night drivers often use only the parking lights, and sometimes no lights.

In the eastern cities, there are not so many autos, yet, and the traffic situation in the cities is moderate.

Driver Beware

Europeans tend to be fast, aggressive drivers, with the exception of Scandinavians. The Swedes and Finns are the most courteous drivers on either side of the Atlantic. But for the rest, watch out for tailgaters riding in your slipstream and general lack of good sense regarding the margin of error. The *Autobahnen* have no speed limits and Germans love to drive fast, pushing those machines to the max. "Doing 200" (meaning 200 kilometers per hour, equal to 125 mph) is not uncommon. Just keep to the right and stay out of their way. It's their road and they will be prompt to remind you with their flashing high beams! Before they use the high beams they turn on their left turn signal indicating their intention to pass if you are poking along in the show off lane.

As mentioned, every other country has speed limits on their expressways, generally 130 km/h (80 mph). The limits are pretty much ignored in Italy and on some roads in France. It can cost you dearly if you are caught. A friend told me that he was a passenger in Holland when the driver was stopped by the *Rijkspolitie* (National Police) driving one of their white Porsche Targas. The driver was ordered to pay $480 on the spot or walk home. They paid.

A significant difference between European and American driving is the variation in speeds. On an American road, most drivers will go at approximately the same speed, say, plus or minus 10% from the posted speed limit. Not so in Europe. There are a large number of underpowered small autos in Europe, along with certain very roadworthy sports cars and luxury sedans. An extra danger in the east, Poland and Hungary in particular, is the large number of horse drawn wagons on the highways. You can be on top of these faster than you expect. On our drive through the mountains of Croatia we were often impeded by large logging trucks. You want to pass just to avoid breathing the diesel exhaust fumes but it's very difficult to find a hundred yards of straightway.

In Portugal, they drive fast and recklessly on the mountain roads, and they toot the horn at every curve to warn whoever might be coming from the other direction.

European trucks do not have the array of night running lights outlining the rig as they do in America. They generally travel slow, especially uphill, so be careful not to run into one at night. Trucks also have a bad habit of quickly changing lanes without warning. Trucks are prohibited from German *Autobahnen* on Sundays until 10:00 pm. Get home before those gentlemen start their engines.

Passing

On all roads, it is strictly illegal to pass on the right. If you're accustomed to metropolitan freeways where you frequently do a right hand pass on those cars poking along in the supposedly fast lanes, break the habit or risk your life. Also, it is strictly illegal to drive in the left lane on any expressway except to pass another vehicle. To announce your approach and intention to pass when the left lane is blocked, turn on your left turn signal. If that fails to budge him/her over to the right lane, flash your bright lights, day or night. All European cars that need it have a switch for flashing the high beams.

In Sweden the law says that the headlights must be on whenever you are driving. Sweden does not have many miles of expressways but does have super wide roads with heavy duty shoulders. To facilitate passing, Swedes by custom pull over and drive on the shoulder (if it is clear) and let the fast guys have the road. Once a driver pulls over to the shoulder he must stay there until the car behind him passes. So don't pull over unless you can see a long clear stretch of shoulder ahead, and if someone pulls over for you, pass quickly.

Italy also requires that headlights be on when driving in daylight. It is a good idea to practice this in all countries since your visibility to other drivers is greatly enhanced when your headlights are on.

Greece has heavy duty shoulders on the tollways. Most people drive with two wheels on the shoulder, leaving plenty of room for others to pass in the driving lane.

The highways in Poland generally have wide shoulders making it relatively easy to pass the horse wagons. In Hungary, there is virtually no shoulder on most roads. If the car behind the horse wagon is one of those under-powered things and his car is typically full of family and friends, he will be extremely reluctant to pass. A long line can build up and slow you way down.

Police

The Dutch and Belgian highway patrols are well equipped in vehicles. Both use Porsche Targas in their fleets. The German highway patrol is fairly easy to spot in green Opels. In fact, most police vehicles are as easy to spot as at home. Virtually all have large emergency lights mounted on top and have *POLIS* or *POLITIE* or some similar word painted in big letters on the side.

In driving through Poland, one thing that you see on entering and leaving every village is a blue police car parked by the road with a very watchful officer inside. I assume that they are there to enforce the speed limit of 60 km/h through the village since it's very easy to fly right through most of these little towns. You'll also notice that the second largest building in most Polish towns, after the church, is the police station. Police presence is so visible in this country that I came to believe that the word "police" is derived from the word "Poland."

Speed limits in Romania are posted as you enter the country. Limits are per type of vehicle in km/hr. The columns show the limits in cities and between cities. [1845]

Sirens

The common American law requiring drivers to pull to the right and stop for all emergency vehicles with siren and lights on is rarely followed. In Europe, drivers race ambulances to intersections. Police and fire vehicles generally get equal disrespect. The only countries where I saw some regard for emergency vehicles were Finland and Spain and the eastern countries. Emergency vehicles usually have blue flashing lights and a two-tone wailing siren. Only in Spain do they have the good old American screeching sirens.

Wrong Way

In Britain and Ireland, all drivers drive on the left side of the road. Steering wheels are mounted on the right hand side of the vehicle so that the driver tends to sit in the middle of the road. An American auto would be a bit difficult to drive in Britain or Ireland.

Pedestrians should be especially wary of vehicles approaching from the right. The streets of London are plastered with signs warning "Look Right" and on one-way streets, "Look Left." It's best to look both ways and over both shoulders before crossing.

One for the Road

Drinking and driving is an extremely serious offense in Europe. Every country has strict laws and strict enforcement. You can be stopped without apparent cause at any time and any place. The police will request your personal and automobile documents. At night, the police will willy-nilly stop anyone and everyone and "request" the driver to blow up a balloon for an alcohol test. Although this test should prove positive after the consumption of more than two beers within the last hour, I have seen a couple of cases where it was borderline on more than that, and the driver was allowed to go on.

Radar Traps

Speeding laws are variably enforced. Radar is becoming more generally used. One of the ultimate big brother devices, being used in Holland, Germany, and Switzerland particularly, is a combination radar/camera set mounted in an unobtrusive dull green box here and there around the country and in the cities. The Germans move them around a lot and usually have a cop hiding in the bushes to make sure nobody jumps out and steals the radar/camera set. This device photographs speeders and has a strobe flash for night operation. Via the license plate number, a notice of violation is sent to the owner. The picture is available on request. Formerly the Dutch police would mail the picture with the notice of violation, but, ah, some drivers were photographed with companions not their spouses, which led to, ahem, some further difficulties when their mates opened the mail. This radar/camera device is also used at traffic lights. Dutch drivers just love to run red lights. I've been photographed for speeding twice in Germany, but only had one notification mailed to me for payment. Locations of the radar camera boxes are posted on various web sites, in the local language.

Somewhere in the Czech Republic the Trabbie in front of us crosses the tracks after a greeting from an American STOP sign. The Trabbie is a wind-it-up artifact of Peoples Demonic Republics, now gone from the European scene. [1802]

Road Help

Help on the road is available in Holland from the little yellow *Wegenwacht* (literally "road watch") cars. These are a service of the *ANWB*, Dutch auto club. They cruise the major roads helping motorists who have mechanical problems. The German auto club *ADAC* has similar cruisers on the roads.

You get pretty used to parking permit dispensers like this, standard all over Europe. This is the French version in Marseille. Instead of individual parking meters, you put money in one of these machines for the time you need, push the button, receive the permit, and put the permit on your dashboard. If you find an available parking place without a parking meter you better look around for one of these dispensers. [1820]

Members of the AAA are accorded some privileges by the various auto clubs in Europe. Check with your local office before departing.

The Swiss automobile club offers outstanding road service for its members. I was a passenger in a car which caught a stone in the radiator on a Sunday at about midnight, way out in the middle of France. That was the end of driving for the night. The Swiss auto club paid for towing to a local garage, a couple of hotel rooms for the night, a rental car for a week, and then delivery of the repaired car back to Switzerland.

Those planning to live in Europe may want to join one of the national auto clubs. Free maps, trip planning, maintenance assistance, and other services are available to members.

Red, Yellow, Green, Yellow

In Germany, some traffic lights change from red to yellow before going green. As soon as the yellow comes on, everybody revs up. By the time the green is on, everybody is moving out. Austria has a similar system.

Between stop lights in many German cities, a small lighted number will be seen on a post by the curb. This indicates what maximum speed (in kilometers per hour) you can drive in order to avoid stopping at the next light.

In Holland, some traffic lights are synchronized for the maximum speed allowed. This will be posted as *Groen Golf* (green wave) on a green sign of course. Don't speed and you don't have to stop.

Circles

Rules governing traffic circles are not uniform. Watch all signs and road markings at circles. The inverted triangle YIELD sign or "shark teeth" on the pavement will indicate whether incoming or circle traffic has the right of way.

On the continent traffic goes counter clockwise, the way we do it in the USA.

In Britain, where the circle is known as a roundabout, traffic goes clockwise. i.e., backwards to us. It scares me even when I'm in a taxi.

On the left door of this courtyard gate in Zagreb you see the standard NO STOPPING sign. The other sign, in Croatian, probably says something like "keep clear or you will be towed." [1817]

Kids in the Back Seat

    Children less than 12 years old must ride in the back seat. In some countries the age limit is 6 or 10. You normally see young men driving around with their wife in the back seat holding the baby. It looks like chauffeur service. Small children must use a child seat.

This notice on a Dutch door proclaims "Exit, do not block, including weekends." There is also an illustration of your penalty. Recovering a towed vehicle is one way to waste time, money, and calm life. [1822]

PARKING

    There are more cars than parking places.

No Parking

    The NO PARKING sign is a blue circular board with a diagonal red band across it. NO STOPPING is a blue circle with two perpendicular diagonal red bands across it — a big red X if you will. Both also have a red border. NO PARKING signs may also be found in the local language posted on gates and garage doors, whether there is a sloped drive at the curb or not. If you see a word like *interdit* or *verboten*, find out what it means before you walk away from your car.

    Europeans park anyplace they can fit their car. Sidewalks and the middle of streets are used. Cars are often ticketed, but usually not towed unless they are blocking traffic. With American license plates, the Haarlem police would often put a kind notice on my car rather than a ticket. In one case when I went to the police station to pay a parking ticket, the official looked at the ticket, looked at me, and asked, "Are you American?" I answered, "Yes." He replied, "American no pay!" and tore up the ticket. However, after having been ticketed a couple of times for parking on the sidewalk in front of my house, the police officers who saw me doing it again one evening angrily announced that they would tow my car away the next time. There was no next time.

The German police can be downright nasty. I stood by my double parked car waiting for Elizabeth to run into the post office and drop off some letters. An officer walked over and told me to move it. I did, but I got a violation notice in the mail anyway.

Pay Parking

Metered parking is available on many streets and parking lots in Europe. In most countries a sign in the local language announces that you must pay to park on the street. The sign points to an *automat* where you buy a ticket which you place on your dashboard. Many parking lots use a similar system. If you don't see parking meters look for an *automat* somewhere on the lot.

Here is a solar powered parking permit dispenser on a street in Brussels, Belgium. Put your money in and put the permit on your dashboard. [1849]

Parking structures are becoming common. Look for a rectangular blue sign showing a large white **P** with a roof over it. In parking structures you often pay at a cashier or *automat* before going back into the garage to get your car. Then insert the validated card in the exit gate machine while driving out. If there is no roof over the **P** it is just a parking lot.

*On entering cities you will often see a sign indicating the names of the parking lots and structures and the number of free spaces available at that moment. Good city maps indicate parking lots and structures with the **P** symbol. [1823]*

Instead of indicating the number of parking spaces available in each of Haarlem's parking structures, this sign is full of Xs indicating that they are all full on Saturday, market day. Park at the city limits and take a taxi to town. [1810]

Street Parking

When available, street parking can be very expensive. It's more than $2 per hour in many Dutch cities.

Free Parking

In the US, the "blue zone" is reserved for handicapped persons. In Europe the "blue zone" is totally different. It allows limited time free parking on the honor system, for everyone. *Zone Blue* parking means that you must place a blue card on your dash board and set the pseudo clock face to the time allowed. You can then park for free for the time allowed as stated on the street sign. Buy it in a stationary store or gas station and use the Blue Zone card in France, Germany, and other countries. Some businesses give them out for free.

When traveling by car, it pays to use the Michelin Red Guides to find hotels and other travel services. These guides show which city hotels have a garage or off-street parking. Very few do, and those which have it often charge extra. Hotels that do have garages rarely have enough parking spaces for all the guests. Claim a space early so you don't have to park out on the street. Most of the motels along the highways have free parking and plenty of it.

If you drive it into Paris this may be the only way you'll be able to park. A glass recycling pentoid also shares the sidewalk and a DO NOT ENTER sign shines bright above all. Livre indicates a book store. [1807]

Bumpered Cars

Finally, in discussing parking, the Paris method comes to mind. It explains the derivation of the word "bumper," as on the front and rear of your car. In the tight parking spaces on the streets of Paris, this method tends to create a larger parking space and helps to minimize the work of turning, backing, and going forward again. Just back in until you hit the car behind you. Then turn in, drive forward and smack the one ahead of you. Turn out, and quickly rip into the car behind you again. Straighten it out and inch it forward. If you're going to live in Paris, I recommend a six-year-old never-washed Peugeot. The Paris method is also practiced in Amsterdam.

No stopping or you'll get towed away pronto in Trieste, Italy. According to Elizabeth, driving in Trieste is a "game of millimeters." [1801]

GASOLINE

Tanking up starts with knowing where the gas cap is located on your car, and knowing how to open it. These minor rudimentary items are not standardized in our modern world. To save yourself some potential embarrassment and frustration ask the auto rental company before you drive off.

Also be clear on their gasoline policy, i.e., how much, if any, should be in the tank when you return the car, and how much will it cost you if it is below that level.

Cost

Gasoline generally costs 2 to 3 times as much as it does at home, throughout Europe. It used to cost four times as much as we pay, but the price in America has doubled in the last few years.

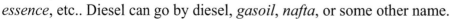

Next to the gas station you find the florist shop on a city street in Ljubljana, Slovenia. [1814]

No Gas

They don't call it gas in Europe. It can be called *petrol*, *benzine*, *benzin*, *essence*, etc.. Diesel can go by diesel, *gasoil*, *nafta*, or some other name.

No Gallons

You can't buy a gallon of gas in Europe. Gas is sold by the *liter*, spelled *litre* in some countries. Our gallon is almost equal to four *liters*. To be more exact, it is

3.785 liters per gallon. You'll see more about the metric system in chapter 27, "Weights and Measures in Europe."

In the Netherlands this Texaco station offers 95 octane "Euro" grade for €1.17/liter (about $4.70/gal), 98 octane "Super Plus" grade for €1.23/liter(about $4.93/gal), and diesel for €0.829/liter (about $3.33/gal) in January 2003. The station has a nachtautomaat so you can pump 24/7. "Ongelood" means unleaded in Holland. [1846]

Octane

High and low octane are sold everywhere. I use *super* (the common name for "high octane") in Europe. Just because the gas cap states the minimum octane to use doesn't mean that you have to use it. I generally use the highest octane to get some extra power out of the engine. This is very useful in passing slower vehicles on some of those winding roads.

Unleaded

Unleaded is sold almost everywhere. The German word *bleifrei* (lead free) is often used in the east. French for unleaded is *sans plomb*.

Service

Many stations are self-serve. Pump your own and go inside to pay. It is becoming more common to be able to insert your credit card at the pump so you don't need to go inside. Some stations allow this even if they are closed. But don't count on being able to use a credit card everywhere for gasoline. Some stations are cash only.

Gas stations provide free air and water, and have all the usual items for sale. Maps are expensive. Restrooms are free and are generally cleaner than in America.

Open Hours

A good rule to follow is keep your tank full, especially on Sunday nights. As with most restaurants and shops, gasoline stations are often family businesses. The general practice is that stations in towns have open hours similar to the hours of other businesses. Europe never was like America with a gas station (or two or three) on every corner. However, there are a growing number of 24 hour stations, attended and unattended. The 24 hour stations usually have basic provisions like the USA's "7-Eleven" stores.

Four grades of gasoline are available at this Czech station. Bleifrei is German for unleaded. The second nozzle is missing so you know what I am pumping. On the left, the top indicator is your total cost in Koruna, the middle is the quantity in liters, and the bottom is the cost per liter. [1804]

MAINTENANCE

Dealers and a large number of independent garages service automobiles. Quality of service ranges as widely as it does at home. The biggest difference is cost and how long it will take to get parts and make repairs. My experience in Holland is that it can take months to get simple items from Germany if the dealer does not stock the part.

I drove over to Stuttgart, Germany to get the Porsche tuned up at the factory, sort of an aside to a vacation trip to the south of France. I left the car at the factory for two days and enjoyed the tail end of a wine festival and some nice sightseeing while they worked on the machine. Apparently the mechanics had a little too much wine festival themselves because 70 miles south of Stuttgart it went dead in a small *Dorf*. Neither of the garages in the town knew what to do so I had to take a room overnight and call the factory the next morning to get help. After getting the supervisor on the line, I handed the phone to a mechanic, he went "Ja, ja, ja," hung up, took a screwdriver over to the car, adjusted something, and I was on my way. About a year later, shortly after I returned to the USA, the timing chain went kaput and the engine blew up, costing some $4,000 for repairs. So much for German quality.

For my German Opel, my company had leased the car and took care of all maintenance expense. I would just drop it off and the dealer drove me to the office. Pretty simple. However, you just about have to know some German to get special items taken care of. Mechanics only speak the native tongue.

Windshields

If you are buying an older used car in Europe, make sure that it has the sandwich-style windshield (safety glass) which does not shatter. Look for "D.O.T." etched on the glass and read the US Customs brochure on importing a car.

This gas station in Rome is chiuso *(closed) for lunch. Most of the major American brands are sold in Italy and throughout Europe. [1839]*

INSURANCE

Only a fool would drive in Europe without insurance, and only a clever fool could get away without it for any length of time. Your home state auto insurance does not cover you. You must purchase insurance valid in Europe.

Two Plans

There are two basic types of insurance. The "all-risk" insurance, identified by the *green card*, protects you against everything. It is required before crossing borders in Europe. The other plan is a limited protection insurance available to residents of each country valid in that country only. But if you have an accident outside that country, expect to be held by the police until you settle up for the damage you caused.

I bought my own insurance when living in Holland. In Germany, my employer provided it. However, they were initially going to provide only the basic service until I requested them to change this to "all risk" insurance.

Special insurance may be required when driving in some of the eastern countries. Rental car companies may advise you that the car cannot even be driven in certain countries.

It is typical in many countries to post a sign like this as you exit the city limits. This indicates that you can resume speed limits in rural area. This sign is in Romania. The lower sign declares that you have the right of way.[1842]

Cost

Insurance is very expensive, upwards of double the rates in a large American city. Substantial discounts are available. Your company may be in a group policy arrangement allowing up to a 30% discount. Furthermore, with a good driving record and no claims on your policy at home, you may be eligible for up to 30% off the balance. Bring a copy of your policy, an affidavit from your agent, and a state motor vehicle report of your good driving record as evidence. Thus, it is possible to be insured for about half the going rate.

Where to Buy Insurance

Insurance is sold by banks and directly through European insurance companies. If you are purchasing an auto for tourist pick up, insurance is an obligatory part of the deal. You will not be allowed to pick up a car at a dealer or at the port unless you have a *green card* with you.

In Lisbon, Portugal I wouldn't park in front of this gate if I was you. There is a BIG sign there with a word on it which looks a lot like "prohibited." [1833]

CRIMINAL ACTS

Theft and Vandalism

Theft and vandalism against automobiles is a common problem in Europe. The large cities are the worst for it, but it can happen anywhere. In Haarlem, The Netherlands my car suffered a stolen antenna, stolen side view mirror, and attempts to pry off the California license plate and the Porsche emblem in various attacks by vandals. One afternoon I caught several drunken Danish tourists trying to roll it into the Spaarne River. I told the owner of the tour boat they came in on that I would sink his ship if his customers ever managed to sink my car. In Aschaffenburg, Germany, my antenna was ripped off along with all the others on our street. One night I caught a weirdo trying to get into the car.

Defenses

Don't leave anything visible in your car. Don't park it on a dark side street overnight. Park it on a busy street under a street light. Don't even leave anything in the trunk. An out-of-country license plate indicates a traveler and tells a thief that there are probably goodies inside. Take everything to your hotel room and leave the thief disappointed.

SAFETY GEAR

Carry a few items of safety equipment when driving in Europe. These should include: a red reflecting triangle, a strong beam flashlight, towing cable, emergency medical kit, and a fire extinguisher. Several of these items are required in some countries. Inquire at the local automobile club or at a police station.

Use of seat belts is required if the car is fitted with them.

Many European cars are equipped with a rear fog light. There is a switch on the dash for this. You'll probably have to look in the owners manual to locate the switch. The fog light is a single bright red light on the left rear. It can be seen from a much greater distance than the normal rear lights. It is also a good idea to use this when there is a light rain because the wheels of your car turn up so much mist that it is hard to see through it.

Another light feature you might find is a roll switch which will raise or lower the beam of the headlights. Keep them down in the city and raise them for country driving. This is not the high beam switch. That one turns on the brights, something that you should rarely use.

It's a good idea to have a car compass. The better quality ones have adjustment screws to let you compensate for the metal in the car. Get one with a night light and lay it on the dash of your rental car. It will come in handy.

Three motorcycle patrolmen of the Rijkspolitie *(National Police) of The Netherlands were three of the few people sober in Amsterdam for the annual celebration of Queen's Day on April 30. [1853]*

"Parking Amsterdam" — somebody could write a song about it. This parker fit it in by the Herengracht, and nearly in the Herengracht. Holland — what a country! Specific hotels are not recommended in How To Europe *but I can say that I would sleep in the Hotel Ambassade again.* [1837]

Chapter 19
Communicating as You Travel
Telephone, Mail, Fax, and Email Are at Your Service

No news is not good news.

STAYING IN TOUCH

Mail and Telephone Basics

We all like to receive mail, and it is even more pleasant when we're overseas and out of touch with daily hometown life. Travelers should be aware of the services provided by the US Postal Service, your long distance telephone carrier, express delivery services, the various *PTT* of Europe, American Express offices, and on-line email services — and the limitations and foibles of each.

Fax and Email

The telephones and the mail work well over there. Faxes can be sent to many post offices in Europe for hand delivery to home addresses. E-mail via the Internet is cheap and fast. A few words from home can really brighten your day.

US MAIL

United States Postal Service

The post office can do one of two things with your mail while you are gone: hold it or forward it. But they will not forward it to Europe.

Vacation Hold: If you will be gone for a short time, request vacation hold service from your local postmaster. The post office will hold mail for up to 30 days.

Forwarding: The post office will not forward mail to an address in Europe because the rate for surface delivery is about 50% higher than for first class domestic mail. So, instruct the post office to forward it to a reliable friend or relative. Give your friend a supply of self-addressed envelopes, stamps, and promises of beaucoup exotic gifts for prompt remailing services.

In lieu of asking the post office to forward your mail, request a neighbor or family member to check the mailbox for you and remail the first class items.

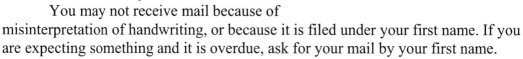

This Ellinika Tachidromeia, "ELTA", *(Post Office) is at Sindagma Square in Athens. Everything inside is written and spoken in Greek and also English. The ELTA is a well run business.* [1912]

Form of Address for Mail to Europe

For mail addressed to you in Europe at *Post Restante* (more about that in a page or two) instruct your friends to address it very clearly. Ask them to print your name in block letters, and capitalize and underline your last name. Do it like so:

> Your <u>NAME</u>
> Poste Restante
> Post Code and City
> Country

You may not receive mail because of misinterpretation of handwriting, or because it is filed under your first name. If you are expecting something and it is overdue, ask for your mail by your first name.

Post code is the same as the American zip code. In Europe it is placed in front of the city name on the same line. For example my post code in Geneva, Switzerland was 1202 and the third line of my address was *1202 Geneva*. In Haarlem, The Netherlands it is *2015 JT Haarlem*.

If there is an alpha character or two in front of the numbers this represents the country. For example CH for *Confederation Helvetica* (Switzerland) or D for *Deutschland* (Germany). My Geneva address could have been written as *CH 1202 Geneva*. Those frontal alpha characters are not required and are not used very often. The alpha characters after the post code in Holland are required because they are part of the local code, not the national code.

If you are living in Europe with a regular street address, the street name is usually written first followed by the number. Sometimes the house number is first but is separated from the name of the avenue by a comma. For example it could be something like:

> *Rembrandtlaan 41*, or
> *141, Blvd. de Gaulle*

It depends on which country you are in.

One Week Service

Airmail takes up to a week to reach Europe, though I have received mail in two or three days. For faster service, type the address or print it out from your computer. The post office uses machines to read and sort mail and this really speeds up the service.

That's the front door of the Amsterdam post office. Post Restante mail can be picked up in the office through the door on the left under the Manpower sign. [1926]

Although it is not required, use airmail envelopes because mail in regular envelopes does not get as much respect. Use a "Priority" sticker on your envelope. Mail service in Europe is "standard" or "priority" and the sticker would be more universally recognized than the words "air mail." Priority can be spelled differently, e.g. *priorité* in French speaking areas. They'll probably understand the English version also.

I can read only a few words of this sign in the PTT at Varna, Bulgaria. There's the French Post Restante, the German Briefmarken (postage stamps), and the nearly universal telephone and telegraph. The rest is Bulgarian to me. [1907]

Three Day Service

"Global Priority Express" from the US Postal Service is another alternate which usually takes no more than four days. Pick up the large or small envelopes from the Post Office and for a flat fee send as much as you can stuff inside. Mail sent to me in The Netherlands from mid-Michigan on Fridays was usually delivered Tuesday morning before 08:00 or Monday afternoon by a special delivery of the Dutch *PTT*. Global Priority Express when I lived in Geneva, Switzerland required an extra day.

Slow Boat

Allow at least a month for mail by boat from the USA to Europe.

RECEIVING MAIL IN EUROPE

There are two popular options for receiving mail when traveling in Europe. One is general delivery and the other is American Express offices. If you are living and/or working in Europe you have other possibilities.

Poste Restante

Poste Restante means "General Delivery" in French and is recognized throughout Europe. In Germany and Austria, you can use *Postlagernd* instead of *Poste Restante*; in Spain, *Lista de Correos*; in Portugal, *Lista de Correios*.

Locations: Mail can be addressed to you at the central post office in any city in Europe. Other locations of post offices in much of Europe accepting *Poste Restante* mail are shown on the maps in the Michelin Red Guides and Michelin Green Guides. Street addresses can be obtained from national and city tourist offices. If you have taken up short term habitation in a large city, go to your local post office to see if general delivery is accepted. Then give your friends the address and post code (zip code) for that post office.

Call for mail, with your passport, at the post office within 30 days or it may be returned. Look for the *Poste Restante* or *Lista* sign in the post office. There is usually a special window for this service.

Collection times are posted at the Edinburgh Post Office. [1923]

I have picked up mail in a number of cities with no problems. But I've seen the clerks go quickly through the stack and miss mail. A sharp-eyed girl in front of me in Madrid saw her name go by and asked the clerk to back up and pull out the letter. It might help if you ask your friends to put a special mark on the envelope with a felt tip pen or use a special colored envelope. That would make it much easier for you to spot your mail over the clerk's shoulder. Say, ask your correspondents to draw a happy face on the front and back of the envelope, and don't forget to capitalize and underline your last name. Write your name on a piece of paper in block letters and show it to the clerk because your pronunciation of your name is most probably not the way the clerk would pronounce it.

Fee: It's usually free but there will sometimes be a fee, equivalent to about 30 cents, for *Poste Restante* mail. When picking up mail, the *PTT* requires your passport for identification.

The PTT in Ljubljana, Slovenia attracts street vendors. The sign advises NO ENTRY to vehicles. It is a pedestrian zone. They won't tow you away here — they lift your offending vehicle onto a truck and drive it away. [1905]

Amex Client Mail Service

A postal facility used by many Americans is an American Express office, available in some major cities. It appears to be a gratuitous service by Amex management who are primarily in the business of selling tickets, tours, and traveler's checks. Mail not claimed in 30 days is returned to the sender. Quality of the personnel at the mail window has been average to incompetent, and it is not open during the entire business day though the rest of the office may be open. Do not count on this service for transfer of money or important messages. As with *Poste Restante*, ask your friends to print your name and address in block letters and capitalize and underline your last name.

Locations: Card holders and those carrying Amex traveler's checks can pick up mail addressed to them at many Amex offices. American Express offices or representatives are located in about 100 cities in Europe, but the representative offices do not offer the client mail service. Get the booklet from American Express listing addresses for all offices and indicating which ones offer client mail service.

Fee: There is a charge for those who are not Amex customers. In Amsterdam it is $3.00. Ouch.

MAIL FROM EUROPE TO THE USA

PTT

PTT is an almost universal appellation in Europe for "Post - Telegraph - Telephone". It is a combination post office, phone company, telegraph office, bank, and central office for miscellaneous government functions. In Italy it is often just *PT*, with the telephone company called the *SIP*. In Spain and Portugal, it is *CTT* or just *CT*, since "Post" is *Correo* or *Correio*, respectively, over there. The post office in Greece is *ELTA* and the phone office is *OTE*.

Form of Address to the USA

Almost everybody recognizes the USA as the USA, except maybe postal clerks. I have begun using the local word for the USA in addition to the letters USA. For example, when I lived in Geneva, Switzerland, the bottom line on my envelopes to the USA reads just like this in big bold print:

Etats-Unis d'Amérique USA

Etats-Unis d'Amérique means United States of America in French.

Put your postcards in the slot of this mailbox in Faro. Correio *is Portuguese for "mail."* [1914]

Postage Stamps

Buying stamps for postcards and letters can be difficult or easy. To illustrate the difficult method, walk into any Paris post office and in straightforward English ask for stamps for air mail postcards to the United States. Mark Twain could have found a collection of words to describe the result more aptly than I — no stamps.

A better way is to bring a postcard to the post office, already written out, addressed, and containing the key words: "United States of America - USA" with the Priority sticker already attached. "Air Mail" (*Par Avion* in France, *Mit Luftpost* in Germany) is no longer an official designation. In Paris, also show the clerk a slip of paper with the word *timbre* written on it. In other cities, the clerk will probably know that you want a stamp for the card, or will speak English. Most Paris postal clerks can speak English but refuse to do it, unless you start up speaking in French in which case they will refuse to speak French. You'll probably have even more trouble in Madrid where the clerks really can't speak English. Over in Rome, do your post office business at the Vatican. There's a post office next to the ice cream vendor at the *Piazza San Pietro* (St. Peter's Square). That ice cream is really delicious.

Nuisance Items

In big city post offices, lines normally develop toward the right of the window. Stay close to the person in front of you or someone will butt in. The inbuttee will usually be a little old woman or a pair of chatting teenage girls. Staying close enough to prevent butt-ins almost requires that you keep your chin pressed to the neck of the person ahead of you. Some inbuttees must consider this a game. They know from a glance that you are an American and that they can get away with butting in. If you encounter one, ask her what time it is. That will let her know that you are already in line. If not, just step in front of her.

Drop your postcards in this mail box in Kiev. It says Posta, in Ukrainian and in the Ukrainian alphabet. [1922]

Clerks at big city *PTT* offices are probably the worst derriere pains in Europe. For better service, and for fewer butt-ins, go to offices in the suburbs or in smaller cities.

On the other hand, one amazing event in my career as a postal customer occurred at the post office in Alzenau, a small town east of Frankfurt, Germany. I went to the window with an airmail letter destined for the United States. The clerk took out a ruler and measured the length, whereupon he charged me about 50% extra. I had used an American envelope which is about an eighth of an inch longer than the German *Bundspost* normally accepts. I howled but it did no good. That was the last time I went to a window with my envelopes. Thereafter I just put normal postage on my envelopes and dropped them in the outside box, with no problems.

Keep in mind that postal workers are not rocket scientists. They are simply bureaucrats and government clerks with life time jobs putting stuff in little boxes. If you need anything more than that you have to spell it out for them.

Extra Stamps

Buy some extra stamps while in the post office to avoid standing in line again. If you can't use them all, bring them home and give them to the neighbor's children. Or frame them as souvenirs.

Parcels

Information on mailing parcels is presented in chapter 24.

EXPRESS PARCEL SERVICES

Reliable but Expensive

Most American businesses have given up on the US post office for everything other than employment rejection letters. Express services like FedEx, DHL, and Airborne Express are the preferred method for sending business papers to make sure they arrive. These services are also available internationally. They are expensive, but can deliver to most European addresses in two to four business days. Prices are extremely high so only use these when you absolutely must have something in a hurry.

Customs Gotcha

If you use one of these express services instead of the post office it is more likely that your parcel will be opened for customs inspection in Europe. This usually adds two days to the delivery time. The express service asks you to fill out the customs declaration, and this can lead to significant expense. Duties on some items exceed the value of the goods.

When Elizabeth traveled with our two-year old Stephanie she needed some additional plastic baby bottle liners. These were not available in Europe. The French duty was about equal to the cost of the liners.

When shipping documents to Germany, the value declared by my company was "no commercial value." The German customs service opened the package to make sure. It was just a rough draft of a sales presentation. On one document they charged about $15 customs duty plus $3.00 tax, and included 12 pages of paperwork with the invoice. That is another example of government clerks with life time jobs at your service. It was unbelievable.

This post office in Helsinki is identified in Finnish and in Swedish, and with the universally recognized French for "General Delivery," Poste Restante. *[1913]*

CALLING EUROPE FROM THE USA

Traditional international telephone services from the United States are handled by AT+T, MCI, and Sprint. These companies are in fierce advertising wars claiming better quality and lower costs and I couldn't begin to figure it out.

The Standard System

All American telephone numbers have 10 digits, three for the area code and seven for the local number. Over there it is a different story. European numbers can have any assortment of digits and arrangements.

Country Code

Every country in the world has a country code. For North America, including Canada, the USA, Mexico, and The Caribbean, the country code is 1. The UK code is 44. You'll usually see the country code written with a plus sign in front of it, for example +353 for Ireland.

City Code

Instead of area codes, all countries use city codes. Each city code begins with zero. For example the city code of Haarlem, The Netherlands is 023. Within Holland, the informal name for The Netherlands, you would dial the 023 plus the local number. But from outside Holland you only dial 23. The zero is dropped. However, Italy has made a change in their system and now requires you to dial the zero on incoming international calls.

City codes can vary from two as in Brussels 02 to five as in Salzburg 06222.

Local Numbers

Local numbers can vary in length from 4 up to 9 numbers. In a small village they don't need many numbers, but in Berlin you've got a couple of million phones.

Rates

For calls from the United States mainland, rates to Europe do not vary from state to state. A call from San Francisco to Paris costs the same as a call from New York to Paris. The rate period is determined by the time at the telephone where the charge will be paid.

Dialed calls from the USA are charged for an initial one minute, not three minutes as with operator assisted calls. You might want to confirm this with your long distance carrier since they are changing things all the time.

10-10 Services

Starting in the late 1990s you have seen more and more advertising for "10-10" services on TV and in your mailbox. These services are decidedly a great deal. My international telephone bill has fallen to the floor using one of these services. Conditions of service vary and can include a minimum monthly fee. Some have varying rates during the day for domestic calls, and international rates for different countries can be significantly different.

The low cost "10-10" services have made life so much easier. You can call Europe for less than the cost of a call to someone only 30 miles away in the USA. I have used several of the "10-10" and similar services and change to another company whenever I find a better deal. You do not need to subscribe and can stop using one and start using another whenever you wish. My calls to Switzerland are down to 7¢ and to Holland down to 10¢ per minute, with a one minute minimum. Not all "10-10" numbers are available in all parts of the USA. Some are restricted to a few states.

HOW TO PLACE A CALL TO EUROPE

From Areas Equipped With International Dialing

Dial the USA international access code: **011**

Then, dial the country code.

Then, the city code, without the zero in front.

Then, the local number.

As an example, to call the Munich Tourist Office:

dial the international access code, *011*,

then the country code for Germany, *49*,

then the city code for Munich, *89*,

then the local number, *233-0300*.

If you call when the office is not open you will hear a clear message in German, followed by the same information in English.

To make a person-to-person, collect, calling card, third number billing, or any international call requiring the assistance of an operator, call your long distance phone company.

From Areas Without International Dialing

If your area does not have international dialing, call your operator to place all international calls. Tell the operator you wish to make an overseas call and give her the country code, city code, and local number. If your call does not require special operator assistance (collect, charge card, person, etc.), the lower dial rate should apply, but I don't guarantee it.

10-10 Number International Dialing

You probably have an instruction sheet describing the procedure for making international calls with your "10-10" number.

I simply dial my "10-10-XXX" number and then

Dial the USA international access code: **011**

Then, dial the country code.

Then, the city code, without the zero in front.

Then, the local number.

The beauty of this is that your area does not need to have international dialing enabled. But you do need to find a "10-10" number for your area. Not all numbers work throughout the USA.

How To Profit From This Telephone Intelligence

How do you apply this information to your advantage? Well, after your travel agent tells you that the lowest cost room in Paris is $200 per night, go home and open your *Michelin Red Guide France* and find a two star hotel for around $70 in the *arrondissement* (section of the city) you want to stay in. Wake up early the next morning and call the hotel to make your reservation. The Michelin Red Guides show city codes. It's the number next to the symbol that looks like a telephone dial, or a daisy if you will. This appears on the first or second line for each city heading. If there is no city code listed here, then the phone number listed for each hotel includes the city code. Hotels in all price categories are listed.

Don't be bashful about calling. You will get a connection within a minute at most times. It is best to call during the week, but not during their lunch time, noon to 13:00 or noon to 16:00 depending on the country. Speak up, right away, slowly and clearly. Here is your script:

> *"Hello! Mr./Mrs./Miss - your last name —*
> *calling from the United States of America.*
> *Do you speak English please?"*

Odds are excellent that an English speaking person will answer the phone and/or be available within a minute or so. If not try another hotel. For less than a dollar worth of telephoning, you should be able to make a reservation and find out what amount of advance deposit is required.

If you have a friend who speaks the language of the country you are calling, you might ask them to make the call for you. This could be especially helpful if you are looking for a room in a small town where there might be only one or two hotels, and where desk clerks are less likely to be fluent in English.

Why can't your travel agent make the phone call and reservation for you, you ask? Because the $200 hotel pays the agent a commission and probably has a toll free (800) telephone number. The $70 hotel pays no commission and it will cost to make the telephone call. You have to make the call yourself if you want to be frugal and stay in a tourist class hotel. If you prefer more than that then it is best to see a travel agent to book your hotel. See chapter 14 for a description of what to expect in European hotels.

TELEPHONE COUNTRY CODES

Here are listed the telephone codes for the 45 countries of Europe, and the city codes for a metropolis or two in each country. If you need more, consult your long distance telephone provider.

Codes for dialing **TO**:
Albania +335. Tirana 42
Andorra +33. All points 628
Austria +43. Graz 316; Innsbruck 5222; Salzburg 6222; Vienna 1
Belarus +375. Minsk 17
Belgium +32. Antwerp 3; Brussels 2; Ghent 91; Liege 41
Bosnia & Herzegovina +387. Sarajevo 71
Bulgaria +359. Sofia 2
Croatia +385. Zagreb 1
Cyprus +357. Nicosia 2

Czech Republic +42. Prague 2
Denmark +45. Aarhus 6; Copenhagen 1 or 2; Odense 9
Estonia +372. Tallinn 6
Finland +358. Helsinki 0; Tampere 31; Turku 21
France +33. Bordeaux 56; Marseille 91; Nice 93; Paris 1
Germany +49. Berlin 30; Frankfurt 611; Leipzig 341; Munich 89
Greece +30. Athens 1; Patras 61; Rhodes 241; Thessaloniki 31
Hungary +36. Budapest 1; Gyor 96
Iceland +354
Ireland +353. Cork 21; Dublin 1; Limerick 61
Italy +39. Genoa 10; Milan 2; Naples 81; Rome 6
Latvia +371.
Liechtenstein +41.
Lithuania +370. Vilnius 2
Luxembourg +352
Macedonia +389. Skoplje 91
Malta +356.
Moldova +373. Chisinau 2
Monaco +33. All points 93
The Netherlands +31. Amsterdam 20; Haarlem 23; The Hague 70; Rotterdam 10
Norway +47. Bergen 5; Oslo 2; Trondheim 75
Poland +48. Gdansk 58; Krakow 12; Warsaw 22.
Portugal +351. Lisbon 1; Porto 2
Romania +40. Bucharest 1
Russia +7. Moscow 95
San Marino +39. All points 541
Serbia and Montenegro +38. Belgrade 11
Slovakia +421. Bratislava 7
Slovenia +386. Ljubljana 61
Spain +34. Barcelona 3; Madrid 1; Seville 54; Valencia 6
Sweden +46. Göteborg 31; Malmö 40; Stockholm 8
Switzerland +41. Basel 61; Bern 31; Geneva 22; Zurich 1
Turkey +90. Ankara 312; Istanbul 1; Izmir 51
The Ukraine +380. Kyiv 44
The United Kingdom +44. Birmingham 21; Glasgow 41; London 1
The country code for the USA, Canada, and the Caribbean is +1.

LOCAL TELEPHONE SERVICE IN EUROPE

Telephone service in Europe is generally excellent, with the possible exceptions of the eastern countries. In all countries telephone service has improved dramatically in the past 20 years. Some of their systems are better than American systems.

Dial slowly, especially where the system is pulse rather than tone. Speak slowly and clearly wherever you are.

On the Meter

In America we are used to having a local toll free calling area. Within a 10 to 15 mile radius around our home we can talk all day and not be charged a penny above our basic service cost. In Europe, it is completely different. Every call, no matter where, is charged by the minute. This will certainly put a cramp in your internet browsing enjoyment.

Telephone Booths

Calls within a country can be made from any phone booth. Just insert some coins or a calling card, dial the city code and then the local number. When dialing a city code from within that country, you must dial a zero first. In Finland dial a 9 first. For example, to place a call to the Munich Tourist Office from any city in Germany, dial the city code, *089*, and then the local number, *233-0300*. They usually speak English at the tourist office.

Telephone booths are not as plentiful they should be, and unfortunately many in train stations have been sabotaged with slugs or have had the handset cut off. What can you do with one of those? If you see someone having trouble with a phone, wait in line at a booth where the person seems to be enjoying a conversation. That way you'll make sure that you get one that operates.

Instructions are usually given in three or more languages or in easily understood pictograms. The method of operation is pretty much the same from country to country. Normally, you lift the receiver, insert some coins or a calling card, get a dial tone, and then dial. The sound of the dial tone varies from country to country. Sometimes it even sounds like the American busy signal. The busy signal in Europe is usually a very short repeating buzt buzt buzt.

Coins and Slugs

When you use a coin phone have a fistful of coins handy. In Holland it costs about 10 cents a minute for local calls from a public phone. If you don't feed the phone enough cash you will be disconnected with little warning.

In France, the *mode d`emploi* (operating procedure) of the older phones makes it easy to lose connections and money. Some require coins, but there are some in cafes and other places that require a *jeton* (slug). Buy the slug from the barkeeper. Do not put any money in the French phone until you get an answer. Have the coin or slug ready and drop it in immediately when the person answers. The other party can be heard over a loud static, but they can't hear you until the coins fall in the box. Then the static will stop and you can begin the conversation, *si vous parlez la française* (if you speak French).

Some phones in Italy require a slug also. There it's called a *gettone. Pronto?*

European Telephone Cards

A new system was started by the French in the mid-1980s and has taken hold in most of the countries of Europe. The French name is *Telecarte*, and goes by local names in other countries, e.g. *Carta Telefonica* in Italy, *Telefonkarte* in Germany, *Telefonnich Jednotek* in Czech Republik, *Telefonkártya* in Hungary, etc. These pre-pay plastic cards are the size of credit cards and contain an electronic chip or magnetic strip which tells special telephones the amount of credit you have.

You found a phone. Now what? Follow the four pictograms: pick up receiver, put in coins, dial, talk. [1901]

Cards are available for about $5 and $10. You buy the card at any telephone office or post office. They might also be available at tourist offices, tobacco shops, money exchange offices, and some other stores. Some cards carry advertising, and a few are gratis. Lufthansa gave me a 20 unit freebee for flying first class.

To use the card, find one of the telephones which accept them. Nowadays that is most phones. It's getting hard to find a coin phone anymore. Put your card in the slot. Some phones have a display showing your available credit as you talk. You can use these phones to dial around the world. A big advantage of using telephone cards is that these phones are generally in excellent working order and are usually available, while the coin/slug phones are tied up by a local teenager or are busted.

American Telephone Cards

You can also use some American telephone cards in Europe. AT+T, Sprint, MCI, and others offer international service in Europe. You usually must dial a local toll free number to use these cards. Each country has a unique toll free system. You won't find 1-800 very often.

Discount Telephone Cards

International telephone service is a fiercely competitive business. Every phone company is trying to get your attention with cheap rates, while at the same time sticking it to local customers with higher rates for calls within their country whenever they can get away with it. For example, the Dutch phone company changed their evening discount calling period. It used to start at *18:00* (6pm) and now starts at *20:00* (8pm). There is a way to fight back. Use a discount service, either with a card or by subscription.

In Switzerland, instead of buying the Swiss Telecom calling card I bought a "Phone Pass" at a newsstand. From any phone I can call the "Phone Pass" toll free number, enter my code number from the card, and call the USA for about one-third of the tariff charged by Swiss Telecom. A 20 CHF "Phone Pass" card will give you 80 minutes of chat with the USA.

In talking with a fellow in Amsterdam, he claimed that he could call a friend in another part of Holland cheaper if he dialed it through a discount phone company via the USA. Back and forth across the Atlantic for less than a call within the Netherlands? I can believe it.

For my phone in The Netherlands, I subscribe to a service which calls itself "One Tel." Rates to the United States average about 4.5 cents per minute compared to 7.2 cents per minute for the official Dutch phone company KPN. These rates are only about twice as much as what it costs to phone your next door neighbor in Holland. Go figure. Phone rates make about as much sense as airline fares.

This card (not coin) phone in Zagreb, Croatia includes four pictograms showing the method of operation. Plenty of graffiti was offered by prior clients. [1908]

Cellular Phones

Maybe you call them mobile phones or cell phones or annoying devices. Nevertheless you see people with one of these to their ear everywhere you go. In and out of stores and offices, on buses and trains, riding their bicycle or on roller skates, the yumpies of Europe are speaking immediately important stuff, no doubt. It is a distraction when they ring in public, but I am getting used to it. Cell phone prohibitions are posted at the entrance to many buildings, so I guess that some people are not getting used to it.

Most American cell phones will not work in Europe, not yet. We can expect universal global roaming ASAP. If you need a mobile phone in Europe, talk to your travel agent. Or you might rent one with your rental car or inquire with your hotel.

Tele-communications shops, springing up all over, lease and sell cell phones. You'll probably need to be a resident of the country and sign on for a year or so to subscribe with one of these firms. Some of the shops sell pre-paid chips allowing you so many minutes of service so you don't need to be a subscriber.

If you are outside the country of registration and you want to call another country, you pay for two international calls. E.g., say you have a Swiss cellular phone and are in France making a call to Belgium, your call is routed via Switzerland. Your bill will be a google of wampum. They allow intra-European dialing, but you pay plenty for long distance charges.

Here are a couple of the many telephone cards I've used over the years. At the top is one from Belgium and below is a Netherlands card. Both cost €5 and can be used to call around the world from any phone which accepts cards, and that is virtually all of them these days. Cards are only valid in the country issuing them, unless stated otherwise. [1920]

Caller Beware

Cell phone charges are handled differently in Europe. It is the one placing the call who pays in most countries. Be careful about calling 06 numbers in Holland, for example. 06 are the first two digits for cell phone numbers and all calls are approximately 40¢ per minute, about 10 times the cost of a regular call. There goes a telephone card to vapor in short order. If you need to call one of these numbers, make it short and ask for a callback.

The caller pays when dialing any 0900 number in Holland also. These are commercial lines providing information or otherwise and make their profit by the phone.

Directory Assistance

Directory assistance ("Information") is available in Europe. In Holland, before getting through to a real operator you will hear a recorded voice which tells you in crisp Dutch how many calls are waiting in front of you. Be patient for a couple of minutes. When the operator comes on, there will be a change in the sounds. You ask "Do you speak English, please?" The answer will be "A little bit, yes," understating her/his ability by a wide margin. The average Dutch operator has a better command of English than many Americans, though all have the typical Dutch accent.

Operators in most other countries are probably capable of speaking English, but the first one you get may not wish to try it. Ask for an English speaking operator if you are in need of help.

Long distance and international directory assistance is also available. These operators always speak English. You can get the number of anyone in the United States with no charge. That's funny — AT&T charges me about $0.75 for these at home. That's the cost of sending 9 faxes to Europe with the "10-10" service I use.

You see more and more shops like this one. This Frankfurt store features discounts of up to 70% on international calls. They also offer a special rate to cell phones within Germany. Notice that the name of the store and its promo are in English. This is extremely rare in Germany so you know that their customers are primarily from outside Germany. [1903]

INTERNATIONAL SERVICE

From Telephone Booths

International calls within Europe can usually be made from public pay telephones. Look for a notice in the operating instructions on the phone booth to the effect that it is an international telephone. The notice will give you the international access code (IAC) for the country you are in and may also give the country code for the country you are dialing to. The IAC for the USA is 011 as was shown in the example for dialing the Munich Tourist Office. Each country has its own IAC. Many, though not all, use 00 as the IAC.

From Your Hotel Room

Most hotels charge an absolutely obscenely outrageous fee for any call made from the room, especially for long distance calls. I heard a hotel desk clerk in London advise a guest to use the pay phone in the hotel lobby rather than make the call from her room. My travel notes show that calls from Paris to Amsterdam cost 2½ times as much from my hotel as from the *PTT*. My hotel in Portugal quoted me over three times as much as I paid at the *CTT* for a call to the USA.

During my house hunting trip, six weeks before our move to Germany, my phone bill was more than the room bill by a wide margin thanks to many calls home discussing the features of the new diggs with Elizabeth still in California. If you must use the phone in your hotel room, try your best to find out what it will cost before picking it up. Also ask for an itemization (it may be called a "specification") of calls. Phone bills in Europe normally do not include anything other than a total, taxes, and a grand total. Don't be surprised if the hotel keeper just shrugs his shoulders at both requests and says he doesn't know. He does know and/or can find out if he wants to.

If you are in Europe on business and must call your office in the USA, make a quick call and ask for a call-back. You can enjoy some nice meals with the money you will save, and avoid a showdown with your company's major-domo of expense reports.

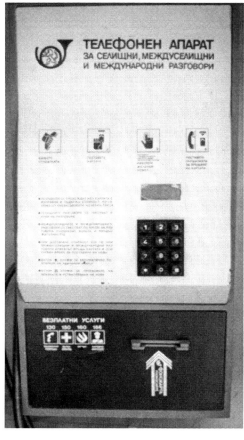

This "telefonen aparat" in Varna only accepts telephone cards issued by the Bulgarian PTT. *Buy your card at the post office. Notice the symbol toward the upper left of the telephone. A stylized French horn is the standard mark for post offices and telephone offices throughout Europe.* [1910]

From the *PTT*

In the old days of coin phones long distance calls to the United States and other countries could be made from any *PTT*. This is obsoleted in most countries by telephone cards and the proliferation of public phones with international access. You can pretty much dial anywhere from anywhere.

But the fallback is to go to a *PTT* and look for the sign "Telephone" or some similar word. If there is none, ask a clerk where you can make an international telephone call. There may be a separate entrance for the phone bureau, or it may be in a separate building a few blocks away. At the phone window or desk, write down the city, state, area code, and local number you want dialed. Sometimes the clerk will dial the number for you and tell you which booth to go to for the call. Alternatively, they may write down the international access code and country code for you and direct you to a booth to dial it yourself. After completing the call, go back to the desk and pay up. If you are having dialing troubles, go immediately to the clerk and let him/her know. The clerk has a meter for each phone line and will charge you for the connection whether the line is dead or alive.

If you don't want to pay in Europe, reverse the charges or use a telephone company charge card, if possible.

Telephone Charge Card

Telephone charge cards are available, free of charge, from your home town telephone company business office, from AT&T, MCI, or Sprint. Call up whoever you have as a long distance carrier and ask for yours. They will be happy to send it out, but it may take a few weeks. I have a couple of these but only use them when I absolutely must. The convenience is great but the cost is equivalent to grand larceny.

You may also be able to use your local telephone company charge card to call back home. Most are honored in the western European countries. In small towns in Italy and Greece, clerks had never heard of the card and would not accept it. It was accepted in Rome but I was told that I would have to wait an hour for a connection. In

Athens I was not allowed to use it on weekends. When overseas, most countries allow the USA telephone charge cards to be used for calls back to the United States only. They normally cannot be used for calls between foreign countries.

The charge card is very handy for making calls from your hotel room. I've done this in several countries and never had to pay the hotel surcharge. Sometimes the hotel will make the call for you, and sometimes they will connect you to an international operator. If your hotel does the dialing, it is best to go to the front desk and write down the numbers for them so there will be no mistake (at your expense).

This Dutch pay phone accepts only Dutch phone cards. A very few phones accept coins. [1924]

From home when we lived in Germany we dialed a special toll free number which connected us to an AT+T operator. We would give her the USA number we were calling and our AT+T charge card number. Our monthly statement included a list of all calls, and we paid in dollars. AT+T now offers toll free connection numbers in many countries of Europe. AT+T is not cheap, but it will allow you to dial 800 numbers which seem to be the norm for American businesses these days. European telephone companies and discount phone passes often will not allow connection to a USA 800 number. If you are calling an 880 or 888 instead of an 800 you can make a connection, sometimes.

Cost

When you compare the telephone to all the other means of communication, it is a real bargain in cost and efficiency. It is much cheaper than the telegraph and far quicker than the mail, and you know you have someone on the other end listening, as opposed to emails which can sit in e-limbo for days before being opened. International telephone rates are one thing seemingly immune to inflation. In fact they have been going down, not up. It generally costs more to call from Europe to the United States than from the United States to Europe, though European rates have been falling over the past few years.

There are three basic ways to pay for your call from Europe: pay direct, reverse the charges, or use a charge card. Within pay direct I include charges to a normal credit card like VISA, MasterCard, or American Express. Many public phones in Europe allow the use of these credit cards.

For a very short phone call, it is probably cheaper to pay direct. There is no three minute minimum as there is for the collect and charge card calls.

When placing a collect call to the United States, there is a charge for the initial three minutes which is usually the same every day every hour. After the first three minutes, the per minute charge depends on the time at the place you are calling to. Check with your long distance phone service for exact conditions.

Charge card calls are billed in the United States at the "operator assisted" rates. This means a minimum charge for three minutes and is usually billed at the "station to station" rate. Each additional minute is billed at the same rate as if it were a collect call.

But a warning is in order. Telephone service has become an incredibly competitive industry. Companies are trying to suck you in with seemingly attractive deals. The bills you receive may astonish you with extras for stuff that you would expect to be in the basic rate. It would be like buying a car for a fixed price only to discover later that you had to provide the wheels, windows, and seats. So get the whole story, if you can, when signing up for a long distance service which you plan to use from Europe.

Telephone Potpourri

An old sea captain I met someplace in my travels told me that when he needs to make a long distance call in a strange town, he goes into a bar, orders a brandy, and asks to use the phone. They usually have toll counters on bar phones to register the clicks for dialed calls. Or dial the international operator to use your charge card or reverse the charges. I did this often in one of my favorite bars in Holland. It's more convenient than going out to try to find a phone booth, and more comfortable since most phone booths are not enclosed. But, there may be a lot of background noise in the bar so ask if there is a back room where you can talk in peace and quiet. There will probably be a higher cost when calling from a bar rather than the *PTT*, so you might want to make it quick and ask for a call back. In fact I still use bar phones when I travel in Holland due to the scarcity of public phones, and if you only need to make one call it is cheaper than buying a phone card. It's still the quickest way to make a call in that country.

Though you must always dial an international access number to make an international call, there is at least one country where there is an exception. In the border areas of Switzerland, e.g. Geneva, you can dial 059 to reach friends across the French border in Savoie. Normally you would need to dial 00 for international access and then 33 for France.

A few ferries and some trains, for example the German *InterCity* trains, now have public telephones on board. I used one of these to call Stephanie's aunt Anita in Italy to let her know that we were on our way from Frankfurt. Later in the day when I tried to call again it wasn't possible to make a connection because the train had passed into Switzerland. The German train phone was inoperable outside Germany. Maybe they will get this glitch fixed before long. The train phone accepted German phone cards, not coins.

Credit card decals on the door of this telephone booth in Geneva, Switzerland let you know of the many ways to pay. At the lower right is an electronic phone directory for all of Switzerland. [1904]

TELEGRAMS

PTT

Virtually all post offices in Europe have an international telegraph office. Telegrams are expensive, but you can save money by allowing them to hold it for a few hours to be sent at a non-priority time. This makes good sense since daytime in Europe is usually nighttime at home and it probably won't be delivered until the next day even if you did pay for immediate service.

Reliability

I've sent telegrams a couple of times from Europe, but I wouldn't recommend it. Besides the facts that they are one-way communications and cost more than a quick telephone call, you don't know for sure if they get delivered. My batting average is one out of two so far. I've retired from telegrams.

Cash

Keep the telegram in mind though if your wallet is stolen. Money can be sent by telegram. Phone home collect and ask your closest relative to wire some funds over. This may keep you from starving on a park bench until your traveler's checks are replaced.

INTERNET AND EMAIL

Communicating via internet email can be one of the easiest and cheapest ways of staying in touch. It can also be extremely frustrating getting connected.

Your Friendly ISP

One way to use the internet from Europe is to bring your laptop if you have an internet service provider (ISP) which has local dial up service overseas. Or you can make international calls to your home ISP to retrieve email. Do this late at night for lower phone charges. On an extended trip of several months I signed up for service from a local ISP in Holland. This entails local phone costs which can be much higher than at home. Since you pay per minute for every call it gets very expensive if you are spending an hour or so every day on the internet. The phone bill is sent every two months. You can be shocked out of your URLs.

Hardware

You will probably need a telephone plug adapter in order to plug your modem into the phone line. Each country has its own version of telephone plugs, and some countries have more than one style. Check your European hotel or residence to see what you need and then go out to a shop which sells telephones and buy the proper plug adapter.

Switzerland's phone plugs are unique. Adapters are more expensive than any I have seen anywhere. In Germany the data connection in the house was different than the regular phone line. This required a different type of adapter.

Fortunately, Holland uses the same phone jacks as the USA. I plug in my phone, fax machine, and modem as if I was at home. Thanks KPN for making it so simple. Italy also uses the American style jack.

This internet café on the Damrak in Amsterdam has several floors of computer terminals. Cost is "market price" - the price can be as low as 25¢ per hour in the morning when it is not too busy and up to $1.50 per hour in the afternoon. One of the ubiquitous ATM cash machines is right next to the front door. [1927]

Hotel Lines

If you are in a hotel you might have a problem between your modem and the hotel's telephone system. There are different types of phone systems and your modem might be cooked on some of them. Check with your local computer store or seek out intelligence on-line to make sure your modem will work and not be destroyed if you use it in a hotel.

Cyber Cafes

Instead of lugging your laptop all over Europe you can have internet access in virtually any city these days at cyber cafes. For maybe a few dollars per hour you can use the café's equipment, ISP, and phone or cable lines. Before you go, sign up for a free email account with one of the major services, e.g., Netscape.net. Then you can log in from anyplace on the planet and email your trip reports back home.

Make sure that the caps lock is off or your password may not work. Also, if your password includes a Y or a Z you may have problems. For example, in Germany where the qwertz keyboard is used instead of the qwerty keyboard you need to know some pretty deep computech to make it work. To ease access, change your password to all numeric for the duration of your trip. Use the first "X" numbers of your favorite credit card, for example.

Since Windows saves every keystroke in special hidden files, be careful about entering account numbers on computers other than your own. Never put personal ID information in a public access computer.

Libraries

More and more public libraries throughout Europe provide internet connections. You may need a library card to use the facilities but usually you can just walk in, register or make a reservation, and log on. The rules may say that you cannot go to chat rooms but you can forego that while in Europe, no? The beauty of library internet access is that it is almost always free so unless you need to spend your money at a cyber café try the library first. Again, first sign up for a free email account with Netscape.net or one of the other services before you leave for Europe.

The entrance to the Haarlem library is in the courtyard through this medieval arch. Ride your bike in and enjoy a half hour of free internet access. You must make a reservation for the internet computers, but normally you only need to wait a half hour or so. Read the IHT and British newspapers while you are waiting. [1925]

FINAL NOTES

Meeting Points

When you're over there traveling around in your newfound world, you might want to meet up with other travelers who you know are going to be in the same area as yourself. Or you might want to split up with traveling companions and regroup later. When you make plans to meet or to reconnect, select your meeting point with care. I recommend hotels rather than Amex offices, PTTs, tourist offices, or park benches. The lounge of a Sheraton, Marriott, or Hilton is a far more relaxing place to sit and wait for the other party. And the coffee shop, bar, and toilet facilities are available if needed.

If you agree to meet someone at a specific time and place, keep the date or send word that you can't make it. It might seem easy to assume that if you don't show they won't care, but it is not so. It will be cause for alarm.

Phone Home

It's a good policy to keep in regular contact with someone who cares about you. Send a card once a week saying where you are and where you plan to be in the next couple of days. Or phone home on a regular schedule. Or drop into an internet café or public library and send an email. Don't break the communication chain or you risk generating unnecessary worry over your safety.

Pick up the phone in Kiev, Ukraine to make a local call. [1921]

Chapter 20
Health and Safety
Travel in Confidence but with Caution

Good health is a prerequisite to a bon voyage.

ON GUARD

Injuries and illnesses while overseas can ruin not only your vacation and your bank account, but maybe your life. Knowledge is your best preparation.

Be Prepared

Thanks to the unfamiliar surroundings, your likelihood of requiring medical help is greater while traveling. Don't take chances on the streets and highways. Stay rested and don't overextend your body's defenses against disease. Guard against catching something from a sneezing passenger on a train or in other confined spaces. Find another place to sit.

Flush toilets before you sit down, and then decorate the seat with strips of TP if there is no seat cover available. Use a paper towel when opening doors of washrooms because it doesn't do you any good to wash your hands if the last person left his pathogenic critters on the door handle. Peel or thoroughly wash fruits and vegetables to remove insecticides, herbicides, and fertilizers. Drink bottled beverages.

Get in Shape

Couch potatoes should consider the fact that they will be doing a lot of walking in Europe, a *LOT* of walking. Visiting the museums, shopping, strolling the streets, and climbing steps in castles all require a lot of foot work. Not only should you be wearing a well broken-in pair of shoes as discussed earlier, it would be a good idea to do a little bit of walking exercise starting a couple of weeks before flying to Europe. If you don't, you'll have discomfort and muscle pain for the first few days of your travels. Even if you do regular exercise, there is a potential problem. I bicycle a lot, but bicycle muscles are not the same as walking muscles. I normally get aches in my first week over there. Combined with the effects of jet lag you can find yourself in misery for a couple of days. So, since you'll be getting in shape anyway, you might as well start it at home. Hurt before you go, not while you're over there.

Speaking of hurting, if you're heading for the beaches get a little sun before going so you don't get scorched on your first day in Europe. A bad sunburn will mess you up for a few days, and probably leave you peeling for another week.

INTERNATIONAL CERTIFICATES OF VACCINATION

The International Certificates of Vaccination (ICV) is a fold out booklet published by the United States Government Printing Office. It is used to record vaccinations and have them certified by your state or county health department. Your doctor can provide you with an ICV. The instructions to travelers in the ICV say:

"International Certificates of Vaccination or Revaccination are official statements verifying that proper procedures have been followed to immunize you against a disease which could be a threat to the United States and other countries. The Certificates are second in importance only to your passport in permitting uninterrupted international travel. They must be complete and accurate in every detail, or you may be detained at ports of entry."

A pharmacy on a busy street in Paris illustrates the traditional crosses above the doors of drugstores throughout Europe. [2009]

Vaccinations

There are no vaccinations which are required for travel between North America and Europe.

However, if your travels include stops in less advanced countries, inoculation or orally administered drugs against yellow fever, typhoid, malaria, or cholera may be required before continuing to Europe or home. Ask your doctor or public health department to see what shots if any are advised. Do this a month or more before departure because some shots need time to be effective, and for some diseases multiple shots over several weeks are required.

A brochure distributed by local health departments warns that typhoid fever, caused by the bacteria *Salmonella typhi*, is possible in some of the former communist countries in eastern Europe. It can be passed on by contaminated water, ice cubes, fruits, undercooked fish, and poultry. It mentions that even watermelon can be a typhoid carrier — some merchants inject water to increase the weight!

This reminds me of a story I heard when first I moved to Holland. A colleague told me about a pre-WWII street vendor in Haarlem who would hold up his grapefruits, cut them open, and squeeze them to prove how juicy they were. As the arrival of the

German army and the Gestapo became obvious, and since he was Jewish, he abandoned his cart and fled to England. Someone took over his cart and took up the business when he left. The new vendor discovered a tube, water bottle, small foot pump, and hypodermic needle in the cart. Just circumstantial?

It is a good idea to get a tetanus booster if you have not had one in ten years, and have it recorded on the International Certificates of Vaccination. List drugs to which you are allergic, your blood type, and other pertinent medical information. Don't forget your eyeglass prescription, if any.

The ICV is in English *et en Français*, and should serve you well in case of special difficulties.

Medical Examination

Whether or not you are getting inoculations, it would be a good idea to have your doctor perform a routine medical examination if you are getting on in years. Your doctor can make a note of anything unusual on the ICV in the section for remarks concerning state of health, medical treatments, or known sensitivities.

If you are allergic to any drug, make sure that is written here as well.

It's usually called an apteekki *in Finland. This one in Helsinki is also labeled with the Swedish and American words for drugstore. The British would call it a chemist. The signs at the bottom of the window give the name of the store. Translated it is the "Three Smiths Drugstore."* [2010]

Prescriptions

If your doctor has prescribed any drugs for one of your problems, carry a letter from your doctor to that effect. An official looking seal or stamp on the doctor's letter wouldn't hurt. It is rare that a customs inspector will search the luggage of an American tourist, but when they search, drugs are what they are usually looking for. If you carry prescription drugs, keep them in the original container.

Even with your doctor's letter, you may be delayed or inconvenienced

MEDICAL HELP IN EUROPE

If you need medical assistance, the nearest pharmacist or doctor will probably speak English. Virtually every educated person in Europe knows at least one foreign language, and luckily that one is usually ours.

But Americans may have trouble communicating with drugstore clerks and doctor's assistants. Even after living in Germany for two years I had a problem getting a simple over the counter drug for Elizabeth. I came home with moth repellent!

Unless you are fluent in the local language, it will be impossible to read the labels and instructions on the medicine they sell you. Ask the person selling it to read it to you in English. If they appear unsure, or if the instruction sounds unusual, question them or have the label read by someone else.

A pharmacy in Prague, Czech Republic is indicated by the nearly universal cross. I guess that the dog's owner has just gone inside. [2001]

Drugstores

Pharmacies are very easy to find in most cities. They usually have a large green cross outlined in neon hanging above the door. In some of the Mediterranean countries, it is a red cross rather than a green one.

If you need a pharmacy after normal business hours, ask your hotel manager or desk clerk. Drugstores in almost every city operate on some sort of a swing shift so that one is always open or on call 24/7. Often, the name and location of the one on night duty will be posted in the windows of the others.

Drugstores in Europe sell medicines and medical supplies of all kinds. You'll see wheelchairs, medical instruments, and devices you won't recognize. But don't expect to find the usual items like toothpaste, nail polish, and lawn chairs in the European pharmacies and apothecaries. On the other hand, I found a *farmacia* in a small Portuguese town pumping gasoline, which proves the rule that every rule has its exceptions.

Doctors

The quality of medical service in Europe is reported to be equal to that in the United States in most countries, but less than par in others. We have had good experience with doctors in Holland and Germany. We even had a home visit in Germany when Elizabeth was too ill to get out of bed.

If need be, the nearest American embassy or consulate can provide you with a list of doctors. These doctors are not endorsed by our government. It is only a list. Your hotel should also be able to direct you to a doctor or dentist.

Doctor's offices are not easy to find. At best they will have a small brass plaque bolted to the front of the building. They can be located in business or residential districts. Medical centers are not common. Sometimes you will see a NO PARKING sign by the curb with the caduceus on it. That symbol with the wings and snakes is the emblem of the medical profession so there should be a doctor's office nearby.

Most of the drugstores in Athens also have the English or French word for drugstore next to the Greek word. This one doesn't, so let's learn a little Greek right now. "F" in Greek looks like an O with a line down through it and "R" looks like a P. With these substitutions you should see a few words here that would sound something like "pharmacy." [2011]

FIRST AID

Travelers should carry a few items for personal first aid. Depending on the season, my list includes:

- Aspirin
- Band-Aids
- Neosporin, A+D, or First Aid Cream
- Vodka
- Bug off
- Lip balm
- Cold sore ointment

Aspirin

Aspirin or a substitute should always be handy. Instead of aspirin, paracetamol is recommended by doctors as a pain killer with no gastric side effects. Paracetamol (a.k.a. acetaminophen) is sold at home as Tylenol, Datril, and Tempra. It goes by other trade names in Europe.

You can buy aspirin in Europe — if you like to pay about ten times what it costs at home. Bring a bottle with you.

Cuts

The other major items to carry are "Band-Aids" and an antiseptic cream. Something like "Neosporin," "A+D," or J&Js "First Aid Cream" should be kept handy when you get a scratch. Left to themselves, almost any scratch can become infected leading to a week of pain. Vodka is also a great antiseptic though it doesn't have the healing power of the creams. The general and medicinal value of vodka was discussed in chapter 6.

Bug Off

If you are going to southern Europe in the summer, "Off," "6-12," or some other bug repellent will be a relief. The mosquitos can be unconscionable savages. Bug repellent is also handy on the beaches anywhere in Europe to ward off sand flies and other nasty critters.

Lip Balm

Lip balm, e.g. "Chap Stick," can save you the discomfort of cracked lips in northern Europe during the winter. On the other hand, a dab of olive oil seems to work just as well. You can also use Italian dressing. In addition to olive oil it has vinegar which is very good for softening the skin.

Cold Sore Ointment

Several products for relief of pain from cold sores and fever blisters are available. Examples are Anbesol and Oral-B. These also make great pain relievers for bug bites and other minor irritations that make you want to scratch the itch. The key ingredient in these ointments is benzocaine, usually at a strength of 20%. If you let yourself be poked by a mosquito a benzocaine ointment gives immediate relief.

Other Recommendations

"Mole skin" was recommended to me as a cure for foot blisters. At the first sign of a hot spot, put on a patch of this stuff and let it wear itself off. The labels say not to use it after the blister has formed or broken. Then you need antiseptic and a Band Aid.

For treating cases of the traveler's trots, some travelers recommend Pepto-Bismol, and others won't leave home without a prescription of Lomotil. It appears that Pepto-Bismol is not available in Europe so you might want to bring some along. I can't recall ever having diarrhea while traveling in Europe, but I have often had it soon after returning to Los Angeles.

A friend told me about a trip she made with several other people a few years ago. Each caught diarrhea except the one who ate yogurt. Coincidentally, part of my travel routine in Europe used to be to stop in a grocery store and buy a cup of yogurt and a couple of oranges every day. My doctor says that once diarrhea starts, oranges and yogurt are the wrong things to eat. Then Pepto-Bismol or Lomotil can come to the rescue.

Lately though, to save time, I request yogurt at breakfast in the hotel and carry a supply of vitamin C (Redoxon by Roche is available all over Europe). At home in Germany and Holland I used a form of vitamin C which dissolves in water like Alka-Selzer. My favorite is the *Blutorange* flavor dissolved in a glass of apple juice. Buy a 20 unit tube of 1000 mg tablets in a drug store or vitamin store.

Some spicy foods can make a quick run through your system, and some fatty sauces can bring on stomach cramps. Before rushing out to a doctor, eat some burnt toast and rest for a while.

Travelers should be aware of the virtues of chicken soup or, if it's not available, roast chicken which is usually on the menu. Unusual fatigue, muscle ache, or fever can normally be chased with a big bowl of soup and a good night's rest. Chicken soup really works.

Pedestrians gingerly cross the rue *and* boulevard *in Paris, France. This typical street scene includes a* Brasserie *with sidewalk seating,* Metro *stop,* P *parking direction sign, magazine kiosk, and the street name attached to the side of the building. [2013]*

TRAFFIC

As discussed earlier, pedestrians should be especially careful crossing streets in Rome, Athens, and Amsterdam. In England and Ireland, with right hand drive, be careful because traffic will be coming from all over the place and very fast.

Sidewalks can also be hazards. With potholes and raised obstructions in some cities, you have to watch the ground to avoid twisting an ankle.

CIVIL DISTURBANCES

Big Crowds

Just about anywhere, large crowds can spawn unruly and dangerous behavior. Guys get drunk and do stupid things. When you attend events with large turnouts be on guard. For example, fireworks are set off by participants at some events. New Years Eve is the big night for fireworks in Europe, and it is strictly an amateur laissez faire affair. Sky rockets and mini bombs seem to be most interesting for the pyroheads. On New Years Eve in Haarlem neighbors start shooting off the sky rockets in every direction. We had a beautiful view of the skyline of Haarlem for a half hour semi-professional display. Meanwhile, teenagers walk around throwing firecrackers at each other. Watch out.

Bastille Day in Paris is another a day for free-lance fireworks. Some characters drop cherry bombs onto the Metro access stairs. There is also an official show. The fireworks display at the *Tour Eiffel* is really spectacular.

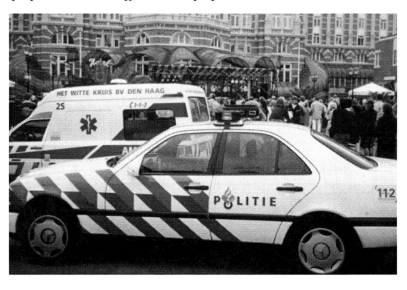

Police and an ambulance are kept on hand for an outdoor festival in The Hague, The Netherlands. [2007]

Breaking Windows

Demonstrations, political and otherwise, can sometimes get out of control. Fashionable shops around the Opera in Paris have been destroyed more than once when groups started voting with bricks. Soccer matches have spawned senseless riots in a number of European cities. The police in Luxembourg once asked the German army to come in to help quash a riot by some British fans. The British "fans" returned and rioted in Paris a few months later.

Yankee Go Home

US embassies and consulates are virtual forts in the capital cities. The State Department has done what it can to defend them against attack. Consequently it is very difficult to get in for legitimate business. Maybe a phone call will take care of your situation. It is often necessary to make an appointment anyway so phone ahead.

Bombs

Within a few countries, groups which have failed to win their way with ballots and negotiation have turned to bullets and bombs. Civilians, rather than government officials, are often the victims.

Spain has frequent attacks from the Basque separatists. I saw a fire they set in San Sebastian, an otherwise pleasant and beautiful city on the north coast of Spain.

Northern Ireland, politically part of Britain, has had decades of medieval style butchery between Catholics and Protestants. The struggle by the Irish Republican Army to unite all of Ireland again goes on, but in a more peaceful mode. Belfast and Ulster still have armed militias and the British Army. They carry loaded guns and shoot.

Murder and Mayhem

Germany, since the unification, has experienced a resurgence of racial hatred and violence. This is directed mainly toward Turks who have lived in Germany for decades as "guest workers" to help power the German industrial engine. Unfortunately, high unemployment in some areas has turned to fire-bombing the homes of the guests and murdering the innocents. Some of this is also directed at immigrants and refugees from the former Yugoslavia.

Middle East

The Middle East hatreds are often exported to Europe. France, with a long history of welcome to all, has found itself the victim of these ethnic and religious conflicts. Throughout Europe, offices of the airlines of Israel and Iran usually have a guard out in front with a machine gun in his hand and his finger on the trigger. El Al jets are guarded by a platoon and an armored vehicle in many airports.

Scamper

When you see these kinds of problems and potential problems, go the other way. Don't get too curious. Once the police start swinging the billy clubs, they don't stop to talk and listen.

A few dozen people met their end in the Mont Blanc Tunnel disaster in 1999. Be alert in there. It is a boring 18 miles. This is the entrance from the French side. The tunnel was closed for a couple of years. [2004]

GROSS ACCIDENTS

Just about every year there is a major catastrophe in Europe. These disasters often involve travelers or revelers. Night clubs, hotels, ferry boats, trains, cable cars, and other facilities with large numbers of people go up in smoke, sometimes with the loss of hundreds of people.

Of course you can do nothing if your Concorde plane crashes on takeoff. But in most other circumstances you have a chance of survival when you follow the safety rules and use good judgment. At the first sign of trouble take action.

NARCOTICS

Street Hustlers

Stuff is sold for smoking, swallowing, snorting, and shooting in many places, and it is illegal in every jurisdiction in Europe. Potentially more serious than a trip to the slammer is a trip to the hospital, or to the morgue. You may be courting an invitation to medical problems with the kind of trash you're going to get from a street seller. It may be more or less pure than whatever you are accustomed to, or it may be spiked. It may be baking powder. It's all dope and made for the genre.

The hustlers at the Dam Square in Amsterdam instantly recognize Americans and, while walking beside you at a distance of six feet or so, will come out in loud whispers — "Hash? Coke?" I even had one fellow ask me if I wanted to buy Viagra! While Amsterdam may be a center for international drug traffic, drug use among the Dutch people is minuscule compared to that in America, even though it is open and accepted. None of the dozen or so hustlers who have approached me were native Dutch.

Here is one of the many shops selling grass in The Netherlands. I stepped inside and nearly gagged. [2017]

"Coffie Shops"

On the other hand, going back to drugs, Holland saw the blossoming of a new line of business in the 1990s. The shops are called "coffie shops" and they are as close to coffee shop as Brooklyn is to the moon. Marijuana is the product for sale. The trade is open and accepted. There is no need to deal with the Amsterdam street hustlers when you can buy branded product in a store. However, if your company has a drug screening program you may be risking your job by going into one of these places, even for a look around. The smoke is pretty thick and wafts down the street when someone opens the door.

Grass is technically against the law. However Dutch police don't cuff a pot head unless the pot head is committing a real crime. I don't guarantee this statement.

US Drug Enforcement Agents

My return to Los Angeles from Amsterdam in the spring of 1999 was greeted by a detail of US Authorities, including a sniffer dog. The drug search was conducted just at the door of the plane as we stepped into the swing-out tunnel leading to the terminal building. The fellow sitting next to me was asked to wear a little sack, presumably carrying some dope, to test the dog. However, some passengers were quite shaken by the sight of a large frisky German shepherd in the narrow corridor. One young girl turned back in fright to find her dad before proceeding. Coming back from Amsterdam at Christmas 1999 and arriving in Washington, DC, there was no sign of dogs or any other kind of inspection. And there was no evidence of exit inspections as I disembarked a flight from Amsterdam in Detroit.

Beware of becoming a "mule." United States narcotics enforcement officers find that dope is sometimes transported and brought home by innocent travelers. If someone you meet overseas asks you to do him a favor and carry a small package home, watch out. If he offers you some money to do it, you can be almost certain of the contents. Direct your "friend" to the nearest post office. If you agree to take a package home for someone you will probably have troubles. Do you have a bail bondsman and an attorney ready to meet you at the airport?

When you need help or directions turn to these guys in Ljubljana, Slovenia. Police in every city are especially helpful to tourists. [2003]

The Local Sheriff

Follow local customs and laws. There are thousands of Americans in jails around the world for violations of local laws. You might be joining them if you believe the glib boasts of others. The mere possession of narcotics paraphernalia may be prima facie evidence of use of narcotics. And such equipment can be seized by US Customs on your return to the USA.

Too bad for those busted and pitched into the slammer overseas. Don't expect American civil liberties to be observed. Police can search and seize without cause. Bail and habeas corpus do not exist in some countries. You are presumed guilty until proven innocent, a serious reversal of the American system. You can be held in jail for months waiting for trial. Punishment may be severe and corporal, and there is just about nothing that anybody can do about it.

The American Consulate is only authorized to offer you a list of local lawyers. The list is free but the lawyers are not.

To your health from Budapest. Photo by Elizabeth. [2015]

INSURANCE

Insurance

If you believe in insurance, don't forget about it during your travels. Check the period to make sure that it covers the time that you will be traveling, or that it can be renewed in your absence. If not, a renewal bill sent to a temporary European address could take weeks to catch up with you. The policy might have expired in the meantime, leaving you, your home, or your chattels exposed.

Before departing for Europe, check your medical insurance policy to see if it covers you while in Europe. Most do, though they have exclusions for war zones, street drugs, experimental aircraft, and other exciting forms of suicide. Ask your insurance company how to go about filing a claim and how they will make payment. They may need a translation of the doctor's report.

Also, the only telephone number you have to reach your insurance company is probably an 800 toll free number. This won't work from many phones in Europe. Ask for an area code number, and ask if they will accept collect calls.

Travel Insurance

You may want to take out additional insurance because of the fact that you are traveling. All manner and size of trip cancellation insurance, travel insurance, travel accident insurance, flight insurance, and luggage insurance is available. If you decide to buy one of these policies, shop around and around. Start with insurance agents with whom you currently deal, and even consider the policy offered by your travel agent.

Travel insurance policies are available which can protect you against loss in case you have to change plans and forfeit a deposit. Most package tours and charter flights require full payment way in advance. Some offer no possibility of refund as the departure time nears, and at the least charge severe penalties for cancellation. If there is any possibility that you will have to change plans, one of these policies might be a good idea.

Bells clang, red lights flash, and the crossing gates come down blocking the street, the bicycle road, and the sidewalk as a commuter train comes flying through. The sign warns you, in Dutch, "WAIT until the red light goes off. ANOTHER train might be coming." This is in Haarlem, The Netherlands. [2016]

Health and Accident Insurance

Your major medical and life insurance policies, if you have them, should provide coverage anywhere in the world except for clearly defined incidents as itemized in your policy. If you do not already have such coverage from your company or through your parents, you'll find that individual policies are ridiculously expensive.

Travel policies can also offer health and accident protection. If you consider one of these policies, look for this coverage in addition to trip cancellation protection. Another special feature of some travel insurance policies is medical evacuation. If you are stricken with a serious problem, particularly in a less developed country, you may need air evacuation to a good hospital back home. Airlines see this as a great opportunity to charge you about $10,000 for ambulatory service. You can save about 50% if you just die over there and they put you in with the baggage.

Travel accident insurance policies of the giveaway style offered by some organizations as an inducement to membership do not fill the need. They only pay for loss of limbs, eyes, or life. No payment is made for care or recovery. A piece of junk mail I recently received offers a good price for "a valuable plan which can insure you or other family members against fatal accidents or felonious assault." The small print says "coverage is not provided for basic hospital, basic medical surgical, or major medical expenses." Great policy, huh? If you think that you are covered by a "travel" policy, read all the fine print about deductions, exclusions, valuations, and limitations before you pay.

A policy you might consider is baggage insurance for baggage checked on flights. But perhaps your homeowner's or tenant's policy already covers this. Your home insurance policy with valuable items rider should also cover cameras and jewelry anywhere in the world. Take photos or videos of these items before departure to assist in making your claim if you have some bad news.

Read your policies before departure.

Auto Insurance

For information on auto insurance in Europe, see chapter 18, "On the Roads of Europe."

Filing Claims

Having insurance and collecting are two different things. Talk to your agent before departure to make sure that you are covered overseas, and find out what to do in case you are hospitalized or if your camera is stolen. It is likely that a European hospital will demand cash rather than accept an insurance card. If you must pay and then file a claim to be reimbursed on your return home a lot of your money can be tied up. If it is a financial burden, seek advice from the nearest American consulate.

Carry your insurance card, and it would probably help to carry a legible copy of your policy. If the claims number is a toll free 800 number, get a regular number with area code.

For lost or stolen items, a police report will probably be required with the claim for reimbursement. My only experience in filing a claim for an event in Europe was for repairs to a camera which fell off the neck strap. The insurance company requested details of the mishap: time, place, circumstances, etc., and a copy of the repair bill. They paid promptly. Make notes of events in your travel record book to help your memory in such cases.

This Jaguar couldn't find a parking palace suitable for his deluxe chrome, except for one reserved for the handicapped. Now it's off to the impound courtesy of the Dutch police. Violating handicapped signs is a no no, big time. By the way, there is never a parking place in Zandvoort on a warm Sunday afternoon, so take the train, or ride a bike from Haarlem. [2002]

Chapter 21
Working in Europe
Travel for Free

Get a job, if you can.

THE JOY OF WORK

If you like to travel in Europe, what better way is there than if somebody pays you to do it? With a job in Europe, you settle in, learn the way of life and the language, make new friends, and open yourself to an experience that will become a major part of your life.

BARRIERS TO EMPLOYMENT

Before discussing the ways of getting a job in Europe, first it is important to state the reasons why you probably will not get one. It can be done and many have done it. But it is as much luck as hard work, and plenty of both.

Unemployment Rate

The first reason that getting a job is difficult is that the unemployment rates in most European countries are higher than in the United States. If Europeans are having trouble getting jobs in their own countries, why would it be easy for someone from halfway around the world? No government has its door open welcoming you to come over and take a potential job away from a local voter.

Work Permit

The second obstacle for Americans is that the European Union (EU) is basically a closed society to citizens from countries which are not members. The EU consists of 15 countries: Finland, Sweden, Denmark, Germany, Nederland, Belgium, Luxembourg, France, Austria, Portugal, Spain, Italy, Greece, Ireland, and Britain. As of December 2002, 10 new nations have been accepted. These are Poland, the Czech Republic, Hungary, Lithuania, Latvia, Estonia, Slovenia, Cyprus, and Malta. The formalities will be officially completed in May 2004.

Getting a work permit is all but impossible except for those with special professions and skills, even in good times. My two work experiences were for

American/European companies which did the work permit paperwork. I had to fill out some forms and the company certified I was needed and that nobody in the European homeland could be found to do the job. For the German transfer, the company stated that I was on a technical exchange program. Ten Germans were transferred to the USA for the seven Americans sent to Germany.

If you are married, your spouse had better like the idea of doing nothing productive for the duration. This caused some grief for us on the German transfer. Elizabeth quickly fond a job that could make use of her language interest and abilities. The German *Arbeitsamt* (Labor Department) quickly denied her the work permit because of the high unemployment rate and the fact that I had a job.

GETTING A JOB

I was lucky to have obtained jobs in Europe twice. The way I did it can probably be described as serendipity, though I did have a plan to explore the possibility when I joined each of the companies which eventually transferred me. There are many professions which are transportable. As with many things in life, it's a matter of being in the right place at the right time. You have more control over place than time, so focus on being in the right place.

European Classified Ads

Job offers in the classified section of the *International Herald Tribune*, a newspaper targeting the American expatriate audience, usually include a statement that you must have valid work papers. This is true even for bi-lingual positions requiring a native English speaking person. These jobs will go to British people because Britain is a member of the EU. The most commonly advertised jobs of this sort are secretaries, English teachers, and translators.

American Companies

A way around the work permit hurdle is to work for an agency of the US government or for an American company. It is easier to find these jobs in the US than in Europe.

American specialists occupy a small number of key positions in the European offices of many American companies. However each company is as individual as it's name. Some will hire only nationals of the country where they are located while others will use Americans in many jobs.

Educational Jobs

Transitions Abroad, a monthly magazine oriented to work, study, and living overseas, regularly publishes articles and advertisements on specific career positions available overseas. This would be a good place for someone with a liberal arts education to start exploring.

Seasonal Jobs

Tourism and agriculture require large numbers of employees for short periods of time. Businesses from vineyards to ski resorts need semi-skilled workers for a few weeks to six months. There are directories and official agencies which can point you to these jobs. The pay is lousy. Many workers in seasonal agricultural jobs are reportedly working illegally.

European Employment Bureaus

Generous social benefits and extreme taxes are a bane of employers throughout Europe. Companies must cope with the decades-old laws giving workers an absolute right to a job and wonderful benefits. Consequently, employment bureaus offering part time or contract employment have started to spring up. It's very prevalent in Holland, a country with some of the highest taxes and juiciest employee benefits. To get around some of the costs of complying many companies employ short term workers on contract. In Holland you'll see many *uitzendbureaus* (literally "send out agencies") offering jobs such as secretary, bookkeeper, or draftsman. You will need a work permit to take one of these jobs, and probably need to speak Dutch. Stop in one of these offices and have a chat the next time you are strolling in Amsterdam.

This series of uitzendbureaus *in The Hague is typical of the Netherlands.* [2105]

My Luck

I'm a chemical engineer, playing roles as process engineer, project manager, and business development manager over the past few decades. In the mid 70's I went to work for a major engineering and construction company which had offices and projects around the world. I was single and was regarded as "transportable" by management. I was soon sent on assignments for weeks to months at a stretch, domestically and internationally. In late 1975 I was asked to transfer to the

Netherlands office for a two year assignment. It turned out to be the best two years of my life on the social side, but not so good on the professional side. Nevertheless, I would do it again.

Then in early 1991 I accepted another transfer, this time to Germany. I was working for an environmental consulting company in Los Angeles. Suddenly it was purchased by a division of a major German conglomerate. Knowing something about what to expect, I grabbed for the opportunity when a transfer became available. This company knew nothing about transferring people overseas so the experience was much different. Being married and with a three-year old daughter at the time contributed to the differences.

These two experiences point out one excellent way for a technically trained person to obtain a paid leave to Europe. Get a job with an American company which has offices in Europe or which is owned by a European company. Then let it be known that you are interested in moving over there. When you hear about transfer opportunities coming up move quickly and get in the front of the line.

One of the reasons I travel so much is business. As a consultant I work at and attend trade shows throughout Europe. This is a view from the balcony of the RAI showing a water technology exhibition in Amsterdam. European fairs operate on a higher level than American shows. Know your stuff and be prepared to deal. [2101]

FINDING A REAL JOB IN EUROPE

The balance of this chapter will focus on approaches that will land you a well endowed job in Europe. It assumes that you are, or will be, working for an American company and have been offered an overseas transfer. You are a professional with a college degree or with equivalent experience in your field. Your field is a specialty in business, finance, science, or engineering. This is the route I took and the one that I can speak to.

Find an Employer

How do you find a European oriented company? Start with the company you are working for. If they have branch offices in Europe, see about obtaining a transfer.

Directories

To locate companies with overseas operations, consult stock market and business directories. These publications list publicly traded companies. They are the biggest companies and the ones most likely to have foreign subsidiaries. Then write to or call the head office and request an annual report. This will give you a PR agent's view of the company with plenty of pretty pictures next to the columns of numbers and loads of footnotes. A good study of the annual report can be invaluable in approaching a company when you are looking for a job, whether here or over there.

A visit to your library will turn up a number of directories listing companies doing business in Europe. The listings in these directories are based on a number of different criteria and they are published on individual schedules. Thus, none of them are complete or totally up-to-date at any one time. It's best to consult several of these directories.

One that I would suggest as a starting source is the four volume World Business Directory. This lists over 100,000 companies in 190 countries, including many listings for all of the European countries. Just look through the directory until you find names you recognize. That's not hard to do if you're into chemicals and sticky paper. 3M seems to be in every country and is usually listed first. Most of the major American companies have operations in Europe, as do many smaller companies. Research the prospective employers to find out where their European offices are located. Other reference materials to look in are Standard & Poor's and Hoover's.

This is a lot of hard work. Success is not guaranteed, but 1,000 failures are history after you score. I've worked with enough Americans overseas, from superbly qualified to sorely incompetent, to be convinced that anybody can do it.

Internet

Try the internet job search engines using keywords that describe your profession and the countries you are interested in.

You can also locate jobs through some bulletin boards on the internet. These services are free, and can offer information on thousands of positions everywhere. Computer oriented jobs dominate the listings but there are plenty of other positions.

Action

When you find potential companies, get the name of the VP of International Operations or European Operations and write directly to him/her with your resume. Do not send your letter to the human resources department. If the VP is interested in you, he will have the HR department contact you. If you can't find a suitable VP write directly to the CEO. Make it brief and business like.

EMPLOYMENT CONTRACT

After you have an offer for an overseas position you will be given a contract to sign. This sets out all of the conditions governing your transfer, your working conditions, overseas benefits, and miscellany. The contract will be 10 to 30 pages in length. Keep a copy where you can find it easily.

Term

All contracts must have a term, i.e. a start date and an end date. Typically this will be two to five years. Typically there will be options to break the contract which can be exercised by either party. Say 30 to 90 days notice is needed to break the contract. Companies sometimes change this as they see fit, and/or fuzzy up the completion date to give them an out if things don't go right. On my first transfer I chose to come home about three months early, and on the second one the company chopped it with about six months to go.

Relocation

The company must pay for your relocation costs, though they limit what can be moved. For a family, normal household items are typically no problem, but may be too restrictive for your personal situation. I had to ask for a reversal on a prohibition against moving our piano, and got it. Most companies will not pay to move your car over.

Relocation assistance for single status is very thin. In 1975 I was given a plane ticket and $246 to cover my expenses, and told to report to work in Holland a week after the following Monday.

Housing

You might or might not be given a house and/or a housing allowance. Housing is very expensive where you will be living, probably in a major city or suburb. This is an important point in the contract. Consider your wife and children when looking for a home since they will be spending 90% of their time at home while you are at work or on the road for business.

Automobile

If you are living and working there, a car is becoming just as indispensable in most of Europe as it is in the USA. Having a company car in the contract can be worth many thousands a year since the cost of cars, maintenance, insurance, and gasoline is much higher over there. You can bring your own, as I did for my single transfer to Holland, or have one provided by the company, as was the case for our German transfer. A second car can be very helpful if you have children unless you are in the heart of a major city.

Be a busker in Basel. The pay is only what passing citizens will throw in your guitar case. I met a street entertainer on a bus from Frankfurt to Luxembourg who was making good money, he said, especially by selling his CDs.

[2106]

Home Leave

Typically you and your family will be given an annual home leave. The company contribution is the cost of the plane tickets to your home base as specified in the contract. You'll probably use your own vacation time. Going someplace other than "home" is probably OK with the company as long as it doesn't cost more. Bring this up after you get over there, or just do it and turn in the receipts after the fact showing that you saved them money.

Bereavement leave and plane fare home should also be provided in a transfer contract.

Conditions

Get everything you want in the contract before you go because it won't happen after you get there, unless you are indispensable and threaten to resign. Personnel department clerks will not change anything for you. You must go to the VP or personnel director who is sending you over there and negotiate anything you want changed directly with him, and do it before you go. Don't expect an easy sell and don't expect a second chance. Your company has probably been using the same contract for years, or they may have just paid a consultant six figures to research the matter and write up a contract for overseas transfers. Your company will probably have little interest in spending time on your special case so handle your appeal with care.

BENEFITS

When you get over there you will find that Americans are treated as a special lot. Not all of the benefits given to European workers will be given to the Yanks, as we are sometimes called. But you will be getting some special privileges, a fact that is best kept to yourself, and you are subject to certain tax considerations.

Some of the following sections will not apply to Americans. I put it here so you know the general flavor of benefits given to European professionals and office workers.

Policy

If you are transferred by your employer to work in Europe, you will probably receive a small booklet of company "policy" relating to the transfer. This will be in addition to the contract and will be mentioned in the contract. Companies which have been transferring people for many years have a good handle on this while companies new to the international transfer arena will have a rough start. They either have no policy or they hired a consultant to write it for them. In this case the policy will not be absolutely universal and is probably subject to negotiation. This depends on your status in the company and/or the number of transferees raising a howl about one or another provision.

Vacations

Vacations are really nice in Europe. The Dutch company gave each employee a minimum of four weeks, plus they gave each vacationing employee a check for the "13th month" so they could enjoy it properly. We Americans were given only our standard two week vacation and the pity of our Dutch colleagues.

In Germany, the standard vacation is about 6 weeks. We Americans were only allowed 4½ weeks, but that was still twice as much as most of us were getting back home.

The German company also gave us an extra week off at Christmas. The standard work week is 37 hours in Germany. Thanks to an agreement between the company Board of Directors and the *Bundsrat* (Employees Council), we worked a 40 hour week and saved up the extra hours for year-end, getting another vacation from about the 22nd of December to after New Years Day. The balance of the hours were allotted as "bridge days," meaning that the office was closed on Fridays after some Thursday holidays. This gave us a few four-day weekends during the year, especially in May. There was plenty of time to go sightseeing in *Deutschland*.

Holidays

Holidays are also especially generous in some countries. We had over a dozen in Bavaria thanks to its Catholic tradition and all those saints and special events. For example, Good Friday and Easter Monday are holidays in much of Europe. There are so many holidays in Germany during May that it's best if you do not plan to do any business there during that month. When the holidays fall on a Thursday, e.g., Ascension and Corpus Christi, many people also take off on Friday, the "bridge day," and make a four day weekend out of it.

TAXES

Income Taxes

Income taxes in European countries are much higher than they are in the USA. Social security taxes are also much higher. Combined income and social taxes can easily take over 50% of your income in some countries. You will have to pay these taxes.

As an indication of the tax burden over there, the average American currently works until May 16 to pay income taxes. This date is known unofficially as "tax freedom day." Tax freedom day in the European Union averages out to July 26. Thus the average European works an extra two months to pay the government. But within Europe, the date varies from June 13 in Britain to August 29 in Belgium! Those people must feel like wards of the state.

When working outside the USA, the IRS still wants you to file a tax return, though taxes on some or all of your income may be avoidable. If you meet one of two requirements, physical presence or bona fide residence in another country, your foreign earned income up to $70,000 can qualify for exclusion from tax liability. Taxes are also applicable to some expenses of relocating and living abroad when these are reimbursed by your company.

To satisfy the requirements for exclusion, follow the rules to the letter. Keep your paperwork up to date. When entering and leaving the USA, make sure that your passport is stamped with exit and entry dates. Sometimes you have to ask for this. Keep a log of international travel with dates and times of arrival and departure, and stash away the boarding cards. I've noticed that many boarding cards do not include the year, only the month and day so write the year on if it's not printed. Keep your overseas residence permit, rental contract, utility bills, and all other evidence establishing you as an overseas resident.

Tax Equalization

If you are working for an American company, make sure you have a tax protection clause in your assignment contract. This specifies that your total tax liability, foreign and USA, will not exceed the tax bite had you stayed in the USA. This benefit is normally referred to as "tax equalization." If you have other sources of income it can get complicated.

Tax Accountant

Your company should also provide you with the free services of an international tax accountant. This is nice in theory. In truth the forms that you fill out for the tax accountant make the IRS forms look easy. I guess the accountants like to do a lot of extra work and run up big bills like the lawyers. It' a good idea to contact the IRS yourself and get copies of their special publications applicable to taxing Americans with foreign earned income. It's hard to believe but the IRS booklets are easier to understand than the stuff the accountants send you.

The big international bean counting firms, one of which will probably be chosen by your company to do your taxes, also publish booklets discussing the tax situation specific for each country. You can call several of these companies and request information on having them do your taxes for you. They'll probably send you their booklet just to prove that they know what they are doing.

Home State Tax

If your home state has an income tax they may try to levy you while overseas. Because of cross reporting of income between state and federal agencies, your state tax board may decide that you should pay even if you are no longer living there. Companies have a habit of continuing to use your former home state address while you are gone for a few years. This can lead to serious problems.

Stay Below Radar

To avoid tax problems Americans living overseas should keep off the radar screens of former home state tax people. To do this, avoid any situation which can lead the state to suspect that your domicile might still be the place you left behind.

For example, by law your bank must report interest income to the government. Close your savings accounts. Also, do not vote in local elections.

If a problem comes up, have proof of your foreign residence. At the very least, get a driver's license after you get a home in your new European country. Register yourself and family with the local authorities as required, and have the proper stamps placed in your passport. These are not sure-fire defenses and other items may be held to be determinant by your state tax board, e.g. if you kept ownership of your home. If you are in doubt, ask your tax board before departing and read whatever publications they have on their rules. Keep the publications covering the years that you are overseas because these things change, usually for the worse.

ON THE JOB

The Frustration

Working over there has some resemblance to working at home and working overseas is not for everybody. Work becomes work after the initial euphoria. Some people are not happy with their new boss, work assignments, or any of a hundred other things. About 1/3 of those going to work overseas get so frustrated within a few months that they start talking about going home. Some do. It is better to hang in there and stick it out. Chances are that you'll get over it and adapt to the new environment.

Language

You will probably be in a bilingual environment. If you do not already know the local language make a strong commitment to learn it, despite the nay-sayers.

One of my bosses in Holland saw me studying Dutch one morning before work. "Why are you studying that? Nobody else in the world uses it." Well, 15 million Dutchies use it and that's good enough reason to know a little of it. It certainly helps to improve your social life, important to me as a single guy over there.

In Germany we attended evening German classes at the *Volkshochschule* (municipal adult education). I also spent every Monday morning for two years at a private school, the local *Eurosprachschule*. I didn't need to know much German in our office, but it was invaluable when I went to Dresden and Leipzig, and to countries in the former Soviet Bloc. It has also enabled me to translate German technical and commercial documents.

In addition to formal studies, you can learn a lot by watching TV and reading the newspapers.

So, the bottom line is maximize your opportunities by learning the local language. Do not give up because it is difficult. Go at your own speed and do as much as you can every day that you are in Europe. These are golden moments which won't come again.

Getting Paid

You probably won't get a paycheck. Direct deposit is normally used. This requires that you have a bank account. Your company's bank would be a good place to open it.

How you are paid can be a dilemma. You may be offered to have part of your pay in dollars and part of it in local currency, at some fixed or fluctuating rate of exchange. It can be distressing if you choose one option only to see the dollar rise or sink against you. There is no way to predict which way it will go. The only thing certain is that it changes every day.

Work Hours

Once you start to work, you are entering a whole new world. Flex-time is very common so you can probably start between 7 and 9 and go home between 4 and 6 in most offices. You might punch a clock, even for lunch break, to keep you honest. This is an advantage over keeping track of your own time and adding up the minutes every month. Be on the premises.

Guten Morgen

On meeting anybody in the office for the first time in the morning in Germany, it is customary to say "Guten Morgen Herr or Frau So-and-so." You can also look them in the eye and shake hands. Very formal, still.

Coffee

The next important part of the working day in Europe seems to be coffee. Pots and cups are full and hot throughout the day. You'll probably find that the building has a lunch room staffed with very helpful people. Coffee may be made by the kitchen staff or secretaries, and cups are cleaned every day.

Whenever you are in a meeting, coffee service is usually the first item on the agenda. It's served with some beautiful chocolate and sugar cookies. I grab those chocolates fast. In some offices coffee is provided by a machine located on every floor. Coffee, espresso, and cocoa are brewed in the machine and it is not bad, certainly far better than you would get from a coffee machine in the USA.

Smoke

Another ever-present feature is smoke. It's everywhere. Not just the usual stuff either. Cigars are not uncommon. I enjoy a nice corona now and then and have given them to my secretary who also smoked them. A guy across the hall from me smoked some funny stuff on a regular basis, switching from clove cigarettes to bad grass as his mood changed. My German boss kept his office in a blue haze.

Social Environment

This is a second hand story. An American I met in Paris was manager of a hospital administrative staff. He could not get over the habit of the French workers spending about an hour each morning drinking coffee and chatting about last nights TV shows, their families, lovers, and anything else in the world. A lot of time was wasted in this socializing.

I didn't see such interest in personal affairs in offices in Holland and Germany. Generally, business is business where I worked.

Work

Work habits of the Dutch and Germans are much different than those of Americans. When I worked in Holland, the Americans could never understand how anything ever got done in that country. There seemed to be an interminable amount of time spent on everything. Nothing was ever released unless it was perfect. 99.44% was not finished and everything got held up for the last touch. The Germans are similar, though they sometimes take some short cuts.

I had Dutch people working for me and I worked under Dutch bosses. I often said that I was caught in the Dutch squeeze. It seemed that the bosses always wanted everything now but the fellows working for me always had a reason why it wasn't ready. *Simpele dingen zijn soms erg moeilijk* (simple things are sometimes very difficult), as they say in the Netherlands.

Business Letters

Writing a letter is different. Salutations and complimentary closings are different in each country. Nobody over there uses "Gentlemen:" or Very truly yours," in a letter. The standard closing in international correspondence is "Regards," or "Best regards," for a more personal touch.

Virtually all correspondence includes a reference number and some other office code marks. When you respond it is polite to include the reference number of the letter you are responding to. Filing is done by secretaries in most offices and the reference system works for them.

It's not a medieval castle - this is the Haarlem train station. Lucky you if you find yourself living and/or working in this charming capital of Noord Holland. There is also a covered parking area and a guarded parking garage for bicycles. Bicycle theft is common in The Netherlands. Lock it or lose it. [2107]

Air Conditioning

Central heating and air conditioning are pretty rare. Open your windows for fresh air. Heating is often supplied by hot water radiators in each office.

Signatures

Letters which are sent to another company require two signatures in Germany. One is yours and the other is that of your boss. Germans and Dutch sign their name is such a way that nobody can ever read it. If the person's name is not typed under it you won't know who it was. Sometimes they sign with all the letters stacked on top of each other. Sometimes they produce a magnificent swirl or two and some more flourish.

Angst

Angst (anxiety) is a German word that is so common that it has become part of the international business lingo. Everything must be analyzed and reverse analyzed as if it were a chess game to avoid error, or even more importantly it seems, a perception of error that can be laid at your office door.

The most aggressive and corrupt German I worked with, or around, was paranoid of any mistake. "We will be blamed" were his watchwords. He tried to cover up his million *Deutschemark* mistake with childish stunts and by blaming others after his incompetence sank his fantasy project.

Devil's Details

It's the little things that will get you.

I wrote a business plan to market a new environmental process during my first few months in Germany. There were 15 appendices labeled A, B, C, etc. Then I went to the supplies cabinet for tab dividers. Sorry, no C tabs. There are so few words in German that start with C that this tab was combined with D. We do the same with X, Y, and Z. Rather than edit the report and change the appendices from alpha to numerical I made the tabs.

A major difference throughout Europe is the size of business letter paper. Europeans use *A4* paper rather than our 8½"x11" size. *A4* is slightly narrower and a bit longer. *A4* dimensions are 21 cm wide by 29.8 cm long, roughly equivalent to 8¼"x11¾". This was a continuing nuisance with the paper tray of the HP III laser printer I brought with me. The paper was always hanging out the back of the tray, unless I wanted to feed it sheet by sheet. Our 11"x17" B-size double sheet is similar in size to Europe's *A3* but slightly off again. *A3* is twice the size of *A4*. This may not seem like a big deal but it can be if you are bringing over pre-formatted documents and address forms in your computer. Stuff may not fit on the page the way you want it to. And documents will probably cause a problem fitting on shelves or in file drawers.

Envelopes are also different. The standard European business envelope is the *DL* which is 22 cm wide and 11 cm high. The standard business envelope in America is the number 10 which is fractionally larger than 9½"x4", and works out to 24 cm by 10.4 cm.

Two hole binders are used universally. There were no three hole punches in Europe except the one I brought with me. My files are about 50% two hole and 50% three hole.

Computer keyboards can be different in Europe. The worst problem I had was with the "qwertz" keyboard in Germany. American keyboards are called "qwerty" for the first six letters on the upper left. The Germans have transposed the z and y. If you are using a password that includes one of these letters you will have a challenge. I bumped into this one and eventually solved it, but it sure is wasted time.

Some computer software will also give you a problem. In spreadsheets, a comma is used instead of a decimal point. See chapter 26, "Languages, Numbers, Alphabets." In word processing programs you are better off to disable the automatic hyphenation because words are syllabified differently. For example you might see your machine printing out was-ted, pun-ch, and sc-hool. This problem is common with English translations made on European software.

COMING HOME

Trauma

Packing up and coming home after a couple of years overseas is going to be a mix of emotions and challenges.

The excitement of adventure you had in going overseas is going to be missing. You're going back, but it won't be the same company. The company kept moving and growing while you were out of town. New people came and some of your former colleagues left. Some of the people you left behind will feel jealous and others threatened and others won't take notice. The day you return will be another work day in their lives, but chances are that it will be the beginning of a major career hazard for you.

The Ax Man Cometh

The anxiety of your return to normal office life is going to dominate your career thinking, and well it should. Some years ago a study found that 25% of all returning expatriates change jobs within one year of returning home, either of their own choice or their company's. This statistic, in my experience, is well understated. Personally, I lost my job within eight months of each of my returns. And, of the seven of us who went in a batch to Germany, four were no longer working for the company within a year of returning to the USA.

Why does this happen? I can only speculate but I won't waste much space here. Figure that if the home company got along without you for two or three years, they can live without you forever. Just be aware of the statistic and make contingency plans. Stay tuned to undercurrents in the office. It may be that you were sent over to get you out of the office. When you return, if head hunters start making unsolicited calls, your job is changed without consulting you, your boss avoids you, your office is moved to the back of the building, or if other inextricable things start happening, make sure that your parachute is packed and ready. People are people and management is fickle.

I was passing through the Côte d'Azur, also known as the French Riviera, a few years ago and came upon set-up preparations for the Cannes Film Festival. If movies are your line of work it looks like this is where you should be. [2104]

Chapter 22
Living in Europe
Travel to the Max

Build a new nest.

THE BACKGROUND

Europe

Europe is a big place, but in truth it is many many places. With about as many countries and languages as we have states and a population greater than the United States by a good margin, it's impossible to offer a definitive guide to every country in a small chapter of a general introductory book. However, many facets of life in different countries are similar, and they are different from ours. The following observations will serve as an indication of the kinds of things you will experience as a foreign resident in Europe. This is written from an American perspective so those things which differ from the way things are in the USA are noted.

My Lives In Europe

I lived in Holland for about four years in three stints, in Germany for about two and a half years, in France for about six months on two occasions, and in Switzerland for two months. My first life in the Netherlands was a company transfer as a single man, with little assistance from the company. The German relocation was another company transfer, a well assisted family move. The others have been do-it-myself efforts.

MOVING OVER

Decisions, Decisions

Moving overseas is a lot more complicated than moving across the country. You must decide what to bring with you because you will find it virtually impossible to get anything from home after you have moved.

Big decisions have to be made, probably in short order, and your company will be the unusual one if it provides more than cursory guidance. Your company relocation specialist has probably never gone through the process of moving overseas, and probably has never even been in Europe. So, you should assume that you are on your own. The best advice you will get is probably going to come from "unofficial" sources. This chapter should give you a head start.

Ex-pat Assistance

There are thousands of Americans living in Europe. Virtually every country has a sizable community of expatriates, some of whom have been there for years. Most of these "ex-pat" residents are working over there, or, at least one member of each family has a job.

Spouses are not likely to be working because of official restrictions. This has contributed to the establishment of American Women's Clubs in many parts of Europe. These clubs can be extremely valuable in providing information for new arrivals, and in helping you get established in the community. As an example of the information you can obtain, the American Women's Club of the Taunus e.V. has published a 200 page book titled *Living in the Frankfurt-Taunus Area*. This book goes into the nitty-gritty of so many things that I can't even begin to list them here.

Before you move over, try to find out if there is an American Women's Club in your area and get in touch. Order their local guidebook(s) and pay for priority mail delivery. For me, one of the important items in the AWC book is advice on bringing over some foods, e.g. your favorite peanut butter. Holland is the only country in Europe where I have found peanut butter that is not saturated with sugar (called "high fructose corn syrup" on the label). Examples of other things that I would bring over are heavy duty aluminum foil and an assortment of your favorite Ziploc bags. These are hard to find in Europe. Also, aspirin is very expensive and Pepto-Bismol is impossible to find, so pack those for your move.

AUTOMOBILE

The biggest item you probably want to move is your automobile. Just about eight months before my first move to Holland I had bought a new car. Selling it would have meant a large loss so I shopped around for the best way to get it over there. Even if your company will not pay for auto shipment, it may be best to ship your personal car. Cars are expensive over there, and you're going to be faced with buying another one when you get back to the USA if you sell yours. I shipped on my first transfer and I'm happy I did.

Shipping Your Car

The procedure is rather simple. Contact an international shipping company. Give them the weight, length, height, and width of the car, make and model, serial number, and license. They will quote a price for freight and for marine insurance. (Your auto policy stops at the pier.) Pay up and then drive to the port on the assigned day. This will be about three days before the scheduled departure of the ship. Make a thorough inspection with the shipping agent for existing dents and scratches, and itemize all accessories on the insurance document. For instance, list the tool kit, spare tire, car cover, and any other loose or easily detachable items. You won't be allowed to ship items such as appliances and clothes in the car because they will probably disappear.

My car, shipped in a container both ways, took three weeks from Long Beach to Rotterdam. It suffered not a scratch. However, a port worker, apparently in Long Beach on the return, stole my auto compass and drained the battery while listening to the stereo.

Retrieving Your Car

When picking up your car at the port in Europe, bring your original bill of lading, passport, auto title, *green card* (all-risk insurance), driver's license, International Driving Permit, a gallon of gas, your keys, window cleaner, towel, and some local money. You need them all.

The original bill of lading will be mailed to you by the shipping agent some time after the ship departs. You must give the agent an address in Europe or wait at home until you receive it. The bill of lading is in triplicate. Bring the original B/L to claim your vehicle.

Port authorities are supposed to disconnect the battery and drain the gas tank before putting the car on the ship. However, it is up to you to get your car going again. So bring a few liters of gas when you go to the port. The car will be decidedly filthy after weeks at sea, so clean the windows before driving out of the Customs warehouse.

And there is always one more tax or fee to pay so bring about a hundred dollars in local currency to bail it out. My fee was about $17, but I have heard of much higher charges even though full service had been paid up at the USA port.

Customs

There might be some problems vis-a-vis Customs, or perhaps other tax collectors over there. You will get different stories from different officials regarding these topics, all of which have to do with prying money out of your pocket.

After living in Holland and driving an auto with California plates for two years, my car came to the attention of the police. Meanwhile I had been parking it on a main street only a few blocks from the police station and was never notified about any violation of the law. I kept my California registration up to date, and told the police each time they stopped me (curiosity questions, not violations) that I was bringing the car home with me when I left Holland. I had no inkling of trouble until three weeks before I planned to leave when I heard from a third party that the police were going to confiscate my car because I had not paid Dutch road taxes. Wow! Panic! It took some Sherlockian efforts to find out which policeman was going to do this to innocent me. After some discussion, he agreed not to take my car if I was going to take it home to California in three weeks. Yes sir, it was on that boat.

Have Car - Must Have Garage

For my move to France, I decided that it wasn't practical to bring a car since my plan was to stay in Paris. I used the excellent public transportation system. A major detriment to having a car in any major city is finding a place to park it. If you bring your car to Paris you will need a private garage. There will never be enough parking places for all the cars in Paris or Amsterdam or any other major city.

Warranty

Another annoyance in bringing your car to Europe is that the warranty will probably be invalidated. Even if you have a European car, as I did, it is normally warranteed by the American importer, not by the factory over there. Check the owner's manual or phone an authorized dealer to review your warranty rights. If your car is still within warranty, make up a moan list of squeaks and rattles to get fixed for free before shipping it overseas. Auto repair is very expensive in Europe.

Company Car

For our move to Germany, the company I worked for refused to pay for shipping our car but offered to compensate us up to "blue book" value for it. In Germany they gave us complete use of a company car, and paid for all maintenance and insurance. So we sold ours before we left. Nevertheless, we wish that we had shipped the car over at our own expense. It would have been very handy to have a second car in the city where we lived, especially when you have a small child. We never got around to buying one because of the high cost of cars in Germany.

Plan Ahead

The bottom line is the bottom line. If you have a relatively new car and you are going over for a couple of years it would probably be best in the long run to ship your car over. That could be less expensive than selling it and buying another one when you get back home, or of paying for storage while you are overseas. You would also have to figure in the cost of buying and then reselling a car while you are overseas.

However, if you are driving one of those jumbo size vehicles it may be best to leave it in the USA. As noted in earlier chapter, Europeans drive smaller cars and there are seldom enough parking places in the cities. Insurance will be expensive, not to mention gasoline. You may also have a rough time finding maintenance service and spare parts.

HOUSEHOLD ITEMS

Except for electrical items (more about that next), ship everything you have and use. If your company is paying for your shipping they may have limits on the amount or types of items. For example, they'll probably not pay for shipment of boats and horses and other bulky pleasure items. Initially they told us we couldn't ship our piano but I proved that it was no big deal, even though it's as heavy as a Mack truck. Ocean shipping costs are based on volume, not weight, so it actually cost less to move the piano than a couch.

Electrical Motorized Appliances

Most of the important points on this subject were discussed in chapter 11, "Electricity in Europe; Travel Voltage Fundamentals." Plug into that chapter again.

As a general rule, do not bring any electrical appliance with a motor. This includes refrigerators, food processors, blenders, electric can openers, washing machines, dryers, stereos, tape decks, dial face clocks, and many other items. Leave them home in the USA, or have a garage sale. The reason is that all electricity in Europe is 220 volt while the USA is at 110 volts, and because theirs is 50 Hz and ours is 60 Hz.

Unless stamped for 220 volt operation, your appliances will need a transformer. You'll have those hot, heavy, and sometimes humming things all over the house if you bring your American appliances to Europe.

All items with a motor will run slower over there due to the lower frequency. The transformer will not correct this, and there is no convenient device which can convert 50 Hz to 60 Hz. Modifying appliances to compensate will cost you time and cash.

Since you will be leaving virtually all of your appliances in the USA, you will need to buy all new ones over there. The $3,000 which my company gave us for this expense covered barely half the cost of replacing household and personal items. Everything is at least twice as expensive in Germany.

You can buy 220 volt 50 Hz appliances at a few specialized stores in the USA. On both sides of the Atlantic, many household items are basically the same except for the electrical requirements. Special retrofit companies install European motors and attach European plugs to new appliances for those going overseas.

Normally that is the end of it. There is an exception. If you have a washing machine you also have water to connect. American washers have connections for hot water and for cold water. European washing machines have only a cold water connection. They have an internal electrical heater to give the exact temperature you dial in on the control panel. So, when you go to hook up that retrofitted American washer in the utility room of your European home be ready to run some new hot water piping also.

Therefore it is probably better to buy a washer over there. We were lucky and bought the used one which was left behind in the house we rented in Germany. In Holland I negotiated a washer into my apartment lease. The downside features of European washers are that they are smaller and take much longer to wash your clothes. The wash cycle in Europe includes an hour or so of soapy soak time. This is probably more efficient than the American way.

Lamps

Take all of the light bulbs out of your regular lamps but bring the lamps with you. American bulbs will flash and burn out pretty darn quick on Europe's 220 volts. Most European bulbs will screw into the socket so you will be able to use your lamps with their bulbs. All you need is a simple plug adapter for the wire. Buy a supply of plug adapters for your lamps before you go to Europe.

Halogen lamps operate on a 12 volt direct current. They come with a small transformer which plugs into the wall socket. Bring the lamp and bulbs to Europe and buy a replacement transformer in an electrical store on arrival. Halogen lamps are very popular in Europe.

Moving in or out in Rotterdam is facilitated by this platform lift. Most buildings do not have elevators and the stairs are as steep as the incline on this device. This is not my move. Fortunately, I had a ground floor furnished apartment in Holland. [2214]

TV

Televisions and VCRs are a special case. The electrical requirement is not the major problem — it's the broadcast system. All American televisions operate on the NTSC system (I do not know, need to know, or even care to know what this and the following acronyms stand for.) In Germany, the PAL system is in use. In France, the SECAM system is in use. There are other systems in other countries, sort of like different languages. The net effect is that an American TV is nearly useless in Europe.

Many of the televisions sold in Europe are "multi system." With the flick of a switch they can be used in various countries on SECAM or PAL systems, or variations of these. We bought a multi system TV and VCR in New York before going to Germany. This was a very expensive TV but still it cost only about half as much as the same model in Germany. Fortunately our multi-system TV included NTSC. Most TVs sold in Europe do not offer this option. If you have NTSC and if you are living close to one of the few remaining American military bases you can watch the World Series and the NFL games on AFN.

Radios operate OK so long as they follow the general rules on voltage and frequency. Radios with digital display and tuning will be an annoyance if the signal is weak or slightly off spec. You may be better off with an old fashioned analog tuner.

Telephones

Telephones are much more expensive in Europe so this would be a good item to bring with you.

Telephone dialing can be "tone" or "pulse." Pulse is the old system where the number is sensed by the amount of time it takes a dial to turn back to stop. Tone uses a different frequency sound for each number. Tone dialing systems began when push button phones were introduced, however push button phones can be used with pulse or with tone dial systems.

Some of Europe is still on the pulse dial system, whereas most of the USA uses tone dialing. Phones sold in the USA have a "tone-pulse" switch so they can be used almost everywhere.

If you are on a pulse system in Europe you will have a little bit of difficulty when you dial a business and receive a recorded voice with a choice of menu items. These menu systems do not recognize pulses. If you are on a pulse system and connect to one of these businesses, slide your phone switch to "tone" after you connect. Then you can use the menu. Switch it back to pulse when you hang up or you will not be able to dial the next time.

If you have a speaker phone, answering machine, or remote handset type phone it will need an electrical connection. Your device must be rated for 50 Hz. Then plug it in with a transformer to reduce the European 220 volts to your machine's 110 volts. Make sure you use a transformer and not the device called a converter. See chapter 11.

However, many of these devices already operate from a transformer which you plug into the wall socket. Bring the transformer, the heavy little black thing, with you to Europe and take it to an electrical or electronic supply store. There you can buy one which works on 220 volts and 50 Hz but produces the same output and has the same plug connector. For example my phone answering machine's transformer puts out 350 ma (milliamps power) at 9 volts DC (direct current) from 110 volt AC at 60 Hz. All I need is a transformer with the same output from 220 volt 50 Hz in Europe. These transformers are easy to find. The same goes for HP DeskJet printers and other small appliances.

Fax Machines

Fax machines are also more expensive in Europe so bring yours over. Pulse and tone dialing options are the same as telephones. A home fax machine is particularly nice to have for speedy and cheap communication. A whole typewritten page can be transmitted within 45 seconds and transmission costs less than half of an airmail stamp. If you use a discount phone system you can send a one page fax for about ten cents. This may be cheaper than an email, especially if you compose on-line in Europe (all phone charges are tolled, whether local or long distance). My fax machine with a 220/110 transformer is running fine in Holland.

There are a few older fax machines and/or telephone systems which cannot accept the latest fax technology. If you are having troubles sending to a particular fax machine, tune down the transmission quality and try it again.

Initially I used a computer fax board, but with less than 100% success. You are better off getting a dedicated fax machine which uses a lot less power than a computer, monitor, and printer, and it is more likely to be compatible with other fax machines. Computer fax boards have other limitations which will prevent them from ever becoming a hot item, especially with the low cost of basic fax machines.

Having said that, one use that will continue is the fax software in laptop computers. This is very handy if you are traveling a lot. I compose a letter in WordPerfect and send it by selecting my fax modem as the printer. It works great. Scan your signature and save it as a graphics file so you can embed it in your letters.

Computers

Computers and peripherals may or may not operate properly in Europe. Check the name plate to see if it will operate on 220 volts and 50 Hz. The frequency is the major problem. If it is not stamped for 50 to 60 Hz you are taking a risk by bringing it to Europe. If it accepts 50 Hz, but only 110 volts, you can use a transformer to convert European 220 v to 110 v for your machine. I found that most computers operate at both frequencies and at both voltages, but most monitors only operate on the American 60 Hz frequency. My monitor, purchased in Germany, was rated for both American and European voltages and frequencies.

You don't want to pay retail for household goods if you are staying for only two years. Find out when neighborhoods have their group garage sales and then go shopping through their surplus items. It is also a great opportunity to meet some neighbors. This is the Ramplaankwartier of Haarlem, Nederland. Second hand shops are becoming more common, also. There are several in Haarlem. And don't forget the fun of flea markets.
[2210]

Transformers

When buying transformers to operate 110 volt appliances in Europe, select ones that are rated at about twice the number of watts as the total power requirement for the devices which you plan to use it on. I.e., if you have a 200 watt monitor and a 100 watt computer, buy a 600 watt or higher transformer. The reason is that all appliances use much more current during start-up. When you turn it on the "inrush" current can be five times as much as operating current, though it lasts for only a fraction of a second. If you have your computer running you don't want another device coming on and sucking up all the electrons, not even for an instant. Laser printers sure do gobble up the electricity. My formerly trusty old HP III can dim the lights in most homes. I used it in Germany with a 750 watt transformer, nearly the size of a bowling ball and the weight of two of them.

Batteries

Devices which operate on rechargeable batteries are no problem, but the battery charger might be. The better quality models can operate on 110 to 220 volts and 50 to 60 Hz. Check the name plate.

THE MOVE

If you are moving to Europe there are several ways it can be done. Those being transferred by their employer will find it rather simple in most cases. Moving companies will be arranged and you kind of follow the directions. Single people are treated rather off-handedly I found, while families are given much better consideration and benefits. Do-it-yourselfers can save thousands of dollars by using a freight forwarder instead of a moving company. Pack your own and bring your things directly to the dock.

Single Status

My first relocation to Europe was on single status. My company gave me a plane ticket and $246 and told me to report for work in The Netherlands on the Monday after next. I left almost everything I owned in storage, packed my clothes and computer and brought them to an air shipment company. On the last day I drove my car to the dock and turned it over to the freight forwarder, took a taxi to the airport, and flew to Holland.

On my self-made transfer to France, I sold most of my household stuff and cars, stored books and computer in my office, filled a couple of suitcases with clothes, and flew over. I had done something similar when I went over for six months while working on the first edition of this book.

Family Status

Our transfer to Germany was far more involved. With a family, tons of furniture, and a three year stay expected, my company provided just about everything to make it as easy as possible. They hired a professional international moving company. Estimators came and surveyed the job, which went to the low bidder. The moving manager came back a few weeks later with instructions on how we should prepare, plus a load of papers to fill out. They showed up on schedule and packed it all directly into an ocean shipping container. We took the shuttle bus to Los Angeles airport and flew to Frankfurt. The moving company, German branch, drove the container up to our house in Aschaffenburg about two months later. They unloaded and unpacked everything.

Moving Day for a House Full of Furniture

Before the movers show up, you should have filled out your inventory and insurance papers for the items which are going on the ship and those that are going into storage.

The mover will show up with a 20' or 40' sea container, a truck full of wrapping paper, and four strong guys. Get ready for the tornado.

The most important thing to do just before the arrival of the mover is to pack your suitcases, briefcase, and purse and get them into a safe place out of sight of the four strong men. Say, lock them in a closet. They must be convenient for access, but not convenient for packing. My movers have told me about incidents where air tickets and passports have been packed. If this stuff is on the boat, you are going to have one heck of a problem when you get to the airport. You might think that the packers will be thinking that he shouldn't pack a purse or briefcase, but if your family is like ours, there are a dozen purses and a few briefcases laying around. How is he supposed to know what is what? When you tell him that a room is ready to pack, *EVERYTHING* gets packed. One of my souvenirs of Europe is the empty box that our German telephone came in. I had left it laying around for a couple of years. It was carefully wrapped and shipped just as it was found by the packer, and is now wall art in my home office.

Also pack or get your valuables out of sight of the movers. Packers and moving men can succumb to temptation and pinch items they like. You won't know it until you are a world away months from now so it is hard to catch the thieves and prosecute them. On various moves in California and Germany I have lost some favorite shirts, dust collectors, a credit card, and a book of beautiful Russian stamps I bought in Poland. The stolen stamp book really burns me. There were news reports of significant thefts from American shipments by German packers during the 1990s. Be on guard wherever you are.

When the container gets to the destination, you have an empty house that will quickly be filled with your bulky wrapped stuff, and it's not Christmas. As the movers bring things to the door they will want to know which room to go to. Try to make sure that all boxes are adequately marked when they are packed, i.e. "kids bedroom" not just "bedroom." For further identification of some items you might want to write the contents on the box as it is packed. You will be busy checking off item numbers on the inventory list and it can get hectic with four guys nearly running in and out with hundreds of boxes. You never knew how much stuff you own until you have to move it. For big and heavy items, they will also want to know where in the room something belongs.

When everything is done, at both ends, it is customary to tip the movers and packers. How much? The job is done so you know how things went, except for the things they stole. If you talk to the moving men about the tip, they will brag about the thousand dollars they got from some company president last week. Of course his family probably had a big lot of expensive furniture. We gave a couple of hundred dollars to the packers at each end, and a lesser amount to the crews which unloaded.

The packers worked for three days while the unloaders finished in a day. We also gave the German packers a beer during their break periods. Germans love their beer.

Students

If you are going over to study, a major part of your belongings may be books instead of furniture and appliances. Books are small and heavy and you will be tempted to bring them as luggage. Instead, consider mailing them over.

Just as the European postal services have a special low rate for up to 5 kg of books to be sent surface mail, the US Postal Service has the same deal. But they have an even better deal if you are shipping more than 11 pounds. If you are shipping a lot of books to one address you can use the "M Bag" and ship between 11 and 66 pounds for about 75 cents per pound. They say it will take 8 to 10 weeks. My sack from Michigan to The Netherlands was there sooner.

FINDING A HOME

Finding a home is the most "fun" you'll have when moving over there. I've done it several times. This section focuses on renting since you are not likely to be buying a home or apartment for a stay of less than five years.

A home can be a house, an apartment, or a room. A furnished house is almost impossible to find in Europe. A furnished apartment is more likely. Renting a room usually means furnished.

Most rentals are offered by real estate agents. Agents have window displays describing their listings, sometimes with an accompanying photo or floor plan. They also advertise in the daily newspapers. In the newspapers there are usually just as many ads from people seeking apartments as there are listings for available apartments, and there is a large difference between the prices of offered rentals and for those requested.

Furnished or Unfurnished

When renting, you will be looking for furnished or unfurnished diggs. Furnished places are not easy to find, and when you find them, they are usually quite extraordinary in arrangement and furnishings.

Unfurnished places are extraordinary in another way — they are *unfurnished!* Typically you won't have a closet in the house, nor a kitchen sink, counter, or cabinets. Light fixtures and switches may have been removed. Moving in may require purchase of stand-up closets for your clothes and installation of a kitchen. Thanks to higher prices for nearly everything in Europe, getting these essentials can easily cost you several months salary. We were lucky that the owner already had a kitchen in the German house and offered to sell it to us rather than rip it out. It was old but functional so we took it. But we left it there when we moved out. He probably sold it again to the next tenant.

Just off screen to the right, the apartment I rented looked out on the Spaarne River and this Dutch lift bridge. Behind and to the right of the bridge in this picture is the Tyler's Museum and like a beacon above it all is the Sint Bavo Kerk, also known as the Grote Kerk ("Big Church"), in Haarlem, The Netherlands. [2209]

Holland

I went to Holland at the same time as a half dozen other people from my company. The company advised us to use a *makelaar* (real estate agent) to find a house. None of us could read the Dutch papers and had no help whatever from our company, a major international engineering firm.

Initially three of us took a small furnished place and temporarily camped in for a few weeks. Each of us had different needs and different *makelaars* to locate a home. Mine showed me furnished apartments and rooms, all priced about twice as much as a Dutchman would pay. Some were rather unusual. One was in an office building. The toilet and shower were two floors below the room. Another, in a private home, required a walk down some stairs and up some others to get to the kitchen. Dutch stairs are similar to ladders, a slight exaggeration.

I finally got lucky with a furnished apartment in the heart of Haarlem for a reasonable price. The owners also had a *Makelaar*, so theirs and mine got together to draft the contract and collect their fees. The apartment had everything. The inventory list was three pages long. The owners lived upstairs and insisted that I also use their maid on a weekly basis. One remarkable thing happened as I moved out. My *Makelaar* could not find one of the items on the inventory list, and in fact he didn't even know what it was. The owner helped out — the missing item turned out to be a plastic spoon which I had long ago thrown away!

Shakespeare & Company is the unofficial headquarters for Americans and other English speakers in Paris, France. Not only will you find new and used books, including How To Europe *at one time, the notice board is full of notices from room seekers and offerers. My little apartment on rue des Trois Portes was just a few blocks away. [2212]*

France

On moving to Paris I went over on my own and took a hotel room while I looked for a place. I checked the postings at the *Alliance Française*, Shakespeare & Company bookstore, American Church, and the newspapers. After looking at a number of unsightly cheap places I got lucky on the Left Bank and found a one room place in the *Quartier Latin* near the *Metro* stop *Maubert-Mutualité*. The owner of the apartment, an American expatriate, lived in another apartment in the same building. She rented it monthly, rather a rarity in Europe. It was fully furnished, complete with TV and kitchen utensils. The utilities were all hooked up including the telephone. It was ideal for a few months during my bachelor days in the summer of '86. That was where Elizabeth came into my life.

Elizabeth went back to Europe a few years later for more research on my book. She based in Paris but had some difficulty finding a low cost apartment for a short period. Finally she found a small place in Boulogne-Billancourt, a suburb in the southwest skirts of Paris. It was not furnished except for the stove and sink. She installed the telephone, got the electricity hooked up, bought a refrigerator and TV, pots and pans, and everything else. For six months it was livable and cozy. From there we made our first expedition to Budapest while the commies still ran Hungary.

Germany

My company's transfer policy for Germany included a house hunting trip prior to our move. That was nice, but the purpose of the trip was changed over there. In the hands of our German bosses the trip became a week-long series of presentations to the "American delegation," with most of it going right past us due to jet lag and unfamiliarity with their organization. The company personnel office was to have helped us find homes, but that didn't work very well. The German office was given totally wrong information about our needs. They thought we were all single guys who could live in just about anything. Most of us were married with families and needed much more.

After a couple days of being led to oddly configured apartments and rooms in private homes by the German personnel office, I took matters into my own hands. I bought some maps and daily newspapers from the surrounding cities and went out on my own hunt.

Rentals are handled by a *Grundstückservice* (real estate agent) in Germany. After selecting my city, it was easy to view a few houses after work every day. A few days of intense searching turned up a beautifully situated old house in Aschaffenburg. My company signed the contract, paid the agent, and gave us the keys. We contacted appropriate offices and had the electricity and telephone lines transferred to our name with no trouble. About every six months we had to order oil for the furnace. Once a year the city chimney sweep in traditional black came around to clean the chimney. When I first saw the guy I thought for a moment that we were in a Dickens' novel — dressed in black with that peculiar hat, he was right out of the book.

The house we rented in Aschaffenburg overlooked the Main River. It was on a bluff at the western edge of the Spessart, near the top center of this photo, and had a partial view of the Schloss further down river in the center of town. [2202]

Lease

When signing up, make sure you can read the contract, or have it officially translated into English and have the owner or his agent sign that version also.

We tried to get out of our lease in Germany. I love storms and was so amazed by a fury the likes of which I had never seen that I made a video of the ominous black clouds, the driving sheets of rain, and the howling wind. It was great. Little did I realize as I filmed the storm upstairs that he was giving us the works downstairs. We were flooded. Our lower floor was a mess, but all we lost was the carpets. The flood was seemingly inexplicable because we lived on a 100 foot high bluff overlooking the Main River.

After we tried to get out of the lease the owner went from smiling nice guy to unpleasant. He fixed the immediate cause of the flooding at considerable expense, but the house situation was basically unrepairable unless a much larger storm drain would be installed by the city.

OFFICIAL STUFF

Permission to Live

You will need a residence permit or visa if you plan to stay for more than three months. Obtain the application from a consulate of the country you are going to live in. Get going on this as soon as possible. Besides your name and other basic data, the form asks about your arrest record, medical condition, and means of support while over there.

Good Guy Letter

Before leaving, get a letter from your home town Chief of Police attesting that you are clean. The letter will simply say that his office has failed to find any record of wrongdoing on your part. Where I come from it's called a "good guy" letter and it's all you need, but it cost $20.

Health Exam

Next, get a good health examination. This will prove that you are not carrying some bugs into the country that will cost the local health and welfare officers some trouble to control. When I moved to Holland the major concern there was TB. Get a chest x-ray and bring the doctor's statement with you.

Even though we went through extensive medical exams prior to moving to Germany, Elizabeth and I had to go through it again once we arrived over there. A couple of weeks after my German exam I had to go back for an interview with the doctor. She was pleased to start the meeting by announcing that I don't have AIDS or syphilis. I was happy to hear that, but didn't even know that they were checking.

Financially Fit

Also, get a letter from your employer or show some other documentation that you have the means to support yourself. If you are working over there, this implies that you also have a work permit. Your company's personnel office should provide you with the proper letters to verify your status for the immigration office and for the labor department.

Where to Apply

Should you mail your application for residence permit from the USA or just go over and find the local town administrative offices to submit your application in person? The foreign government consulate will advise you on this. In at least some cases you are required to obtain the permit before going over.

For Holland and Germany, I applied after going there. I think that this is the fastest way of getting it done. There are always at lease two registrations required. The immigration people want to know who is coming into the country, and the local police want to know who is living in town. You are going to need some extra passport photos for all of these forms.

Staying American

As mentioned in chapter 21, "Working in Europe," you're still liable for paying US income taxes while in Europe. You're also still eligible to vote. Contact the nearest American consulate for information on registering and casting your ballot to cast the rascals out to get different rascals next time. You might have better assistance from your political party which tries to keep its voters voting. The Republican and Democrat parties have "abroad" organizations to help you vote.

Driver's License

When living in Europe you may be driving to work every day. Most countries allow you to drive for a period of time with your home state driver's license, and some require that you have an International Driving Permit. One year is generally the maximum that you can drive before you must get a license from the country where you are living.

I obtained a license in Holland simply by presenting my California drivers license. As long as your home state license is valid, you can obtain a Dutch license without taking expensive lessons and a rigorous test.

Obtaining a driver's license in Germany was not as simple as in Holland. You must make application within a year of taking up residence and take an eye examination at a regular optometrist's office. They use sophisticated instruments to check your eyes, not one of those wall charts. Unfortunately my test resulted in determining that I needed eye glasses. Not for me again, I decided, and talked the doctor into changing the results of the exam based on the fact that I had been partying the night before at local *Fasching* events and couldn't yet see straight. He bought my story and gave me an OK to drive without glasses. The technician who gave me the test was not happy. She gave me one of those looks. By the way, *Fasching* is a time when Germans drink and party hard. It's one of the German names for *Mardi Gras*, known in some countries as *Carnival*.

If your license has expired or if you wait too long you will be required to take expensive driving lessons and pass written and driving tests. In Holland you need 30 hours of driving lessons at 40 euros per hour, then take a multiple choice test of 50 questions followed by a strict driving test. Many people fail and must start again from start. If you are successful on your first shot the whole procedure will cost about $1,500. It is reported that Britain requires everyone to take lessons and pass the tests before being given a license, whether you have a valid license or not. The cost of lessons and tests runs over $1,000. Brits drive on the wrong side of the road so lessons would be a good idea. The pass rate is less than 50%. Many people with years of experience driving elsewhere don't pass the test and must repeat it.

GETTING SETTLED

Appliances

Once you arrive there are a number of things to get settled right away. First off you are going to need replacements for the refrigerator, TV, and other electrical necessities you did not bring over. Since the ocean shipment will take a month or two to arrive, you are going to be living in a hotel and eating out initially. Start shopping the major department stores in your vicinity for the things you need.

If you are on a company move, your European branch office probably has special discount deals established with certain vendors and stores, but they won't tell you unless you ask. Ours had a deal with an electrical goods store which sold everything from refrigerators to electric wire, and published a catalog listing all of it. We picked out the refrigerator and had it delivered the day after the furniture arrived. Later we went in for a vacuum cleaner, steam iron, and all the other items. When you buy, select major brand names so you can get parts and service when/if you relocate to another country. We bought a great vacuum cleaner but the company has gone out of business. Buying replacement bags has been impossible.

Ovens are a bit different in Europe. Even though the Celsius temperature scale is used, ovens usually have no temperature settings. They have numbers from 1 up to 7. Cooks grow up knowing what number to use for what. An American would be well advised to bring an oven thermometer when moving over. Also, some ovens have an internal fan to move the air around inside. Food will cook faster or at a lower temperature. You'll save gas or electricity with this feature, but getting the food properly done may require some experimentation.

Utilities

You are also going to need electrical service, probably gas or oil for home heating, telephone service, maybe cable TV, and maybe an internet service provider. Telephone service can be very expensive. You pay by the minute even to call next door, and you pay exorbitantly when you dial a mobile phone. The highest rates are in effect during business hours, just like American long distance service, so try to place your calls in off-peak hours. Besides that, in Holland at least, the bill is sent every 2 months and can knock your socks off if you've been talky or used the internet excessively.

Water, sewer, and garbage service fees should be included in your rental agreement and be paid by the property owner, but make sure. Especially make sure the owner is paying for water if you are expected to keep his grass watered.

Discuss these items with your landlord or real estate agent. Also, talk to your company's relocation or personnel officer, though these people are not too helpful on such items. You might be lucky but they will certainly not offer to hold your hand, and are not likely to give meaningful assistance when you ask. Talk to colleagues in the office or neighbors for real help. These new friends are usually very supportive to new arrivals from the "States." The local branch of the American Women's Club can also give definitive guidance, or tell you where you can get it.

SHOPPING

Shopping for daily necessities in Europe is a bit different than it is at home. Each country has its own peculiarities and you'll quickly learn the local customs and rules.

A Few Examples

In Germany stores close at 6 pm every day during the week, except for one day when some of the stores are open later. Even on that day it's pretty much impossible to buy bread and milk since the grocery stores don't follow late closing hours. On Sunday almost nothing is open in Germany except in airports and train stations.

Holland is pretty much the same as Germany, except that the Albert Heijn grocery stores are now open until 8 pm every day. Stores stay closed on Monday mornings and some types of stores take an afternoon off during the week. This is local custom and is normally not posted on store windows. In beach towns like Zandvoort and Noordwijk you'll find many stores open on Sunday throughout the year. Things sure have changed since my first time living here in the 1970s. The country was welded shut at 5:59 pm every day and totally all day on Sundays.

In France stores generally close at 7 pm though small Paris markets run by Algerians stay open until 10 pm selling basic food staples, beer, and essential household items. Bread, but little else, can be bought on Sunday mornings in Paris. A day without a fresh baguette would be a bad day. Supermarkets in some cities are open on Sunday morning.

Instead of using the grocery stores, it's convenient and interesting to use the farmers markets in Europe. These are open on different days in different parts of major cities, or in different cities. Ask a neighbor when the market is open, and where it is.

"Standards"

Though every country has it's own peculiarities as noted, there are some general ways of doing business which are the same in most countries.

Meat, chicken, and fish can be bought almost "on the hoof" in farmers markets. You may even see live chickens in some markets. Or you can buy everything precut and wrapped in styrofoam trays and cellophane just like home. The cost of beef is very high throughout Europe, and it is tough. Cattle are fed on grass and not corn so there is little fat in the beef, and it is not tender. Fat is what gives American beef much of its flavor and tenderness. Invest in a meat hammer to tenderize your steaks, and learn the art of slow roasting for most other cuts.

In small markets and in farmers markets the vendor usually selects your produce for you. In most large grocery stores, fruit and vegetable bins are arranged so customers can paw over the goods and pick their own. Each bin of apples, broccoli, etc. will have a number. Make a mental note and go over to the scale, put your bag on the scale, push the button, and a bar-coded price sticker will spit out. Slap the sticker on the bag and put it in your cart. Some items like cucumbers, avocados, etc., are priced by the piece.

Egg sizes in Switzerland are graded by weight, e.g., 55+ grams, 53+ grams, etc. Free range chicken eggs are also noted on the package, and cost about 50% more than cooped chicken eggs. And eggs are sold in packages of 10, not a dozen. Eggs and milk are normally not kept in refrigerated cabinets in the stores. They're just stacked along the aisles.

Most cities have a farmers market once or twice a week in the town square. On Tuesday, Thursday, and Saturday the market in Aix-en-Provence, France, is open for business. [2217]

Metric System

It's a good idea to keep the metric system in mind when shopping; see chapter 27, "Weights and Measures in Europe; Travel with Grams, Meters, Liters, and Celsius." Most items are priced per kilogram, though some of the more expensive things like meat and fish can be priced per 100 grams (the same as a hectogram) or per 500 grams so it doesn't look so expensive. Pricing is always in the local currency which means that you have to do two calculations to figure out what it costs in greenbacks per pound.

Coin for a Shopping Cart

Carts generally require that you insert a coin to unlock the chain holding it to the others. This pretty much eliminates the need for store owners to go around the block chasing their carts since everybody brings the cart back to the rack to retrieve their coin, equivalent to a dollar or two.

BANKING

Account

If you are living in Europe you need to have a bank account. It is rather simple to do this since most banks are only too happy to have another customer putting cash in their pockets. When you sign up, make sure you understand the full package of services available, and that you can figure out (in the local language) how to use them.

Automatic Teller Machines

The most important thing is to have an ATM card. These work just like those at home and let you draw cash from your account from virtually any bank in virtually any country. However, they are not called ATM cards in Europe. More likely it will be some local version of *euro-card* or *euro-pass* or *eurocheque card*.

Besides the usual magnetic strip which we have at home, *euro-cards* also have a memory chip which looks like a brass spider on the front of the card. They also have a double hologram. This security feature shows the face of some long hair from the last century flipping with the expiration year of the card.

All banks in Europe recognize four digit PINs, but almost none of them recognize anything but 4 digits. If you are using a 5 or 6 digit PIN with your ATM card, change it before you go to Europe and make it a numeric code, not an alpha code. You can use most American ATM cards and credit cards in European cash machines. See chapter 8 for more input on money in Europe.

Checks

When you open your account request some checks. You rarely need these but now and then they can save you money since banks charge extra if you pay a bill without an imprinted check. Checks are not the same as in America. When you get a bill, do not mail the payment to the creditor. In Europe you pay your bills at the bank, either automatically or by check.

Most statements, e.g. your phone bill, include a check which is already made out for the amount of the bill and payable to the creditor's account. So all you do is fill in your account number, sign it, and take it to your bank. Sometimes you'll receive a statement of your account without the check attached. This is when you need your own checks. You fill in the creditor's account number which is on his bill, his name, name and routing number for his bank, and a notation regarding the reason for the payment, e.g. his invoice number. Bring it to your bank and it is taken care of. You hope it is taken care of. Follow up with the one you made the check out to about a week later. I have experienced sloppy bookkeeping in Germany and have been billed twice for some items.

Automatic Debit

You can also have automatic electronic debit of you account. I do this for my international phone bill and for my internet service provider in Holland. You don't have to do anything, except to keep an eye on your bills and your account balance.

Credit Cards

Banks also issue credit cards. You can get a locally branded MasterCard or Visa card in most countries. You may find however that they don't work the same as in America. The charges on our German MasterCard were automatically deducted from our bank account every month. The banks do not carry credit balances on which they would be charging interest. So a credit card appears to be little more than an extended ATM bank card with the debit from your account coming once a month rather than at the time of purchase.

Because credit cards are expensive, few Europeans use them. Most large and medium size stores, restaurants, and hotels accept payment via your *euro-card*, the card we would call an ATM card.

Bank Routing Number

You'll probably have a need to transfer money between the USA and your overseas home now and then. This is when you learn a new term — "bank routing number."

When you are transferring money between continents, the safest and fastest way is to let the banks do it for you. So, before leaving home for relocation, talk to your bank and verify the data you need to make sure that everything goes according to plan for electronic money transfers between your European bank and your home town bank.

Every bank should (a few don't) have a bank routing number. You will find this number imprinted on all your checks, at the bottom next to your account number. You probably never needed this number for anything, but the bankers need it. In Europe you will be using that number fairly often. In Germany it is called the *Bankleitzahl*, your "bay-el-zet" as they say for BLZ.

Money Transfer

Find out which bank, usually a monster in New York, your bank uses for sending their international transfers. In Europe you might get lucky and find a bank which uses the same monster bank. This might speed your transfers but probably won't save you any money. The monster bank is going to take a cut no matter what, and the biggest cut at that. The banks at both ends are also going to take a cut. It pays to shop around to find the lowest fee, which will probably be at a medium or small bank since big banks got that way through tried and proven larceny.

The transfer usually takes less than 48 hours.

Other Services

Banks provide a number of other services, many of them not found in American banks. You can buy auto insurance, for example. You might also be able to buy stocks, commodity futures, and other risky investments. Electronic internet service is widespread and in many cases is better than anything available in the USA.

Stephanie completes her kindergarten year in Germany at the annual ceremony followed by a picnic. That's her in the front row, having just seen my camera. Her best friend, Tina Böhmer, is second to the left. Stephanie would only speak German when we returned to California, until she started school again. [2205]

SOME POTPOURRI

Neighbors

It is not especially easy getting to know your neighbors. People will nod or say hello if eye contact is made, but more than that needs a good reason. When single I spent a lot of time in the local pubs and had plenty of local company. When married I had no time or interest for that and met almost nobody outside the office.

Chances are that your neighbors will be watching you, and talking with each other about you. New arrivals, no matter where you are on the planet, are the subject of natural human curiosity. For some of your neighbors this will be the first time they have seen an actual American in the flesh. Some will want to meet you, but shyness and inhibitions will get in the way of most of them. The first step, if any, must be taken by you, in whatever way you choose to do it.

Television

Our family may have been *Schwartzsehers* (literally "black watchers") in Germany. Some countries impose a monthly tax on all residences which have a TV. We never paid this in Germany because no official asked us to. Several people in my office told me that we should be paying, but a neighborhood friend said that we only had to pay if we had more than one TV. We preferred to accept that interpretation of whatever law there was. Besides, public TV in Germany for the most part is fit for corpses.

I once saw an American news report which showed a special British police vehicle equipped with high tech electronic gear and whose job it was to prowl residential neighborhoods scanning for TVs by detecting the electronic waves they emitted. If the police found anyone who had not paid the TV tax the resident had to pay a stiff fine. George Orwell was certainly ahead of his time.

Hidden in the trees above the glass recycling bins in Geneva is a box with two dark rectangles. This is a surreptitious radar/camera box designed to photograph those running the traffic light at this crosswalk. If you can't find it in this photo, look to the right of the traffic light on the left side of the bright tree trunk. These devices are also used in Holland and Germany with strobe lights for night time operation. [2206]

Living Habits

Many Americans like to wash their car in the driveway on Saturday. You'll rarely if ever see this over there. Europeans take their motor to the car wash.

At home, room doors are normally kept closed within the house. Rooms which are not used much are not heated because of the high cost of gas and oil. You can catch a case of the shivers in Holland every winter morning just going to the bathroom. A colleague in Germany once commented disapprovingly that his neighbor kept his doors open. On the other hand, blinds are often kept open. When you walk past a house in Holland you can see straight through to the back yard because many houses have a combination living room and dining room with bay windows on each.

Residential doors in France have locking systems which remind you of bank vaults. The closest I have seen to Paris fortifications are those in New York City apartments. Nevertheless, the burglars often get in.

On moving out, renters are responsible for leaving the apartment in such a condition that new renters can move in within minutes.

On moving out of our house in Germany, the owner demanded new wallpaper throughout the house. The ugly stuff we tolerated for 2½ years was probably there for decades. We didn't know about a clause in the lease requiring us to leave new wallpaper. But I didn't sign the lease anyway. My company signed and they were responsible. I still don't understand this. Six months earlier we had asked the landlord about changing the wallpaper and he replied something to the effect that "Why do you want to do that? You are leaving soon anyway." This was the first indication that our three year transfer was going to be less than three years. The company told the landlord long before they ever intended to tell us.

Internet

Getting reconnected to the internet in Europe has been one of my biggest hassles in the last five years. In Holland in 1998 I subscribed to a local internet service provider (ISP) for about the same cost as back in California. However, the Dutch phone company, the PTT, charges by the minute for all calls. There is no such thing as a "local calling area" in which the calls are pegged by call, not time. Thus, an hour on the internet can cost one or two dollars depending on the time of day. Since it's easy to spend several hours on line and phone bills come every two months, you can be shocked with a bill of several hundred dollars. Cable internet may be less expensive than dial-up phone internet if you are on line a lot. Cable is also much faster.

From Switzerland in 1999 I only planned to stay for a couple of months so I did not get a local ISP. Instead I would dial my ISP in California, quickly download my email, and then hang up. I would compose new email off line, dial, sign on, send, and sign off - just about that quick. With a discount phone card in Switzerland the cost of a call from Geneva to Los Angeles was about 15 cents per minute.

Garbage

The problem of garbage disposal has become one of worldwide environmental concern. Too much stuff is being thrown away and there is a growing need for waste reduction. Garbage dumps, now termed waste disposal sites, are filling up and new ones are difficult to install so something must be done to halt the amount of refuse generated. On thing for sure is that the number of pizza boxes will continue to go up, along with the average waistline.

Europe is just as aware, if not more so, of this problem than any community in America. Our experience in Germany was very interesting. We had eight separate containers for household waste by the time we left in mid 1993. The objective was to recycle as much as possible. We segregated all paper, plastic, clear glass, brown glass, green glass, *Bioabfall* (biologically degradable waste), and batteries for recycle or special handling. Everything else went into the "garbage." The main reason was that our city had run out of space in the local landfill and could not get approval to install an incinerator due to strict environmental regulations and the "nimby (not in my back yard) syndrome." All waste which could not be recycled had to be hauled about 300 miles east to another landfill. This was very expensive so the recycling program was instituted.

In practice, we had various containers for each waste and different collection schedules for each. Once a month the paper and plastic were collected. I had to take the cans and glass to special containers set up around the city. Every grocery store parking lot had containers for different colored glass and cans. It's basically the same in Holland and many other countries in Europe.

Insects

There are gazillions of crawling, slithering, and flying critters in Europe, especially during the summer. Window screens are not in common use so these bugs can get in everywhere. One night we had a huge flock invade the bedroom through an open window. I used the vacuum cleaner extension tube to suck them all in. Our back yard was home to the most amazing slugs and snails I have ever seen.

When garbage collection was switched to biweekly from weekly in Germany we had a strange sight one morning. A fly had laid her eggs in the can and the extra week gave them enough time to hatch. There was a stream of maggots slithering out, which I promptly controlled with a can of bug spray.

For flies, one of the most effective bug sprays I have found is carburetor cleaner. Use the six inch long nozzle to aim right at the thing and it will be on its back in moments. Be careful about what you spray it on because this stuff is a powerful solvent and can affect paint and other surfaces.

Here are paper and glass recycling bins in Prague. Recycle glass is not picked up at your home. You must bring it to bins like these which are usually parked near the store where you bought the wine or mayonnaise. Beer bottles in most countries are returnable and require a deposit. Disposables never became popular. There is usually a recycle container for cans and paper. [2201]

Mail

Chapter 19, "Communicating as You Travel" gave a general rundown on the mail situation. Review that chapter. Also, go to your local post office after moving in to inquire about mail provisions. Each country has its own rules.

Magazines

There is a minor inconvenience which you should be aware of if you subscribe to magazines. The costs and delivery times will be different in Europe. When you change your address to Europe, magazines follow one of the following procedures;

a.) Keep the subscription at its present term and change the price at the next renewal.

b.) Shorten the subscription period to compensate them for the extra costs of postage.

c.) Send you a bill for the increased cost on the present subscription.

If your magazine is on plan a.) above, sit down before you open the renewal bill when it arrives. I formerly subscribed to one of the technical magazines published by McGraw Hill, "Chemical Engineering." The US domestic rate is $30 per year. The rate in Europe is $177. Air mail postage for 12 copies is much less than the difference of $147 so where does all that money go? They would never answer that question. Funny thing though - I met the European editor and was later given a free subscription.

Therefore, one of the perks you should negotiate into your relocation contract is remailing postage for your professional journals and hobby magazines from your home office. This shouldn't be a big burden for your employer but can save you bundles. Many companies already use a weekly courier dispatch or express shipment from the home office to their overseas offices. Your secretary or the mail room could put your magazines and newspapers into the overseas mail bag.

MOVING BACK "HOME"

After living in Europe, leaving is likely to bring on mild trauma. Arriving home in the USA is going to be a let-down, and give you a few shocks.

Unplugging

Just as when you left the USA, you'll have to send out change of address cards, get a mover or do it yourself, disconnect the telephone and utilities, clean house and settle up with the landlord, say your good-byes, and go to the airport. I write this matter-of-factly, but leaving is an extremely unpleasant thing to do, for me at least.

My first departure, from Holland after two years of living there, was an event. I let my friends know I was having a going away party at my favorite brown bar, scheduled for the night before my flight home. After packing up my apartment into eight oak barrels and delivering it all to the dock in Rotterdam, I checked into a hotel owned by the father of a good friend. Then I went to the bar and the party began. I woke up the next morning well past departure time for my flight. That evening I went back to the pub whose owners, Jan and Ellie, were surprised to see me. Ellie told me that I still owed about $50 of the $200 bar bill from the night before. I rescheduled my flight for two days hence and scheduled another going away party. This was not as extravagant, but I would have missed the plane again had my friend not awakened me, almost carried me to his car, stuffed me in, and drove me to the airport.

Our family departure went a bit smoother. Before leaving Germany we took the maximum one-month vacation in the company car, all the way to Istanbul and back with plenty of zig-zags along the way. On returning to Aschaffenburg after the long drive, I made reservations and we were on the plane the next day. We were still a bit tired from the trip, and our going away party was a quiet affair with our best German friends on the evening before our departure.

Replugging

When you return home after a couple of years out of the country, things look the same but have a different complexion. You have another perspective, and comparisons with your European experiences are always creeping into your thoughts.

One of the striking things is that you can overhear and understand conversations around you.

There are two major changes that you can do little about. The cost of auto insurance is much higher and you are probably going to lose your job.

Auto Insurance

Everything else being equal, one thing that may cause a lot of grief on return is signing up for auto insurance again. If you've been out of the country for six months or more, you'll be treated as a new customer. You begin to feel like you're starting at the beginning of the evolutionary chain when dealing with auto insurance salesmen. One way to make it easier and less expensive is to obtain a notarized statement from your European auto insurance company that you had no accidents or claims. You might also try to get a statement from the agency issuing drivers licenses that you had no violations.

It would be a good idea to find out what your insurance company's policy is before going over. You might be better off storing your car in a neighbor's back yard and paying for minimal insurance while you are out of the country. Otherwise, no matter how long you had insurance before you went overseas, you'll probably be treated as though you never had it when you return.

You're Fired

As mentioned in the previous chapter (so here is a redundancy worth taking note of), another thing that may affect you is a new perspective in your job. Things keep changing while you're out of the country, and since you're not around, you're not figured into the equations.

Both of my returns have been met with less than enthusiasm back in the home office. On returning from Holland, I lasted about three months before being laid off. On returning from France, I wasn't laid off because I was self-employed at the time. Then the problem was to re-establish client contacts which took a few months. On returning from Germany I lasted about eight months before the idiots threw me overboard.

Use this information to keep yourself alert to changes in yourself and/or your company so that you can be prepared for the high probability of a new job. Be especially alert to changes in management back home. If your boss has moved on, you are probably on the same track.

So why is this fleet of garbage trucks parked on the town square in front of the beautiful historic city hall? Because one of the drivers is getting married in there. This is the Grote Markt *of Haarlem, The Netherlands. Friday morning is wedding day in Haarlem and there are often dozens of people standing around to get a glimpse of the couples and their entourages. At the far left is the Amadeus Hotel, recommended in many guide books so it is often fully booked. Noisy party animals pouring out of bars late at night make the center of Haarlem less than ideal for getting a good nights rest. [2208]*

Chapter 23
Shopping in Europe
Buy Your Souvenirs, Gifts, and Necessities

The emptor must caveat.

THE DIFFERENCES

With higher taxes built into the price of everything and per capita income about the same as in America, you just won't find many bargains in the western countries of Europe. In the east you can still find good deals. In both areas you will see many unusual items, designs, materials, and fashions not found at home.

TOURIST SHOPPING

Caution

Tourists are immediately confronted with airport duty free shops and souvenir shops. Additionally, the folklore of flea markets gets the juices running. It is usually better to hold off on spending sprees until you have browsed the major department stores and other stores where the locals shop.

Duty Free Shops

There are duty free shops in major international airports, on most planes, and on board major ferries crossing international borders. Prices of goods in these shops may be duty free, but there are few bargains. If you are considering a major purchase, say a camera or electronic device, plan far ahead. Write to the duty free shop, care of your European gateway city airport (home-bound), and request a price list at least two months in advance. Compare prices with those for the same items in your local shops or through mail order. You can also shop in the duty free shop of your outbound airport for a last minute gift.

The only bargains I have seen in duty free shops are on alcoholic beverages and tobacco products, though this depends on the duty free shop and on the country. A pretty good rule would be that one should not enter any of the Scandinavian countries without carrying the maximum of duty free booze, if you enjoy drinking. The same is not necessarily true for Holland where the retail price of most spirits is less than the price in America, except for American products.

"See, Buy, Fly" is the catalog of Amsterdam's Schiphol Airport duty free shop. Since you can only buy in a duty free shop with a boarding pass for an outbound international flight in your hand, pick up the catalog on your arrival and browse through it in your leisure. They also have an internet site for browsers. Make your purchases when you return to the airport for your flight home. The subtitle of the booklet "voordeel voordat u vliegt" sort of means "save before you fly." [2305]

On board some ferries, bottles look like fifths and pints, but the exact quantity is not shown on the bottle. Except in the major airports, don't expect very good selections. The same limited number of brands show up in most duty free shops. One lesson I have learned is do not buy brands you are not familiar with, unless you can afford to experiment. Don't even buy new products from known brand names. I have tasted disasters.

All goods bought in duty free shops are subject to duty, if any, when you land at your destination. The duty saved is the duty of the country where you bought the item.

Souvenir Shops

After you land you are confronted by shops almost from the moment you're off the plane. After clearing passport and customs control the first hall you see will probably be lined with all kinds of stores. Don't expect any bargains. You might want to invest in a roller dolly for your suitcase if you've just discovered that it is too heavy.

High prices for stuff made in Brazil or Hong Kong can be found in the eighty thousand souvenir shops swarming around the tourist centers. These places are stocked with junque, but do have some useful items like Heineken T-shirts.

Consumer protection legislation is not as thorough in Europe as in America. Trinkets that appear to be of local origin may be imports from Pakistan and available at home in your five-and-dime for half the price. Items are identified with country of origin only when they want you to know. In Greece and the eastern European countries most of the craft work is locally made. Street markets with no overhead are the best places to shop.

When shopping for trinkets, offer a price lower than that marked. Sometimes a shopkeeper will accommodate you. If you like an item but you think it costs too much, say so. That is the easy indirect way to get some negotiations started.

Flea Markets

Some books on Europe boast of the great buys available at the Paris Flea Market and the Amsterdam Flea Market. Those were the old days. These places are now among the biggest rip-offs. The only customers are tourists. For bargains, go where the local folks shop.

There are scores of outdoor markets in Europe where the greenbacks are not grabbed so readily as in Paris and Amsterdam. Inquire at tourist offices. Look for small markets which are not so institutionalized. Permanent, roll-away, or knockdown structures occupy most of the acreage in the overpriced markets, while the cheaper markets feature merchandise displayed on old boxes or lying on the ground.

Flea markets are becoming more popular in Germany but are usually held at intermittent times, say every month or so at certain locations, usually a parking lot near a large shopping area and usually on a Sunday. These German *Flohmarkts* usually have a large number of vendors from Poland selling all manner of goods, some of which look like throw-outs from the Russian army.

I love these authentic flea markets. This one is in Budapest, Hungary. [2311]

When buying items at flea markets, start negotiating way below the asking price. Even though the vendor sees you as a rich American tourist, there's no need to throw money at him. If something catches your fancy buy it now because you'll never see it again.

Oh boy — an open market in Varna, Bulgaria. You can find almost any household item in these markets, plus some unusual foods. [2306]

Street Vendors

There are a few places which still have the classical fellow who comes up to you on the street with an armload of wrist watches up his sleeve. If you buy a famous brand name from one of these vendors, it's certainly a forgery. If it keeps running long enough for you to take it home with you, U. S. Customs can confiscate it.

In Lisbon, I was approached at least once a day by chaps trying to sell me a "gold ring." Each ring looked identical, and each probably would have given me a case of green finger.

In eastern Europe there are a large number of street vendors who have set up tables in town squares or on busy boulevards. Books are the most common items of merchandise in Kiev and some other cities. In Budapest, one street used to be lined with women selling embroidered cloths. It looked like a human clothesline and disappeared quickly when a policeman appeared. I bought two books of beautiful Russian stamps from an enterprising fellow in the main square of Warsaw and some brass inlaid wooden boxes from another. At first it seemed rather blasphemous to be dealing in such a beautiful place but I couldn't pass up those bargains. Distilled spirits are another common item. I bought a half liter of Stolichnaya vodka for a dollar from one vendor in Bulgaria. The same bottle in a store in L'viv, Ukraine cost me 25¢ (L'viv is spelled L'vov on many maps).

Postcards and Posters

You'll find a great variety of postcards: art reproductions, photos of cathedrals, nudes, and watercolors of 19th century street scenes. Prices of similar cards can vary considerably from shop to shop. The best prices can usually be found on the side streets and in open-air markets. Many cafes in Holland have a rack of free postcards, though they may not be to your taste.

If you are planning to buy posters on the street, maybe buy a mailing tube at an office supply store. Tubes are usually available at museums for the most expensive prints but generally not at poster stores or from the dealers along the Seine in Paris. Tubes can be crushed in the mail. One defense is to stuff them as full as possible before mailing them home.

The City Galerie enclosed shopping center in Aschaffenburg has 50 specialty shops, four department stores, and plenty of covered parking. Stores in Germany close at 2pm on Saturday so get up and shop early. [2303]

REAL SHOPPING

Department Stores

A visit to a major city isn't complete without a shopping trip through the major department stores and downtown specialty shops. Here you'll find the culture of modern civilization, descendants of the crude tools and pottery you went to see in the museums. Even if you're not buying, go and take a look.

For instance, in Munich visit the *Kaufhof*; in Paris, the *Galeries Lafayette* and *Printemps*; in Stockholm, the *NK* and *Aehlens*; in London, *Harrods*; in Amsterdam, *de Bijenkorf*; in Madrid, *El Corte Inglés*. Other major cities in each country have branch stores of the same name. Some of everything can be seen in these major department stores, and they often have a supermarket in the basement. My favorite is

BHV (the "bay hash vay") on rue de Rivoli across from the Hôtel de Ville in Paris. The basement is a fascinating hardware store. Handyman types will find an incredible assortment here, and in other hardware stores throughout Europe.

Crowds gather outside the El Corte Inglés *department store in Madrid, Spain for the annual "Cortylandia" window display. Christmas shopping in Europe is just as maddening as it is at home. [2314]*

You can almost always find a clerk in the big department stores who speaks English. In some stores, clerks wear name badges with miniature flags of the nations whose language they speak. Don't look for the American flag though. Look for the British Union Jack.

Browse through clothing stores, sporting goods stores, bookstores, and furniture stores for unusual and useful items that suit your fancy and are not found in the United States.

This is inside the beautiful Galleries Lafayette *department store in Paris, France. Have fun! [2315]*

First Floor

Note that in stores and hotels and offices all over Europe, the "first floor" is what we call the second floor. Don't stand there confused when you walk in asking for gloves and are directed up to the first floor. The floor at ground level has various names, depending on the country. Many large department stores have one or two floors below ground level. This is usually the bargain basement and/or a grocery store.

The large and specialty stores will ship purchases home so you don't have to carry them. When they do this, the value added tax which is already included in the posted price can be refunded, but a shipping charge is added which approximates the amount of the tax. See chapter 24.

"Pots and Pans" in Prague is open on Monday from noon to 6 pm, Tuesday through Friday from 9 am to 6 pm, Saturday from 9 am to 4 pm, and closed on Sunday. The Czech Republik is famous for its beautiful cut stemware. We brought home some champagne glasses. [2302]

Grocery Stores

Grocery shopping can range from modern supermarkets to shop hopping for bread, meat, dairy products, and fresh produce in a half dozen provincial-type shops and open-air markets. There are some advantages to the provincial way of life, but you can eat up a whole afternoon just buying a sack of groceries. Goods, especially bread, are usually fresher at the individual shops. But open hours are limited and the quantity of goods is limited. Shop early. Enclosed shopping malls are becoming more common in Europe. These usually include a super market and/or various specialty food shops. Super markets are springing up everywhere and the days of the small shops might be numbered.

You'll notice some differences as you shop. For example, fresh produce may be selected for you by the shopkeeper, or by an attendant in large supermarkets. You can't always paw over the fruits and vegetables to get an unblemished, perfectly ripe item. In some stores milk and eggs are often left out at room temperature, not kept in refrigerated cases; room temperature in many stores is often quite cold. The Dutch dairy products shops are a treat. Each cheese can be tasted before you buy. One of my favorites is *Boer kaas*, "farmer's cheese."

In the basement supermarket of a large Stockholm, Sweden department store, take a number for service at the meat, fish, or cheese counters, or help yourself to packaged products just like home. [2313]

Bring your kid when you go to a German meat counter and the toddler will be given a small piece of sausage or hot dog. Yes, they are fully cooked so you can eat them "raw."

In the eastern countries, the situation is different. I've seen scores of people standing in stores in some cities waiting for whatever they can get at government controlled prices. Meanwhile, at the farmers market, all sorts of meats and vegetables are for sale at free market prices.

The butcher shops are hardly different from the meat counters in some delicatessens at home. Meat is left open and unwrapped in glass cases, sometimes refrigerated. Point to the item you want, or try to pronounce it. Same goes for the fish shops, though the fish is always on ice.

One problem with all these butcher and baker shops is the waiting lines, or mobs. When you walk in, look around and note the people who are present. Keep your eye over both shoulders checking out new arrivals to make sure that no one makes an end run to the counter. During busy shopping hours, there may be ten customers for each shopkeeper. Keep inching forward or you could be in there all afternoon. If there's a large mob in a store, look around for the "take-a-number" dispenser. These are becoming more common.

You wanted to buy a dozen eggs? Sorry, they come in cartons of ten in Holland. [2317]

Usually in Europe you must bag your own groceries, in your own bag. If you didn't bring a bag, the store will usually sell you a sturdy plastic one for the equivalent of about 25¢. It can carry about 15 bottles of beer. Then you have a panic job of bagging your groceries before those of the next customer come shooting down the ramp. Don't expect consideration, much less smiles, from the cashier.

Usually shopkeepers select your produce for you, but at this little market in Salzburg pick your own. Notice that the customer has brought her own shopping basket. These wicker baskets are so common in Germany that I nick named them "Frau baskets." We bought one too. Very handy. [2316]

Warranties

Items purchased outside the United States are not covered by warranties issued by American manufacturers or distributors of those products. And there is a small chance that foreign purchased products do not meet United States safety standards, and may even be inferior goods with forged brand labels.

On the other hand, manufacturers and stores in Europe can bend over backwards to make the customer happy. I bought a used bicycle in Holland from a bike dealer. About six months later, the crank hub broke off. The frame was completely ruined. I went to the bike shop and was told to bring the bike in and the manufacturer would repair it. I did and they did, except that they gave me a completely new frame and reassembled the bike. Cost? Nada. That's the Sparta bicycle company in Holland for you, the kind of company you wish there were more of. I never heard of any other firm which would completely rebuild a broken item for free. And mine was years old when I bought it second hand. That was the third bike that I bought in Holland.

BARGAINS

Although almost everything costs more in Europe, there are a few items to be had at a lower price than at home.

Elizabeth's favorite souvenir of the places she visits is a locally painted plate to hang on the wall. Here she is in Istanbul's bazaar negotiating a new find. Of course she also bought a carpet and that nice leather backpack. A gang of brazen gypsies nearly had their hands in her backpack as we walked on a busy boulevard. I couldn't believe it as Elizabeth suddenly started swinging at these girls on the street without warning. I didn't know what had transpired. The gypsies didn't succeed in getting anything, and they jumped into a waiting car and were off before I could get a good picture. [2308]

Where To Buy

Prices are normally lower in the country of origin, and lower yet in the city where made or at the factory itself. One notable example of this is Swedish table crystal and decorative handmade glass articles. These are sold at about one-fourth of the American retail price at factory showrooms. The major brands are Boda, Kosta, and Orrefors, which are also the names of the towns in southern Sweden where the glass is made. A number of other towns between Vaxjo and Kalmar are also in this business. The items on sale are seconds, but are hardly distinguishable from those on display in fashionable American stores.

Cut glass is also a specialty in the Czech Republic and the prices are very good, even on major boulevards in *Praha* (Prague). Other glass items are also well priced. I bought a couple of glass laboratory condensers for a couple dollars each in a side-street shop.

Eastern and southern Europe have more bargains because the prices of nearly everything are lower in those areas.

Not only are the prices lower but the selection is much greater for Swiss watches and Swiss army knives when you shop in Switzerland.

Freebees

There are a few "free" souvenirs. One item that I indulge in is the paper coasters used in bars and cafes throughout Europe. Each carries the emblem of the house brew. There is usually a stack of them within easy reach on the bar or on the table. Or take the wet one under your own glass. If you're a label saver, ask your waiter to steam the label off your dinner wine bottle. Usually they will accommodate you. Matches are also a nice free souvenir when you find them. Most matches in Europe, even book matches, are wooden.

At the Kiev, Ukraine farmer's indoor market meat is left out on butcher block tables for your selection. [2320]

I do not take towels from hotels, but I do liberate ash trays from restaurants. I ask for the glass and ceramic ones but I just pocket the plastic ones. At one of my favorite restaurants in Amsterdam I asked the waitress for one of their nice ashtrays. She went to the kitchen to check on it and came back with a comment that they are running low on them and couldn't let me have it. Later, the *maître d'* came by as I was admiring the candle holder. I wasn't going to ask, but she told me that I couldn't have it, and then volunteered the ashtray! Thanks. On my way out our waitress said that she was sorry that I could not take the ashtray. I smiled.

If you enjoy cigars, stop in any Dutch tobacco shop and look over the selection of fine Sumatra smokes. I buy these little "Wilde Havanas" at the Jan van der Pigge shop in Haarlem. They are 100% tobacco with none of those chemicals used by American companies. Some wilde havanas contain 10% Cuban tobacco which would probably make them illegal to import to the USA. [2318]

WILDE HAVANA

Anno 1880

50 stuks
100% zuivere tabak

CAVEAT SHOPPING

Embargoed
Some items for sale overseas are prohibited from entry to the United States, or require a permit for entry. A few examples are: firearms, fruits, plants, meats, uncured cheeses, drug paraphernalia, and a long list of other items. Violations can be expensive and embarrassing.

All goods from some countries are prohibited. Cuban cigars are sold throughout Europe but you cannot bring them home. Beautiful and expensive Iranian carpets are sold in Istanbul but are not admitted to the USA.

Chapter 25 will introduce you to regulations of the US Customs Service.

You can spend some time shopping for kitchenware here. WMF shops are located throughout Germany. Other manufacturers also have their own retail shops. [2301]

Forged Labels
Forgery of trade marks is a serious problem for producers of high fashion, entertainment goods, computer software, and other overpriced items.

When you return home, US Customs can confiscate any forged or copied item.

Unusual Offers
While it was still communist, Elizabeth and I visited Budapest for a week. We did the city tour, bought some souvenirs, and splurged for dinner a couple of times. At lunch in one restaurant we admired the coffee cups. They included a small "hat" to place over the cup to keep the coffee hot. Elizabeth asked where she could buy these and after some discussion between the waitress and the manager, he offered to sell them to us.

We bought a set of six, but before leaving the restaurant a rather portly gentleman appeared from the kitchen. He was the owner and had come out to look around. We didn't know it at the time we made the deal but it seemed that the manager had sold something that was not his. He already had our money, and we had most of the coffee set in our day bags. But, Elizabeth had rejected one cup due to a defect and she wanted a good one. We waited some 20 minutes for a good cup to appear. Finally, from a nook near the stairs, the manager signaled us to leave and discreetly put the last cup in my conveniently unzipped day bag as we walked past him out of sight of the owner. I guess it could have been jail time for all of us if we had blinked.

We were driving by so I stopped in Burgundy again to taste and buy. This region has a magnet out for me. Stephanie shot this as I waited for my wine purchase paperwork. A certificate is issued when you buy en vrac (in bulk). You can buy 10 or 20 liter containers from the merchant, or bring your own. Get free labels, and buy bottles and corks separately if you want to bottle it and put some away. Drinking French wine helps you speak French ;>). These are my summer driving clothes in Europe. [2310]

Wine

Buying wine and returning it to the USA is a worthwhile diversion. It is relatively easy to find wine shops in the major cities who will help you select some good souvenirs and package them for your return as carry-on luggage.

Many states restrict or prohibit entry of alcoholic beverages. Review chapter 25, "Passing Customs," for more information.

Go window shopping after the stores have closed. This is a typical scene in Holland at sundown. [2312]

*Formerly the classic Amsterdam post office, this building is now a boutique shopping mall called the
Magna Plaza. From the* Dam *it is behind the* Koninklijk Paleis *(Royal Palace). [2323]*

Chapter 26
Languages, Numbers, Alphabets
Encounter The Tower of Babel in Europe

Ja, Oui, Si; 1, 2, 3; A, B, C.
It's not quite that simple for Americans in Europe.

LANGUAGES

American or English

Americans speak English, we say. Actually it is a dialect of English. It differs in a number of ways from the language as used in England.

When in Britain you'll notice the differences right away. Grammar and vocabulary can be a bit strange. One of the major differences involves pluralizing words that apply to a group, e.g. they say "the team are playing." Also, Britishers don't "go to the hospital." They "go to hospital." Many words are different on the Island, including *spanner* (wrench), *bonnet* (automobile hood), *loo* (toilet), *lift* (elevator), *torch* (flashlight), and scores more.

Going colloquial, Americans are Yanks, short for Yankees. Bull to Yanks is rubbish to Brits. When an American is pissed he is angry. When a Britisher is pissed he is drunk.

Before going to Britain, I recommend an interesting hour of reading in the front of any college dictionary. There is usually a chapter there on the subject of the history of the English language. Read it. Among many other things, you'll find out why Bostonians put an "r" in many words that don't have it (remember John Kennedy's "Cuber"), and leave it out of words that do have it ("khah" for "car"). Some people from New York do likewise. Britishers have the same habit, only more so.

European Languages

There are dozens of languages in use in the countries of Europe. While it is generally not necessary to know anything more than English, it certainly helps to know a little bit of the language for those countries you plan to spend some time in. In the eastern countries, a little bit of German can be quite valuable. People you come in contact with at airports, hotels, restaurants, and train stations in western Europe usually speak excellent English. But occasionally, the people you would really want to speak with know only broken English. Then some familiarity with the native tongue is a great help.

Almost everything in Ireland is posted in Irish, known there as Gaelach, *and in English. This is an "Exit" sign, in case you are not familiar with the British translation,* Way Out, *which means something different to George Carlin and our 60's generation. [2613]*

Rudiments Are Appreciated

Learn a few simple phrases in the local language. For instance, use the native for "please" and "thank you" as a minimum. When you start up speaking in English and they don't understand, you'll get a frown and a wave off in a few seconds. Then point to yourself, say "American" with a smile, and ask if someone speaks English. Nine times of out ten someone will come forward or the one you are talking to will run into the back room and bring out a teenager who has learned it in school or picked it up from American rock 'n' roll records. American is the language of the future throughout the world.

When using English, speak clearly and slowly and keep your ear tuned because the reply could be distinctly accented. If you know one of the romance languages you might try to use it in another romance language country. French, Spanish, Portuguese, Italian, and Romanian have the same source.

Double Language Nations

Political boundaries do not always equal language boundaries. In several countries more than one language is in use. Belgium and Switzerland, two of the smallest countries, are examples.

Besides the major languages, there are a number of regional and national languages which have survived invading armies and prohibitions. Notable among these is the Irish language. Basque is coming back to northern Spain after decades of government prohibition.

Phrase Books

Phrase books are fun reading, but not so much fun trying to use. Once you find the phrase that you want to use, you'll probably botch up the pronunciation. Then you'll show the book to the native and point to the phrase you were trying to say. The native will look, nod his head, smile, and then ramble on in the native tongue for a minute. Now what? These books can be very helpful, but I find that a pocket translating dictionary usually works better. I use both.

Talk about self service. Aperto *(open)? The owner had locked up. The machine on pump 5 island lets you pay and pump while he has his lunch at home.* Senza piombo *is the local dialect for unleaded. Prices are in* euro *per liter (a liter is about a quarter of a gallon). Stephanie watches the nozzle while I take the picture. We were heading upward in the Italian Alps near Aosta for a drive through the Mont Blanc Tunnel into France.* [2608]

Dual Language Dictionary

I wouldn't travel in a foreign country without a pocket translating dictionary. You can find lingua/language paperbacks in any bookstore or department store in Europe.

When using your translating dictionary to hunt up the foreign equivalent of an American word, also look up the reverse translation to see if it is the meaning you want. Many American words have more than one meaning and several foreign words may be presented.

For instance, in my Portugues Ingles / English Portuguese dictionary, the American word "bill" is followed by half a page of Portuguese words. Looking them up to find the reverse meaning, I find: *conta* meaning "count, computation, calculation, reckoning; account, bill; note; report, statement; esteem," etc., for another half a page; *nota* meaning "a note, mark, sign, memorandum, bill, memorial," etc., for ten lines further; *factura* meaning "invoice, bill of parcels;" *lista* meaning "strip of cloth, ribbon, slip of papper (sic), shred of linen," and a load of other words including *podao* meaning, among other things, "a clumsy, awkward man." When asking your waiter for the bill, I don't think you want to use that last one.

Pronunciation

Speaking foreign languages is far beyond the scope of this book, but a few tips here may help you pronounce a word or two.

Words are divided into syllables differently in most foreign languages. Polysyllable words are usually broken after a vowel or between double consonants. For instance, monopoly would be mo-no-po-ly rather than mo-nop-o-ly.

Pronunciation of *e* can be like *i* or *a*, or mute at the end of a word. Then *a* can be like *o*, *u* like *oo*, and *i* like *ee*. Combinations of vowels, diphthongs and triphthongs, are generally impossible to express except in speech by a native.

Consonants are also different. The letter *g* can sound like *y* or a cough. Often *k* can sound like *c* or *ch*, and *t* like *d*. The letter *r* is the most erratic of all. It can be mute, trilled, coughed, or even spoken where it isn't seen.

Also, all languages have a rhythm and character which seems to go with the people who speak it. German is noted for having, to most ears, a rather brusque tone. Some of the Mediterranean languages, reflecting a more relaxed life style, have an almost poetic rhythm.

This morning the dining car on my EuroCity train from Paris to Cologne features breakfast in three languages, but not ours. If you can't manage in French, Dutch, or German ask the waiter. He is probably fluent in English and wants to practice. [2609]

LANGUAGE LESSONS

Learning a foreign language is one of the reasons some people go to Europe. Teachers use the summer to brush up on their language specialty. For transferees it's a must-do because you are working over there and need to communicate. For first timers in any language, it's hard work, mentally intimidating, and worth close to nothing when you get home.

At Home

Many Americans had two to four years of foreign language study in high school or college. Then they go to, say, Nimes and can't even make the *garçon* (waiter) understand that they want a glass of wine. Well, you turkeys probably copied the homework from someone else and cribbed on the exam. Anyway, the best way to learn a foreign language is to go there, and speak it or suffer.

Berlitz

The famous name in language lessons is Berlitz. It's also expensive and used primarily by business people who need to get started in a hurry. We used Berlitz in getting prepared for our transfer to Germany. I would rate our experience as pro-forma. We learned about the difficulties of learning the language, but little else in about six weeks at a couple of hours a week with a one-on one instructor. It's about as effective as learning to cook without a stove.

This school, the Alliance Française *in Paris, teaches French language and culture at a very reasonable price. I studied French here in 1978 and came back in 1986 for a few more months.* [2614]

Alliance Française

I have attended the *Alliance Française* in Paris twice. It is cheap and good and fun. Classes consist of a maximum of 20 students from all over the world. No English is spoken — everything is taught by sight and sound. With four hours a day in class and four hours a day studying, plus the environment of Paris, on my first visit I finally understood the teacher in my third week. It was an amazing feeling when all that darkness and confusion fell away in the light. I would expect that three months at this pace would bring most people to a fairly competent level in French. I regretted that I only had time for one month, so I went again eight years later. That's where I met Elizabeth and *amour*. It's over now, but as Bogart said, "We'll always have Paris."

My French ability is still rudimentary, but it's satisfying that I have done this. To study at the *Alliance Française* just go there and sign up on the first of the month. You'll be given an entrance exam so they can place you at the right level. I'll be going again when I have the time.

Volkshochschule

On moving to Germany, we took German at a private school in one-on-one lessons. I also signed up at the local *Volkshochschule*, a kind of adult education type of school in Aschaffenburg. This seemed to work better for me. I was in class for three hours a week for two years. Only German is used in these schools and it sinks in after a while. Elizabeth had continued with intensive study at the private school and progressed faster than I did. She also used her German more frequently, in shopping and in talking with Stephanie's kindergarten teacher and the neighbors.

Dutch

I took Dutch lessons at a private institute, the *Talenpracticum Dreefzigt*, when I lived in Holland. This was an almost comical arrangement due to the informal setting and the highly individual character of our teacher. I also used a teach yourself book and studied every morning for a half hour at my desk. One day my boss came in early and asked me what I was doing. When I told him he scowled "What are you learning this language for? Nobody speaks it except us!"

I ended up learning most of my Dutch by hanging out in the local cafes, watching TV, and by dating Dutch girls. Learning Dutch was my first experience with a foreign language, except for two years each of high school Latin and German. Picking up Dutch is very difficult because everybody in Holland wants to, and can, speak English. And some of them have an attitude about foreigners learning their tongue, as my boss demonstrated. Another time I was washing my car in the street when a car pulled up and stopped. A spry old man leaned out and asked me how to get to the train station. I started to tell him, in my best Dutch of course, and was nearly done when he abruptly shouted back in English "In your own language! In your own language!" And again, I was back in Amsterdam after my first month of studying French at the *Alliance Française* in Paris. In a bakery I ordered a loaf of that beautiful Dutch bread, speaking Dutch. The owner replied in English. I replied in French. Then she retreated to Dutch. I won! Oh, that felt so good.

They don't expect Europeans to know all the languages either so signs like this are becoming more common with increasing travel between the 45 or so countries and languages. Reading this from the left you have toilets, waiting room, restaurant, baggage carts, money exchange, train information, exit left, exit right, baggage storage, parking, busses/trams, tickets, seat reservations, and couchette reservations. You'll see these signs throughout Europe. [2607]

Babel No More

There are a number of schools in all countries which specialize in teaching the local language to foreigners. French, German, Italian, and Spanish lessons are readily available in the respective countries. Russian language study has recently become popular and schools have opened their doors in major cities.

If you are interested in studying in any country, obtain information from the official tourist office of the country you plan to visit.

Language Lessons by Tape

Taped language lessons provide a convenient and inexpensive way to learn a few words of a foreign language. We have used several of these and have found big differences in the approach and the value of the tapes.

For German, we used tapes from Berlitz, SyberVision, and "Just Listen 'n Learn" (Passport Books). By far the best, and the most expensive, is SyberVision. Tapes are available for all the major languages. Many are available at your bookstore, library, and through mail-order. Check the internet.

Potpourri

A couple of nuisance items on languages should be mentioned.

Americans in France should get used to saying "yes" or *"oui"* (pronounced "whee") when giving an affirmative answer. Never say "yeah." To the French ear, "yeah" sounds like *"ja,"* the German word for "yes." Many French don't care much for Germans.

Finger language should be avoided. Americans start counting with the index finger, go up to the pinky and then hit the thumb. Europeans start with the thumb, and count through to the pinky. This may seem innocuous, but in some countries, our number two with raised index and middle finger is equivalent to the American middle finger high sign, popularly known as "the finger" or "the bird." Our way of showing two might be interpreted as the "finger salute."

I found this bilingual notice in my hotel room in Munich, Germany. Number 6 says "Impress you exact our site," and number 2 is "Do not throw away careless your butts." Note that lift *is the British word for elevator. Since British are the more common of the English speaking foreigners on the Continent, preference is given to their word usage over American. [2615]*

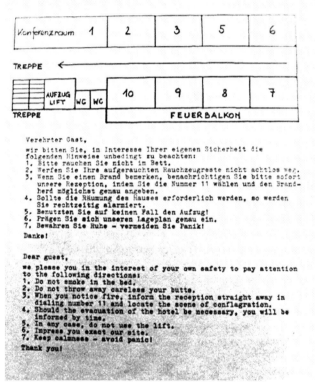

NUMBERS

There are some small but potentially significant differences in the way numbers are expressed in Europe.

One and Twenty

Beware of numbers like *neunundfünfzig* and *negenenvijftig*. These are respectively German and Dutch for fifty-nine (59). The literal translation of both is "nine-and-fifty." Thus, these languages employ the "olde English" system of counting from 21 up, that is, one-and-twenty, to nine-and-ninety. Some shopkeepers who are not too smart, or who are flustered at meeting an American, may announce a price as 59 when they actually mean 95. It will sound like a bargain until you get 5 *euros* change from a 100 *euro* note. This happens often so be alert.

To avoid misunderstandings, ask for the price, bus number, address, taxi cost estimate, or whatever to be written down. If it is not convenient for them to do it, pull out your notebook and pen, write down your interpretation, and show it to the other person for agreement. Heads talk. The smiling, affirmative nod and the frowning, negative shake are almost universal language. But your interpretation of the written numbers can also be different. See below.

The streets and public buildings in Brussels, Belgium, have two names, one in Walloon *(French) and one in* Flemish *(Dutch). In English, these translate as the "Meat and Bread Street." The direction to* Toone *is accompanied by a DO NOT ENTER sign below the street names.* [2616]

French 70

The French have a peculiarity in their number system which anthropologists may be able to explain. They can't count past 69. To the French 70 is *soixante-dix*, literally translated as "sixty ten," and so on up to sixty-nineteen for 79. At 80, a new system takes over. The French for 80 is *quatre-vingts*, literally translated as "four-twenties." This continues as four twenties-one for 81 all the way up to and including four-twenties nineteen for 99. Those who feel that they may have seen something like this before may recall Abraham Lincoln's opening words at Gettysburg: "Four score and seven years ago..."

Decimal Point

Numbers are written differently. The decimal point is usually a decimal comma in Europe, i.e., "78.5" is written as *78,5.*

And the comma separating thousands can be a point, e.g. "8,642" is written as *8.642.* However, if a number is given to you verbally as *seventy-eight-point-five*, it means *78,5* to them and 78.5 to us. If you are working on a computer spreadsheet in Europe, you'll come across this situation right away. Change the default settings for your program to the decimal point/comma protocol of your choice.

You may occasionally see the decimal point located halfway up the number rather than at the base. Don't be confused.

1,000,000,000,000

If you're talking big numbers in Britain, remember that a billion over there has twelve zeros. Our trillion has twelve zeros and our billion has nine. The American billion is a *milliard* in Britain.

Handwritten Numbers

Your bill (*l`addition* or *rekening*) at a restaurant or café may look like a bunch of crazy squiggles. The number one (1) is usually written as an inverted *V* and is easily mistaken for a seven. Seven usually has a slash across its middle, or looks like a *Y* or a *4*. Two, three and five are often garbled. Eight is started with the lower loop. Zero is usually impossible to decipher except by excluding all other possible translations.

The PTT in Varna has Post-Telegraph Telephone written out for you — in Bulgarian of course. Note that the letter L is very similar to P in Bulgarian (and Cyrillic) except that L has a small ball on its left foot. Legally parked there you see the trusty Opel that carried us from Germany to Istanbul via Switzerland, Italy, Slovenia, Croatia, and Greece, and back again through Bulgaria, Romania, Hungary, Slovakia, Poland, and the Czech Republic. [2603]

Roman Numerals

Fibonacci is credited with bringing the Arabic number system to Europe in the 12th century. Prior to that, Roman numerals were the only means of counting in Europe.

Roman numerals have been trashed almost everywhere. There are few places where they are still in public use. *Arrondissements* (districts or wards) in Paris are normally indicated with Roman numerals. They are sometimes used as the month indicator in dates, as in 6.IV.02, April 6, 2002. Other than that, Roman numerals are engraved in stone.

Fibonacci also developed an interesting sequence of numbers. The first two are 0 and 1. Subsequent numbers are formed by adding the two previous numbers in the sequence giving you 0, 1, 1, 2, 3, 5, 8, . . . The interesting part of this is that the ratio of one number to the one previous approaches the "Golden Ratio" of 1.618... This ratio is frequently found in the structures of flora and fauna, and in famous artifacts such as the Parthenon on the Acropolis in Athens, Greece.

This train board indicates that the train goes from Varna to Sofia, the capital city of Bulgaria.[2618]

ALPHABETS

So you think that everything is a, b, c? Wrong! There are very few languages, if any, which use all of and only the 26 letters in the English alphabet.

This ladies room sign in Athens, Greece is translated into English for you. [2619]

Code Breaking

In western Europe it's usually not as bad as alpha, beta, gamma. Irish puts the lie to that statement with a thoroughly unique set of alpha characters. Three alphabets in eastern Europe also fail to follow the Latin version. Greek is the one you are most familiar with. Another is Cyrillic, used in Russia, Ukraine, Belarus, Moldova, and Serbia. The unique hybrid Bulgarian alphabet looks like Cyrillic and Greek. The two monks, St. Cyril and his brother St. Methodius, who invented this cipher are celebrated as national heroes and given a holiday in their honor.

If you are going to spend an extended time in one country, make an early stop in a bookstore and buy a local English bi-directional translating dictionary. You'll have a much wider selection of dictionaries available in European bookstores than you will find at home. In the eastern countries these books cost pennies compared to their prices in the USA.

You are probably going to need some help reading the train departure board in Varna, Bulgaria. The destination names are given in the Bulgarian alphabet. [2610]

Latin Alphabets

Following is a summary of some of the major differences you'll find, and ways to cope with sometimes strange looking signs and menus. Use this as introductory material only.

We can be very thankful that the Germans and Swedes have abandoned their old medieval script, *Fraktur*, which makes Greek look easy in comparison. But both languages have retained some features which are strange to us. In **German**, the three "umlaut" vowels *ä*, *ö*, and *ü* are used in addition to the basic five: a, e, i, o, and u. When used with the umlaut, spelling order is mixed in with the regular vowel. However, the umlaut is gradually being dropped with the spelling changed to *ae*, *oe*, and *ue*, respectively. So the umlauts are de facto diphthongs. For instance, Munich is spelled in German as *München*, and is sometimes written as *Muenchen*. This gets the spellings to fit into the 26 character international telegraph system and the ASCII computer system. A practical consequence and nuisance of this pops up when you are looking for a street on a map or a name in a phone book. *Koenig* would come after *Köln* and be mixed in with *König*. Just regard any spellings with *ae*, *oe*, or *ue* as the single letters *ä*, *ö*, and *ü*. German also has an extra consonant which looks like *ß*; it is equivalent to an *ss* in pronunciation and alphabetically lies between *s* and *t*.

Heading north, the **Danish** alphabet runs from *a* to *z*, and then adds *æ*, *ø*, and *å*. Equivalent characters are: *ä* for *æ*, *ö* for *ø*, and *aa* for *å*. You'll find *ü* mixed in with *y*. The **Norwegian** alphabet is identical to the Danish. **Swedish** twists this a bit. After the normal *a* to *z*, they have added *å*, *ä*, and *ö*. Thus, look for *råka* after *ryka* in your Swedish to English dictionary. **Finnish** only adds the *ä* and *ö*, but has very little use for *b*, *c*, *f*, *q*, *w*, *x*, and *z*.

Brussels uses a lot of paint on their bilingual signs. Each board has the French and Dutch name for the place indicated. [2620]

The **French** have done little to the alphabet, except to add some accent marks to help them pronounce it. You'll see *é*, *è*, *ê*, *á*, *â*, *ô*, and *ç*. Don't sweat there — I can't pronounce them either. The letters *oe* in sequence are run together as in *œf*, the French word for egg, pronounced something like oof. French also has the accented *ë* to indicate that it is in a new syllable and not part of a diphthong, e.g. *Noël* (Christmas).

Portuguese uses *é*, *ê*, *á*, *à*, *ã*, *õ*, *ú*, and *ç*. All of the marks are strictly for pronunciation. The **Italians** have no unusual letters or arrangements, but have no use for the letters *j*, *k*, *w*, *x*, and *y* except in words of foreign origin. **Spanish** has four additional consonants: *ch*, *ll*, *ñ*, and *rr*. They come right after *c*, *l*, *n*, and *r*, respectively. The *rr* combination does not rate a separate chapter in the dictionary, but each of the others does. Thus, you can look for *rechazar* after *recusor* in your Spanish to English dictionary.

Dutch, more properly Nederlands, is spoken in **The Netherlands**. It uses most of the normal alphabet with one oddity. The combination *ij* isn't sure yet whether it's a *y* or just a humble *ij*. In dictionaries it sits between *ig* and *ik*. But in modern usage, such as in telephone books and street indexes on maps, it is equivalent to *y*. Its pronunciation is very similar to our *y*. Thus the Dutch word *dijk* sounds almost the same as its English translation, "dike." Another quirk of this combo is that if it begins a proper noun both letters are capitalized, as in *IJmuiden*, a city on the coast of Holland. Dutch also uses the "umlaut" e, *ë*, where they want to break a word between vowels for pronunciation, for example *cliënt*.

That was all of the easy stuff. Now we'll take a quick look at the strange alphabets used further east.

The eastern European languages which use the basic Latin alphabet have additional characters. Special characters involve various marks on the standard characters, combinations which receive separate chapters in the dictionary, and changes to the word order because of the new characters. In short, it's more of the kind of thing you see with Spanish. When you travel to any of the former eastern European countries, one of the first things you should do is buy a translating dictionary. Study the alphabet first and then learn a few of the polite words.

On this train departure board in Prague, "platform" is given in Czech, Russian, and German. [2601]

Other Alphabets

The classic **Greek** alphabet has contributed its first two letters to make our word "alphabet." Even though the Greek symbols are familiar to those in science, mathematics, fraternities, and sororities, they aren't in the daily diet of most of us. Look in the front or back cover of a college dictionary for a tabulation of the Greek alphabet. This may look forbidding, but it's really not so bad. In fact, with the street signs and many other signs in Athens using both the Greek and the Latin alphabets, you start to learn Greek by assimilation after a few days in town.

The **Cyrillic** alphabet is a bit more difficult to assimilate. You might also see it listed in a table inside the covers of your college dictionary, though it might be labeled **Russian**. They use it in Russia.

The **Bulgarian** alphabet is similar to Cyrillic but you won't find it very easily in reference books. If you are in Bulgaria, buy a dictionary and ask someone how to pronounce it for you.

Punctuation

There are a couple of strange punctuation marks in use in European languages. As examples, the Germans put the first quotation mark in the subscript position rather than the superscript position. Sometimes quotation marks are shown as double angle brackets, <<like so.>>

Spanish uses two question marks, the normal one plus an inverted one at the beginning of the question. To be consistent they do the same with exclamation marks. ¿Why do they do this? ¡Because this way you'll know what's coming!

The axe rouge *(red X) in Aix-en-Provence is accompanied by a notice in French that all violating vehicles will be towed immediately. This "No Stopping" and other critical signs are further illustrated in chapter 18. You can purchase a parking coupon from the machine next to this sign and put it on your dashboard, if you can find a valid parking place. [2612b]*

Clint Eastwood spricht gut Deutsch *in Salzburg, Austria. This movie is obvious\y dubbed. Those with foreign subtitles present a good opportunity to learn a bit of foreign language. [2617]*

Chapter 27
Weights and Measures in Europe
Travel with Grams, Meters, Liters, and Celsius

You'll have to go metric in a hurry.

BRITISH SYSTEM

The first stop for Americans is often England. There is where you'll find your first confusion. The British formerly used the same names for weights and measures that we do but this is now generally illegal. Britain has joined the metric club, with limited exceptions to the old system.

METRIC SYSTEM

Metrics in America

Most Americans have heard that the United States is converting to the metric system. Europe is already there and has been for a couple of centuries. Actually, the United States legalized the metric system in 1866 but after a century of yawning it just didn't come alive here. However, for the past 10 years or so all product labels now have the metric equivalent of the weight or volume in parenthesis next to the good old American way of measuring things.

The touted benefit of the metric system is that units are converted to higher or lower units of measure by factors of ten only. On the other hand, the American system has twelve inches to the foot, three feet to the yard, and many other odd divisions of units. One small absurdity of the metric system is that almost nobody uses half of the named units, e.g. *dekagrams* and *decigrams*. *Hectograms* are rarely used. I've only seen them in produce and fish markets in Italy.

Another problem with the metric system is the size of the basic unit of weight, the *gram*. The only place where it is at all meaningful is in the post office for weighing mail, but even there an ounce makes more sense than 28 grams.

Most products in Europe are sold by the *kilogram, kg* which is 1,000 *grams*, and equal to about 2 pounds. But in Holland the word *pond* is used colloquially to mean half a kilogram. Meanwhile a British green grocer went on trial for selling bananas by the pound. The Dutch also use the word *ons* for 100 *grams* when its true translation is ounce, and that is only 28 *grams*, not 100.

On the road in Slovakia this sign gives the distances in kilometers. The 191 km to Bratislava works out to 118 miles, roughly three hours of leisurely driving. [2701]

What Is the Metric System?

The metric system is a decimal system of weights and measures in which the *gram* is the unit of weight, the *meter* is the unit of length, and the *liter* is the unit of volume.

These units are conveniently related: one *liter* of water weighs 1,000 *grams* and one cubic *meter* contains 1,000 *liters*. One cubic meter of water weighs 1,000 *kilograms*, which is a metric ton.

Amounts greater or smaller than *grams*, *meters*, and *liters* are expressed by adding prefixes derived from Greek and Latin words for ten, hundred, and thousand. Thus you have:

Units	Prefix	Example
1000	kilo-	kilogram = 1000 grams
100	hecto-	hectoliter = 100 liters
10	deca-	decameter = 10 meters
0.1	deci-	decimeter = 1/10 meter
0.01	centi-	centiliter = 1/100 liter
0.001	milli-	milligram = 1/1000 gram

Additional prefixes are available for millions and billions but you won't see those on the store shelves, well, except in computer stores where everything is mega-and giga- these days, but you already know that.

The centi- prefix is one of the most common you will see and always means 1/100th of whatever. This is easy to remember because the American cent is 1/100th of a dollar. Cent shows up in many other places as well, such as century, centipede, centurion, centigrade, and *cent*, the French word for 100.

Gasoline is sold by the liter all over continental Europe. Here we are tanking up in Greece, and getting the window washed by the attendant while his son talks with Elizabeth. [2705]

Abbreviations

We seldom write out pounds and gallons but usually use lbs. and gals. They do the same with metric units. Here are some common abbrs.:

Unit	Abbr.
gram	g
kilogram	kg
liter	l
centiliter	cl
meter	m
kilometer	km

Using Metric

The conversion factors for the basic units into nearby American units are:

One *gram* equals 0.0352739 ounces.

One *meter* equals 3.280833 feet.

One *liter* equals 1.056710 quarts.

Six place conversion factors are of little use to the traveler. You want to be able to relate quantities in the European units to American units in a flash. It's like learning a foreign language, but far easier because you don't need to learn any grammar.

Think in metric units, approximately. For example, consider the following conversions and the round off approximations in the next column:

Conversion Factor	Round Off
1 ounce = 28.349527 *grams*	1 oz = 30 g
1 *kilogram* = 2.204619 pounds	1 *kg* = 2 lb
100 *grams* = 3.52739 ounces	100 g = 1/4 lb
33 *centiliters* = 11.15884 ounces	33 *cl* = 11 oz
1 *liter* = 1.06573 quart	1 *l* = 1 qt = 1/4 gal
1 gallon = 3.785332 *liters*	1 gal = 4 *l*
1 inch = 2.538998 *centimeters*	1 in = 2.5 *cm*
1 foot = 30.48006 *centimeters*	1 ft = 30 *cm*
1 *meter* = 1.093611 yards	1 *m* = 1 yd
1 mile = 1.60931 *kilometers*	1 mi = 1.6 *km*

These approximations are close enough to get you through the day.

Familiar derivations of American units are also much different. For instance, we rate automobile engines by cubic inch displacement and Europeans use liters. One liter equals 61 cubic inches equals. Our horsepower is equal to 3/4 of their *kilowatt* (kw). Americans use kilowatts to measure electricity, not automobile horsepower. For the tires, 30 psi equals approximately 2 atmospheres, 2 bars, and/or 2 kg/cm^2. For you boaters, wind speed is measured in *meters* per second. 10 *m/s* equals 19 knots. On land, 10 *m/s* equals 22 mph.

TEMPERATURE

Fahrenheit

America uses the Fahrenheit temperature scale. On this scale water freezes at 32° and boils at 212°.

Centigrade

The *Centigrade* temperature scale is used in Europe. It is also called the *Celsius* scale after its Swedish inventor. In *Centigrade*, water freezes at 0°C and it boils at 100°C. That is a 100 degree span and thus, *centi-*.

Fahrenheit and *Celsius* temperatures can be converted back and forth with a simple algebraic expression. To convert *Celsius* to Fahrenheit multiply °C by 1.8 and add 32. To convert Fahrenheit to *Celsius* subtract 32 from °F and then divide by 1.8.

I know that is too much math for a few of you, and I seldom do it myself.

Instead, keep some benchmarks in mind. Easy points to remember are:

$$0°C = 32°F$$
$$5°C = 41°F$$
$$10°C = 50°F,$$
$$15°C = 59°F,$$
$$20°C = 68°F,$$
$$25°C = 77°F,$$
$$30°C = 86°F,$$
$$35°C = 95°F$$
$$100°C = 212°F$$

For every five Centigrade degrees add nine Fahrenheit degrees.

Key Temperatures

Normal body temperature of 98.6°F is equal to 37°C. The only temperature at which Centigrade and Fahrenheit are the same is 40° below zero. You won't find me in town when that happens.

On entering Bulgaria you are greeted by this sign giving maximum speeds in km/hr. [2706]

Down the street 80 meters (87 yards) in Stockholm, Sweden you'll reach a point where the overhead clearance is 3½ meters (11½ feet). There is the familiar NO PARKING sign on top. [2707]

This sign at Le Havre, France points the way to Rouen and Paris, and gives the distances in kilometers. It does not give the distance to Etretat. The arrow on the pole in the background shows a tent and trailer indicating the direction to a nearby campground. [2703]

Chapter 28
Time and Dates in Europe
Travel in a Different Time Zone

On the clock, Europe will always be ahead of the USA.

TIME

There are two baselines regarding time on the planet. The International Dateline runs north-south through the middle of the Pacific Ocean. This line determines the turning of one day to the next.

The other line, the Prime Meridian, runs north-south on the other side of the world through the English city of Greenwich. The time at Greenwich is Greenwich Mean Time, a.k.a. G.M.T. It is also called Coordinated Universal Time, or UTC for short.

Time at places east of Greenwich can be expressed with a plus sign in front of the G.M.T., e.g. Moscow is G.M.T.+3 hours. Time west of Greenwich is expressed as G.M.T. with a negative sign. Example, New York is G.M.T.-5 hours.

Knowing this is not especially important, but it won't hurt you either. On the other hand, I recall the time I phoned a major airline to buy a specially discounted ticket. The special offer was due to expire at midnight. So I called on Friday evening from Los Angeles. The special offer had expired. That airline used G.M.T. as its clock and it was already early Saturday morning G.M.T. With some begging on my part the agent gave me the special anyway.

The prochain *(next) train in France is posted in 24 hour format, but the clock is a 12 hour timepiece. In some European stations you will see digital 24 hour clocks.* [2806]

- 429 -

Time Zones

     Because Europe is about a third of the way around the world toward the east, the time in Europe is always about a third of a day ahead of ours. To find the time in countries of Western Europe from the United States, use the following tables:

Table 1	
The four European Time zones are divided like so:	
Western WET	Iceland, Ireland, Portugal, United Kingdom
Central CET	Albania, Andorra, Austria, Belgium, Bosnia, Croatia, Czech Republic, Denmark, France, Germany, Hungary, Italy, Liechtenstein, Luxembourg, Macedonia, Netherlands, Norway, Poland, Serbia (Yugoslavia), Slovakia, Slovenia, Spain, Sweden, and Switzerland.
Eastern EET	Belarus, Bulgaria, Estonia, Finland, Greece, Latvia, Lithuania, Moldova, Romania, Turkey, Ukraine
Moscow MSK	Western Russia
See the notes on Daylight Savings Time.	

Table 2 To find the time in the European Time Zone below:	add the number of hours corresponding to your USA Time Zone - - - American Time Zones - - -				
	Eastern GMT+5	Central GMT+6	Mountain GMT+7	Pacific GMT+8	Alaska GMT+9
Western GMT	5	6	7	8	9
Central GMT-1	6	7	8	9	10
Eastern GMT-2	7	8	9	10	11
Moscow GMT-3	8	9	10	11	12

Examples:

What time is it in Paris, France when it is noon in Chicago? Solution: Table 1 shows that France is in Europe's Central time zone. If you live in Chicago you know that it is in the USA Central Time Zone. Find the intersection of the row and column in Table 2. This shows that there is a 7 hour time difference between Chicago and Paris. Then add seven hours to noon, 12:00, in Chicago and you get 19:00 on the 24 hour clock in Paris. Deduct 12 and the answer is 7:00 pm in Paris.

What time is it in Istanbul when it is 10:00 am in Los Angeles? Los Angeles is on USA Pacific Time and Istanbul is on European Eastern Time. Table 2 shows that the time difference is 10 hours. Add 10 hours to 10:00 am in Los Angeles and you have 20 hours on the 24 hour clock. Deduct 12 and the result is 8:00 pm. So, at 10:00 am in Los Angeles it is 8:00 pm in Istanbul.

Get on quick in Holland for the typical two minute stop. This Dutch train is two minutes late and might take off at any moment. The timepiece looks like ours, but the departure time, 14³⁰, is based on the 24 hour clock. The box with the arrow shooting out of it indicates an exit, in this case down a stairs. [2805]

Daylight Savings Time

Daylight Savings Time is practiced in most countries of Europe. It is called *Summer Time*. Some countries have adopted it only recently, and some haven't tried it yet.

The period for Daylight Savings Time in the USA is the first Sunday in April to the last Sunday in October. The period for *Summer Time* in most European countries is the last Sunday in March to the last Sunday in October.

These are more in agreement than they used to be, but there is still a week in the spring when the time differences according to the tables above will be an hour off.

Consult the current *Thomas Cook European Timetable*, especially the notes in the front, for information on which countries have adopted *Summer Time*.

It is always a good idea to check the local time when crossing borders. I once missed my breakfast in Italy because I had not reset my watch after crossing the night before from Switzerland, before Switzerland adopted Summer Time. But not all local clocks are on time. Clocks in train stations in Portugal and Italy can be out of synchronization by several minutes.

G.M.T. does not go on daylight savings time.

Open hours for this store in Kiev, the Ukraine are weekdays 10:00 am to 7:00 pm with a lunch pause from 2:00 pm to 3:00 pm, Saturday 10:00 am to 6:00 pm, and closed on Sunday. [2807]

ХУДОЖЕСТВЕННЫЙ
САЛОН

РАБОТАЕТ   С 10 ДО 19
ПЕРЕРЫВ   С 14 ДО 15
СУББОТА   С 10 ДО 18
ВЫХОДНОЙ — ВОСКРЕСЕНЬЕ

24 Hour Time

Time is officially kept on the 24 hour basis on train schedules, on NO PARKING signs, and on other items of importance. But most clocks are 12 hour clocks.

If a time of *1300* or greater is stated on a schedule, subtract 12 and add pm. Get used to the concept of *14h00* being 2:00 in the afternoon, and *2100* being 9:00 in the evening. Even some Europeans get confused and can slip into thinking that 14:00 is 4:00 pm. Your train left at 2:00 pm. I use my trusty alarm chronograph when traveling in Europe with the time indication set on 24 hour notation.

If it is a whole number of hours, the time may be written simply as *15h*. If it is 3:30 pm, it may be written as *15.30* or as *15h30'*.

Note: I've deliberately mixed up and written these 24 hour times in different ways. There is no uniformity in Europe either. This is more training to prepare you for the various ways of doing things in Europe's 4 dozen countries.

Telling Time

Time is expressed in different ways. For instance, 2:30 in America is "half past two." In Britain it is "half two." In Holland it is "half three." And in Holland, *tien voor half drie* (ten before half three) is 2:20. Be careful that you don't miss an appointment because of these little quirks of custom.

DATES -- INTERNATIONAL SYSTEM

Flipped

There is a major difference in the way dates are written. Europeans use the *day/month/year* arrangement rather than the month/day/year system used in America. Thus, to you *6/2/04* is *June 2, 2004*. To the hotel keeper in France that is *February 6, 2004*. You didn't intend to spend February in Paris, and he certainly won't hold your room until June.

Dashes and Slashes

The date is commonly written with points, as *6.2.04*, rather than the dashes or slashes common in the USA. To avoid mix-ups, get into the habit of writing dates with the month abbreviated rather than numbered, i.e., *6 Feb 04*. Due to the common Roman origin of calendar month names, the three letter abbreviations are almost universally recognized. A system that is coming into general use in timetables is to use a Roman numeral for the month. Thus, *February 6, 2004* would be *6 II 04* and *June 2, 2004* would be *2 VI 04*.

You might still see free parking in some cities, as with this "blue zone" in Germany. Buy a parking disk in a gas station and use the clock face to indicate your arrival time. Park here with a wheel on the curb, work days (werktags) from 8:00 am to 6:00 pm (8-18 h) for a maximum of 2 hours (2 Std..) In some cities parking is only allowed for local residents, and this restriction is only written in the local language. [2808]

Your Documents

You can do little about your driver's license or birth certificate if it is dated in the American system. Just be prepared for official headaches if you need to show these in the small towns. It would be helpful if AAA would get into the habit of using the European date system on International Driving Permits. Insist on it, or at least have the month written out. A little number that looks wrong to a bureaucrat or police officer can be a mighty big headache.

Calendars

Last but not least, here is one more thing that is different between the USA and Europe. American calendars start with Sunday and run across the page to Saturday. In Europe, calendars start with Monday and run across to Sunday. I sent an American wall calendar to my friend Paula in Holland. She made a note of a party just by the position of the day on the calendar, out of habit. When she prepared to go she followed the column headings giving the name of the day. She sure surprised the host being a day early!

Even worse, some European calendars run the days of the week down the side rather than across the top. These also start with Monday. Very very confusing. It is easier to read rune stones.

This Milan shop's open hours are more or less the general rule in southern Europe. The lunch pause lasts from 12:15 to 15:00, which is 3:00 pm. When you see "non-stop" it means that they are open for business the entire day. [2803]

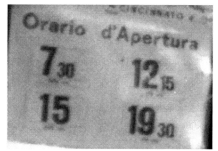

Fremdenverkehrs-
auskunftstelle
LINZ

HOTELZIMMER

GEÖFFNET: 8⁰⁰ — 19.⁰⁰ h
MITTAGSPAUSE: 13⁰⁰ — 14⁸⁰ h

The hotel reservations office in Linz, Austria is open from 8:00 am to 7:00 pm, but takes a mid day break from 1:00 to 2:30. [2809]

Chapter 29
The Weather in Europe
Travel with Your Umbrella

The sun is always shining, but it may be behind a cloud at the moment.

FAIR IS RARE

Travelers need to have some idea of the general flavor of the temperatures and precipitation. Should you take along a mackintosh or a bikini, or both?

The Gulf Stream
Most of Europe is north of Chicago, and none of it is as far south as Atlanta or Los Angeles. However, this information won't tell you much about the weather.

The warm Gulf Stream, starting out south of Florida, crosses the Atlantic and passes all the way up the West Coast of Europe. This stream moderates the temperature throughout northern Europe. Norwegian harbors located hundreds of miles north of the Arctic Circle rarely freeze. Meanwhile cold winds sweep down from the Arctic and clash with the vapors from this warm water. This creates a virtual constant drizzle over much of western Europe. The result is generally cooler and wetter summer weather than in most of America, but the winters are not nearly as harsh.

A light snow visited Edinburgh, Scotland the day before I arrived in January. An L on the roof of a car anywhere in Europe indicates a student driver. Steer clear. They drive and park on the left side of the street in Britain. [2906]

Take London for example. It's about 800 miles further north than Chicago but has average January temperatures about 15 degrees warmer, and it seldom freezes. Chicago can be sub-freezing for weeks on end, and intermittently for six months.

When you go east you get away from the influences of the ocean. It can get mighty fierce out there in the Ukraine.

This tranquility in the center of Paris is the Jardin Luxembourg (Luxembourg Garden) *After a few days of pounding the pavement, go in for a sit in the sun.* [2903]

Off Season

Summer is when most Americans go to Europe because that's when the school teachers get a two month vacation. They deserve it. Summers in northern Europe can be warm, though seldom scorching. Average July highs run in the seventies and rarely hit ninety. The summer of 2003 was an exception with weeks of 100 degree plus throughout Europe.

Often the best weather to be had is in some month other than July. In northern Europe, April, May, and June tend to be the driest months, though they will be a bit cooler than July. I prefer to travel in the spring for this and a few other reasons.

Sunshine

None of this applies to Europe south of the Pyrenees and the Alps, the two mountain ranges forming the French/Spanish border and the country of Switzerland, respectively.

In many areas of Portugal, Spain, Italy, Greece, and Turkey there is hardly a drop of rain during July and August and the thermometer runs in the high eighties. It is no wonder that planning for an annual one month vacation on one of the southern beaches is the preoccupation of many northern Europeans for eleven months of the year.

Summer is not always the best weather for travel. We drove across Greece to Istanbul in blistering heat. It can really knock you out if you're not used to this. And I've sweated it out in the heat and humidity of southern France where it is also buzzing with mosquitos and flies in the summer. Visit a cathedral if it gets too warm for you. It is usually 10° or 15° cooler inside.

Wet streets indicate that the shower just passed through Düsseldorf, Germany. Keep your umbrella handy. Park wherever, but read the signs first. They are written in German only.[2904]

The Rush

Most European schools are closed for only six weeks, typically mid-July through August. Most workers enjoy a four to six week vacation. So everybody goes at the same time. The result is a procession heading south in middle and late July that reminds you of the Oklahoma land rush. The dates are infamous in Holland as a convoy of caravans heads south on the *Route du Solei* in eastern France. I was stuck in that traffic several years ago.

Stop to tank up and to enjoy the azure skies and wisps of vapor over the crystalline Alps. This is Hall-in-Tyrol, Austria. Go north toward Munich, Germany or south toward Bolzano, Italy for more fantastic scenery. Bolzano is also known as Bozen, its Austrian name. German is widely spoken in the valley south of the Brenner Pass because this area was once a part of the Austro-Hungarian Empire. [2905]

WEATHER DATA

Weather Map

Weather maps and data are printed in the major European daily papers. The European edition of *USA Today* provides one of the best weather maps available anywhere. It can't keep up with the changes in Holland though. Really terrific storms can come in off the North Sea faster that you can say *Tot ziens* ("See you later.").

Local TV also has periodic weather reports, usually coming just after the news and sports. Dutch TV has a feature called *teletext* which allows you to look at weather maps and data at your pleasure, 24/7. The controls for *teletext* may be inside a special slide-open part of the remote control device. *Teletext* also has dozens of other pages featuring news, financial and market data, sports, and many other things.

For an excellent review of what makes the weather work in Europe, see *Fair Weather Travel in Western Europe* by Edward D. Powers. This book has historical weather data for scores of European cities giving average temperatures and precipitation. It also has some very interesting maps showing why it is the way it is. You'll be a meteorologist in a week. Look for this book in used book stores or on the internet at Amazon.com or Alibris.com.

Dress down for local weather conditions. This is in the resort city of Varna, Bulgaria. They have also adopted the American stop sign. That's a post office on the left with the French horn symbol at the bottom. [2901]

Chapter 30
Melding with Europe
Travel Is Interesting and Entertaining

What's going on?

MANY CHOICE CHOICES

Selecting from the cornucopia of Europe requires careful preparation. It's all a matter of personal taste. You don't have to visit museums if you would rather go on a balloon flight or go to a bull fight or relax in a café and meet someone new.

Uh, No Thanks

As an example, one of the most highly recommended items in all of the popular travel guidebooks, TV travel shows, and guided tours is the Amsterdam Canals Boat Excursion. I took this ride and I have a different opinion. It is a waste of time and money. You're stuffed into this long boat with a plexiglass roof, you and 80 other tourists. In four languages, over a miserable speaker system, you listen to a tape recording of stupendous facts and statistics about the places you are floating by. Good luck ever finding these places again as you walk around. I was not the only one bored on board. On top of that, it seemed that the boat was going to be swamped by a huge freighter when it got out in the middle of the harbor What in Amsterdam's name were we doing out in the harbor?

I'll never set foot in one of these Amsterdam boats again. [3047]

It's Amazing

On the other hand, one of the most fascinating exhibits in Europe is usually left out of the popular guidebooks. Sins of omission are far from the major problems with these books. A premier site to visit is the intact 17th century armory at Graz, Austria. It is stocked with 29,000 weapons and sets of armor of all sorts, some dating to the early 1500s. I wouldn't have known that this place exists except that the Michelin Green Guide *Austria* gives it two stars, worth a detour. I bid three stars and worth a return visit.

Your Million Dollar Trip

This chapter presents a few of the things that I have seen and/or done in Europe, from the somber to the frivolous. You'll learn something about me from this, but you'll also learn a bit more about Europe.

If you are looking for a ring-in-your-nose guide, this chapter will be a disappointment. There are literally hundreds of books wherein the authors give their perspective on the sights and events. My recommendations for good guide books (and there are plenty of bad ones) are to be found in chapter 10, "Guidebooks, Maps, Dictionaries."

In advance, learn as much as possible about the places you will visit and only do those things that suit your personal fancy. It's impossible to see and do everything, unless you have five years and an extra million dollars burning a hole in your pocket.

This line of thousands waits to enter the Tower of London. The two week period bracketing Easter is a popular holiday time in Europe because Good Friday and/or Easter Monday are public holidays in most countries. [3028]

HOW TO TOUR

Basically there are two ways to travel — on a package tour or on your own.

Package Tour

The tourist on the packaged 15-day tour will have already decided what he will see and do by having placed him/herself in the hands of a tour operator. The bus will be parked in front of your hotel with the engine running at 6 am. All you have to do is get your suitcase to the curb, have breakfast, and then get on board. Enjoy the ride. When you arrive in another city down the road, after passing hundreds of worthwhile places to visit, you and the other bovines are herded off the bus into your luxury or budget hotel, as your case may be. You probably won't know where you are. Collect your bag and key, and unpack again. Later on, a guide will meet your group and tour you through the sights as listed in the tour booklet.

Tour buses make regular pit stops where you have a chance to buy trinkets, use the potty, and have lunch. The shops and cafes probably have annual contracts with the tour operator which bring them the captive business.

I have never done one of these tours but have seen plenty of them in action in my travels, and I've read many tour brochures. If you want to sit on a bus looking out a window for up to six hours a day, some of the time stuck in the impossible big city traffic jams, this is for you. You are hardly seeing Europe any more than if you had stayed home and watched the travel channel. If you take a package tour, I hope that you have set aside enough time after the tour to actually see some of Europe on your own.

One of my favorites, and Stephanie's, is Madurodam. This fascinating exhibit is a miniature Holland in The Hague. [3020]

City Tours

If you are traveling on your own you have the opportunity to select individual city tours. In any city the number of guided tours is more or less proportional to the size of the metropolis. In big cities you'll also find tours of neighboring regions. Pick up brochures in city tourist offices and in commercial tour offices located in downtown areas. Your hotel desk clerk will probably be trying to sell you a tour, and look for promo brochures on the table in your room.

I have taken some of these city tours. They are good for openers, but in all of them the guide mechanically recites the lines describing the place, along with data and dates of questionable relevance. The guide is on a schedule so there is little time to dwell on an interesting exhibit.

The guides usually speak English, with a heavy accent. I have been on some guided tours of museums in France where only French and German were spoken. When the guide held out his hand expecting a tip for the tour, I kept my hand in my pocket. On a walking gastronomic tour of Haarlem the guide spoke only Dutch but I could understand most of it. We ate so much I could hardly move.

Strategic Positioning

When taking a guided tour, it is essential to get in the front of the bus. Stay next to the guide on a walking tour. This way you can get in questions about things you don't understand, or inquire about interesting objects which aren't covered by the standard speech. The guide usually has time for a little chitchat between sights and exhibits and welcomes the opportunity to reply to curious visitors. It indicates that you are interested and gives the guide an opportunity to use some words that aren't in the standard dialogue.

Self Touring

All of the things on a guided tour can be seen more cheaply with the help of a good guidebook and the public transportation system. The do-it-yourself traveler has to find his own way about, find a hotel, locate restaurants, and handle a number of mundane chores in order to enjoy the paintings and cathedrals. Since you have read this far in *How To Europe*, you know the basics and are probably anxious to start putting some of these do-it-yourself traveling techniques to work. Be an independent traveler and become a part of the scene, thus the title of this chapter, "Melding With Europe."

This is the famous Hofbrauhaus in Munich on a quiet night. One of those quart-sized mugs of beer should start to get your attitude properly adjusted. [3030]

The Guide

The first thing you need for self touring is a good guide book. Use the Michelin Green Guides for France, Britain, Italy, Germany, Holland, Spain, and the other countries for which they are published. Michelin Green Guides are available for different regions of France, e.g. Burgundy and The Riviera, and for Paris. If buying your copy in Europe, make sure that it is the English language edition, unless you can read French. These books are classics for travelers. They include historical sketches of the country, short vocabulary lists, general maps of the country and regions, useful information on local laws, customs, prices, driving, suggested itineraries for one to three week auto tours, bibliography, and a detailed discussion and map of every significant city, town, and region in the country. This includes scaled maps showing tourist offices, post offices, and city halls, along with museums, cathedrals, and other items of interest. Major museums are discussed in detail, giving floor plans. locations, open hours, and descriptions of the works in each room. Go with Michelin Green.

Free Guides

When traveling on your own, you may occasionally be offered native bilingual guide service. An individual guide may sound like an expensive way to travel, but I have had several and at absolutely no cost. It was with a bit of luck I admit, but ordinary citizens in some cities that don't see many Americans have proudly marched me through the town and its cathedrals, helped me find a hotel, and bought me coffee or a beer. One was an unpleasant experience (which I should have recognized beforehand), but many others were favorable. In L'viv, Ukraine I had probably the best help of any city I have been in. Thanks, Orest. If you are offered free guide service, seriously consider canceling your previous plans, if any, and accepting the offer.

BASING

By "basing" I mean where you are going to sleep and store your luggage while you are out seeing the sights and doing the town.

Gotham City

Most travelers go to the major cities because that's where the big cathedrals and museums are parked. But you don't have to put up with the big city all day long. With excellent public transportation available everywhere, you can stay in a medium sized city nearby and commute to the big city. Eurailpass makes this especially convenient. In a smaller city, you are off the beaten tourist trail and more out of the way of pickpockets, high prices for rooms and food, and pushy hucksters. Things you can't measure are the friendlier atmosphere and genuine welcome from almost everyone you meet in the smaller out of the way places. You'll also find it more convenient to visit other sights and events in the countryside.

This building is a steam engine, the Cruquius Expo in Haarlem, the Netherlands. Speaking as an engineer, it is amazing. [3044]

Bucolic Living

As an example, when you are in Holland base yourself in Haarlem rather than Amsterdam. There are six trains an hour making the 15 to 18 minute trip to the heart of Amsterdam.

Besides being convenient to the heart of "A'dam," Haarlem itself features a couple of impressive cathedrals -- the *Sint Bavokerk* which is usually referred to as the *Grote Kerk* (Big Church) and the *Basiliek Sint Bavo*. Museums include the *Frans Hals* and *Tylers*. The *Cruquius Exposition* is a huge 150 year old steam engine used to pump the water out of Lake Haarlem. This lake is now a *polder* in which Amsterdam's Schiphol Airport resides, about 15 feet below sea level. Near Haarlem you'll find Keukenhof (magnificent flower garden in spring), Zandvoort (beach, casino, and race track), and Kennemerland (dunes with bike paths). There are many other sights dating back to the 17th century.

The city is convenient to Schiphol Airport. Use Connexxion bus number 300 or 300R from the airport direct to the Haarlem train station. Right in front of you on the southwest corner of the train station is the *VVV* Tourist Information office of the city of Haarlem. They'll get you oriented and help you find a hotel, hostel, or B&B. Several budget hotels near the Big Church offer a good choice, along with a couple of upscale business hotels in the city. Get a map of Haarlem and the booklet *Uit Met Info* tourist guide at the *VVV*. The Haarlem train station rents bicycles with daily rates for less than the price of lunch. You'll never find a better place to ride a bike.

These are a few specifics about a place I am fortunate to know well. I first lived in Haarlem from 1975-77, and have spent another couple of years here since then. Not all major cities can boast of a nearby jewel like Haarlem, but all do have suburbs easily accessible by public transportation and which offer tourists unique and favorable experiences not available in the capital cities. You will get a much more balanced image of the people in each country. After all, would you think that a European visiting the USA should go to New York City and/or Washington D.C. and home again? Duh.

My favorite artist is Frans Hals. Here is one of the reasons, his De Vrolijke Drinker *(The Merry Drinker) in the Rijksmuseum, Amsterdam. [3024]*

SIGHTS AND PURSUITS

My catalogue of things to do and see in Europe is presented in no particular order. It is meant to be a mere introduction to the nearly infinite range of activities possible in your travels. It is certainly not complete and it does not dwell on the subjects that you can easily learn about from traditional information sources. These sources include travel agents, official national tourist offices, home sports and hobby associations, guidebooks, travel magazines, Sunday travel sections in major newspapers, TV shows, and other info.

Museums

There must be a thousand museums in Europe. Though we usually think of museums as art museums, there are scores of other types featuring everything from warfare to windmills to wine making. There is usually an entrance fee, though many state-operated museums allow free entry one day a week. In a very few museums, e.g. those in castles, entry is only allowed in the company of a museum guide. You might have to wait a few minutes for enough English-speaking people to show up and make it worth their while to walk the tour.

Typically museums are closed one day a week to allow the staff time to dust off the artifacts. Then the rush is on at other museums and sights. For example, the Museum d'Orsay is closed on Monday and the Louvre on Tuesday. Therefore, wait until Thursday to visit a Paris museum unless you like big crowds of tourists.

Sometimes a surcharge is made if you are bringing in a camera, and sometimes cameras are prohibited. Tripods and flash are always prohibited.

Most museums have shops where you can buy posters, postcards, books, jewelry, and other mementos. If there is an entry charge for the museum, you can usually talk your way into the souvenir shop without paying.

This is the beautiful St. Vladimir Cathedral in Kiev, the Ukraine. I walked in during a multiple wedding ceremony. [3043]

Cathedrals and Mosques

The many ancient cathedrals are main attractions throughout Europe. The architecture and engineering that went into these structures is overwhelming. You might say that these were the first skyscrapers. There is rarely an entry fee though a donation basket is usually conspicuous near the door.

Visit the mosques in Istanbul, Turkey. What are the differences between mosques and cathedrals? Mosques have carpets, no seats, geometric decor designs, and minarets for the call to prayer. Cathedrals have stone floors, pews or chairs, statues of the saints, and bell towers for the hourly ringing. [3017]

All of these churches are still in use as houses of worship. Use discretion when taking photos and talking even if there is no sign advising of a service in progress. Many tourists visit to pray, and you will occasionally walk in during a service. You are welcome to visit the mosques in Istanbul. Women are admitted. Everybody must leave their shoes at the door to walk on the carpets inside.

A lot of people are buried in those cathedrals, in crypts along the sides and under the stone markers near the altars. The kings usually get the best positions. In English churches, you can often buy materials on the spot to make brass rubbings.

There sure are a lot of castles in Europe. This one happens to be Kronborg Castle, the reputed setting for Shakespeare's "Hamlet" in Helsingor, Denmark. [3032]

Castles

Some former houses of royalty are open to visitors. These may be empty shells or fully furnished, or converted for use as museums, hotels, or restaurants. The famous *Schlösser* along the Rhine are only a fraction of the possibilities in Germany. The *chateaux* in the Loire Valley of France are also major tourist attractions. The most spectacular castle I have seen is at Sintra, Portugal. It's the kind of place you envision a castle should be, and it is fully furnished. The king had a short bed. Other tourists in the group I was with dwelled over the queen's commode. In the same breath you can regard the walled towns of Europe. Most cities have torn down the ramparts, or invading armies did it for them. One of the most famous and beautiful of the survivors is Brugge, Belgium, though it is extremely touristy. Rothenburg, Germany is the same. I have stumbled upon several walled towns in France which have not exploited their unique features. In other words, there were no crowds of tourists when I arrived. There are scores of others scattered about, usually on top of a hill with very steep sides.

Here is one of the most chilling sights in Europe - the Dutch exhibit at Auschwitz, Poland. It features the rail car sign plate for the train which brought Holland's Jews to their death. The design of these placards is basically the same now as it was 60 years ago. The former World War II Nazi killing camp is now a memorial museum. [3001]

World War II

I don't go out of my way for memorials to the carnage that engulfed Europe in the 1940s. It seems so senseless that millions of people died so horribly and for what. But I have come upon some cemeteries and war museums in my travels so I stopped to have a look. There is a massive memorial to the American Army in Belgium that gripped me for hours.

Sports & Games

The common denominator in Europe is soccer, generating more interest and fervor than American baseball and football combined. Primarily of British interest is rugby, an amazing bone-crunching game using a ball similar to our football, but the players wear no helmets or body armor.

The familiar American pastimes of golf, tennis, and bowling are found, but on a limited basis to travelers. These are usually private club sports, or require reservations well in advance if open to the public. It is best to know somebody and get invited if you wish to play, or make arrangements through your travel agent.

Ice skating and skiing are national pastimes in the colder locales during the winter. Ice skating is very democratic. Just find a frozen pond or river and make sure the ice is thick enough, or pay hourly at an ice rink. Scandinavia and the Alpine regions of France, Germany, Italy, Switzerland, and Austria feature hundreds of ski slopes. Affluent Europeans put the rush on the good spots, so plan and reserve early. The cold climates also feature toboggan racing, curling, and other frozen water events. Non-athletic types can build a snowman or snowwoman, or enjoy the fireplace in a cozy mountain chalet.

Summer events which are internationally publicized are the *Grand Prix* auto races and others. Bicycle races are held throughout Europe, the most famous being the *Tour de France* every July.

There are horses for hire at a few stables, but no welcome for cowboy riders. Saddles, stirrups, and horse training are strictly English style. There is a horse in Holland who was happy when I got off, I'm sure.

Boating, sailing, and water skiing are popular along all the coastal areas and inland waterways of Europe. Sailboats, cats, and power boats can be rented or chartered in most ports and resort areas by the hour, day, or week. Surfers can shoot the tubes on the Atlantic coast of southern France. Wind surfing is popular where nature provides no waves.

Fishermen and hunters can have a go at it. You will need a license. In Germany you must take lessons in order to get a fishing license.

Additional activities for participation or viewing are handball, field hockey, and canal jumping (Dutch amusement). The Dutch are also into baseball, called *honkbal* in Holland. Nearly every account I've ever read says that bullfighting is bad. I saw an afternoon of it in southern France and it was OK by me. Actually, I thought that it was pretty exciting.

Backgammon, bridge, checkers, and chess have millions of ardent players in Europe. Expect an intense win or die effort. They love to beat Americans. Billiards have a cult following, and championship matches are broadcast on TV. These games and others are often played in bars or cafes just like in the USA. If you find a free table, check the local rules of play before making any wagers on your skill. Game rules are sometimes different over there.

Café Sitting

This often promoted traveler's sport is as good as they say it is. In most of the countries of Europe, café owners put up tables and chairs on sidewalks and in the streets during good weather. And in many cities, the café owner has glassed in a good piece of the sidewalk so that he doesn't depend on the weather. It seems to be the inverse of eminent domain.

Enjoy outdoor café sitting at the Leidseplein in Amsterdam. Sooner, more probably later, a waiter from one of the surrounding kroegjes (brown bars) will appear and take your order for coffee, beer, or jenever, the traditional Dutch gin. Ask for a jonge, meaning the "young jenever," which is palatable to any martini drinker, but much cheaper. Incidentally, a "martini" in Europe is simply dry vermouth — neat with no gin or olive. [3033]

Before sitting make sure that a pigeon has not made a deposit, then relax and let yourself be amused. The waiter will arrive before dusk. Draft beer, table wine, coffee, tea, or mineral water generally cost a couple dollars, maybe more depending on the exchange rate. Getting a second one is usually more difficult than the first.

Entertainment varies from zero to plenty. In a good location you will have a constant parade of local citizens going about their business, other tourists looking as uncertain as you about whether or not to sit down, and assorted entertainers with fifteen minute repertoires after which they pass the hat and leave the sidewalk stage to the next busker, troubadour, mime, or magician. You'll love it!

The ambiance of Paris must force creative types to let it all out, and it needn't be at a café. In riding the *Metro*, you'll often see soloists or five-piece string groups board, blast away, pass the hat, and split at the next stop. Alas, the good old days of this unique form of entertainment may be ebbing. Signs in the *Metro* stations now say "For your tranquility, entertainment and passing the hat are forbidden in the Metro cars. Please do not encourage it." (free translation from *le français*). *Metro* access tunnels are favorite habitats for violinists and flutists. The echo chamber is real. But the city has imposed new restrictions. Musicians must have a permit to play, and they must audition to receive one of the few hundred available permits.

In the evening, Paris streets come alive with some pretty unusual stuff. I have seen 15-piece brass bands in the Montparnasse area. And the winner of them all was a rat circus in which two very normal young men had a dozen huge rats climbing ladders, walking the high wire, jumping through burning hoops, and all manner of other acts on a Paris sidewalk! The price is only what you want to toss in the hat.

There is more to life than Paris. In many German cities, the *Altstadt* (Old Town) features outdoor café sitting and street entertainment. The relaxing atmosphere of a German beer garden on a warm afternoon is all the more pleasant because local citizens want to practice their English. Stores close in mid afternoon on Saturdays in Germany so you have plenty of time to get revved up for Saturday night.

This is not from a western movie. This is a modern day Gypsy camp that we drove past in Romania. Some Gypsies still live and travel in Conestoga wagons (not made in Pennsylvania). [3018]

Shopping

Although some points on shopping were discussed in chapter 23, do not overlook its recreational value. The central shopping streets in many cities of Europe are forbidden to automobiles. Window shopping after dark is excellent because most of the stores have lighted window displays, and the crowds are all at home watching an American movie on TV. For inside browsing, mornings are best. In some countries, impatient salespeople are on your heels and expect you to buy the first one of anything you look at. If you don't buy, you are slammed out the door. Conversely, in other countries you won't be noticed unless you scream.

If you are looking for a special item, get an authoritative translation of its name, an illustration, and/or a description of its features in the local language. Then go for it. Many items are not displayed.

In Istanbul, go to the bazaar and shop for Turkish carpets, leather goods, and dust collectors. Haggle, haggle, haggle, and keep on haggling.

While sport shopping, don't forget houses, apartments, and automobiles. Walk into showrooms and real estate agencies and start chatting. It helps to be well dressed. You will be amazed at the features, size, and cost of living quarters, and you will be glad that your grandfather or great-grandfather got off his duff and emigrated to America. One of my great-grandfathers did it twice.

Beaching

Public swimming and sunbathing beaches are spread along coasts throughout Europe. Most are sand, though you will sometimes find a stony place like Nice, France. Inland lakes and rivers usually have grass banks and plenty of crawling critters. Beaches are popular, so if it is a warm Sunday, arrive early if you have a car to park.

Resort beaches often have cafes and bars right on the sand. These cafes rent beach chairs by the half day. Just sit in one and sooner or later some fellow will be around to collect a fee in local currency. He can bring you a beer or sandwich or you can walk inside to order it. Or you can bring your own sand mat and your own picnic.

A nice feature of beaches is that Europeans wear considerably less on the sand than Americans. A large number of girls in Europe wear nothing above the navel, and almost nothing on the derriere. Also, you can strip and go naked at one of the hundreds of nude beaches.

Take a dip in the Black Sea. Here's the beach at Constanta, Romania. The harbor entrance is just beyond the first breakwater. [3003]

    In discussing beaches, I should mention Zandvoort. It is overlooked by most guidebooks but is really an experience. You might be lolling around Amsterdam on a warm sunny day when you notice that the town is virtually deserted. Most likely everybody went to Zandvoort aan Zee, and so should you. There are frequent trains from the Amsterdam Central Station which can get you to Zandvoort in about 30 minutes, perhaps with a change in Haarlem. Walk out the front door of the station, go straight ahead two blocks and you're splashing in the North Sea. The water will be warmer than the water off southern California thanks to the Gulf Stream. Turn left (that's south) and walk the length of the town, about one mile. Along the whole beach "club" cafes and traveling wagons are selling good Dutch beer, herring, and other delicacies. Sailing cats and wind surfers are available for rent. The beach and water will be packed with Dutch and German people, at ease.
    In the summer you're likely to find more Dutch and other northern Europeans on the beaches of France, Spain, Greece, and Italy. In fact, you're likely to find too many and they already had all the hotels, pensions, and campgrounds at the popular places booked solid months ago. Do as the Europeans do — book early.

Music

    Music lovers will have no end of things to do in Europe. You have your choice almost everywhere. Major cities have opera houses, though performances do not coincide with the summer tourist season. A visit in fall or winter is necessary. But summer is the time for free open air jazz and rock n' roll in the streets and band shells throughout Europe, with beer and wine going down the gullet of everybody in sight. You'll love it.
    Jazz bars are popular, friendly, very down-home, and drink prices are reasonable. There is sometimes an admission charge, but usually the jazz bars are the best free entertainment in town. Piano bars are also very nice, though smokey as hell. Almost all the music is from America, and some of the entertainers are American

expatriates. If you can rumble a keyboard, you might think about living off the land as you travel. When you are in a hot place, ask if you can do a few "guest numbers" and try to work your way into something. The worst they can do is say is "No" and you've survived that word before.

Popular musical groups tour during the summer. If you have the chance, attend one of these concerts for a look at the young life. At an outdoor performance of the "Eagles" in Stockholm a number of years ago, I saw what must have been half of the teenage population of Sweden.

Kick back with the group "Sky Ranch" at the Café des Amis in Carouge, a suburb of Geneva. I haven't heard country music like this since I lived in Wichita some 30 years ago. This café has different groups every Friday, except in summer. It is sometimes jazz. I was a regular. [3007]

Bill Smith, on trombone, leads his group at the Café Central in Madrid, Spain. Admission was free, though the bar levied a small entertainment surcharge on each drink served. The barkeeper saw me talking with Bill and thought that I was a friend of his, so they didn't surcharge me. Heck, I'm a friend of everybody. [3037]

Festivals and Carnivals

One of the biggest parties in the world takes place in Munich, Germany for 16 days every September — it's the famous *Oktoberfest*. It is truly an amazement, but it isn't the only party. There are hundreds of lesser ones scattered throughout Europe. Many of these celebrate the harvest of the grape. It would appear that they often drink most of the crop straight away and have nothing left to export. For a darn good time, drop by and help them taste the beverages at any German wine festival. The French are more subdued, even drinking the raisin juice.

Ljubljana, Slovenia is one of the most beautiful cities in Europe. I refer to it as the Petite Paris of the East. [3013]

Revelry and ridiculous parades occupy the residents and visitors of some cities from the Friday to the Tuesday before Ash Wednesday. I was on duty in Maastricht, The Netherlands, for several days of *Carnaval* some years ago. The costumes and unbridled behavior of the citizen actors are unbelievable. The memories will keep you laughing for decades. *Mardi Gras* is the way this period is known in New Orleans.

Bar none, my favorite party is *Koninginnedag* (Queen's Day) in Amsterdam on April 30 every year. It seems like the entire country comes to town to drink beer and/or sell the family junque. The streets are mobbed curb to curb. It is just unbelievable that a major city can turn into such debauchery for an entire day. Unfortunately for many, Amsterdam was so crowded in 2001 that all train service to the city was shut down early in the afternoon. The weather was so bad in 2002 that there wasn't such a crowd.

Amusement Parks

Some major cities have amusement parks and zoos. For many years probably the most famous of the amusement parks was *Tivoli Garden* in Copenhagen. This is only open during the summer, and is definitely worth a day and evening visit. Started in 1843 on the outskirts of the city, *Tivoli* is surrounded by city now, and the train station is across the street. You'll be reminded of Disneyland when in *Tivoli*, and it would appear that Walt Disney was inspired by some of what he must have seen there. The admission fee to *Tivoli* is much less than for Disneyland.

Speaking of Disney, *EuroDisney* opened near Paris in 1993 and has become somewhat infamous. There was great hoopla and great moola, except the moola went the wrong way. The park was rejected by the French en masse and was a disaster for the investors, ranking up there with government projects. EuroDisney lost about $1 billion before starting to earn some of it back. Then Disney sold half of their stake to an investor in Saudi Arabia to cut losses and then renamed it Disneyland Paris to further insult the French. I guess that the word hubris was invented to describe such behavior. Mouse brain at work

Stephanie loves the Duinrel water amusement park just north of The Hague, especially this "Water Spin" ride. She is up there somewhere in the middle of that contraption with the rippled edge. Those people are spun around upside down, over and over and over again. I would have dumped my lunch. Kids should be at least ten to get full value at Duinrel (pronounced "down-rell") because some of the rides have minimum size limits. I get my kicks on the three story water slides over at the swimming pools. [3026]

.

You'll find much more reasonably priced amusement centers set up in many cities as part of their annual fair. These are usually summer events and are a lot of fun, especially for the children. As you travel keep your eye out for posters advertising these mini carnivals and circuses. If you see a Ferris wheel in the distance you'll know what's happening.

In Evian-les-Bains I came upon the source of that bottled water just outside the train station. The Heineken sign on the hotel restaurant on the right is getting to be as common as the Coca-Cola sign. [3010]

Movies

Movies are very, very popular in Europe. Most American movies appear in Europe shortly after they open in the United States, sometimes at the same time. The local language is usually dubbed in. But in Holland, Portugal, Greece, and Scandinavia you'll probably hear the original sound track and see a subtitle with the local translation. Check with the box office before entering. Simply ask the ticket seller or another customer in line if the sound track is in English.

Breweries & Wineries

Breweries throughout Europe welcome visitors. The famous and not-so-famous Danish, Dutch, and German breweries will admit you, normally for a small fee, and give you a tasting and snacks at the end of the tour.

Wineries are different. They are smaller and have a different market. They might not appear so hospitable but you will be warmly welcomed as a customer. When we lived in Germany we drove over to France about every six months, bought the ruby liquid *en vrac* (10 to 30 liter plastic barrels), loaded up the trunk of the car with as much as 120 liters, and then drove home where I bottled it in our cellar. You can also buy it bottled and bring it home to the USA, up to the limits of your home state alcoholic beverage rules. Our trips were to Burgundy, the area in the environs of Dijon. In Beaune and the surrounding villages and countryside you can find scores of *Caves de Dégustation* where you taste the beverage before buying. This is a nice way to really experience the ambiance of France and come home with delicious souvenirs, while extending your life span according to the latest medical research. When in Dijon we also bought the mustard, decidedly sharper than the stuff made in Connecticut under the same name.

For information on a wide variety of wineries, consult *The Winetasters Guide to Europe* by Anthony Hogg.

WHERE IS ACTION CENTRAL?

Up to here, this chapter has focused on the mild side, except for that mustard. What do you do after dinner in Europe? Hit the sack? How about hitting the wild side first?

Traditional Cafes

I experienced Europe first as a single man in the 1970s and 1980s. The "bar scene" over there is not exactly what you have in the USA. In general, it is a relaxing socializing atmosphere with plenty of whatever. Serious talk predominated over "game playing." Our games were backgammon and liar's dice. Solo girls could walk into a café and order a drink without stigma, though they would certainly get attention proportional to their appearance. Cafes were and are a social center of Dutch life. Activity picks up right after the shops close, at 6:00 pm, and lasts for about two hours. Dutch TV broadcasting would stop at about 11:00pm. Then I might put on my shoes and go over to my favorite café, call it a pub, for a nightcap. So did a bunch of others. Even though TV is on 24 hours now, the old traditions continue. Many Dutch, and I suppose people in other countries, consider a few neighborhood cafes as extensions of their home. I see regulars in the places I visit every time. The atmosphere has not changed much, nor have the hangings on the wall, in the 25 years I have known Holland. Some of those cafes have been there for a hundred years or more.

The European Bar Scene

In the gamut of establishments from dope dens to luxurious piano bars throughout Europe, I prefer the stand-up talking bars where I can find them. These places generally have enough chairs for less than 1/3 of the clients, enough stand up floor space for another 1/3, and the last 1/3 have their head in somebody else's armpit. Finding these places is not easy, especially when you're traveling and still having trouble finding your own hotel and shaking off jet lag after three days in town. One thing certain is that the good spots do not advertise because they are so busy that it's almost impossible to get in, especially on Friday night. With a lack of fire marshals, they usually allow anyone in who can get through the jovial mob.

These places are not well staffed behind the bar, and you may get pretty thirsty before being served on a busy night. The bartender will serve his familiar patrons (standing behind you) and may completely ignore you. Be patient, wave your hand, and yell, "Hello!" One or two nights practice and you'll get the hang of it.

Rue Huchette in Paris is one Greek restaurant after another. I lived a few blocks away and often found my way to the Caveau de la Huchette for a few beers and a night of dancing to the rock band in the cellar. [3025]

I didn't find most of my favorite places, I was led to them. And of those that I did find, virtually all were stumbled upon by pure accident. A few features common to popular places, are: steamed up windows, too many cars and/or bicycles parked on the street and sidewalk, taxis standing around, light-headed wobbly people walking out, loud laughter, a din of voices, and cheap drinks. People like cheap drinks.

For first time visitors to Europe, a good place to start, and to finish it all, is Amsterdam. The often mentioned Leidseplein is a favorite of the Dutch and tourists alike. In addition to the bars (some with outdoor seating) at the Leidseplein, the whole area is peppered with restaurants and cafes. The Dutch love to practice their English and buy a beer for a "Yank," so it is very easy to get acquainted and find leaders to other cozy places. Most bars in Holland are open until 2 am. After that it is disco fever till dawn.

Almost every city and town in Holland, England, Ireland, Germany, Austria, Switzerland, and the Czech Republic has similar establishments serving brew, food, and good times. In Germany, the *Altstadt* revelry starts early on Saturday since stores close at 2 pm (except for the first Saturday of each month).

In Spain drinking is nice and inexpensive. Many bars serve gratuitous saucers of olives, cakes, seafood, and other nice munchies with the drink in mid afternoon and early evening. The Madrid tourist office has a convenient guide map to these *tapas* cafes.

Beverage Budget

What you drink can have a big influence on your budget. In general, Europeans drink beer. A bartenders job is rather simple - pull the handle. Even the French drink beer, but the Italians are big on wine. Beer is cheap, except in Scandinavia.

A shot of locally distilled spirits is usually about the same price as a local beer. Prices increase dramatically for foreign distilled spirits so it is far cheaper to drink the local firewater, especially in the eastern countries. Distilled spirits are often dispensed in 2 cl or 4 cl amounts from special measuring cups on the bottle, or in equivalent amounts expressed in grams. Except in Spain, do not expect a generous splash from a friendly bartender.

Carbonated drinks and fruit juices in abbreviated bottles can be had almost everywhere, and these drinks usually cost more than beer. If you are traveling with a child you can save money if you carry a few of his/her favorite beverages that you bought in a grocery store.

Roll out the barrels and convert the Nassaulaan bus stop in Haarlem into an outdoor bar. It was another one of those typical Dutch festivals. In the middle, Paula is holding two beers, one of which I consumed. Beer is food, made from grain as is bread. [3046]

Measure and Head

Beer drinkers should not expect the "American pour" — down the side of the glass to minimize the head. In Holland, they pour a tall head, let it settle a minute and top it off. Then a plastic knife is used to shear off the head at the brim. In Germany, "pilsner" takes 7 minutes to pour in successive draws, each one after the head has settled a bit. If you order "export" you get immediate service without the seven minute ritual. It is said that "export quality" denotes the stuff that the locals won't drink.

The normal glass of beer in Europe is 25 cl, equal to about 8 ounces. You can also find it poured as 33 cl equal to 11 ounces and 50 cl equal to about 17 ounces. In Finland, beer is dispensed in automats at the bar giving exactly one half liter. In Greece it is poured as 500 grams and 330 grams, roughly equal to 50 cl and 33 cl. In Britain and Ireland it is poured by the pint, the Imperial pint that is. One pint over there is about 19 American ounces.

As in America, if you call your brand to a waitress, you can expect to be cheated with inferior goods many times. If you insist on a certain brand, sit at or near the bar so you can see what is being poured.

Wherever there is a beautiful tourist site there will be vendors of home made jewelry and art. This is the Charles Bridge in Prague, Czech Republic. [3045]

Discos

Live music for dancing is virtually nonexistent in Europe. For years, they have been dancing at the discotheque, a French word for "record collection." In some cities they are called "night clubs," sometimes in the local language.

Discos don't get going until after 10 pm and then stay open until 4 or 5 am. They often advertise in the local newspapers and are mentioned in the "This Week in . . ." booklets which are published in the major cities listing current events (booklets are free in the major hotels and in city tourist offices).

Depending on local custom, discos may or may not charge an admission or membership fee. Virtually all have locked front doors, door bell, and peep hole. If they don't like your looks they just don't open the door. In Spain, they leave the front door open, but have two huge doormen collecting an admission fee. This typically includes one drink. In Holland, the doorman expects a tip on your way out.

Discos are dressy, snobbish, expensive, crowded, and don't seem to attract a very intelligent class of people. Watch out that your drink is not stolen by another patron in the Scandinavian countries. This has happened to me several times in Sweden and Norway where a beer costs about what we would pay for a case of 24 at home. And speaking of the price, I was standing at the bar in a Monte Carlo disco quenching a busy thirst. The young lady was running a tab for me. After six or seven beers, I asked her how much a beer costs. She looked at me and looked at the tab and said "Normal price is 20 francs each, but since you drink so many, I give you a special price — 15 francs." That's discount drinking, but it still left the price equal to about $4.50 for a 12 oz bottle of beer, way back in 1976.

For the record book a shot of Scotch on the rocks in a Paris disco cost me $15 in 1978. I protested and got another one for free. In a Geneva night club in 1999 one beer cost me about $11. They take your money with a straight face. In the same place the over eager waitress cleaned out my ashtray while I was out on the floor dancing. There went half of a Monte Cristo, a gift of another patron and the most beautiful cigar I ever smoked. I was not happy.

Casinos

Casinos are scattered throughout Europe in the haunts of the wealthy and idle. None of the European casinos compare in glitter and glitz to Las Vegas. The typical European casino is sedate and quiet, with a dress code requiring jacket and tie or turtleneck, and evening dress for ladies. You will need your passport when entering and normally must pay an admission charge. Roulette, 30/40, blackjack, and baccarat are usually the only games on the tables.

The casino at Monte Carlo, Monaco, is probably the most famous in the world. Go in for a look around even if you don't feel lucky. [3040]

Estoril, Portugal claims to have the largest casino in Europe. You must decide on entering this one whether you want to play bingo, slot machines, or the gaming tables. For a nominal charge I was admitted to a large hall with roulette, French bank, and blackjack.

Holland is a relatively new arrival in the casino business. Their first one was a cozy little place in Zandvoort in the 70s. They also have one in Schiphol, Amsterdam's international airport. If you have a layover you can play cards or roulette. Casinos are scattered throughout Germany, generally in places whose names start with Bad (that's German for "bath"). The most famous is in Baden-Baden, a beautiful little city in the Black Forest. France has casinos in Nice and a number of other resort areas. Budapest has a boat casino.

Note that game rules vary and are not the same as those you may be familiar with. Get the brochure detailing local game rules before you start putting your money down.

In major cities of Spain and Holland, slot machine parlors have been established. You'll also find slot machines, black jack, and roulette on international ferries. Some of the luxury hotels in Helsinki have a blackjack table in the lobby. Ties go to the dealer.

Red Lights

Charlemagne outlawed prostitution in 801 AD, the first year of his reign as Holy Roman Emperor. Was this wise? The business has continued and the poor women of pleasure have simply become criminals. Outlawing prostitution continues to have the same effects as did the 1920s law against alcohol in the USA and the continuing prohibition of Maria Juana since 1937. Politicians will never get it right, including those who don't inhale.

In a few places, notably Holland, prostitution is legal. Amsterdam has a red light district, and it's a busy tourist attraction. It is heavily patrolled by the police, but exercise caution. It does have red lights, and ultraviolet lights. It does have real prostitutes sitting in the windows and standing in doorways wearing not much more than a smile. They wink and beckon and quote you a price. There are also red light districts in many other Dutch cities. My neighborhood in Haarlem had six "windows."

These window displays and the activity behind the curtain are perfectly legal in the Netherlands. The ladies, euphemistically called "sex workers," are licensed by the city government to engage in business, and must be medically inspected and certified healthy on a regular basis in order to keep their business license. You have to hand it to the Dutch for their pragmatic attitude toward the world's most tenacious "profession." The Amsterdam red light district is a popular tourist area but be careful when taking pictures.

Besides having sex for sale, the red light districts also have sex shops and live sex shows. In America, a sex shop would be called an adult book store, with window displays. You'll also find them in Scandinavia and Germany, especially Copenhagen and Hamburg. Gaudy neon lights and the hawker at the door advertise live performances inside at the sex shows. Years ago, I introduced a couple of my former girlfriends who met up in Amsterdam. I had asked my Dutch friend to show my Filipino friend around the town. The report I got back was more about the live stage act than about anything else in the city.

Major cities all over Europe have hookers on the side streets. Milan, Paris, Stockholm, and even Amsterdam have girls standing in the shadows winking at potential customers. Out on the highways in Hungary from the Romanian border to Budapest there are one or two girls standing at every rest stop. Truck drivers coming up from the Balkans must be good customers. You'll also see the come-on as you drive toward Germany from the Czech Republic.

Prostitution is controlled by characters on the other side of the law, thanks to the fact that has been put on the other side of the law in most places. Not only do you jeopardize your life to health risks, there are other dangers as well. Let the buyer beware since purchased sex is no more reputable in Europe than it is in America.

No matter where you go, there are two things you can't get away from — Coca Cola signs and the Goodyear blimp. Here is the blimp hovering over St. Peter's at the Vatican in Rome, Italy. [3042]

Last Call

Hey! The taxi is waiting and your flight departs in a few hours. What did you forget? Here is a last minute set of checklists to help ease you into your seat on that big silver bird.

___ Mail. Stop delivery, give forwarding instructions to the Post Office or have a friend or neighbor save it for you.

___ Stop newspaper delivery.

___ Ask a friend or neighbor to pick up ad flyers which get thrown on your doorstep.

___ Disconnect electrical appliances.

___ Disconnect or turn off water to automatic ice maker.

___ Set thermostat to 50°F heat or 90°F cool.

___ Secure house plants.

___ Kennel or loan pets.

___ Ask a neighbor to keep an eye on your home and to call police immediately if men start moving furniture.

___ Lock up windows and doors, including second floor. Remove hidden door keys.

___ Service automobile. Change oil, change coolant, disconnect battery, and put it up on blocks if you will be gone for more than a month.

___ Make arrangements to keep current on your rent or mortgage, accounts, phone bills, utility bills, insurance, etc.

___ Review the next batch of lists.

Have a good trip!

BUDGETED EXPENSES
(Chapter 2)

Basic Biggies
[ ] lodging
[ ] food
[ ] transportation

Thirty Miscellaneous Cost Items
[ ] Guidebooks
[ ] Maps
[ ] Souvenirs
[ ] Medicine
[ ] Gifts
[ ] Toilet tips
[ ] Guitar case donations
[ ] Fees
[ ] Cleaning
[ ] Money changing
[ ] Film
[ ] Guided tours
[ ] Museum admissions
[ ] Bus, tram, and metro tickets
[ ] Taxis
[ ] Bike rental
[ ] Film processing
[ ] Shows
[ ] Telephone calls
[ ] Internet café time
[ ] Smokes
[ ] Entertainment
[ ] Drinks
[ ] Postage
[ ] Toothpaste
[ ] Postcards
[ ] Soap
[ ] Haircuts
[ ] Taxes
[ ] New shoes
[ ] New clothes
[ ] Casino losses
[ ] Pickpocket losses
[ ] Whatever else

PACKING LIST

Clothing: (Chapter 5)
(season & locale dependent, and
including what you are wearing)
[ ] umbrella
[ ] mackintosh
[ ] jacket
[ ] sweater
[ ] two shirts or blouses
[ ] two slacks or skirts
[ ] four sets underwear
[ ] two pairs shoes
[ ] belt
[ ] _____
[ ] _____
[ ] _____

Personal Care Items: (Chapter 6)
(You do not need all of these, and you
do not need to bring all the items you
need — buy them in Europe)
[ ] razor
[ ] nail clippers
[ ] toothbrush
[ ] toothpaste
[ ] comb or brush
Optional
[ ] hair blower
[ ] shave cream
[ ] cosmetics
[ ] _____
[ ] _____
[ ] _____

Cleaning Supplies: (Chapter 6)
[ ] Woolite or dish detergent
[ ] Clothes line
[ ] Clothes pins
[ ] Shoe polish
[ ] Shoe brush
[ ] _____
[ ] _____

Supplies: (Chapter 6)
[ ] Alarm chronograph
[ ] Calculator
[ ] Coin purse
[ ] Compass
[ ] Condoms
[ ] Earplugs
[ ] Flashlight
[ ] Mirror
[ ] Plastic bags
[ ] Plastic utensils
[ ] Portable radio
[ ] Swiss Army Knife
[ ] Tape measure
[ ] Telescope or binoculars
[ ] Toothpicks
[ ] Vinegar
[ ] Vitamins
[ ] Vodka
[ ] Wash cloth
[ ] Water cup heater (buy in Europe)
[ ] Wire ties
[ ] _____
[ ] _____
[ ]
[ ]

Repair Kit: (Chapter 6)
[ ] Glue
[ ] Needles and threads
[ ] Latex gloves
[ ] Oil
[ ] Leatherman tool
[ ] Pliers
[ ] Scissors
[ ] Screwdrivers
[ ] String
[ ] Tape
[ ] Tweezers
[ ] Wrench
[ ] _____
[ ] _____
[ ] _____

Guidebooks and dictionaries:
(Chapter 10)
[ ] Guidebooks
[ ] Pocket dictionaries
[ ] Maps
[ ] Rail Timetable
[ ] _____
[ ] _____

Electrical Hardware: (Chapter 11)
[ ] Plug adapters
[ ] Transformer
[ ] converter
[ ] rechargeable batteries
[ ] battery charger
[ ] _____
[ ] _____

Photographic Equipment:
(Chapter 12)
[ ] 35mm automatic SLR
[ ] 35-105mm zoom lens
[ ] 21mm lens
[ ] 2X multiplier
[ ] polarizing filter
[ ] 35mm miniature camera
[ ] loupe
[ ] lens paper and brush
[ ] bean bag
[ ] lens hood
[ ] film
[ ] X-ray film shield bag
[ ] _____
[ ] _____

First Aid: (Chapter 20)
[ ] aspirin/Tylenol
[ ] Band-Aids
[ ] antiseptic cream
[ ] lip balm
[ ] Lomotil/Pepto-Bismol
[ ] _____
[ ] _____

IN YOUR POCKETS   NOTES:

Money: (Chapters 8,19)
[ ] cash
[ ] traveler's cheques
[ ] personal checks
[ ] credit cards
[ ] ATM card
[ ] _____
[ ] _____

Identification:
(Chapters 3, 14, 18, 20)
[ ] passport
[ ] driver's license
[ ] international driving permit
[ ] international certificates of vaccination
[ ] visas
[ ] school I.D.
[ ] AYH card
[ ] insurance card
[ ] _____

Tickets: (Chapters 4, 14, 17)
[ ] air ticket
[ ] hotel confirmation
[ ] Eurailpass
[ ] car rental reservation
[ ] _____
[ ] _____

Travel Records: (Chapter 9)
[ ] travel record book
[ ] tape recorder
[ ] VCR
[ ] _____
[ ] _____

Miscellaneous: (Chapters 3, 25)
[ ] Customs registration certificate(s)
[ ] _____
[ ] _____

Now, get going!

Index

Ready to cast off lines the Stena Line ferry is set to sail from Göteborg, Sweden. It docks in Frederikshavn, Denmark 3½ hours later. [3102]